The Life and Times of Ernest Dobson

GRAINER ◆ MARBLER ◆ DECORATIVE PAINTER

including

122 MASTERCLASSES

RESEARCHED & COMPILED
BY
JOHN FLEMING & TERRY TAYLOR

Robert Woodland
F.F.D., A.P.C.T.
Freeman and Liveryman of the Worshipful Company of Painters Stainers otherwise Painter Stainers and Freeman of the City of London
L.C.G.L. of City Guilds

ROBERT is a world figure in graining and marbling, demonstrating all types of work at salons where the world's best work is on view.

In 1999 Robert was awarded at the Salon in Sweden a lifetime achievement award to graining and marbling by the organisers of the International Salon.

He is a member of the Faculty of Decoration which is a group of decorators who are notable exponents in the field of applied decoration.

Robert is third generation of decorators and is training his son in the craft. Most of his work is carried out at such places as Westminster Palace and many other prestigious buildings in the public and private sector.

Robert is a member of the Painting Craft Teachers Association and gives generously of his time to the association.

He is that rare combination of businessman and craftsman.

John Fleming & Terry Taylor

Forward

I am pleased that the works of Ernest Dobson have been researched and published by Taylor and Fleming.

Without their efforts the works would have been lost. They are now available to present and future generations wherever graining and marbling is carried out.

Since I was an apprentice I have always thought Dobson was one of the finest grainers and marblers this country has seen, fit to take his place with the likes of Kershaw, Bradley, Taylor, Valentine, Barnet and Zeff Carr.

This book will be of great use in all types of painting classes, i.e. preparing for City Guilds exams, for grainers and marblers to take it out on jobs.

To have this book in your tool bag must give you confidence when you start a graining or marbling job.

I strongly recommend this book to anyone at any level in graining and marbling.

Robert Woodland

The Life and Times of Ernest Dobson
GRAINER ◆ MARBLER ◆ DECORATIVE PAINTER
INCLUDING **122 MASTERCLASSES**

RESEARCHED & COMPILED
BY
JOHN FLEMING & TERRY TAYLOR

Copyright John Fleming & Terry Taylor
2006

Published by John Fleming & Terry Taylor
1 Sydney Avenue, Whalley, Clitheroe, Lancashire BB7 9TF

Typeset and Printed by
Hargreaves Steel Limited
133 Henry Street, Church, Accrington, Lancashire BB5 4EP

First Edition 2006

ISBN 0 9553028 0 3

Acknowledgements

Dr Spenser Dobson
Son of E. Dobson who has been most helpful to us in the preparation of this book by letting us have access to memorabilia of his father's works.

Whalley Library
Our thanks to them for tracing works of E. Dobson through the national network of the Library Service.

Patrick N. Richardson, National Secretary of the Painting Craft Teachers
For his encouragement in the early stages and for his help in advertising the book.

Mr David Pescod, of Professional Painting
For giving permission to publish Mr Dobson's works. Mr Dobson wrote for the JDA which became Painting & Decorating and now Professional Painting.

George Ball F.I.B.D.
Member of the Painting Craft Teachers Association and Past President of the British Master Painters and Decorators, for his loan of copies on The National Master Painter.

Also our wives!
For all they have put up with over the last two years: the house full of papers and many nights of floors covered with notes. Anyone who has published a book will understand this.

And to our printers who gave us lots of help and advice. Thank you Chris Hargreaves and Bob Steel.

Mention must also be made of Bill Luker, a colleague from our days at Blackburn College. Bill attended several of Mr Dobson's lectures and was strongly influenced by his work.

Contents

Forward by Robert Woodland 3
Acknowledgements 5
What the Experts Say 9
About the Authors 10
Cartoon 12
The Life and Times of Ernest Dobson 13
A Successful Lincrusta Pattern 16
Press Cuttings 19
Obituary 23
Snakes & Ladders from the S1 Grainers 24

The Journal of Decorative Art
August 1948 – July 1955

Introduction 28
Tools and Brushes for Graining 30
Graining Mahogany 32
Graining Mahogany (cont.) 34
Graining Mahogany (cont.) 36
Graining Rosewood 39
Grand Antique Marble 42
Breche-Verte Marble 44

Sienna Marble 46
Ash 48
Ash (cont.) 50
Carrara Marble 52
Levanto Marble 54
Maple 56
Maple (cont.) 58
Poupre Violette 60
Grey Maple 62
Irish Green Marble 64
Pitch Pine 66
Rouge Royal Marble 68
Curly Pine 70
Granite Marbles 72
Figured Oak 74
English Figured Oak 76
English Figured Oak (cont.) 78
English Figured Oak (cont.) 80
Oak Trees 82
Marbling Vert Campan 84
Sandstone 86

Turkey Oak	88
Verde Antique	90
Reproduction of Stone of the British Isles	92
The Graining of Walnut (1)	94
Alabaster: Marble Limestone	98
The Graining of Walnut (2)	100
A Grainer of 1851	102
Oak Graining: The Heavy Figure	110
The Graining of Walnut (3)	112
Skyros Marble	114
Oak Graining: Heartwood Markings	116
Italian Walnut	118
Italian Walnut (cont.)	120
Cipollina Marble	122
Italian Walnut (cont.)	124
Graining of Obeche	126
Napoleon Marble Limestone	128
The Graining of Sycamore	130
The Marbling of Breche Violette	132
Graining of Brown Oak	134
Blue Fleuri Marble	136
The Graining of Teak	138
Breche Blanche	140
Heartwood Markings of English Oak	142
Walnut	144
Black and Gold Marble	146
Graining of Pollard Oak	148
Graining of Pollard Oak (cont.)	150
Serancolin Marble	152
Oak Graining: Larger Figures	154
The Mottled Graining of Teak	156
Convent Sienna Marble	158
Satin Walnut	160
Black and Gold Marble	162
The Graining of Mahogany	164
Drawings of Brushes	166
St. Anne Marble	168
Bleached Walnut	170
Knots in Graining	172
Dark Dove Marble	174
Knots in Graining (cont.)	176
Graining of "Natural" Oak	178
Waulsort Marble	180
Graining of Bleached Rosewood	182
Knots in Oak Heartwood	184
Australian Walnut	186
Swedish Green Marble	188
Graining of Beechwood	190

National Master Painter
July 1956 – July 1960

Juniper 194
English Walnut 197
Sandstones of Britain 200
Willow 203
Light Oak and Linen Fold 206
Mahogany (Sapele Variety) 209
St. Anne Marble 212
Scotch Pine 215
Lacewood 218
Crown Elm 221
Verde Antique 223
Satinwood 226
Californian Red Wood 229
Breche Violet Marble 231
Brown Oak 234
Colour Combing 236
Graining a Flat Door 239
A Quick Method of Graining Walnut 242
Vert-de-Mer Marble 245
Maple 247
Alabaster-Marble Limestone 250
Bleached Heartwood Markings of English Oak 253
Wood Grain by Pencil Rubbing 255
Bleached Italian Walnut in a Bedroom 258
Feather of Oak 262
Poupre Violette Marble 265
English Ash 268
Makore Curl 270
Limed Oak 273
Connemara Marble 275
Walnut Burr 277
Oak Heartwood 280
Rose Campan Marble 282
Feather of Walnut 284
Pencilled Figure of Oak 287
Henrietta Marble Limestone 290
Pine Laths 293
Australian Silky Oak 296
Rouge Royal Marble 299
Silver Spruce 302
Skyros Alpha Marble 305
Hungarian Ash 308
Bog Oak 311
A Glossary of Terms 313
A Look at Watercolour 325
Index by Subject 326

What the experts had to say . . .

JEFF BROWN, Secretary of Scottish Painting Craft Teachers Association: *These works are going to be amongst the World's greatest on graining and marbling.*

CECIL SEALE, Teacher, Craftman member of Painter Stainers Co., London: *A wonderful effort preserve for furture grainers.*

PATRICK RICHARDSON, National secretary painting craft teachers Assoc: *An excellent work that must be published.*

ANN COOK, Past President P.C.T.A.: *It is essential to preserve and further promote craft skills and I fully support the publication of this book which contribute to this.*

FRED HARGREAVES F.I.B.D., Head of Department Painting & Decorating, Burnley, after Mr. Dobson: *Most grainers have a style of work that they repeat and almost sign their name on the work, Mr. Dobson had many styles, and the only way of knowing it was his was by the quality of the work.*

He did intend to write a book but led such a busy life giving lectures and demonstrations. However his works are safe in the hands of Terry Taylor & John Fleming. I recomend this book to First year apprentices and to eighty year old grainers & marblers. The work of Mr. Dobson will live forever.

MARTIN HORLER, Past President Painting Craft Teachers Association: *Well done Terry & John now the works of E. Dobson will live forever.*

GILBERT DOWLING, Teacher, Grainer, Marbler: *The book will be a great asset to all craftsmen.*

RON BETTS, Past President A.P.T.C.: *A must for everyone in graining & marbling.*

GEORGE BALL, F.I.B.D, Past President of British Master Painters Association and member of A.P.T.C.: *Taylor and Fleming have done the trade a great service by publishing the works of Dobson.*

JON LATHAM, Conservator Brighton Pavilion: *These works must be published for future grainers and marblers.*

STEVE DAWS, Vice-President Painting Craft Teachers: *The Painting Craft Teachers welcome this book to use in City Guilds decorative treatments.*

FRANK. B. SIDES, President, Facilty of Decoration: *This work will be well received by all craftsmen.*

G.W.D. OLD, City & Guilds (London), M.F.B.(ret), Hon. Ass. I.C.W.S.(ret). Head of Technical Advisory (ret) Walpamur Co. Ltd./Crown Paints: *I find this to be an excellent book on the art of Graining and Marbling by one of the finest craftsmen I have been pleased to have known during my time in the decorative trade.*

Reading this book brings back many memories in attempting to emulate the great masters during my apprentiship. I thoroughly recommend this book to all craftsmen, tutors and students; wishing them the enjoyment and success achieved in work well executed.

MR. BRIAN BOTTING, The master of the Worshipful company of Painter-Stainers: *The Worshipful Company of Painter Stainers support T. Taylor & J. Fleming in publishing the works of E. Dobson. Without their efforts the works would have been lost.*

BILL HOLGATE was one of the elite band of grainers and marblers. He saw the start of the book and approved of it. He died three years ago but his work can be found all over the world. He was a big fan of Mr Dobson and often used his methods of work. Bill's widow June has had his panels on exhibition at his Clitheroe studio and they can be seen by appointment. His work has been awarded a place in the Painters Stainers Company who also gave Bill the Freedom of the City of London. His panels must be seen by any student of graining and marbling.

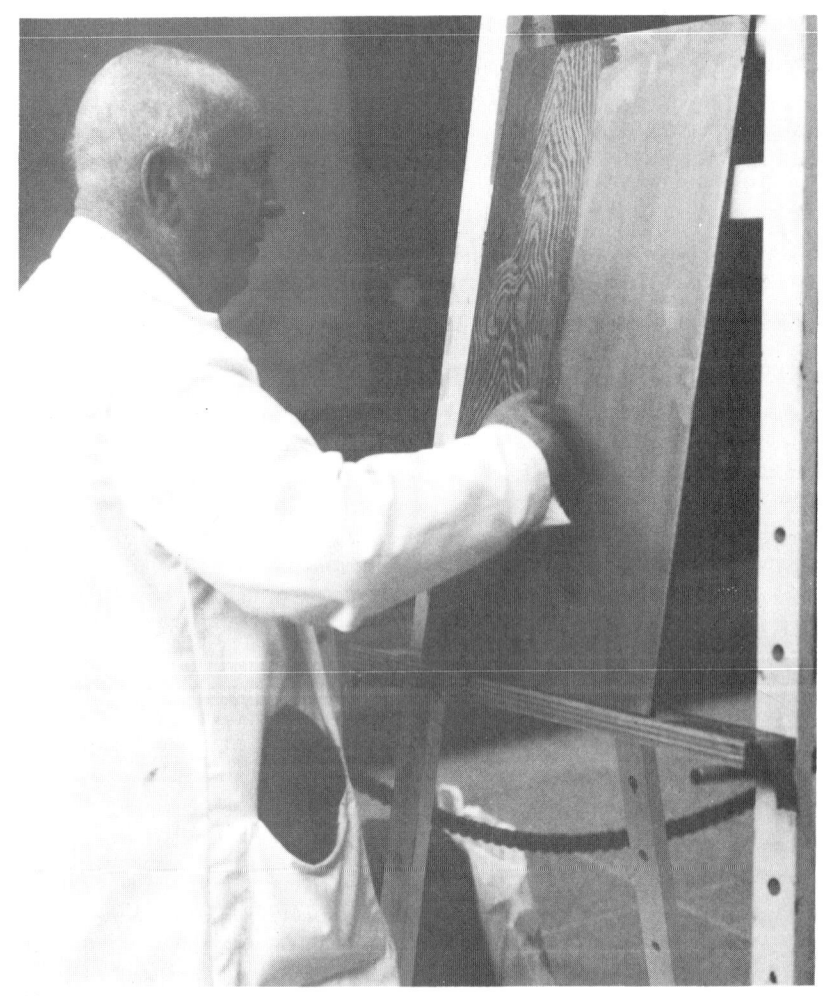

John Fleming

F.T.C., member of City & Guilds,
Insignia Award Gold Medal,
Further Education Teachers Cert.
Visiting Lecturer, British Paint Research Association, London.
Member of Painting Craft Teachers Association & demonstrator to Painting Craft Teachers Association at seminars and exhibitions.
Part time lecturer at Blackburn College.
Demonstrator to international exhibitions with the "Salon"
National Service R.A.F aircraft painter
Retired painting superintendent to Blackburn Corporation employing 120 painters.

Whoever reads this book I want to encourage them to practice.

I am now seventy years old but I practise as often as I can, and try to learn new techniques.

You must never think you have reached perfection. Always think the next graining or marbling job will be better.

So use this book and PRACTISE, PRACTISE, PRACTISE.

John Fleming

Terry Taylor

AFTER serving a recognised apprenticeship and graining trade qualifications up to and including C&G Advanced Craft Certificate, Terry worked on all types of painting and decorating projects and for a number of years ran his own business.

In the mid 1970s he decided on a change of direction and studied full time for a B.A. degree in History and Politics, and also a teaching certificate in Further Education. He later joined the full-time staff at Blackburn College.

In his early days at the college he designed a course for students and the general public in graining and marbling, and building on this he later designed and implemented week long courses for teachers in further education, and a two year part-time course which was externally validated and assessed.

Terry has taught students the techniques of graining and marbling from all parts of the U.K. and from abroad.

He has exhibited his work widely and at Painters Stainers Hall in London and at the Association of Painting Craft Teachers craft awareness weekends.

He strongly believes that in Mr Dobson we have a person whose knowledge of graining and marbling is unrivalled, and his skill at presenting the subject in written and visual form is probably the most comprehensive work of the twentieth century.

He says: "In this book we get a marriage of all that is best in British and Continental methods of imitating woods and marbles."

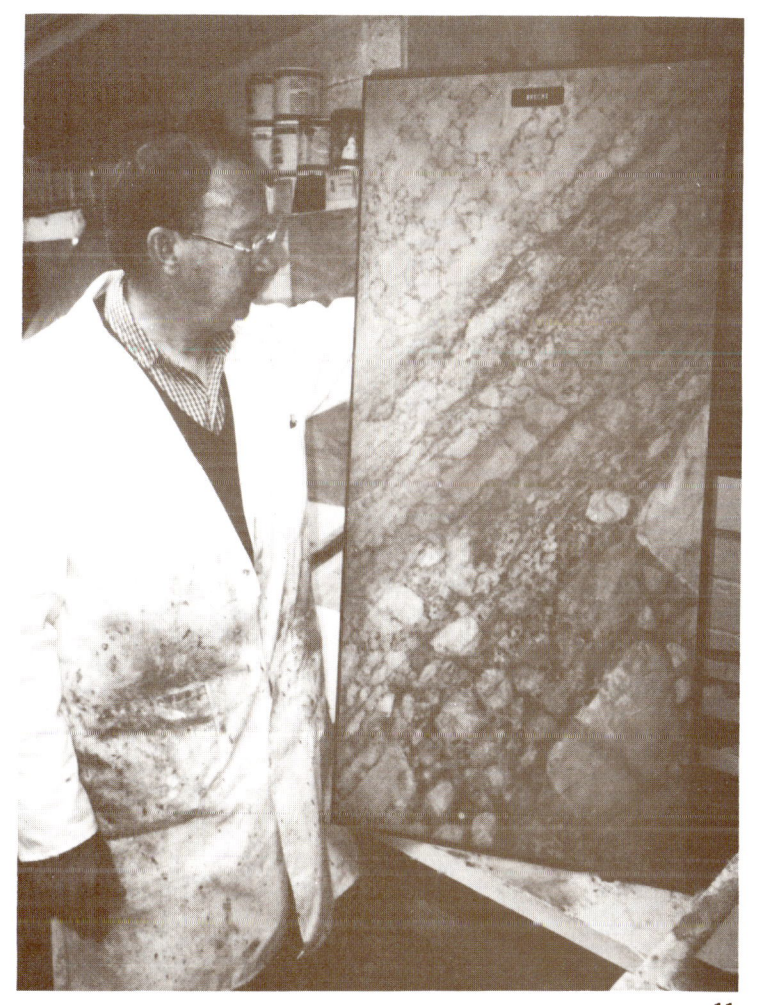

THE HOME DECORATOR 1890

"Now I comes to you, and I say, 'Meogginy', I says. 'Werry Well', you says, and you combs it so and puts twiddles with a rag. There!"

"Then I changes my mind and I says, 'Oak', I says. What do you do? Why you up and combs it lighter and puts tha twiddles t'other way."

"Then I says, 'Wornut', I say; and you makes it werry dark and turns the twiddles upsey down! And there's yer wornut."

"Then I up an I says, 'Marble', I says. Then you paints it black and shies a hegg at it, and there's yer marble!"

GRAINING

THE process known as 'graining', by which painted surfaces are brought to resemble natural woods, is open to a number of objections, but if well done is at least decorative, if not artistic.

In years gone by, the work of the grainer was much in demand, though it was scoffed at by the 'moderns' of thoses days. We make no apology for introducing a copy of a comic strip cartoon by a well-known humorous artist of the 1890's, J.F. Sullivan, taken by permission of the piblishers, Messers. Macmillan & Co. from Joseph Pennell's book *Pen Drawing and Draughtsmen*.

The Life & Times of Ernest Dobson

Ecole Supérieure de Peinture de Bruxelles – Année 1913 - 1914
Directeur: Pierre Logelain, 67, Rue du Conseil
Ernest Dobson is arrowed in the picture

PHOTOGRAPHS

Left: A Sunday afternoon "somewhere in France".

Bottom Left: A celebratory dinner in the Sergeant's Mess

Below: Comrades in Arms

Left: Mr Dobson (right) and his English colleagues in Brussels.
Above: Post-war training in Germany.
Below: Warrant Officer Dobson supervising trainees.

A successful Lincrusta pattern

ONE of the most successful Lincrusta patterns in recent years is No. 1827, a very true representation of oak panelling.

This pattern has a history which is more than likely to interest "P. and D." readers.

Every such pattern must result from a combined operation, and in this case the basic drawings of the sections were prepared by the design staff of the Relief Decorations Branch of the W.P.M. at Darwen.

Then someone had the bright idea of calling in, as collaborator in the important matter of the graining, no less a person than "our" Mr. E. Dobson, who appreciated, as he always does, just for what the situation called. The result has been the success noted above.

The interest of readers in this fine and very usable Lincrusta oak will be enhanced by the knowledge that the grainer involved was none other than "the" Mr. Dobson.

The Grainer

Just a skib by occupation

Whose forte is wood imitation

And you'd ne'er think to see him smile

That he possessed such guise & guile

But, truth to tell, the marks he makes

Look almost real, although but fakes

Mahogany, walnut or ash

To imitate he'll "have a bash"

Though Ruskin-ites revile him, we

Delight in his dexterity

                E. Sanderson

Ernest Dobson retires

MR E. DOBSON who until a few months ago was a regular contributor to this journal, retired from craft teaching in December.

On leaving day school he was trained in his father's painting and decorating business at Thornton, Bradford.

He also attended as a part time day and evening student at the School of Art, Bradford, under Mr E.R.S. Andrews.

While at the school he obtained many certificates, diplomas and prizes, and perhaps his biggest success in that respect was the gaining of a City and Guilds first class final certificate at the age of 17 years and, by obtaining a number of board of Education certificates for drawing, the technological certificate at 18.

At twenty years of age he was awarded a travelling scolarship to the Royal College of Arts and the Principal School of Painting, Brussels.

The late Mr. Edward Preston, of Huddersfield, and Mr. William Burton, of Kettering, were at Brussels at the same time as Mr. Dobson, and were the only other English speaking students.

Mr. Dobson's first offer of a post was at Monte Carlo, but he returned to England and settled in Lancashire.

He remained with Messrs. Kendal Milne & Co., Manchester, until he joined the forces as an infantryman in the Duke of Wellington's (West Riding) Regiment, in the first world war.

After a brief training he was on active service in France and Belgium.

In five engagements his battalion was reduced to less than 100 men, three only of the seventy recruits with whom he was trained returning to England after hostilities, the remainder having been killed or severely wounded.

In 1919 he was appointed Inspector of the painters' and decorators' scheme under which disabled men and others were trained by the Ministry of Labour.

On the formation of the Army Educational Corps he was given post as Warrant Officer attached to the Northern Command.

Although trained to become a master painter, Mr. Dobson became a craft teacher and commenced as such at the Technical College, Cologne, and has just finished his teaching career at the School of Art, Burnley, Lancs., after having taught at seven schools and colleges in all.

On the retirement of his father in 1927 he took over and developed the well established family business.

Mr. Dobson has always given freely of his services to the betterment of the craft and has sat on many local and national committees.

He has undertaken the setting of examination papers and adjudicating.

He is a Past-President of the Association of Painting Craft Teachers.

Many readers will join with us in wishing Mr. Dobson a long and happy retirement.

• *Personal Pars from Painting & Decorating, January 1956*

17

Architectural, sporting, scenic and still life subjects were used for early wallpapers in the 18th century – drawing by Ernest Dobson dated Oct. 29, 1960

Dobson's drawings of motifs from early wallpapers 1545-1645

Press cuttings...

From the Painting Craft Teachers column of The Journal of Decorative Art, September 1937:

MR. DOBSON of Burnley, created a desire, on Tuesday afternoon, July 20th, by all those who saw his marbling demonstration, to go home and try out his methods for themselves. It was the only practical demonatration give on the Course, and even the inspectorate was thrilled.

From the Painting Craft Teachers column of The Journal of Decorative Art, September 1949:

Marbling

A NEW feature of this year's course was the inclusion of lectures by Mr. E. Dobson, of Burnley, who spoke on "Continental Methods of Training in Graining and Marbling".

Whilst admitting the limited use of marbling to-day, Mr. Dobson stressed the importance of the subject in awakening an interest in drawing and colour in the young apprentice.

Mr. Dobson illustrated his lectures with many interesting demonstrations which proved his great competence and knowledge of the subject.

From the Painting Craft Teachers column of The Journal of Decorative Art, December 1950:

Mr. Dobson on Graining

ON RETURNING to the college the first lecture was by Mr. E. Dobson, on Continental Methods of Graining.

Mr. Dobson's work is, of course, well-known to J.D.A. readers, but as usual, he contrived to find many fresh treatments for our interest.

He showed us first a number of charts illustrating the grain of various woods, and stressed the need for good drawing by grainers.

At the Brussels Academy, he said, the professors were not only skilled grainers and marblers, but good landscape and portait artists and expert linguists.

Discipline in Continental schools was strict, and students were expected to compile notes after the day's work, which was from 8 a.m. to 9 p.m.

Drawings of wood grain were made on graph paper, and Mr. Dobson said it was useful to apply this to our own teaching technique.

Students could not be expected to produce orginal work; they should be provided with a diagram of simplified and basic shapes from which to work.

Continental Methods

A demonstration of Continental graining methods then followed. The first specimen was bleached mahogany, working on a white ground with white, black and umber and a gilp of turpentine, oil and glaze. The warmer hues were added with crimson lake, applied sparingly with a piece of rag.

It was pointed out that the general practice in Continental schools was to run a cross-grained border round a panel to make for neatness.

Next came figure oak, the figure being dark. The ground, of deep buff, was coated with white lead and the figure wiped out, after which the panel was glazed.

Cedar wood was next dealt with, working on a deep, warm buff ground with burnt sienna crayons. It was stressed that glaze should not be mixed in the gilp for a crayon process, as it caused the crayon to slip and slide.

Canvas, said Mr. Dobson, was better than

rag for most graining purposes, as it did not pick off the colour to the same extent.

An Unusual Wood

The next wood imitated was a rather unusual one, Redwood burr. The ground was similar to that for mahogany, made up of venetain red and white. The graining was in water-colour medium with crimson lake and vandyke brown as strainers and the effect obtained first with a rubbing-in brush and then with a sponge.

In glazing a pitch pine panel Mr. Dobson showed how the mottling and glazing on the continent differed form ours.

The mottler was kept on the surface all the time, the effect being obtained by twisting the wrist and varying the pressure, giving a much truer effect than that grained by lifting the mottler from the surface, but it requires some practice to know the precise amount of water colour to use; otherwise the markings flow out.

The last example was of walnut, worked in oil colour on a flogged water colour ground. The stainers used were Indian red and black and a tool, made up of two spliced water colour brushes, was employed.

Mr. Dobson emphasised that he did not believe in students using makeshift tools for graining; a good kit helped to make a good job.

From the Painting Craft Teachers column of The Journal of Decorative Art, date unknown:

"Graining To-day"

THOSE who believed that the craft of graining was a dying art would have had reason to revise their opinion had they been fortunate enough to attend an entertaining series of lectures recently held in the North-East under the sponsorship of British Paints Ltd.

Under the title "Graining To-Day", Mr. E. Dobson, well-known authority on this subject, gave two lectures at the Sunderland College of Art and a further two on the 11th and 12th March, in the lecture Room of British Paints Ltd. new Colour Centre in Newcastle upon Tyne.

Attendances by master painters and apprentices were excellent and certainly refuted any suggestion that professional interest in the subject was lukewarm.

His listeners were obviously fascinated by Mr. Dobson's practical demonstrations of new techniques, developed to comply with modern decorative requirements.

He proved to an amused though greatly admiring audience that elaborate & costly equipment was not necessary – certainly not, at any rate, to one of his confident ability – for with a few homely tools, crude perhaps in appearance but employed with a splendid skill, he reproduced with deceptive ease true-to-life impressions of modern oak, mahogany and walnut finishes; his marbles – a form of design much used on film and T.V. studio sets – were masterpieces of craftsmanship.

British paints Ltd. are to be congratulated on their enterprise in making speakers of such calibre available, and further lectures of similar quality are planned for the future.

Their new Colour Centre, which is already proving to be a success, had a lecture-room incorporated for the express purpose of providing a convenient meeting place for discussions of professional interests.

It is an advice bureau with a refreshingly practical approach to the problem of colour selection for domestic and industrial purposes, and the well-known B.P.L Colour Advisory Service, which has done so much to stimulate industry to an appreciation of the practical value of colour in the factory, is now accommodated at the new address.

Several hundred schemes are planned and submitted every year and it is significant that well over 90 per cent. are accepted.

From the Painting Craft Teachers column of The Journal of Decorative Art, April 1952:

Painting Craft Teachers

THE Associaton held its Annual Luncheon on Saturday, March 15th, at the Cathedral Schools, Bradford, the new home of the Bradford classes.

At the outset, Mr. J. E. Deady, President, was in the Chair, but the meal over, and the Loyal Toast duly honoured, he invested his successor, Mr. E. Dobson, with the badge of office.

Mr. Dobson, he said, was a Bradford man, and was trained side by side with Mr. E. Sanderson, the fame of whose work was widespread, and whose old students were teaching in all parts of the country.

During the last 18 months said Mr. Deady, he had noted rapid changes in methods and in the outlook on decoration. Thus their methods of teaching colour and design must be in line with contemporary thought.

In investing Mr. Dobson with the chain, he asked for him the same enthusiastic support which he had himself received.

Mr. Dobson thanked the members for their confidence and for the honour they had conferred upon him. Theirs was a key job; the work they did to-day would be discussed and assessed 40 years hence, just as they discussed the tuition they had received many years ago.

He followed a line of splendid men, not the least of them being Mr. Deady, to whose work as President he paid a fine tribute.

He advised his hearers to "do each day's work as well as you can and give the best of yourselves".

The Lord Mayor of Bradford, Ald. H. Hird, J.P., spoke next, in racy and lively vein, but he touched on a serious note when he spoke of an estimate for decorating his house.

Had it not been for the address it might well have been for the decoration of the Town Hall. Clearly their craft was faced with a cost problem.

Two other spokesmen for the municipality were Ald. Revis Barber, J.P., Chairman of the Further Education Committee, and Mr. H. Abbott, Inspector of the Further Education.

Both were clearly proud of the Bradford classes, and the former had heard a recent lecture by Mr. Dobson, on graining, and had been greatly impressed.

So had Mr. H. Magson, President of the Bradford Branch, N.F.M.P., and he too expressed pride in the fame of the Bradford classes, and was eloquent in praise of Mr. Sanderson and Mr. Reg. Wilson, who had deputised ably during Mr. Sanderson's illness.

Then Mr. W. G. Sutherland, after referring to the distinction which Mr. Deady had lent to the Presidency, and the eminence as craftsman and teacher of Mr. Dobson, spoke of the pleasure they all felt at the presence of Mr. Charles Eaton, looking surprisingly well.

He went on to propose "The Ladies", and Mrs. Deadly's response delighted the company by its confident delivery, clarity of phase and sureness of touch.

These Annual Luncheon have their own very happy atmosphere, and are a most pleasant prelude to the General Meeting which follows, and at which the serious business of the day is transacted.

Postscript . . .

"This book will be welcomed by grainers and marblers the world over. Researched by two men known throughout the trade. Well done, Terry and John."

– Walter Riley, BA (Hons.) Fine Art, Grainer and Marbler, Member of the Painting Craft Teachers Association, Writer and Demonstrator for *Professional Painting* (this magazine used to be the *Journal of Decorative Art*).

A man called Dobson!

THE cynics who decry everything and anything that is connected with craftsmanship in the painting and decorating industry, especially graining, presumably have never heard of a man called Dobson.

What a pity some of them did not go to the Liverpool College of Art on Wednesday, 11 January, 1956, to a lecture/demonstration by Mr. E. Dobson, organized by the Northern District of the Institute of British Decorators and Interior Designers.

Displayed on portable screens and on most of the available wall spaces in the lecture theatre were examples of Mr. Dobson's graining.

Mr. Dobson proved by reference to his specimens how graining had altered during recent years, and he made it clear that, although the work had become quicker in execution and in many cases a one coat process was required for economic reasons, the study of the wood was very necessary.

He spoke of the pride in gathering together one's own personal kit of tools and he demonstrated the correct manner in which the graining tools should be used.

Light woods were of two kinds, those which were naturally light in tone, or those which were bleached. Mahogany was of the latter group, and this wood responded excellently to bleaching and was immensely popular.

The first wood to be demonstrated was bleached mahogany feather, one reason for this choice being that it could be imitated very quickly and pleasantly with a sponge.

Working in water colour and using burnt sienna, a touch of Vandyke and a touch of red, the panel was laid in with a deeper tone down the centre. The sponge was first dabbed on the heavy portion of the work and then worked from the centre up and down each side in a fountain formation to make the feather; the rubbing-in brush used to draw the side grain downwards.

He demonstrated with a three-inch mottler how the mottling is bought down the sides and all the work lightly softened. He pointed out that because a water medium was used there was no need to panic about it going off; it was possible to work in sections.

The use of a feather was next explained by a demonstration of bleached Italian walnut. The type of feather used was dictated by the closeness or otherwise of the work, a turkey feather being used on this occasion.

The feather was pared off until only the working part remained. When dipped in water and used on a water scumble of Vandyke brown to draw the hearts, the feather certainly appeared a magic tool.

A good deal of softening with the badger softener and an occasional mottle with the side of the badger as it was drawn over some of the work, gave a very pleasant effect in very little time.

The next demonstration was the method of overgraining pitch pine, and a warning was given never to overdo the glazing. A useful tip was to keep the mottler on the work all the time it was brought down, but slightly varying the pressure. Mr. Dobson suggested mottling on a counterchange method from one side of the panel to the other.

A warning was given to the younger students never to use a mottler for rubbing-in, as it was only really effective as a mottler when the edges were sharp and straight.

Bird's eye maple was next demonstated and Mr. Dobson's specially prepared rigger, with the centre burnt out to create the eyes, gave the work a very natural appearance.

The art of using the mottler with the fingers well pushed into the mottler to create two cup shapes, and the necessity to leave some unmottled spaces was emphasized. Mr. Dobson preferred to soften before the eyes were put in, and he did not approve of the use of the fingers to create the eyes.

Mottling being such an important part of the work a demonstration was also given of the method of mottling satinwood. Raw sienna was used on a cream ground, and the cutter this time was kept on one side and lifted off the other.

• **Painting & Decorating, February 1956.**

OBITUARY
Ernest Dobson

Mr Dobson died December 13th 1965.

MR DOBSON was for many years a contributor to the Journal of Decorative Art. He was a member and president in 1952 of the Painting Craft Teachers Association. He retired from teaching in 1955.

A contemporary of his, Mr. E. Sanderson, F.I.B.D., F.R.S.A., wrote at the time:

The death of Ernest Dobson is not only a loss to the painting and decorating craft but his passing virtually ends an era of craftsmen who dedicated their lives to the promotion of a standard of craftsmanship which has become a source of pride to our industry.

The skill of graining and marbling are yet again in fashion.

The standard which he attained will prove to be an invaluable source of inspiration to the rising generation of young decorators who are aspiring to excel in their chosen craft.

He was a Fellow of the Institute of British Decorators and Interior Designers.

There are many men holding responible positions in both industry and teaching whose success is due in a large measure to Mr. Dobson's thorough methods of tuition, and all who were privileged to be his friends will regret the loss of his warm personality and likeable companionship.

– Ernest Sanderson

Snakes and Ladders

IT IS now February and we have had them for five months.

The great blow has fallen for them and they have at last realised that it will be a long time before they become Shop Grainers.

We are wondering, and perhaps they are wondering too, if there has been a "slip-up" in the explaining and training they have received during the past eight weeks.

They are a grand crowd, abour fifteen of them in all, still with that scoolboy-cum-apprentice look and carefree, happy manner which is peculiar to their age and makes the poor old teacher feel he would glady exchange places with any one of them and start out again on the wonderful road of Apprenticeship.

It has previously been pointed out that there are not fifteen grainers in the whole of the town, but a look drifts into their eyes and they give the impression that that state of affairs is soon about to be remedied.

"Just let me get at those panels", they seem to say.

However, they are held on the leash yet awhile and first introduced to the various aspects and approaches to the art of graining.

The impression thay have of the craft is the same as that of a class of Plumbers or Bricklayers – a few notes, some practical work and the rest will come easily.

Comes the rude awakening when they are told there are no aids for them such as plans, specifications, plumb rules, chalk-lines, or even a Clerk of Works to put them on the right path.

No! Nothing but their own acquired skill and knowledge carried around in their hands and head.

A Secondary School, or even College, education gives no advantage, or easier way to the desired standard of craftsmanship in the art of graining, over the Elementary Schoolboy.

The senses of sight and colour take the place of mathematics and Latin.

To be able to look into a piece of figured oak and see wonderful pattern and colour it contains, to match it and build up their work means that these senses have to undergo long and steady training.

Confidence and Youth

If these pupils were to have watched an art student painting an oak tree or a pattern of acorns, they would have been thrilled at the student's skill and would have thought it quite beyond their possibilities, but not so the painting of the tree inside.

That is a job (they thought) such as any other in the Painting Trade.

They now know that they must not only reach the art student's standard but must even surpass it, before they may hope to become expert in their craft.

Having brought them to this frame of mind, the drawing of an oak tree, leaves and acorns, was carried out quite successfully.

The next step was the cutting up of the log and explaining how the grain is formed; the history, growth and uses of the tree from "Hiding King Charles" to the smoking of kippers and the utilisation of sawdust for cleaning furs.

They are now "wood-minded". By this, we do not suggest that they are now a class of "Archie Andrews" or "Blockheads" but that they have now reached the second stage.

"Cheers!" they say, "we have reached the second stage".

This happens also, to be the annoying stage; annoying for their employer, their colleagues at work and their teacher.

They can be seen during working hours, gazing into the windows of furniture shops, no doubt assessing their chances of matching some of the figured woods on view.

At work, they have to be told twice to "get

from the S.1 Grainers

that oak sideboard covered and take the cart back to the shop".

Now also, the classes are becoming merely sessions for a Debating Society which, with the teacher as chairman, decides which boys are fortunate in that they are working in the same shop as the "best grainer in town"; on the other hand, perhaps the teacher is first called upon to decide who is the town's best grainer, Mr. Brown or Mr. Jack Crow.

First Attempts
The first attempts are now made on paper with yellow grease crayon and washed over with water colour and "ticked" with sepia ink in place of the graining roller.

A demonstration of tools and their uses and the mixing of colour and ground, is given.

The completed work of each boy, i.e the oak tree, acorns and leaves, cutting of the log, sample of ground, tools and colours used, panels done in grease crayons and washes of the figure and sap, is then cut into the most favourable shape and mounted on brown paper.

Some of the exhibits show excellent work and we feel sure that these belong to the "window-gazers".

Having completed the previous studies, the Great Day, or perhaps we ought to say the Great Evening, arrives.

Most of the boys attend class armed with a large piece of cloth, a thumb nail that has been carefully nursed for the preceding two months and every intention of showing the teacher that his very apparent worries had all been needless and now all he must do is sit back, relax and watch!

Of course the opposite occurs.

In actual fact, the teacher almost begins to think he has forgotten to show them how much colour was needed to "rub in" the panel after noticing that one pupil has enough in the brush to grain a street of houses.

And the boy with the poultice, or whatever it is, on his thumb? Had the teacher folded the cloth like that and then stuck his thumb in the centre?

No. He was not dreaming. He had folded it and left his thumb partly exposed to show how the cloth could be easily moved after each marking, or set of markings.

He is beginning to wonder also, whether his teaching had been on "how to tar a gable end" or "how to apply creosote to rough undressed timber".

Had he explained the methods of breaking up the ground? He feels sure he had, and yet some of the boys were making marks as clear as chalk on a blackboard – stark, hard patterns with no variation in the colour.

Where was the balance and run, so many times mentioned and demonstrated?

Why so many interpretations of a Snakes and Ladder board? Why? Why? What had he done to deserve such treatment?

Sanity returns with the arrival of several S.2 grainers, who saunter into the classroom, cast a disdainful look at the work in progress, a pitying look at the teacher and proceed on their way with stage whispers of "flippin' kids", altogether forgetting, of course, that the teacher they pity had passed through exactly the same nightmare with themselves as the "flippin' kids".

Well, the panels are cleaned off, tools and materials put away, and with a cheery "Good Night, Sir", the boys are off, leaving the teacher to light his cigarette and wonder, as we are wondering – will there be another fifteen grainers?

Have they started in the proper way and how can he, the teacher, best help them to proficiency in this branch of the trade, or at the very least, how can he help them to appreciate good workmanship, and make them keep striving to that end for the rest of their working days.

Only time will tell.

C. S. CLARKE

The Journal of Decorative Art

79 articles between

August 1948

to

July 1955

Continental Methods of Training – 1

Introduction

ONE summer evening when I was twenty I sailed from Hull down the Humber, past Spurn Head, to the open North Sea, and across to Zeebrugee.

I was accompanied by another Bradford student and we were to be away from home for a year, to study painting and decorating at the Brussels Academy.

We had completed our course at the Bradford College of Art, and had spent several years on drawing.

The Continental schools were much talked of in England about that time. They were running fulltime p. & d. courses. In England all p. & d. classes were part-time, the remaining time being spent in art classes.

Our venture to the Continent was encouraged by the Principal and the head of the P. and D., Mr. Andrews.

After correspondence with Brussels we were admitted on the standard of our work and our examination results. We were also awarded a grant by the Bradford Education Committee.

On the boat were students going to schools all over Europe. They included two young men from Scarborough bound for Malines to study music. We saw them often afterwards.

When we returned to England, however, our friendship was short-lived; all four joined the Forces, and I am the only survivor.

The Continental people of that day cannot have heard of Ruskin. They clearly liked elaborate painted ornaments of the Louis XIV and Rococo styles in full colour and gold, and used it to good advantage.

Wood and marble imitations were widely used in a most pleasing manner. The work was done quickly, and executed with good taste, accurate colour and good design.

It was always quiet and dignified, and did not hit one in the eye as too often our English work did – and does.

In the Academy every form of decorating was taught thoroughly in every detail, to a high standard.

For the first few lessons we were graded until our level of ability was found. Many of the students were teachers who had come from the great cities of Europe to improve themselves.

The professor in charge of wood imitations was a first-rate artist and a fine linguist, speaking English, French, German, Spanish, Italian and Dutch, with Flemish or Walloon thrown in.

Most of the students were excellent at some branch of the craft before they came to Brussels, so they helped to raise the standard of the work, and the competition amongst them was very keen.

In the classrooms we always occupied the same places. On my right were two students from, respectively, Germany and Luxemburg, while on my left I had a Frenchman and a Dutchman. The latter had studied at the Van Der Burg school of painting, and was a first-class craftsman.

The first thing that impressed one about the graining was the size of the areas we tackled. The large scale, however, was good training and gave a breadth to our work, which made it easier afterwards to fill any space.

Most students looked upon graining as a stepping-stone to decoration, or as a very necessary subject to a teachers' curriculum.

At this time all firms of any size on the Continent employed at least one decorator who had gone through a full-time course at one of the schools.

They were better paid, of course, than ordinary journeymen. They dressed well and smoked cigars (which were duty free).

On the completion of my training I was found a post at Monte Carlo, in the South of France.

I had, however, other interests in England at that time, and I settled in Manchester as decorator to a well-known firm of decorators, furnishers and drapers.

Here most of my time was spent on decoration in theatres, churches, banks, law courts, and large mansions all over England.

It was a most interesting time and fine experience.

I spent altogether four years on the Continent, one year teaching the craft in Germany. This was the first of my many teaching appointments.

Classification of the Woods

It was general, on the Continent, to divide the woods for teaching purposes under the following heads:

Decorative Woods

Burr walnut, maccasar ebony, curly pine, the feather of mahogany, pollard and root oak.

Light Woods

Acacia, maple, sycamore, beech, light oak, and satinwood.

Fruit-bearing woods

Rosewood, olive, plum, cherry, apple, citroen

Resinous Woods

Pine, spruce, fir, cedar.

Hard Woods

Oak, elm, ash, teak, jarrah, walnut, mahogany, and birch.

I don't intend, however, to describe the detail of all these woods, but to select a few for attention. I intend to give as many sketches and examples as possible, with the minimum of written matter.

This short series will, I trust, be useful to teachers and students alike.

I intend to devote one article to the construction and composition of the wood itself.

Illustration number one is of oak figure, just to give a wood flavour. In the next article I will deal with the construction of the heartwood from a decorative design point of view.

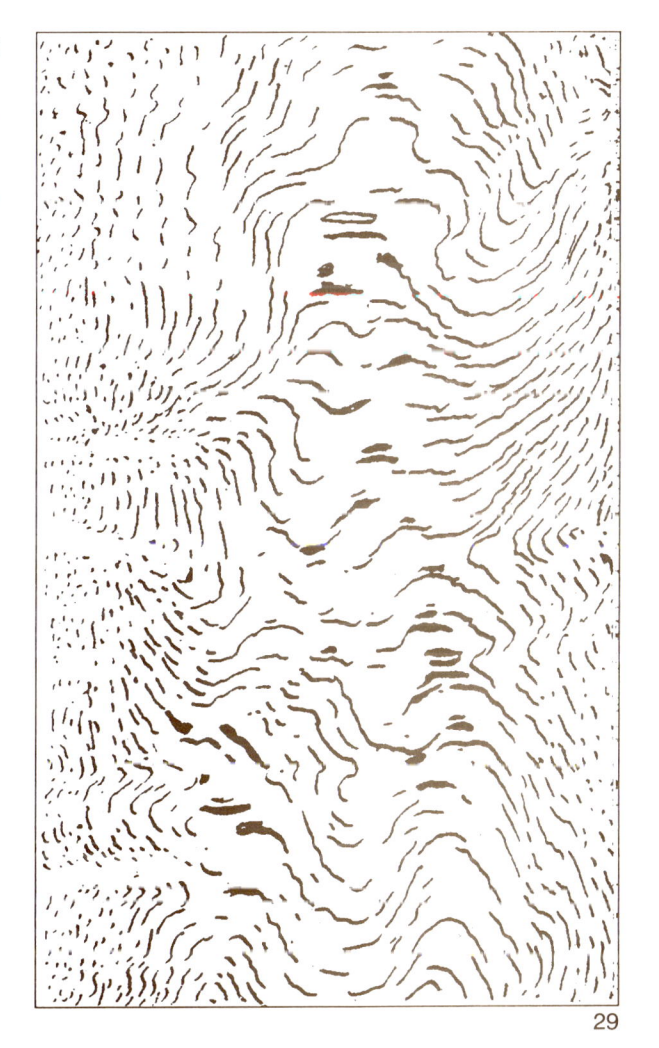

Tools and Brushes for Graining

THE following is a brief list of the brushes and tools used by the Continental decorator for graining purposes. Some are the same as we have always used, whilst others are slightly different.

(a) The badger hair softener 4in. wide, set in ivory with detachable handle. Used mainly for water colour work.

(b) The hog hair softener, 3in. wide, with 4in. bristle. Has a long handle, and is used only for softening oil colour.

(c) Hog hair fitches as in England.

(d) Set of steel graining combs; graining horn of bone with a fair amount of spring; coarse hair comb, used for dividing the bristle of the overgrainer.

(e) Brushes for glazing and overgraining, made from hog hair 1½in. long, 4in. wide and ¼in. thick. A pair is always included, and they are very useful, serving the same purpose as our mottler.

(f) Brushes for drawing the veins. 1½in. and 2in. wide. 1½in. bristle, ¼in. thick. Strong, firm brushes.

(g) About three tools are carried for applying the colour. Grey or black hog hair are satisfactory for this purpose. Under no circumstance should the mottlers, or marking brushes be used for rubbing in. This blurs the edges.

(h) Camel hair water colour brushes are used for marking in turpentine. These are bound together with wood and string.

Continental Methods of Training – III

(i) A cutter made from other hair is used for sharp water colour work. This brush has a long handle, is about 2in. wide with short ½in. bristle or hair, cut very sharp. Very clean and quick in use.

(j) A dotter for maple, consisting of a hog hair pencil ⅛in. diameter, cut short, and with the centre burnt out with a red hot needle.

(j) Sponge, pieces of cork, 3in. square and ¼in. thick, for cutting to different widths, to be used for coarse combing. Hessian canvas, billiard cloth, rag, well worn but clean washed.

(k) Palette board, knife and two large dippers to take a 2in. brush.

THE GRAINING OF CEDAR

Origin: West Indies, North Africa and the Himalayas. Cedar is a coniferous tree of great beauty. The wood is a light red-brown colour, pleasantly marked, with a difference of markings and colour in each country. The wood is extremely durable without any paint treatment.

Cedar will grow in England, and many fine trees are to be seen in old parks. The trunk divides early into upward-spreading branches, covered with great, flat, impressive foliage. The lowest of the branches droop down almost to the ground.

No. 8

Ground: A warm buff colour, composed of white, yellow ochre, Venetian red and a touch of lemon chrome.

Palette: Vandyke brown, burnt sienna, crimson lake, all ground in oil. Vandyke in water.

Dipper: One part linseed oil, three parts turpentine, and a few drops of terebine, with a touch of megilp or glaze.

Brushes: One two-inch tool, fitches, hog hair softener, badger and mottler.

Sundries: Two burnt sienna Conte crayons. 6 in. square jute canvas.

Method of working: Oil in the ground with mixture from the dipper. Afterwards brush on just a touch of burnt sienna and Vandyke, with very little crimson. The colour should be very faint, but heavier down the sides, where the heartwood markings are going to be placed. Wipe off any excess of colour down the centre, or where the markings are to be placed, as the veining may run during softening.

Knots: Put in your knots with Vandyke and a fitch. They should be small, but quite dark in colour. Draw in the veins round the knots, working from the centre outwards. Most heartwood centres are adorned with a knot, generally two. Knots also occur at intervals of nine to fifteen inches all up the sides as well.

Drawing: In drawing the veins, two Conte pencils may be used side by side for speed, and by holding at varying angles and widths a better effect is obtained than working with single pencils. The lead pencil type Conte is better than sticks, as our line is only about 1/16 inch thick.

Generally the heartwood markings are pointed and narrow, whilst on the finished work they are subdued by the prominence given to the glazing of the knots.

Drawings five, six and seven show the knots and the drawing to be worked with the Conte. These are shown as studies only; the markings are small in scale and are deliberately overemphasised, so that they may be clear and easy to work from. Practice on paper before attempting to work on an oiled ground.

Side Marking: The sides are drawn down with the piece of canvas that has been neatly folded into a square pad. This portion is left white on the 5, 6 and 7 sketches, but is shown on number 8. The small amount of colour that we used in the glaze is sufficient to leave a soft-wood grain effect. By varying the pressure a lighter or darker effect can be obtained. Colour can also be drawn around the knots. Cotton rag or sponge will not answer. Both pick up the colour.

The knots should be outlined with a light line, and cracks made from the centre by using the end of the fitch before the colour sets.

Softening: The whole is now softened carefully with the hog hair softener. All

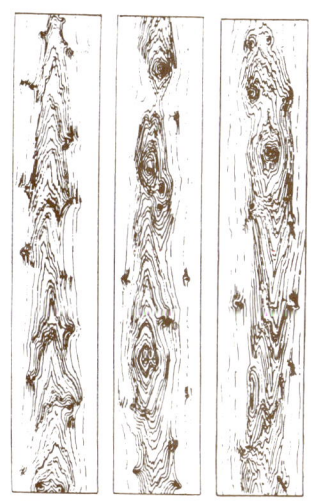

No. 5   No. 6   No. 7

softening is done with the grain. On the Conte markings the softening should be inwards towards the knot; any softening across will produce a woolly effect.

Glazing: The work should be dry in 24 hours, when the glazing should be done with Vandyke in water. No binder is required within this time. Glazing is only light generally; the greatest weight is used round the knots, and then down the centre of the heartwood markings: mottling is used very little, and fine waves are the only ones required. Soften gently with the badger, drawing the colour under the knots, which show up more prominently than the veining of the heartwood.

Graining Mahogany

Cherry Mahogany

MAHOGANY is grown in Spain, Africa, the West Indies, and South America. It is comparatively easy to imitate, and has been popular with decorators almost from its introduction into England some 180 years ago.

Mahogany is a hard, durable wood, takes a high polish, or may be flatted down. It is well suited for panelling.

It belongs to the cedar family and its botanical name is Sweitena mahoggni, after the famous botanist, Gerald V. Sweiten, who discovered it.

The trees grow to a great height, often eighty feet to the lowest branches, with trunk sixteen feet in circumference.

The crown of the tree is wide, spreading awkwardly, with shiny lanceolate leaves, in threes and fives.

The flowers are carried between the leaf stalks, turning to large fruits which contain the seeds.

Colour

Mahogany varies from a light cherry red in the African variety to the deep purple red of the Spanish. With age mahogany deepens very much in colour, with the exception of the British Honduras variety, which is usually well figured and of a yellow-brown colour.

Continental Methods of Training – IV

In the green state, mahogany is so heavy that it will not float on water.

Varieties

Let us now consider the different types of figured mahogany.

There are four, i.e. Cherry, Sapele, Heartwood and Feathered.

Let us consider them separately.

1. Cherry Mahogany – Acajou Moire

This is a wavy-shaded variety, almost covered with mottling.

The Ground Colour should be a reddish buff, prepared from white, venetian red, ochre, and a touch of chrome. The ground should not be flat; a drop of varnish helps to harden it, and there should be two parts of turps to one of oil.

The Palette is vandyke brown, burnt sienna, and mahogany or crimson lake, ground in water.

The Brushes, etc., required are two 2-inch tools, sponge, mottlers, cutter and badger, plus a bucket of water.

Method

Cherry mahogany is usually grained in watercolour; it is simple to work, as the same forms are repeated every few inches. It consists of long dark shaded parts, well mottled down the edges of the shadows.

Lay in the darkest colour with vandyke, using a tool. The wavy streaks should be 1½in. to 2in. wide and about 15in. long.

Keep the colour on the wet side and arrange the streaks 3in. or 4in. apart.

Fill in the remainder with sienna and lake. The marks of the tools are useful, and should not be brushed out. Soften gently in a vertical direction.

Now proceed to mark with the mottler, which should be clean. Dip frequently in the bucket of water, shaking out any excess.

Work down the edges of the dark parts; then soften in a horizontal direction only.

The cuts should be made with just a twist of the wrist; in this way the marks will be all slightly tapered, and not thick or square at both ends, as they are sure to be if the mottler is removed each time.

If the cutter is now used in the same manner a few cleaner marks can be made, leaving a lighter line in places.

When dry, fasten with goldsize and turps.

Glazing should be done with the same colours. This will give depth without making the colour too heavy. Parts can be cleaned off with the sponge, and additional mottling added if required. Soften well with the badger.

2. Sapele Mahogany – Acajou Mouchete

This is a spotted variety with dark red spots all over the veining; the veins are not very prominent.

The Ground is slightly darker than for Cherry Mahogany, and is prepared by using the same colours in varying quantities.

The special features of this wood are the many dark knots which are scattered over the surface.

The Palette is black, burnt sienna, and lake in oil, vandyke and lake in water.

The Brushes and Tools needed for oil colour are the graining horn and clean rag, hog hair softener and fitches; tool, mottler and badger for watercolour.

Method

Rub in a thin glaze of oil colour, using burnt sienna and a touch of lake.

Put in the dark knots and markings where required with black and soften with the hog hair softener. Grain the heartwood marking around the knots, some in alignment down the sides. The marking of the veins is again narrow.

When dry, glaze in watercolour using vandyke and lake; draw the colour below the knots and soften with badger softener.

Sapele Mahogany

Graining Mahogany (continued)

Mahogany Heartwood – Acajou Femelle

THIS is a plainer, quieter type of mahogany, representing the heartwood markings only. The figure is akin to walnut in size and shape, but the heartwood shapes are rounder than those of most woods, with very few knots, and those dark in colour and small. The markings on the heartwood rings are narrow, and lighter than the ground or glaze. To imitate we have to wipe out, instead of, as with other varieties, adding darker colour. The whole effect is simple and calls for really good drawing of the shapes, to obtain any real quality in the work. The general colour is a burnt sienna brown, not a lake red.

The Ground

A medium to warm buff composed of white, Oxford ochre, orange chrome and a touch of burnt umber.

The Palette

Burnt sienna, crimson lake, and black, ground in oil. Vandyke brown and burnt sienna in water.

Brushes and Tools

Flogger, badger, hog hair fitches, mottler, graining horn, rag and hessian canvas, plus a few tools and water.

In the Dipper

Oil and turpentine in equal quantities, with a few drops of terebine.

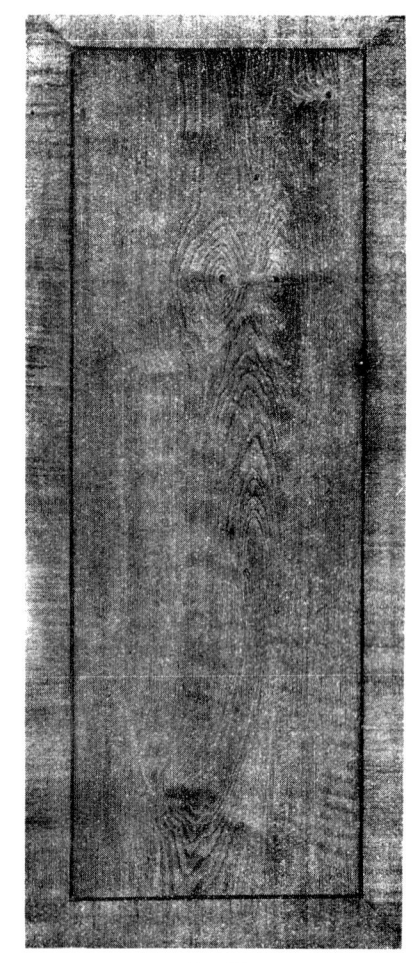

No. 15

Continental Methods of Training – V

Method

Flog in the ground very lightly, using three parts sienna to one of brown, well flogged upwards to a fine texture.

Bind with a few drops of acetic acid, as neither gold size nor varnish will be used for fixing. The flogged ground is not only intended to give texture, but to hold the subsequent glaze from running.

Rub in a transparent glaze of oil colour, composed largely of burnt sienna, with a touch of lake and black in parts. The balance of medium to pigment calls for much skill, as does the correct amount of brushing, which should be done sparingly. The drying should be slow, to allow ample time for the graining, which is not so quick as water colour.

The centre of the work, panel or door, should be a little darker than the outer field. Wipe off any surplus colour with rag, brush up and lay off again. This should he done slowly, deliberately and with the grain, with the minimum of brushing.

Graining

The marking of the grain is done with a narrow, round, graining horn, using rag or billiard cloth. Commence graining round the centre of the knot nearest the base, working outwards and upwards.

Much imagination can be used in the drawing; many unusual shapes occur. The centres are often nine to fifteen inches long, with two or more knots at the ends. The design is fairly large, though the markings are fine and near together.

The sketches and finished examples give a fair basis on which to work. I do recommend, however, that students should draw in a sketch book any good examples they may come across, for future reference and use.

The drawing of the heartwood is confined to the curly portions, the sides being drawn down with the hessian canvas, which gives just enough grain marking.

With a worn fitch now proceed to remove colour from the inside of the wider view, graduating to nothing before the next view is reached; this is effective without being striking.

The whole is softened very gently with the hog hair softener, with the grain of the wood.

The few knots may now be strengthened with black and lake.

A star shape is often seen in the knot; this may be drawn with the end of the fitch. The outline of the knot may also be emphasised in the same manner. Then soften again.

Glazing

The glazing is done with vandyke brown and burnt sienna, ground in water. All the surface is laid in first with an even coat, a little thinner being added in the centre, where the markings are assumed to be.

Proceed to execute the mottling, with very gentle, soft, shadows, making it shady in parts. One side only of the knots is shady; the other is usually plain. The outer sides are almost straight, without any mottling.

The softening with the badger should be thorough, across the grain where fine mottling is showing, but gently upwards and inwards towards the centre of any knots.

No glazing should be so dark as to cover up the previous graining.

The whole effect, to be satisfactory when completed, should show the gentle waves in parts, and it should be darker down the centre where the heartwood markings occur, and the colour should be quiet, and not a lake red.

The markings of the grain are clear in the illustrations 12, 13 and 14, which are intended for purposes of practice and study. Number 15 is a finished painted example from No. 14 drawing.

Note:

I have had many kind enquiries asking if the reproduced examples are from real wood. They are not; they are and will be, reproduced from painted examples.

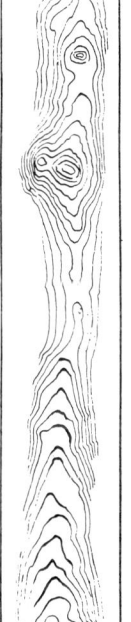

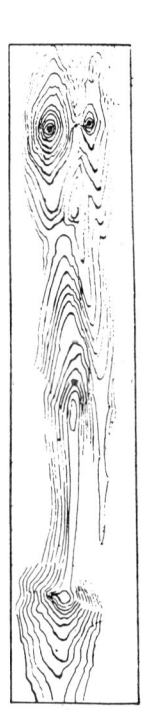

Nos. 12, 13 and 14

In continental schools no natural examples are to be seen. When I was a student the lecturer or demonstrator always worked the example before the class, and this was the only one we were allowed to study at that time.

We were, however, encouraged to make sketches in our own time, from the many large public buildings in the capital.

Graining Mahogany (continued)

FEATHERED Mahogany is a fountain-shaped arrangement of the grain, very showy and decorative.

The English translation of Gerbe is of course "sheaf of corn." "Garb" in heraldry has the same meaning; both words aptly describe the graceful flow of the lines of radiation.

This feather of Mahogany only occurs in a few trees, which command a high price. The wood is, however, weak structurally, and is used mainly for veneers.

The size of the feathers varies from one foot to five or six in length, with proportionate width. I had one recently that was much higher than myself.

It is a mistake, however, to use a large feather crushed up on a panel. Both the examples executed to illustrate this article would be better with more surrounding space.

Colour varies from the dark purple red to the now more modern bleached cream colour. These are the colours used in my two illustrations, 16 and 17.

The very bright red colour that we often have to work from is not a natural colour, but may have been treated with a bichromatic of potash solution.

The tone value of the colour is important; the darkest tone is down the centre of the feather, the medium on the outer field, whilst the lightest is between the two, on the edge of the dark centre – the top, of the curl of the feather marking.

All the previous types of mahogany are used to a smaller extent with the feather, as the upper portion works into plain grain or heartwood markings, and if the panel is wide, mottling often develops down the sides.

Continental Methods of Training – VI

Ground Colour

This should be a red-buff composed of Venetian red, Oxford ochre, white and a touch of orange chrome, the quantities diminishing in the order given.

Tools and Sundries

Badger softener, tools, mottlers, overgrainer, cutter, sponge and a small piece of leather.

Palette

Blue black, burnt sienna, crimson lake and vandyke brown, all ground in water.

Method of Working

This wood may be worked in oil, water or in several combinations of the two.

No.16 Bleached Feathered Mahogany

Oil colour was most favoured on the Continent, where time was not a deciding factor, as it often is here.

Both the examples shown are carried out in water colour, the method I intend to deal with in this article.

Take your tool, assisted by the wash leather, and wet your ground over; a little fullers' earth or whiting may be used to stop cissing.

This is caused by the grease on the face of the paint film, which in turn is valuable, as it assists in binding the water colour.

Lay in your colour, both in the tones and places required, taking care not to cross, but to work with the grain.

Use black, vandyke and crimson for the centre of the feather, and for the sides, sienna and vandyke.

Keep your design firmly in your mind, or better still make a small sketch of it on paper and fix it near you for reference.

As you will be a few minutes working on each different process, make sure your colours are all very wet, or they will set before the work is complete.

Graining

On large surfaces I often divide the work into two or three portions, working out my divisions, with the grain of the wood.

Now with the badger softener draw the primary grain, carefully following the feather shape round. Take great care not to let the sides of the feather bulge out unduly.

The graceful shape depends on good drawing at this stage.

The top ellipse must be narrower, and smaller, than the one at the base, which is not easy unless you keep them well in check.

Try to have a good wide base, with your dark colour very wide at the bottom, and finish with your vertical sides as straight as practicable.

A craftsman must be very good indeed to make a satisfactory job of any work that finishes with wavy lines, even down one side of a panel.

We must aim at an appearance of stability in our work.

On the dark centre, we should now work some black, or vandyke, with the overgrainer.

It is only required on the darker portion, but the first lines of the badger must be accurately followed.

With the moist sponge draw the sides of the feather, again following the first grain marking made with the badger.

Hold the sponge loosely, paying particular attention to the top, which you do first; give it a slight roll to get some fine accidental markings.

These form a natural jagged edge, all down the feather.

Don't be tempted, to go more than two thirds up a panel with the sponge marking, at which

No.17 Red Feathered Mahogany

height the two sides should be touching and working away to nothing.

With the badger, soften the work quickly and lightly all up the centre, gently pushing the dark colour towards the sides.

The side should now be softened vertically with the grain.

Should any more accidental marks be required they must be put in with the sponge or leather.

Colour may be added to the sides with the sponge only, and softened into the other work.

With your sharp civet cutter dipped in water and shaken out, make the clean fine lines of light down the centre.

These should merge into each other in gentle curves; they should not cross over or be stiff and straight.

A little mottling may be done down the sides with the same tool; this must not be overdone, or the general effect will be spoiled.

Soften this mottling gently across the grain only.

Glazing

Allow the work at least two hours before fastening with goldsize and turpentine, the longer the better.

Glaze in the same colours again, darkening the centre of the feather.

Glaze the sides only a little to allow the mottling to show.

All mottling should be done at this time, and not with the graining when glazing is subsequently carried out.

Thus the marks are kept quiet and in keeping.

No.16 was completed in one operation, whilst No.17 was glazed with a second and quite separate operation.

A fine cutter is an essential tool in good graining or glazing in water colour.

The fine fur of the civet or polecat makes the best. Hoghair is too clumsy, and coarse.

Other substances, such as perspex, or the sharp edge of cardboard, make quite good substitutes.

Of the colours used both in glazing and graining, in No.17, nine tenths consisted of vandyke brown, with one tenth divided between black, crimson and burnt sienna.

MAHOGANY
See also:
The Graining of Mahogany
164
Mahogany (Sapele Variety)
209

In the bleached mahogany example (16) three quarters of the colour was blue-black, and a quarter, vandyke brown.

This example was worked from a white ground.

As this subject is far from exhausted and is a favourite with painters, I propose to return later to the water and oil process, giving at the same time a sheet of sketches of different types of the feather.

Next month we will study the Rosewood of India.

Graining Rosewood

Continental Methods of Training – VII

ROSEWOOD is a deep transparent brown to crimson coloured wood, of great beauty in both colour and markings.

It gives a good decorator plenty of scope in the use of colour and good drawing.

The French name is Palissandre.

The vein markings are all one colour, black; they are narrow and often complicated.

Glazing plays a very important part in the success of the finished effect, each shape having a different tone, which requires to be worked separately.

This is one of the very few woods that gives off the fragrance of a flower. This fragrance is very evident in new unpolished wood.

On account of its high cost however, it is only used for first class furniture, then only in veneer.

Examples from which one is called to work, have often been stained heavily with crimson lake to obliterate the heartwood markings, which, of course, is unnatural.

The full page drawing is a typical example of the way complicated markings appear to grow from the side or from under each other.

Only a few woods do this. The trunk of the vine often grows in this manner.

Examples of Rosewood are sometimes plain, sometimes straight grain and sometimes simple heartwood with markings down the centre.

Inlays of Maple or stainwood harmonise well with Rosewood.

Origin

The country of origin is India. The most popular species is Dalbergia latifolia, and is the one that I discuss.

Other species are grown in smaller quantities in Jamaica, New South Wales, and Burma.

The Ground

This should be a warm buff, from medium to deep in tone, prepared from Oxford Ochre, a touch of Umber, Venetian Red, and a little white.

A drop of varnish is desirable to harden the ground.

Palette

Vandyke Brown, Crimson Lake and Blueblack; all ground in water.

Tools and Sundries

Fine black crayons, flogger, tools, mottler, hog hair and badger softener.

No.18

In the dipper, 1 part oil, 1 part turpentine and turbine driers.

Preparation

Rub in a thin light transparent Vandyke wash, beat with the flogger, working upwards to a fine texture.

Bind with a suitable binder and allow ample time to dry and harden, preferably overnight.

Gently rub in mixture from the dipper to oil the ground for the subsequent graining. Apply liberally.

This oiling is partly intended to bind the flogged ground and the vein markings. It also helps with the softening of the dark markings which must spread slightly with the oil.

It should be kept under the running stage, though it should not require rag to dry up any surplus.

No colour is used with this oil glaze.

Graining

The grain markings are now drawn with the two black crayons held side by side; two give far better results than one held singly.

One, of course, may be used for a centre or for small finishing touches but it is better to do as much as possible with two.

I always used black stick conté crayon, but this is now difficult to obtain.

40

My finished example, No.18, has been worked with two crayons of the "Black Prince" type.

Commence your drawing near the base with the centre of a knot. Work outwards and upwards until the shape begins to form.

Next draw the strong outline at the outside of the complete heart.

Now return to the inside and fill in the spaces with finer veining.

You should now have the cue for the second from one of the knots on the outer edge; this will form the centre for your next shape.

Advantage should be taken of the heavier markings to give design to your work, a good length gives elegance.

The dark markings are obtained by running over the lines a few times with the crayon; unlike the brush extra pressure makes little or no difference.

The fine veins are drawn nearer together or wider apart to give variety.

Continue with one shape springing from the side, end, or top until the centre of your panel or door is covered.

The sides should now be completed with long wavy lines, conforming to the inner shapes.

Fill in the spaces with short light wavy lines; only a small degree of waviness is required.

Amongst the complicated markings a number of plain portions may be left void; these will be almost hidden by the glazing.

Another point to note in the drawing is a number of semi-circles down the edges of the heavier lines; they occur both inwards and outwards and often contain a knot.

The drawing, No.19, contains about the maximum number of complications encountered in this wood.

When the drawing is completed it should be softened with the hog hair softener along the grain, very gently at first, but more vigorously if the oiled ground is setting.

The sides may be softened more than the centre where the small detail is required to show.

Should any darker lines require strengthening, more crayon may be added at this stage and again softened.

Glazing

The grain markings all show prominently but the glazing tones them down.

The glazing is best done in water colour. To do this procceed as before, with leather or sponge almost dry, to remove the surface grease and to stop cissing.

Next apply a thin glaze of vandyke over the portions to be finished in the lightest tone; work the shaded parts with the mottler and soften.

Three separate tones are used in my example which also vary in colour. Vandyke is the the lightest; black, the medium and crimson the darkest tone.

Work the crimson second and bear in mind that lake colours are fugitive and it is therefore advisable to use more than is finally required; it will tone down to a warm brown in a few days.

OTHER WOODS
See also:
Graining of Obeche	126
The Graining of Sycamore	130
Graining of Bleached Rosewood	182
Graining of Beechwood	190
Juniper	194
Willow	203
Lacewood	218
Crown Elm	221
Satinwood	226
Californian Red Wood	229
Makore Curl	270
Silver Spruce	302

The whole should be worked quickly, in a cool room if possible, the tones and colours being applied roughly with a tool. Soften before any part is allowed to dry.

On large surfaces it is better to work a few shapes down the centre, then glaze the sides (which are always lightest), last.

Joinings among the knots often add to the desirable accidental effect.

Should a very deep glaze be required, particular care must be taken with the badger softening.

It is safer to fasten with goldsize and turps if a reglaze is required in order to obtain an even depth.

With skill and care it is possible to wet the surface over and to add more colour even without fastening.

In my finished example, the shapes are too large to make a good proportioned panel.

A larger amount of plainer work down the sides would improve the panel.

In my office I have a rosewood table the top of which is 6 ft. by 3 ft. It has been used as a model for many fine jobs.

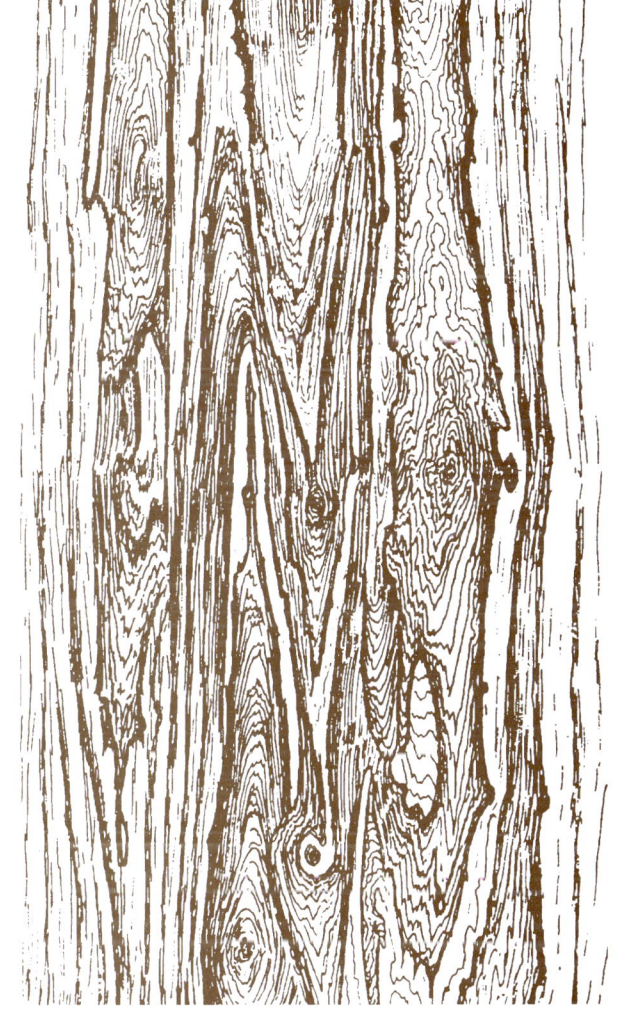

No.19

Continental Methods of Training – VIII

Grand Antique Marble

THE use of marbling on painted interiors is much older than wood imitations, which have only been used since the softer pine replaced hardwoods in building.

Marbling appears to have originated in Italy, where many of our real marbles are obtained.

Often marble was used for the lining of the lower portions of walls, the upper parts being plastered and treated with painted imitations.

Many fine buildings abroad still receive this treatment, the colour and craftsmanship being so remarkably good that detection is often difficult. The use of large scale marbling on plastered wall surfaces is still very popular in most European cities.

The large scale of the work calls for more simple, open, treatment than is appropriate in small panel work, where beauty and detail are developed by the use of many small glazes and fine vein markings.

For speed in working two brushes are always used on the Continent, sometimes bound together, sometimes held loose, but held about two inches apart. They give wonderful accidental effects.

The numbers of types of marble used are not numerous, Grand Antique is one of the most vigorous of the Breccia type.

Most continental decorators look on this marble as we regard figure oak in graining, i.e., as basic; the colours are neutral, and thus all our attention can be devoted to the markings.

Description: Grand Antique which is black and white, is a cheerful, showy marble. The best marbles of this type I can recall are in the Hotel des Invalides, Paris, which is open to visitors, and is well worth a visit.

The sharp pointed broken stones are the result of volcanic eruption, which has shattered a bed of black carbon, into which a matrix of white cement filling has filtered.

The whole has been compressed with the weight of earth over a long period of time. The shape of the stones varies much; generally they are angular. I give this angular variety first, to overcome the painters' weakness for the round oval types, which are sometimes overdone.

There are many sizes of stones, but three at least, large, medium and small should be aimed at. In the larger figures or stones, which are up to three feet in height, one side is clean and almost straight, whilst the opposite is very much broken by small stones or a network of fine veins. Observe how a black, medium-sized stone usually has on one side only, a fine line of white; this keeps the whole effect delicate. A broad white line around each stone would look clumsy.

The smallest stones are about one inch long, but are still sharp and angular, forming fine chains across or down the largest stones.

It will be noted that the medium stones are the most irregular in shape.

No.20

Design: Marbling on a large scale, to be a success, must be treated as a design, and the direction of the pattern must first be decided.

In the two examples (Nos. 20 and 21) the pattern runs from right at the top to left at the bottom, i.e., from corner to corner.

Left to right, and vertical, are also used, to give variety when a dado or wall surface is being cut up.

The large stones should be placed first in chalk, allowing from three to nine inches for the white matrix containing the medium and fine stones.

These are grouped together in a certain way. On the large white mass a fine vein or crack of black often connects the smaller stones together.

There is a sparkle of white or yellow grey on the large black stones, with a thin broken glaze of black on the white chalky parts, both being so delicate as not to upset the clean appearance.

Origin: France and the Pyrenees mountains.

Ground: Black, but occasionally white, when not many of the large stones are desirable.

Palette: Black, white, and yellow ochre.

In the Dipper: One part oil, three parts turpentine and liquid driers.

Tools and Brushes: Two squirrel or fine hair pencils, about ¼in. diameter, fixed about one inch apart. Two worn No.3 sable pencils, again fixed. One No.4 and 5 sponge. Hog hair softener and 2in. tool.

Method: Rub in a glaze coat (with the tool) from the dipper; wipe off any excess with a rag.

Pass a thin stipple of grey, using black, white and ochre, all over the surface, using the sponge. Abroad we used a fine brush named a "chequeter" for this purpose; it was much cleaner than a sponge.

Using the two squirrel pencils, proceed to paint in the white portions on the large areas, working round the stones as it were.

The drawing should be started in the top left hand corner. Take care not to fill in the work too much or too quickly. Try to keep both brushes working at the same time; this gives a far more accidental effect that is possible with a single pencil.

The smaller pencils should now be used double for the finer work. Use a single pencil for the final shaping of the outside of the stones.

A few of the smaller stones are filled in with dark grey. When hard and dry the large masses of white require a second coat of white, which is quickly applied.

Glazing: Soften the surface with an oily rag. Proceed to "granite" the insides of a few of the larger stones more vigorously. Block in a few smaller stones if required. With the sponge, pass a broken glaze of grey over some of the white parts. Mark around some stones with a very faint tint of ochre. With a pencil put in the fine black veins from stone to stone in a wavy line.

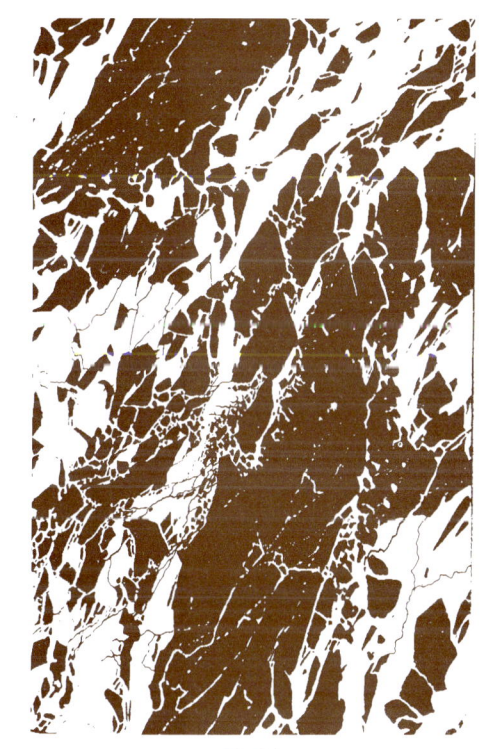

No.21

Harmonies: Many other varieties may be used with Grand Antique, including Grey Grave, Sienna, Hevouto, Breche Violette, Skyros, Breche Verte, Vert de Mer, Serancolin and Breche Caroline.

Breche-Verte Marble

Description
BRECHE-VERTE, as the name implies, is a green brecciated marble, breccia being a type of marble consisting of angular fragments united by a matrix or cement-like substance.

The shape of the components indicates that they have been produced by a fracture and have not been subjected to rounding by attrition – the act of wearing or rubbing. This produces round or oval shapes.

The general effect is green. The largest stones are cream colour, shaded towards the edge with gold and divided over the surface with pale gold veins and with almost white centres, well softened, to blend with the cream and gold.

A medium green is the filling colour of the average stone, whilst the smallest shapes are of cream colour.

The shapes are less angular than Grand Antique and not so wild in their distribution.

The matrix, or binding cement, is more varied in colour and consists of blues, greens and gold with their tints and shades.

All are applied in glazes, with a sparkle of the light ground showing through.

Composition
A bed of white calcite lying deep in the earth is stained with an iron solution to a creamy yellow or pale gold colour.

Continental Methods of Training – IX

This bed is shattered by a volcanic explosion when green coloured organic matter percolates into the opening in liquid form.

This binds the broken stones into a solid mass and the heavy pressure of the earth above slowly hardens the whole.

Country of Origin
Italy.

Ground
A creamy white.

Palette
White, chrome yellow, golden ochre, Brunswick green, Prussian blue and black.

In the Dipper
Turpentine three parts, oil one part and liquid driers.

Brushes and Tools
Sponge, hog hair pencils, a few fitches, worn sable pencils, tools and hog hair softener.

Method
Soften the ground with the mixture from the dipper and a piece of rag to prevent a raw or vivid appearance in the finished work.

No.23

Glazing

The glazing is carried out with the same colours and brushes.

Soften the ground all over with a glaze from the dipper.

With a clean sponge charged with white, stipple over most of the surface, add a little chrome and stipple remaining parts, but leave some stones untouched.

With a fitch lighten the centres of the largest shapes and darken the edges with ochre; more of the medium stones may be filled in with tones of green.

On the darker parts glaze with a green made from Brunswick and black and, in places, ochre.

The aim should be variety with harmony in colour and tone.

Much or little may be made of the work, according to the time spent in glazing.

On a large wall filling little, or no, glazing will be required, whilst more is required on a dado where columns or small panels are decorated with marble; more labour would be put into the glazing.

Common Errors

The common errors that occur in this work are:

(1) Making the green too bright;
(2) Making the shapes too regular;
(3) Having the colour too monotonous.

Harmonies

Other marbles that harmonize well with Breche Verte are St. Annes, Skyros, Grand Antique, Rouge Royal, Breche Caroline, Black and Gold, Levanto and Paonazzo.

Sketches

The large reproduction, No. 22, is taken from a sketch that I made from a slab in Brussels.

It measured seven feet by four feet; this makes the scale about one inch to one foot.

All the lines show up clearly, making it useful for practice and study purposes, but it is all of one tone.

No. 23 was painted in colour, and gives the tone values correctly.

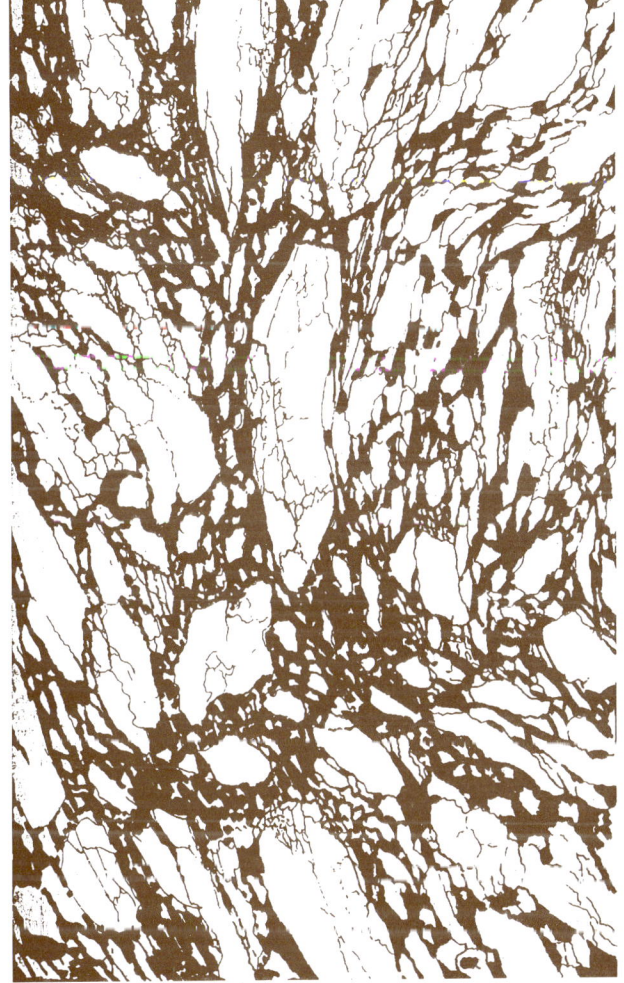

Breche-Verte Marble No.22

> Continental Methods of Training – X

Sienna Marble

THERE are many yellow marbles but none is as beautiful, or as rich in colouring, as Sienna marble. I shall always remember the richly painted Sienna marble imitation in the main entrance and large staircase of an Hotel in the Dom Platz, Cologne. This Hotel belonged to an English tourist company but was probably decorated by a Cologne firm. The bright orange, yellow and sienna did not appear to have faded in the least, but had developed and darkened all to good effect.

Sienna varies form a light greenish cream colour to an almost orange brown. A fine example of the dark Convent Sienna is to be seen at Winmarleigh Hall, Lancashire, recently taken over for a college by the Ministry of Agriculture. The Sienna marble most favoured on the continent, for large scale wall decoration, is medium to light in colour, well softened, and containing large stones of rectangular oval shape divided from each other by chain formations composed of medium to small stones.

The general colour of the veins is a yellow brown, some reds are used but are not prominent. Much white is found in fairly heavy chains crossing the large stones at random. The breccia matrix is very narrow and only occurs in the medium and dark varieties.

In the lighter varieties, pale grey, cream, white and greenish yellow occur on the light golden yellow, with a faint sienna outline for the veining; this could be described as a brocotel marble. The design is steady to solid, with a more even arrangement of stone in two sizes, large and medium. Very few small stones are found as the matrix is very limited. The shape and size of the stones are partly dependent on the cutting of the marble; I will, however, consider this with the brocotel type later.

Owing to the large size of the stones, the drawing requires a fair amount of accuracy, the angular breccia and the elongated brocotel give Sienna a distinct character of its own. Almost all the colours in the rainbow are to be found at times in sienna. These occurs largely in the veins and are caused by oxides of metals that have percolated into the cracks after an earthquake. The larger stones are lighter in colour, the darker tones follow the veins all of which are narrow compared with the previous examples.

Origin: Italy; named after the town of Sienna in the province of Tuscany. Many varieties are named after the quarries from which they are obtained.

Composition: This marble is composed of crystallized calcite, coloured with the salts of such metals as iron, manganese and cobalt. Vegetable or organic substances form the darker parts.

Tools Required: Fitches, tools, rag, pencils, sponge and hog hair softener.

Palette: White, Lemon Chrome, Yellow Ochre, Black, Raw Sienna, Prussian Blue, Crimson Lake.

In the Dipper: Two parts turpentine, one part oil, a few drops terebine.

Method: Soften the ground first with the oily rag. Proceed to lay in glazes with ochre, a touch of lemon

No.23

chrome, zinc white, and in parts orange chrome. Fix your mind on your direction and the position of larger stones or, better still, draw them on paper before you start.

Keep some areas a cool grey colour broken with the sponge and softened. Make others a clear lemon chrome cream, shaded light towards the centre of the stone. The Largest area should be tinted a good rich yellow made from ochre and a touch of chrome. I find a tool used firmly and vigorously, with turns of the wrist, quite satisfactory for laying in these glazes. A rag or sponge should be used in conjunction to wipe out at the same time, which gives a charming shaded effect. The accidental effects that can be obtained in marbling are delightful but well known principles in the use of colour must be obeyed to obtain good results. Aim at getting many tones, tints and colours of cream to rich orange gold, clearly defined in separate areas; these will be outlined later by veins.

The fitch should be used to apply stronger tints of Raw and Burnt Sienna, Vermilion and Purple. The sponge moistened with turps should be used to break up and spread these deeper, brighter colours which are used sparingly and only where the heavy matrix markings are to be placed.

The background glazes should give a clear picture of what the finished work will be like; the marbling is now almost three parts completed. Soften vigorously the larger areas where the largest stones will be placed with the hog hair softener, but only lightly in the darker small stone areas. These preliminary glazes can be put in quite successfully with water colour for smaller work and followed by oil colour for the veining.

The veining is done with one or two pencils, working near together, for the best accidental effect. The colour used is largely Raw Sienna which is semi-transparent. Work with the sides of the pencil as well as the point, alter the amount of weight continually and so obtain a broken or wider line in places, not the clean-cut line we require in lettering.

The large stones are surrounded by chains of smaller stones all falling in the same direction to keep the balance and steady effect. Part of the veins may be done in Burnt Sienna, Purple, and Crimson lake in diminishing quantities. Wipe out with the rag all the colour from many of the smaller shapes to show the cream coloured ground.

Splash with turps in places to open out the colour. This can be done by charging a fitch with turps only and striking it with a tool or knife allowing the turps to speckle different places on the panel. The rag again will pick up more colour from these newly softened places and at the same time will soften the work. Sienna marble lends itself to spray gun application. I have many times carried out panels up to twenty feet in height and six feet wide. The ground work was applied with brushes in coloured glaze as previously explained, using tools, sponge and rag, the veins were applied with the gun in Raw Sienna. A round nozzle was used and the gun held near the work. The effect is soft with no hard edges. Shading can also be carried out. Orange, burnt sienna and, finally, the white were applied with the gun.

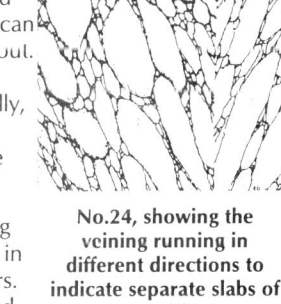

Glazing: Glazing should be done in the same colours. Oil in the ground and sponge stipple with thin white all over the large stones. On the small stones use Sienna or an Umber. Take a fitch and fill in the centre of most of the large stones and a few of the small ones with a light cream. Shade around some edges with Ochre and Chrome. Now work up the veining in a few darker tones; in places a little light green may be used on the broader veins and in others a little Burnt Sienna. Continue with small areas of glaze until a satisfactory arrangement has been produced. Finally, with dove grey and white, paint some cross veins similar to open Black and Gold veins.

No.24, showing the veining running in different directions to indicate separate slabs of marble

Origin: Ash is distributed profusely over most temperate climates; Great Britain, Southern Europe, and the United States of America. There are three types, two of which, Ash and Mountain Ash, are grown in these Islands.

Description: The trees grow to a great height. I have examined many on Towneley Park, Burnley, which lies in a sheltered hollow. Several are 100 feet high with boles over 10 feet in circumference, some are forty feet to the lowest branches.

This lower portion, unlike the oak, is very straight. The lowest three of four feet are, however, knotted and gnarled and produce very interesting grains. The lower large branches curve downwards, then upwards again towards their tips.

I recently counted the annular rings of one tree that had blown down during a gale, they numbered two hundred and thirty-one. The park superintendant suggested the age would be higher than this as some rings were too close for clear definition.

The sketches (No.25) were drawn from timber one hundred to one hundred and twenty-five years old. I found them in a timber merchant's yard adjoining the grounds of the house where Charlotte Bronte was born.

The leaves of the ash are composed of seven to thirteen leaflets, one terminal and the remainder opposite in pairs; the average length is about one foot. The trees bear

Ash

flowers of a greenish yellow colour which grow in dense clusters.

Ash is a pleasant light coloured wood from an almost white to a pale brown in colour and is occasionally found with a pinkish tint.

The general colour is no darker than pale maple but the dark variety is a medium cool oak colour. Being light coloured, and comparatively easy to execute, makes it popular to-day. The strong yellow colour, which we sometimes see in old examples, is due to age and the use of deep coloured spirit or oil varnishes.

The heartwood markings of ash are broad and open, composed of fine lines of light coll brown. The texture is closer than oak; it does, however, have lines of light running through the veins as though a steel comb had been drawn through after graining. The point of the heart grain are rounded, never sharp. This is one means of distinguishing the wood from light oak heartwood, and chestnut.

Tools and Sundries: Tools, pencil, leather or well washed rag, rubber and steel combs, fitches and hog hair softener.

Ground: Off white, prepared from white lead and a touch of raw umber. For the pink variety a touch of Venetian Red is added to the lead. For the medium Ash use lead, a

Continental Methods of Training – XI

touch of ochre and a little Raw Umber. A little mixing varnish or gold-size should be added to the paint to give a clean wipe out.

Palette: White, Raw Sienna, raw umber, black.

Gilp: Prepare a gilp as for light oak white touches of raw sienna, raw umber and, if required, a little black. Thin three parts of turpentines, one part linseed oil, one part flat varnish or glaze medium and a few drops of bine, according to the speed of work.

Method: For the open grained British Ash the wipe out is the simplest method. The glaze will help the gilp to "stay put" so commence by laying on a good coat without undue brushing out, this also gives a cleaner wipe out. To prevent the ground being "shady" rub in with the grain. A fair amount of this ground scumble will show in the finished work so care must be observed.

With the same colour used in the gilp, prepare a stiffer mixture on the palette board. Proceed to draw in the principal veins with a sable pencil. Commence the drawing from the bottom of the work, or from the lowest knot centre, and build up. Keep your lines narrow.

Next proceed with wiping out. As the work is pale the wiping must be clean and firm. A piece of hard rubber is best for the graining horn, and wash leather for a covering. This can be washed clean after use so is not as extravagant as it first appears. As you proceed with the wiping out take roughly two-thirds of the distance from line to line leaving part of the gilp ground to show, thus producing three tones of colour.

Change your rag or leather by slipping it over the end of the rubber about a quarter of an inch each time you remove it from your work. The rag should be used double; the leather single.

Always work with both hands to get a firm grip of the loose ends of rag and facilitate the changing each time. This ensures a clean wipe out and prevents a brown line forming at both sides of the wiped out portion.

The wiping out completed, proceed to soften the inside edge. This is best done with a short worn hair fitch.

The sides should now have attention. Select a rubber or steel comb with a wide section, cover with clean rag and draw down the sides following the contour of the outer markings.

Watch carefully for both tone value and direction; if unsatisfactory brush out and repeat again using more pressure and less colour, or vice-versa, until a good match is produced.

Now take a medium steel comb and work in places over the centre of the panel. A fine comb is often used in a "jumpy" manner on the plain grained sides. Soften inwards with the hog hair softener or with a soft clean paint brush.

The graining may be done on a clean oiled ground, without rubbing-in where the heartwood markings are placed. The effect is not so natural, though it is much easier to do and does not require the same dexterity.

Keep all colours pale and all contrasts soft; this helps to get a woody appearance. Also the softening should not be overdone or left too late. It is best to make only a few well placed and carefully worked heartwood shapes; joints should be clean.

Working in water colour would only be attempted by an expert and he would only used it when drying time was to be reduced.

Glazing: This may be done in water or oil; water would be my choice. This could be done with vandyke only or with blue black as an addition.

Rub in with the sponge and water, draw the colour about with the mottler and soften with the badger. Very few knots are found in ash, but radiating shadows are reflected from the oval centres and the waves in the grain.

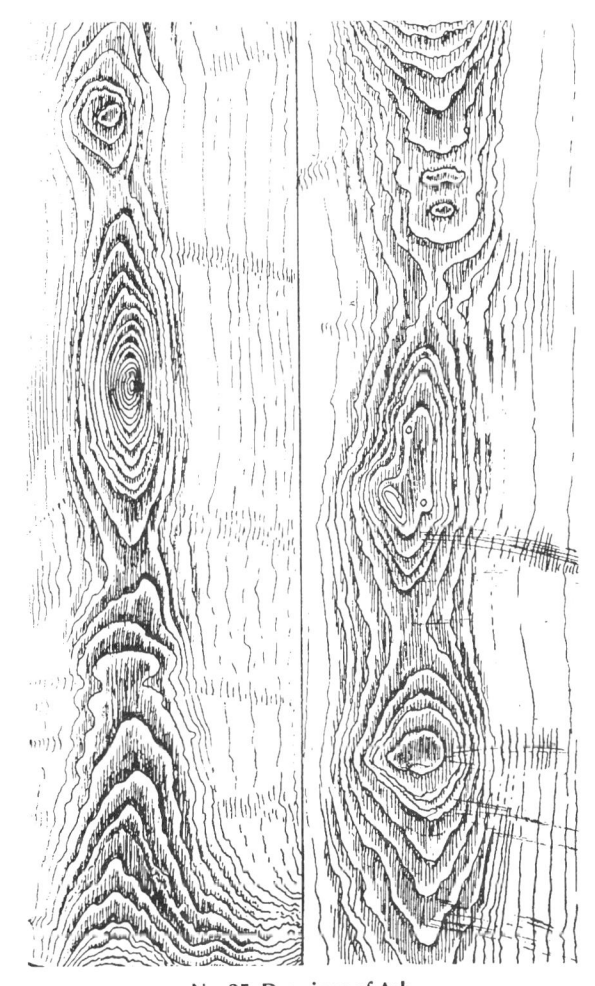

No. 25: Drawings of Ash

Continental Methods of Training – XII

Ash (continued)

IN the large British variety, Fraxinous excelsior, the heartwood is moderately open and well defined; it produces a small feather and burl.

Feather of Ash: In the example of Ash, No.25, of last month, the sketches were made from the lower part of the tree. Higher up amongst the branches I found three to five small feathers on each board; these occurred under the large branches. They were growing in the opposite direction to the way in which they are usually grained. The feathered portion was twelve to fifteen inches wide and two feet six feet.

The markings and shadows were quite vigorous for such a small feather and showed through the grime which had settled on them during seasoning. The feather shape is similar to mahogany, though I found the centre portion not quite as dark. The "cuts" of light on the dark centre were much longer than we associate with mahogany and they were broader on proportion.

For a quick, accurate representation, the imitation should be carried out in water colour, use Raw Sienna, Black and a little dry Zinc White. Tools and methods used are as described for mahogany. The example, No.26, has been carried out in this manner.

Burl Ash: This is the gnarled portion of the tree that occurs near the base, it is very delicate in colour and stength. It is used on panels or small cabinets, and consists of a number of fine knots. They are not so pronounced as in burr Walnut though they are of the same type. It is impossible to obtain a very large piece of Burl as it only occurs on the outside of the tree a few inches deep.

The fine knots are not grouped, as in Oak or Walnut, they are single and near together.

Graining may be carried out in oil or water colour, providing a sponge is used. I prefer oil myself, partly because my first teacher, Mr. M. Rhodes, of Batley, used this method in Burr Walnut, and partly because of the development of aluminium stearate glaze medium which makes it possible to work slowly and accurately in oil colour.

Mix a gilp as for Ash graining. On the palette prepare a colour rather darker and rounder than your gilp. Soften a sponge in clean water and squeeze out. This helps to keep it clean and to make clearer markings. Rub in a panel with the tool; wipe off any surplus with a rag.

Using the coarse side of the sponge commence to work from bottom upwards. Grasp the sponge firmly, twisting the wrist about a quarter turn. Work until most of the colour is exhausted on the sponge before replanishing from the palette. The best markings are made when you take the sponge off the work. One advantage of a sponge is that the colour can be added or removed, on any part, without making an unsightly mark.

One edge may be left wavy, working into heartwood formation if the surface is very wide. No softening is required as the colour and makrings are only delicate, all the sharpness we produce is required. The wood may be worked in water colour in the same manner. The work is complete in one operatoin without glazing.

Feather panel, Burl Ash Border

Mountain Ash: This variety of Ash, Eucalyptus regnous, grows a greenish cream, sweet scented flower and has fine red berries in the autumn. The wood has plain heartwood markings resembling utility oak in appearance and colour.

The small amount of heartwood marking is much closer than in ash. As in some other varieties, very few knots are found; most of the veins are again rounded off. The side grain is equally compact and the specimen from which I worked the examples, Nos. 27A and 27B, was very similar to fine oak in texture.

Method: Using a gilp prepared as for Ash, rub in a medium coat. It should not be too liberal as the grain is fine and liable to close over if too wet. A corase rubber comb may be used to wipe out most of the grain. The graining horn and leather should be used to wipe out parts which are not parallel and where changes of direction occur.

The rubber comb may be used uncovered or covered with rag. If it is used covered, change the position of the rag frequently; if uncovered, wipe after each application. On the sides use an uncovered steel comb.

There are no darker markings on the edges of the veins which merit extra pencil work.

Softening or drawing the hog hair softener through the grain, towards the centre of a shape, will remove sufficient colour to make one edge light. Carried to the opposite edge, it makes it slightly darker. This gives us all the tones required for such a narrow graining wood. Soften the sides gently, then comb over in a jumpy, wavy manner.

Workings inwards a 1in. medium steel comb should be used down the centre according to taste. The combing should not be overdone as it softens out the heartwood markings.

Glazing: Glazing should be done with Vandyke and raw sienna in water. I prefer a milky appearance so I use a few grains of zinc or titanium white. This helps to hold the thin pale colour onto the vertical surface. It also allows more stainers to be used without undue darkening of the work which, in turn, prevents subsequent fading of the glazing.

All the darker parts are found near to the wavy portion of the grain. The centre or open portion of the grain is slightly darker than the sides.

The heavily shaded portions in Ash and the more violent wavy grain (which is not suitable for decorators' grained work), are found near the junction of the branches to the trunk.

Hungarian Ash: This is grown on Southern Europe as its name implies, and is the most decorative of the Ash family. The markings are interesting and consist of a number of oval shapes not unlike pitch of curly pine. The markings are, of course, broader and more open, but conform to Ash widths and weight.

The method of working and colour are simialr to Ash but with the addition of a little more yellow in the ground and raw Sienna in the gilp.

The glazing forms an important feature in graining this wood. I prefer water glazing, which can be done satisfactorily either before or after graining.

27a 27b Mountain Ash
28 Hungarian Ash

Carrara Marble

Description

CARRARA is a soft grey white colour, with delicate pale blue grey veins. Often a few veins are coloured a warm yellow grey and are quite striking against the cooler tints.

The centres of the large stones are a pure zinc white colour, shaded to pale grey near the edges and up to the darker veins.

The whole effect is soft and pleasing; wide, open stones occur as well as closely packed narrow ones.

I remember the carrara marble effect on many of the large, high halls and staircases of numerous flats in converted mansions, round the outskirts of Brussels and Cologne.

Specimens, to study, of large areas are fairly common. Many progressive stores, offices and restaurants lined their premises with this marble a few years ago.

Country of Origin:

Italy. From the days when Augustus ruled Rome, the white marble quarries at Carrara have been famous.

In 1937 over 30 tons of black powder were used for one blasting operation. This powder lifts without shattering, so it is very valuable for dislodging marble.

On this occasion more than one million tons of Carrara was lifted and started an avalanche

Continental Methods of Training – XIII

down the slopes to the valley. The supplies appear almost inexhaustible, which keeps the cost at a very reasonable level.

Composition and Formation:

The white marble base is of limestone, the bed of which has been subject to crushing by volcanic eruption. The lava under the mountain is thrown out by the volcano and deposited on the mountain slope. This serious transfer of weight causes the marble to crack in two directions, vertically, and with the slope of the mountain.

These cracks are gradually filled in with various metallic and mineral substances that happen to lie above the limestone bed. Feldspar is the colouring matter tinted with iron that is usually found in Carrara. The carrying agent is water, the darkest marble is the deepest in the bed.

Type:

The type is known as "brocotel," we have a few other colours and names that are marked in this manner.

Tools and Sundries:

A tool for rubbing in. Hog hair pencils or riggers, sponge and rag.

In the Dipper:
Turpentine only. This is very important as the turps pushes the scumble glaze to one side when the colour gets a good grip on the ground and allows vigorous softening without losing the drawing.

Palette:
Zinc white, black, ochre, cobalt or ultramarine.

Ground:
A good, lead free, ground, consisting of half zinc white and white gloss on enamel paint.

Method:
Rub in a thin transparent white similar to the ground. The enamel is a bit sticky but leaves a good finished surface without subsequent varnishing.

On this, work in patches of very pale grey with a brush in some parts and sponge in others.

Soften well, with the hog hair softener, in the same direction as the marble runs.

Draw in the veins with two riggers, working together, they should be kept moderately dry as the turpsy colour is liable to run if too wet.

The large, long, main veins, should be worked in first: they run diagonally as well as vertically.

Draw in the large stones, next the medium and last, the smaller ones.

Use several tints of grey; the lines should be broken and jagged in parts. Soften well with the grain of the work.

Glazing:
This should be carried out with the same colours.

Soften the ground with a clean oily rag. Sponge in a snow flake effect all over with thin zinc white. Fill in, with white, the centres of all the larger stones.

Strengthen the colour of a few main lines and veins where required. Much of this work is finished without glazing.

Harmonies:
Blue Fleurie, Breche Caroline, Verte-de-Mer, Napoleon, Secancolin, Jaune Lamartine, Verte Campan, etc.

Next month I propose to describe the Red Levanto marble, after which I shall return to a wood.

No.29 (far left) painted example of Carrara marble with rouge royal border
No.30 (right) drawing of Carrara marble
The finished work would require vigorous softening so that half tones would be produced from many of the hard lines

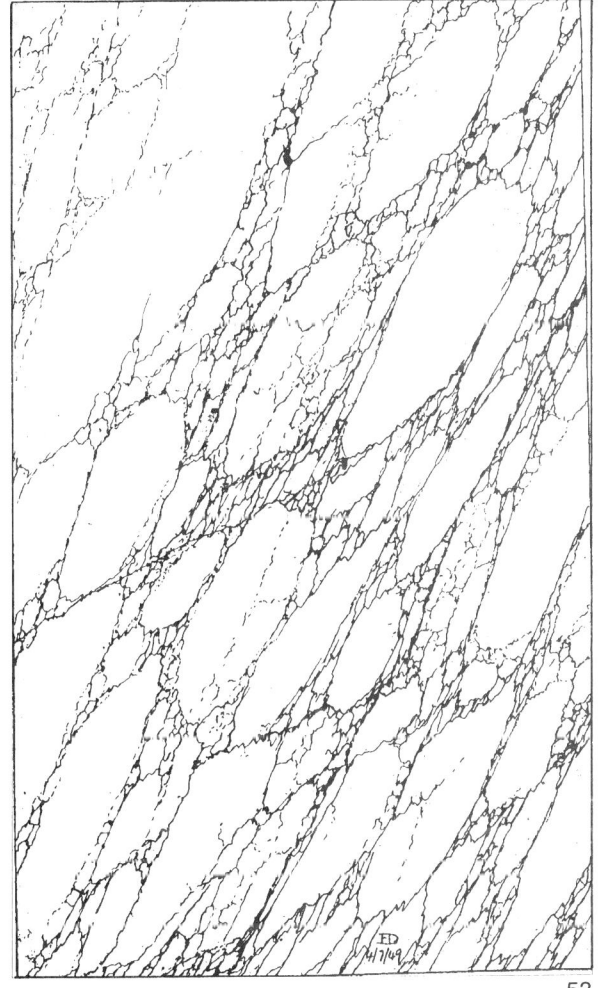

Continental Methods of Training – XIV

Levanto Marble

Description
Levanto Rosso, or Red Levanto, is a heavily marked dark red marble.

The markings are bright, gay and lively in light tints which give a splendid show and harmonise well with the dark red background.

The markings consists of flecks of feathery broken veins arranged in a spider web formation.

The veins are coloured in a delicate manner; cool cream and pale green with touches of red in the background.

None of the colours are solid and they change many times in a few inches.

Levanto is classed geologically as a serpentine marble; it contains a fair amount of that mineral.

No stones are present; all the markings are fine lines, points and flecks.

They are arranged, however, in such a manner that they leave large pebble shapes in the darker places.

The lines are few in parts, giving the impression of deep, open spaces which are always left darker.

Inside these shapes the colour and texture varies, whilst outside it is both fairly even and much lighter. The whole is held together by broader, lighter lines.

Levanto is often used on good shop fronts. Fine examples are to be seen in Westminster Cathedral, London.

Origin
Italy: This marble is quarried in the province of Liguria and takes its name from the small seaport town of Levanto.

Composition
The base is of vegetable origin, coloured with iron, whilst the lighter veins are caused by crystalline flakes of glittering bastite.

The green parts are composed of the mineral serpentine which gives the marble its classification group name.

A few other marbles come under this class of serpentine, all of which contain this mineral and many of them I hope to deal with later.

Tools Required
Sponge, sable pencils, fitches, feathers, tool, a hog hair softener.

Palette
White, Lemon Chrome, yellow Ochre, Indian Red, Vermilion, Dark Brunswick Green and Black.

In the Dipper
One part of linseed oil to three parts of turpentine with a few drops of terebene.

Ground
A deep maroon colour, made of Black and Indian Red.

Method
Oil in the ground with the mixture from the dipper, using the tool and removing any excess with a piece of rag.

With the palette knife prepare a dark red. This should be slightly lighter than the ground and is made of Indian Red, Vermilion, Crimson, and a touch of Black.

Apply the colour with the sponge in a series of dabbing motions on the oily ground in such a matter as to produce a large number of fine spots of colour. Keep the colour on the outside of the sponge. Do not press on too hard and do not twist the sponge. Continue with a few tones of red and well cover the area.

In places a dull green made from Brunswick, Ochre and Black may be used. This may cover, in patches, up to one-fifth of the total area. These colours should not be thin as to be transparent.

On the Continent a spotting brush is used, but as mine is now worn out I have to use a sponge and I find that it works quite well.

Drawing

With two sable pencils, charged with a pale tint of ochre and White, draw in the main shapes of the large veins.

These cross each other leaving large open spaces, which serve as guides to the changes in tone and colour for the outline round the sponging.

It will be noticed that a broken colour effect is obtained with the cream on the spotted red ground; this becomes more pronounced with the subsequent use of the feather and with softening.

With a little practice, and a reasonable knowledge of materials and colour, this marble is easy to work.

Take a strong feather with the end cut off, charged with thin cream colour.

Work in short strokes backwards and forwards across your work.

Variety of texture and colour should be your aim.

With a shorter stroke apply more, or less, colour in places and use a dabbing, stippling motion in parts. These treatments will give variety.

With the fitch again charged with cream, almost dry, sharpen up the main lines and clean up the inside edges with the feather. All this should be done before the background stippling dries.

Glazing

For general work glazing is not always called for, but for a fine representation of colour we must glaze.

The aim is to subdue most of the colouring bringing out only a few of the more prominent lines.

Proceed to oil in the ground, wipe off, and sponge with a dull green. The green can be made from raw Turkey Umber and Prussian Blue. Apply this colour more heavily in some parts than others. The surface should be well covered, particularly the more open spaces. Soften very gently as this glaze without white spreads quickly.

Take a fitch and some almost dry white to bring out the main veins and to add spots in places at the junctions of the veins.

Common Errors

Having the main veins too straight. Using too crude colour; red with green needs careful handling. Making tonal contrasts too violent.

Harmonies

Black and Gold, Paonazzo, Sienna Marble, Serancolin, Breche Verte, Golden Onyx, and Breche Caroline.

Continental Methods of Training – XV

Maple

ORIGIN: Maple is a very important Canadian wood; the leaf is used as the National emblem and many Canadian soldiers wear the maple leaf as their regimental crest. It is grown in England but only for its decorative foliage; English maples do not grow to a useful size for timber.

The Japanese variety, which I saw growing recently in the Ribble Valler, had bright scarlet leaves in full colour rather smaller than the Canadian leaf. Maple produces its best growth on the fertile well-drained fields of Canada from Nova Scotia to Ontario. It is also grown in the West Indian Islands and Switzerland.

Description: Maple belongs to the family Aceraceae, which is prolific and possesses one hundred members. Some members produce sugar (Acer Saccharum), from which the painter's lunch time sweetener gets its name.

The maple tree grows to 80 or 90 feet in height and four feet in diameter. The bark is rough, having a ploughed appearance. The leaves are similar to the sycamore having fine lobes, with notches rounded at the crutch; each lobe has a few teeth.

The flowers occur in clusters and are mostly yellowish green in colour. The fruit is a small nut with a long wing or key at the end.

The colours of maple wood range from a pale pinky white to a medium honey yellow. A few tints of greys, all of which are pale, are also found.

The heartwood markings are all fine and narrow and are a few tones darker than the ground. The divisions are narrow to fine except down the centre of the tree. There they are simple in pattern with very few curly complications; "Birds-eye" is an exception. The shapes of the heartwood markings are round, even at the ends and are not difficult to draw.

The mottling in Maple is always a pleasure, both on the straight and the well marked heartwood. The cuts are almost at right angles to the grain; they are never dark in colour but are cut clean to the ground in all cases. They should be near together, pointed at the ends and never square.

Painters think of Maple as being full of small knots or "birds-eyes." Whilst most varieties have a few eyes, very many are without, and the profusely eyed variety is comparatively scarce.

Tools and Sundries: Badger softener, tools, mottler, the hog hair overgrainer, coarse hair comb, sponge and leather, dotter.

For the dotter, a rigger or hog hair pencil is cut down to 1/4 in. of bristle. The centre is then burnt out with a red hot needle or nail leaving a hollow with bristles on the outer edge only. If you wish to experiment further, small knotches may be cut from this outer circle of short bristle, all to good effect.

Ground: Off white to a pale yellow, prepared from a zinc white tinted with ochre and a touch of chrome yellow.

Palette: Raw Sienna, Vandyke brown in water. Zinc or titanium oxide.

Method of Working: Maple is traditionally worked in water colour, fairly good results, however, can be obtained in oil colour, using glaze medium.

Rub in a thin wash of raw sienna and a touch of

Canadian Curly Maple

vandyke for a warm tint; a greater proportion of vandyke is used for a cool effect. A touch of white will help with the milky appearance which is so desirable.

Charge your mottler with thin mixture from the palette and commence mottling at the bottom left hand corner, working upwards.

I prefer to work from the palette with the mottler to give more variety in colour, as compared with the even mixture prepared in a kettle. Should the mottler become too moist it should be partially dried on the sponge.

Leave part of the ground without mottling, though most of it should be covered. The success of Maple graining depends on the quality of the mottling and softening more than anything else. Keep the panel wet until a satisfactory ground mottle is completed.

If any portion of the work is not up to standard, wet it up quickly and start again.

The water wave effect requires much practice before a reasonable amount of skill is attained. The ripple of the wave should be varied by slightly altering the angle of the wrist whilst working.

Another good point to obtain interest is to alter the width between the waves slightly in different areas. Try to cover the square end that the mottler leaves.

Softening: This should be done quickly before the colour sets. First in a horizontal direction, fairly vigorously, then lightly with the grain, in a vertical direction.

In the parts where the heartwood markings are later to be placed, soften more vigorously, subduing the mottling very much.

The heartwood markings are mostly worked in with a pencil crayon of Burnt Sienna colour.

This is clear and safer than working with a sable pencil and produces just the correct weight of line for the drawn markings.

The plainer work, down the sides, can best be put in with the hog hair overgrainer in water colour.

Make up colour lighter than the single lines as these are near together; many more being used they appear darker and of the same tone.

Charge the brush with colour a little on the dry side, draw through a coarse hair comb of the plastic variety to separate the bristle.

Place lightly on the panel commencing at the top and bring down the side of the previous work.

By altering the angle of your wrist you can make your lines narrow in places or, starting wide at the top, finish narrow at the bottom, in a gentle wavy motion.

The work should be fixed with varnish and turpentine, between the mottled ground and the graining if one is not sure of success, but after a while this may be dispensed with.

Another point of interest is that the pencil crayons contain wax as a base, this requires some few hours to harden or the spirit in the varnish will act as a solvent and cause the markings to weaken or disappear.

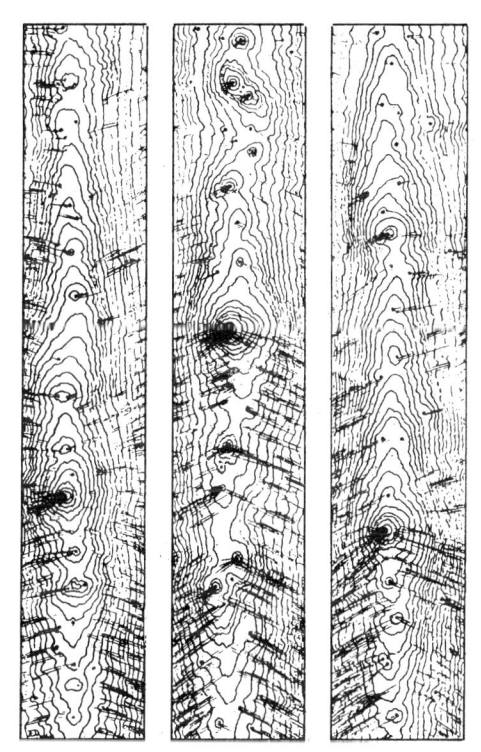

Drawings of Canadian Curly Maple

Where it is not desirable to use a hair overgrainer for the line marking, the veins can be all drawn in with the crayons using two side by side for speed.

A slight bend occurs at each eye or cut of the mottler. This can be drawn with the crayon but not with the mottler.

57

Continental Methods of Training – XV1

Maple (Continued)

I PROPOSE in this series of articles, to deal with three members of the Maple family. Last month I gave the family name but overlooked the French one; it is "Erable."

Birds' Eye Maple: This wood is used more in decoration than the plainer varieties. The cutting on a rotary cutter shows up the beautiful and characteristic grain to advantage.

Birds' eye maple is of irregular, and rather rare, occurrence. I have examined this week the flooring in a large dance hall which is being decorated and found one block in every fifty contained the famous "birds' eye."

It may be found in one tree and not in another adjoining one, and, peculiarly enough, though sometimes scattered over the whole tree, the birds' eye markings may be confined to one side only, or to irregular strips and patches.

There was for a long time no satisfactory explanaton as to why these markings occur. Some attributed it to insects and others to woodpeckers; finally it has been discovered that a fungus feeds on the growing cells under the bark in such a way as to produce a retarding of the growth in localised areas.

A large number of small depressions are formed in the wood and these are subsequently filled up by fresh growth of wood. The result is that when the timber is cut tangentially, a number of circular markings is seen.

Origin: Canada, West Indian Islands and Switzerland.

Description: Birds' eye maple takes its name from the small knots that are distributed over the surface in an orderly manner. These small eyes are fairly prominent, being darker in colour than the grain or the mottle and having a light centre.

They vary little in shape and size. They are almost round and about $1/4$in. in diameter. Generally they are not found in groups but follow indefinite lines, after the manner of figured oak.

On the upper side of the eye, we find a small light patch with a dark wavy shadow left by the cutter or mottler on the underside. The mottling is vigorous, more than two-thirds of the area being cut out; all the tones are delicate and the pattern wavy.

The grain is very complicated, small round or oval markings enclose the knots down the centre on to one side. The remainder of the wood is just wavy grain. The direction of the grain appears to change across every cut in the mottle or round every eye. The general effect is very complicated but delicate.

Ground: The colour may be off-white, pale yellow, or pale grey, according to the finish required.

Palette: For off white; Raw Sienna only. For pale yellow; Raw Sienna and Vandyke Brown. For pale grey; Cobalt Blue and bleu black. All colours ground in water.

Tools and Brushes: As Maple.

Method: Rub in a pale glaze of colour; take a mottler three or four inches wide, moisten with water and a little colour from the palette. Grip the mottler firmly, push two or three fingers, well opened out, into the side of the bristle.

Examine the ends of the brush to see if there are two or three small semi circles before commencing to work. Adjust your fingers until the straight line of the bristle is well broken up. Should your fingers be too

Birds' Eye Maple

near together they merely push the bristle over to one side.

Commence at the bottom left hand corner, hold your mottler at an angle and work upwards; draw the mottler down in strokes of from one to four inches apart.

The most important place is where you take the mottler off.

The widest mottle should be down the centre where there are fewer eyes.

Gradually change the angle of the mottle as you would flow of the figure in oak.

The work must be done briskly and must be kept wet, as more has to be put in before it sets.

With the badger softener work first in a horizontal direction, going gently where the cuts are near together.

In the wider parts, finish by softening upwards, this will draw the colour to the top of the cuts.

Softening should be vigorous and firm, but not unduly slow as it assists the water to evaporate and does not allow sufficient time to put in the eyes before it is all set.

The eyes are put in with the dotter.

First dip into the water bucket and wipe off any excess on the sponge.

A little colour may be added though the dotter usually picks up quite sufficient from the wet ground.

To put in the eyes hold the dotter carefully at right angles to the work, just touch the wet surface and slide down at an angle of 50 degrees for a distance of from 1/8in. to 1/4in.

This slight sliding motion cleans out the centre of the eye and gives us the light on the top both at the same time.

We should try to finish the eye on the top edge of a dark cross mottle effect; this will form a shadow line under several eyes at once.

Where the eyes are near together two dotters may be used for speed, one in the left hand and one in the right hand.

The placing of a few eyes may be continued after the work has dried but no light parts will show and a little colour must be used.

The direction of the slide is important; in nature the light varies on account of the rotary cutting, in decoration it is safer to leave out many small points that occur in nature or a very wild effect is obtained. I prefer to work the sliding motion in one direction only on each panel or door.

The heartwood, or vein markings, are next put in with the Burnt Sienna pencil crayon. Commence with the most important centre eyes, working a few shapes before attempting to connect them up.

The drawing of these small heartwood shapes is a young grainer's dream, as it is first rate practice for many other woods. The side markings of the grain can be carried out with the overgrainer and water colour as described in last month's article.

For smaller panels, or fine work, I prefer the

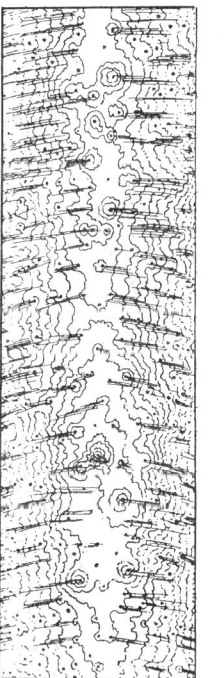

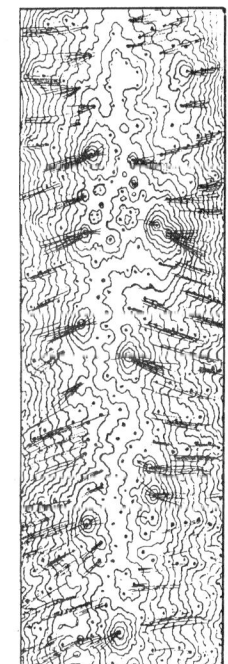

Drawings of Birds' Eye Maple

pencil crayon. The direction changes at every eye and every cut in the mottling and this cannot be done faithfully with the overgrainer.

Maple gives the decorator ample scope to show his ability and is a very charming wood when well carried out. The flush door is a suitable place to show it off to full advantage.

59

| Continental Methods of Training – XVII |

Poupre Violette

Description

Poupre violette, or Pavanazzo, is a striking yellow cream marble of great beauty. The shapes are, generally speaking, large, only a few medium sized and small ones occur. Three feet by twelve to eighteen inches is a normal size for the larger stones

Paranazzo is of the breccia type. The matrix is a true complementary, purple to black in parts, with faint gold or green stains. Large patches of the dark matrix are found attached to the side of the larger stones without the usual accompanying smaller ones.

Another marked feature of this marble is the softening of the semi-tones. When the veins are deep in the transparent yellow marble it rather greys the purple but has little effect on the reds and ochre yellows.

The larger stones are fairly even in tone and they merge into the dark matrix around the edges; the contrast is not sharp. A few smaller stones are lighter in colour, in some cases they are almost white.

Many fine buildings are lined with this marble. The National Banks in Europe and the U.S.A. favour Pavanazzo. The lower portion of the staircases in the Victoria and Albert Museum, South Kensington, are adorned with this marble.

Pavanazzo is rare and expensive. It varies slightly in colour in different countries. Owing to the soft nature of the darker parts, it is difficult to handle, cut, and move.

Origin: Algeria, France, Italy and the U.S.A. Pavanazzo is found only in a few quarries.

Explosion, subsidence or shrinking having shattered the white marble, dark matter percolates in to form the matrix. The American variety usually has larger stones, the yellow ground including towards green.

The Poupre Violette of the Pyrenese has more crimson with the dark veins. The variety from Tuscany possesses a fairly light yellow brown matrix, whilst the Algerian numide has much darker stones and they are more broken than in the other varieties.

The one to which my notes chiefly apply is the Pavanazzo of the Pyrenese, Poupre Violette.

Composition: The main background, formed by the large stones, is composed of crystallised calcite stained with metallic oxides, whilst the dark matrix is of vegetable origin tinted with iron in parts.

Palette: White, Chrome Yellow, Ochre, Crimson Lake, Prussian Blue, and Black.

Ground: White, flat finish.

In the Dipper: Oil, turpentine, and liquid driers, it is difficult to state exact quantities, but it should be on the oily side. The heat of the room, the size of the work, and the speed of the craftsman all have a bearing on the amount of oil used. It varies from one-third to a half.

Brushes and Tools: A 2in. tool, a few large fitches, hog hair pencils, black chalk or soft crayon, hog hair softener and sponge.

Method: Lay on a medium coat of white paint without much brushing. Tint, in some parts, with the Chrome or,

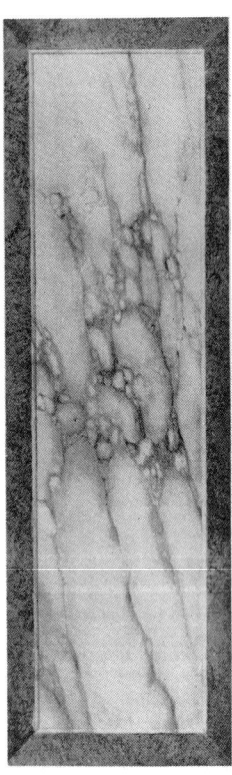

An example of the imitation of Pavanazzo Marble with Napoleon Border

where a warmer cream is desired, with Ochre.

Draw the main veins round the stone shapes with Crimson, Purple (made from White, Prussian Blue and Crimson Lake), and Ochre. Work them on the dry side with the hog hair pencil, soften in a vertical direction.

Most veins are of a purple colour, a few of the large straight veins are backed with Crimson whilst the smaller faint shapes are stained with ochre. A few lines are without a coloured background.

With your black chalk (which should be soft), or No.3 Conte crayon, proceed to draw in the outline of the stones. A few short cracks, loose at one end, should be drawn; they merge into the background colour at the loose end.

The dark lines, on the coloured outline, are very uneven in weight. Make quite sure of your drawing before attempting to soften.

Soften lightly, first in a vertical direction, to let the black mix with the ground colour. Where the small work is thickest, very little softening can be carried out or a grey smudge will result.

In the open parts you may soften more vigorously. The softening process accelerates drying by causing the turpentines to evaporate and by forcing oxygen into the oil.

The finish depends on the good effects obtained from the softening, this, in turn, depends on the correct amount of oil and the wetness of the ground. Practise and knowledge of your materials alone will help you here.

The centres of a few larger stones, and smaller ones in places, may have a little white rubbed in, this should be thinned towards the edge and softened.

Glazing: Soften the surface with oil and turps spread thinly with a rag. Sponge in a stippled effect in parts with thin white, paying special attention to the semi-tone veins to push them further back.

With a fitch, strengthen the darker parts of the purple or black which have become dirty with the softening. Fill in with more white in a few of the smaller stones and again clean up the centres of the large ones.

Harmonies: Other marbles that harmonise with Poupre Violette are: Napoleon, Rouge Royal, Comblanchien, Blue Flueri, Vert Campan, Golden Onyx, Levanto, and Breche Vert.

Drawing of Pavanazzo

Continental Methods of Training – XVIII

Grey Maple

DESCRIPTION: Grey Maple is a light, delicately coloured, grey wood and is used for the finest of furniture and panelling. It is rare and decorative. The markings are plainer than the two previously discussed varieties of maple.

The "birds' eyes" are fewer and further apart; many fine examples are entirely without them.

There are numerous delicate mottles or undulations. The open centre portion has very little other markings. The pale, combed wavy lines of overgraining are scarcely visible.

Grey maple varies in colour from a pale, warm, almost yellow grey, to a blue grey.

Origin: Switzerland, and the West India Islands.

Palette: Black, Ochre, and Ultramarine blue.

Ground: White, to off white.

Method: As previously described for Canadian maple. The greys being obtained by using (1) Black and Ochre, (2) Black and Ultramarine.

With all examples the black predominates, but the blue may be arranged to suit the scheme of decoration. I find small water colour tubes very useful for this work.

The coloured pencil crayon should be changed to blue and the overgraining should be carried out in the same colours.

Allowance should be made in all colouring of delicate work for the yellowing effect of the subsequent varnishing.

The coloured crayons or pencils are often difficult to obtain. Art shops are the most likely source of supply, they are 4d. each or 4s. per dozen assorted in a good firm box. The blue pencil required for this month's

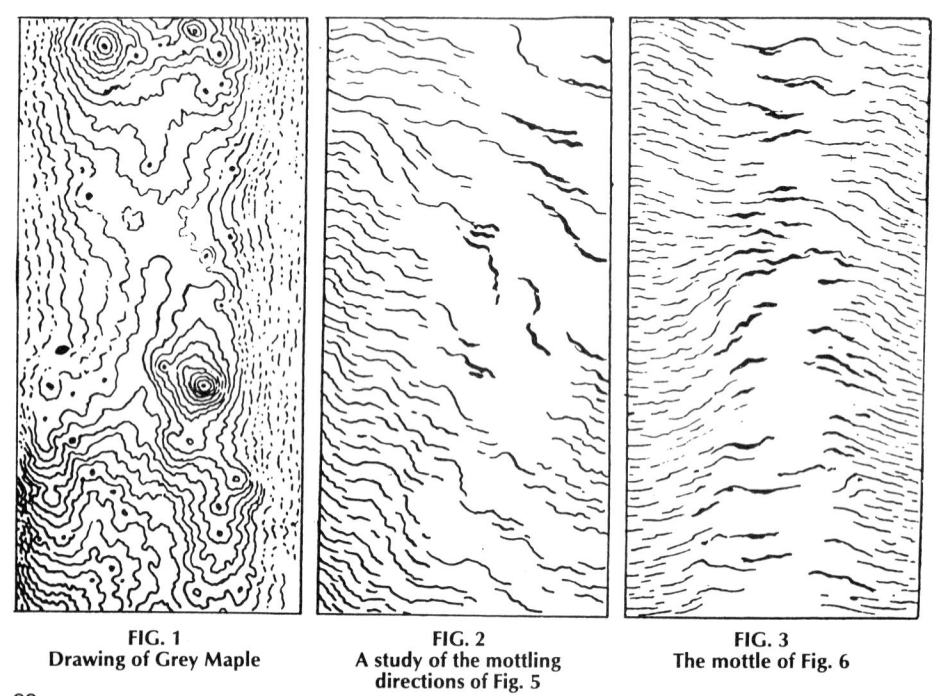

FIG. 1
Drawing of Grey Maple

FIG. 2
A study of the mottling directions of Fig. 5

FIG. 3
The mottle of Fig. 6

example should be found without much difficulty, being in greater demand than Burnt Sienna ones. It is the same as is used for marking school work.

The drawing of the grain of Grey Maple was made from a typical example in Paris, the size of each panel was about 11in. x 16in.

True examples are difficult to find as they are often stained from the yellow variety, thereby losing much of their beauty.

At the request of many readers I have worked a number of painted examples in four stages.

In No. 4, which shows the mottling only, the panel was rubbed in with an even glaze of grey, the upper right portion still remains to show the depth of colour.

At the bottom left, a light curly portion of markings is produced. This was done by forcing the fingers well into the brush whilst using very little pressure on the mottler.

The centre portion was carried out by pressing fairly hard on the mottler, thus forcing out more colour and leaving harder, darker streaks with each cut.

The work was not softened in order to show clearly what to expect from the mottling.

In No. 5 example, which is mottled and softened all over, we find how the darker marks come up with softening, the colour being well pulled up to the lighter parts. Use has been made of hard mottling to advantage. The bottom portion has been "dotted." All the waves of mottle and eyes are running across the panel falling from left to right, as found in oak graining.

In No. 6 we find the waves of mottle running wilder, but according to an intended design. On the right side they are all sloping or failing outwards, whilst on the left they change direction from top to bottom, radiating from a point near the centre. The bottom portion has been grained with the heartwood markings.

No. 7 shows a plainer example of mottling, working from wider to finer waves in the width of the panel.

The overgraining has been carried out with a comb passed through a mottler well charged with colour; the wavy bands show clearly.

The heartwood markings down one side were carried out with the coloured pencil crayon.

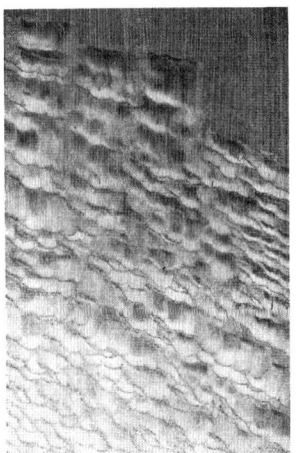

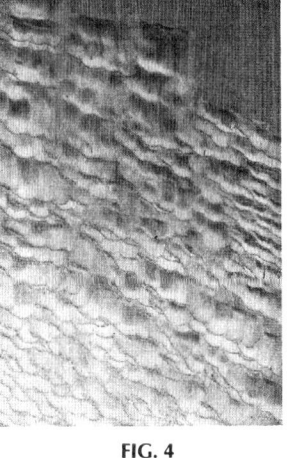

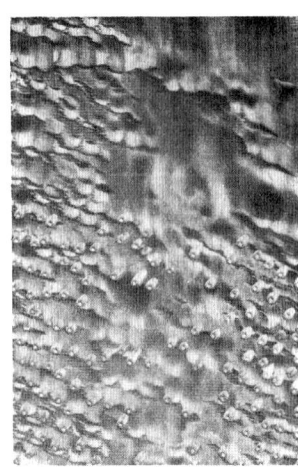

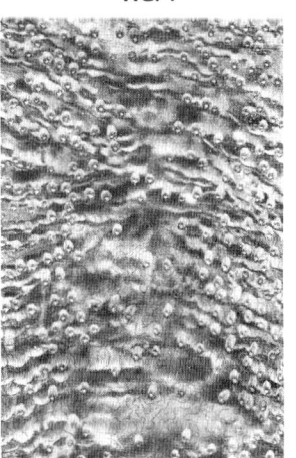

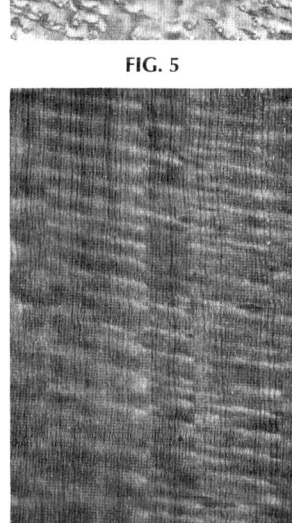

FIG. 4

FIG. 5

FIG. 6

FIG. 7

Continental Methods of Training – XIX

Irish Green Marble

IRISH Green marble was not in the curriculurn of any of the four Continental Schools with which I was connected. My knowledge of this marble dates back to my student days at the Bradford College of Art. A very large specimen, from which I worked as a boy, is to be seen in the painting and decorating department there.

Irish Green is frequently demanded in the trade and in school work. On that account I decided to deal with it so that it may be of use before the end of the winter session.

It is to be found in several fine churches, built during the last hundred years. In university buildings, banks and clubs it is often used for columns, but its wavy bands of colour do not make it very suitable for wall fillings. In the building trade this marble is known as Connemara or Galway Serpentine.

Description: The colour is of medium tone, broken with grey, black, brown and white, but tints of green predominate and cover most of the surface. The wavy bands of green are often six inches wide; they twist and sometimes interlace. The darker portions are narrow; the contrasts of tone and direction are always less than they appear at first glance. The texture is usually broken and fine, but can be very uneven in size.

It is a serpentine marble and no stones are large enough to be worked. There are no chains of light colour running over the coloured waves.

It differs from Verde Antique in the absence of stones, whilst the white bands, shaded to medium or grey green, make it clearly different from Onyx Marble. The darker portions often show some resemblance to pollard or root oak.

Palette: White, raw sienna, light Brunswick green, Prussian blue, black and Vandyke brown in oil colour.

In the Dippers: (1) One part glaze or aluminium stearate to two parts of turpentine.
(2) turpentine only.

Grounds: According to the depth of example required.
(1) White to off-white.
(2) A pale grey-green.
(3) A medium grey.
Method: Many of the colours in Irish Green are opaque. Prepare a few tints of greys and greens on the palette board.

Coat the panel first with a glaze from the dipper, this prevents the darker colours from getting a firm hold on the ground. With a large fitch lay in the lightest colours first; these pale warm tints of green will

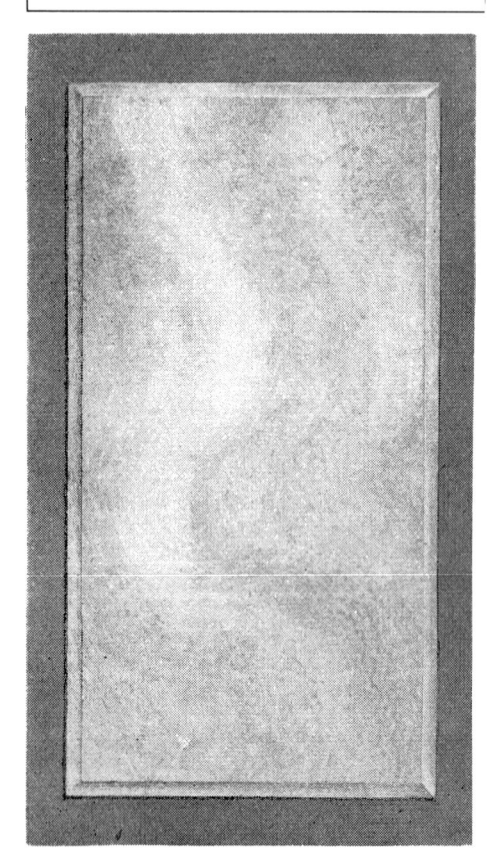

FIGURE 1

form the drawing. Half the surface should be covered with the pale tints, all following in one general direction as in Fig. 1. Continue to lay in darker tones of greens and greys; these may be added to one side of the panel on the top of the pale green.

Take a sponge lightly charged with turpentine and work with a sliding and dabbing motion. This should break up all the surface into a soft texture. All working must follow the direction of the drawing.

With a fitch now add darker broken lines in dark grey and brown, almost to black. These should not spread over the panel but should be confined to one area.

A handful of rag, roughly held together, should be used to assist in softening and to give soft edges. Continue to work with sponge, rag and hog hair softener until a satisfactory effect is obtained.

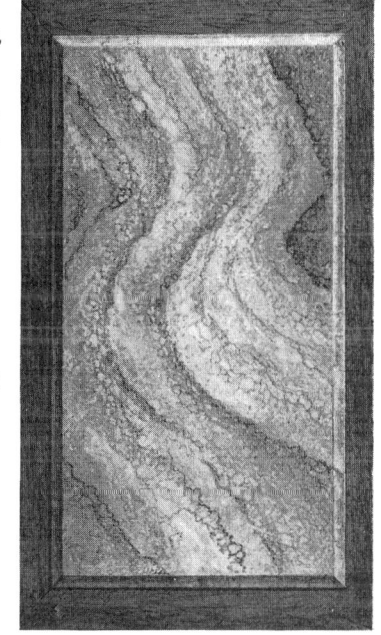

FIGURE 2

Glazing: This should be carried out with the same palette. Oil in the surface, add glazes of green, green blue, and vandyke in parts, following the meandering lines.

Wipe out with rag in parts and soften well; try to keep the ground (which shows through in the lighter portions), clean. Cleaning up with white at this stage gives a muddy appearance. Splash with turpentine from a fitch, struck against a larger brush, to open out finer areas where required.

A little practice is required accurately to gauge where the turpentine will hit. The method is a bit messy at first but it is useful for giving a finer texture where it is needed.

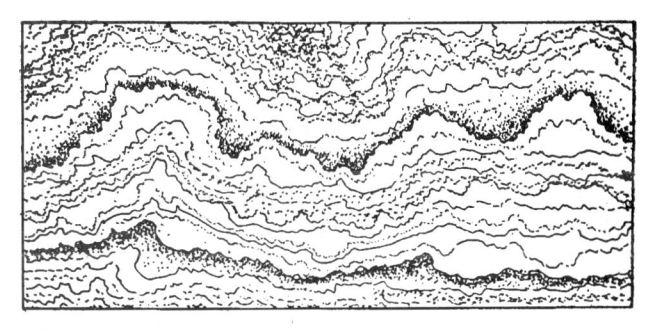

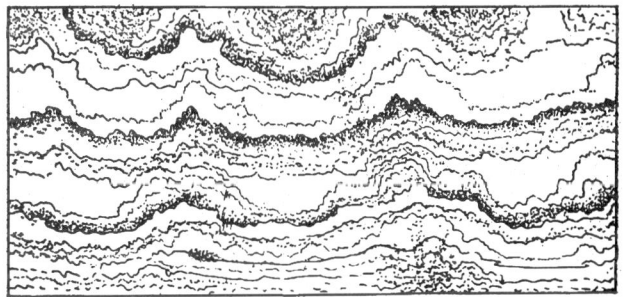

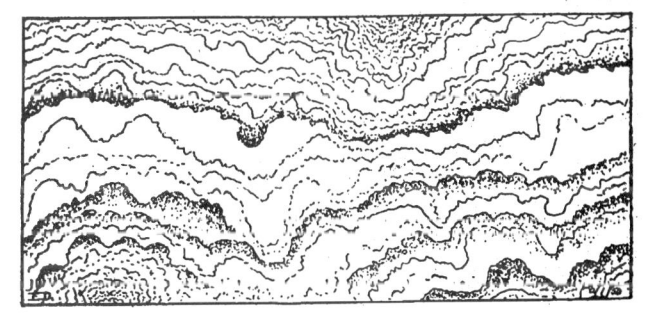

Drawings of Irish Green Marble. Size of the panels is 18in x 42in

Continental Methods of Training – XX

Pitch Pine

IN continental schools, the warm coloured pitch pine is the subject of the first lesson given in graining to painting and decorating students. The clear, well-defined lines of the grain markings are easy to see and are of good shape.

Pitch Pine is a long leaved pine, its Latin name is pinus polustris; there are several other varieties. The name, "long pine" is apt, for the leaves or "needles" are nine inches or more in length and may be found up to half-a-yard long in young vigorous trees. It is a coniferous or cone bearing tree.

The trees grow straight and tall, up to 100 feet or more, and have a rough bark. The branches occupy the top quarter of the trunk. The needles grow in tufts like turk's head brushes.

In the United States of America, north of the Gulf of Mexico, there is a strip of forest where pitch pine is grown abundantly. During the Past half century heavy fellings have reduced the stocks.

75% of the world's supply of turpentine was obtained from the Georgian pitch pine forests. The stripping and cutting of the tree, year after year, eventually kills it, but the timber is still sound and useful.

The wood is heavy for a pine timber and corresponds in hardness and toughness with its weight. This accounts for its use in public buildings and for school furniture. It is a showy timber standing up well to hard wear.

Grained Pitch Pine Panel

Description: The markings of the grain are all plain and clear, almost blatant. It calls for good drawing; even the combing of the sides requires skilful treatment.

The colour of the ground is of medium toned buff which deepens with age. The heartwood markings are of tones of raw and burnt sienna, with touches of darker vandyke lines in places. The dark line indicates a good wet, warm, growing season in the life of the tree. The wavy, shaded, mottled effect of the glazing breaks up the strong grain.

The heartwood drawing is broad and often straight. Variety is obtained by using wide and narrow lines. The large and usually well-filled centres are very interesting, they offer quite a variety of changes and sizes. The first two lines are fine and near together whilst the third and fourth spread out with a knot, perhaps to the side, around which is some good drawing.

In pine there are quite a number of small patches of dark colour that cannot be called knots; they are simply portions of grain which come near the surface. Another unique feature is the fine curly grain that occurs down the edges beyond the straight grain.

Method of Working: Oil in the panel with medium from the dipper; this oiling of the ground helps to give a softer appearance to the work, is easier on the sable pencil, and keeps the background clean. Rub out well or wipe off any excess of oil with a rag.

Charge a pencil with raw sienna and commence drawing the principal knot near the base of the panel. As the grain is open and clear, great care must be taken in the drawing; keep the knots more round than oval in shape. Should the raw sienna be on the warm side, you can work with white for the lighter parts and add vandyke for the darker veins.

If old examples are to be matched, burnt sienna and vandyke will be much in evidence. Colour about every fourth vein stronger than the remainder.

The broadest and deepest coloured markings always occur about half way from one knot centre to the next. Work up the panel starting another knot before the heavy lines become too long. The heavy veins require a lot of room, particularly where they join.

When the drawing is completed take a fitch to soften or thin out the colour on the inside of the line. This should be done in an uneven manner.

After the work is partially dry, or is setting, draw the hog hair softener gently through, working from the centre outwards. This moves part of the colour to the outside edge of each vein making it slightly darker.

Combing: The grain down the sides is clean and well pronounced and is carried out with a cork comb. A piece of cork, about 4in. x 3in., is cut straight along the edges; the notches are cut out to allow the colour to flow through and to leave dark lines. The cut out portion should be half to one-third of the portion left in. This gives a wide, clean line, with a narrow dark one. The cork combing method is clean in action, wiping out well to the background without dragging.

Before combing, rub into the oil ground a little raw sienna; cut in carefully up to the edge of the heavier veins. Keep the combing glaze pale and on the dry side. The combing pulls the colour together making it appear much darker.

Draw the comb firmly down the sides, following the contour of the graining. If this operation is new to you, it is best to experiment first, both with the cutting of the comb and the amount of colour required, before you commence graining.

If the thin, flat ¼in. cork is not available, a cork from a large bottle can be cut in half, or a cut rubber comb may be used as second choice.

A sable pencil overgrainer, or fantail, may be brought into service for the side grain, but these are not so clean, or quite as reliable, for long accurate work.

Glazing: This may be done in oil or water. Oil colour is the softest an gives most chance of success for a student. For a light glaze, use raw and burnt sienna; a dark glaze requires burnt sienna and vandyke or umber.

Rub in a faint glaze of colour, heavier down the centre, on the grain markings. Take a wide mottler, charged with a little colour, draw down the centre first with a rocking motion passing the weight from side to side. The side mottling should be worked more exactly. The cuts are made accurately, about where the curves in the grain markings occur. Colour may be removed from the top of the knots with a short fitch.

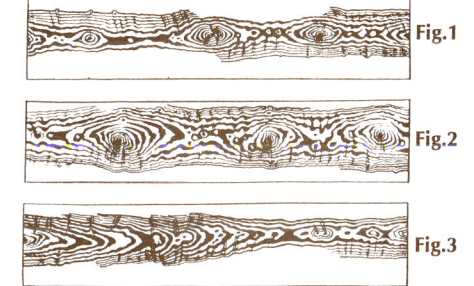

The side mottle should be different on opposite sides; simple or open down one side and much closer work on the opposite one. Soften well before the colour sets, with the badger softener in water colour or the hog hair in oil colour.

Drawings 1 and 2 are typical examples of well-marked pitch pine. Number 3 is of a plainer type; most of the markings are of this order. The painted example is rather overdone for such a small panel, it should have much more plain work around it.

Curly Pine will be dealt with in a future article.

Fig.1

Fig.2

Fig.3

Continental Methods of Training – XXI

Rouge Royal Marble

WHILE on a walking tour once in the Ardennes, a mountainous district in south-west Belgium, I saw Rouge Royal marble being quarried. This red marble is found in large quantities in this district only, the marble quarries extending for several miles. All the processes of cutting, polishing, carving and turning are carried out in buildings adjoining the quarries.

Many good examples of Rouge Royal are to be seen in English buildings. As it is considered to be difficult to paint it is often required for advanced examinations. On that account I was anxious to deal with it before the end of the winter session of the P. and D. classes.

Like most red marbles it belongs to the "Devonian" age – this is a very deep strata of the earth's crust below the carboniforous. Red sandstone with shales and limestones that are broken and squeezed all form part of this marble, together with coral, crinoids and fossils. Rouge Royal is classed as a fossiliferous marble. It also contains grey and red granite that has been forced upwards into it during earth tremors and quakes.

Description: Rouge Royal – royal red – is the general colour of this showy marble. The colour is made to look brighter by the surrounding blue grey. The red itself is actually dull in colour.

In some examples grey predominates, only a few small patches of red are found. The red in all cases is milky, being largely a tint of Indian red, and it is often dulled with burnt sienna.

The design of the marble is based on a number of grey shapes, distributed fairly evenly every foot or eighteen inches over the entire surface. They are drawn with veins of grey or red running around them and have a little white or yellow in the centre. These grey masses are about 9 in. in length by 3 in. wide and have wavy or curved edges, resembling heavy knots in woodwork.

The remainder is composed of stipple or sponge work and is a good example to study for this type of effect. Red predominates but part is left grey.

Rouge Griotte is a similar marble though brighter in colour and the markings are more pronounced. Other varieties of marble come from the same district.

Running over most of the surface is a network of white lines; these veins are heavy and in parts quite solid in colour. Along with the grey fossil shapes they call for much attention, careful study and good drawing. Examples of Rouge Royal are found with large cream to yellow shapes and very soft

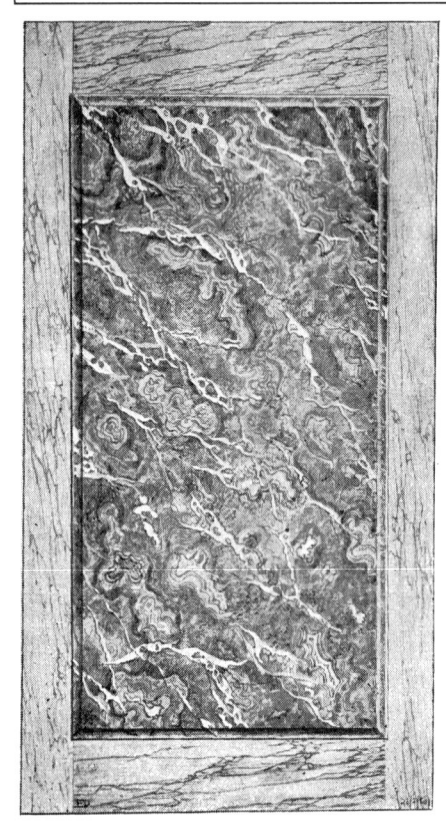

Printed example of Rouge Royal with blue Fleuri border

shading. Such examples are without any hard grey lines of outline.

Country of Origin: Belgium

Palette: White, Indian Red, Light Red, Burnt Sienna, Yellow Ochre, and Black.

Brushes, etc.: Tools, fitches, sable pencils, sponge and hog hair softener.

Ground: White or light grey.

Method: Rub in a thin glaze of greys prepared from white, black and a touch of yellow ochre. A sketch should be drawn and coloured and the tints applied according to the drawing.

Draw the larger of the fossilised shapes with the sable pencil, charged with a medium grey colour. To avoid the marble appearing too wild they should run in one general direction. Now, with the fitch in grey, paint in the veins on the inside of the pencil lines, keep your colour on the dry side. With the fitch continue to put in darker and lighter tones of grey, both inside and outside your shapes.

Change over the colour to tints of light and Indian red. Make a few separate smaller shapes in red. Also place red lines on the outside of a few of the grey ones, according to taste. To draw these parallel veins the fitch should have long, new bristle and should be held firmly with only tips of the bristle touching the surface. Work slowly.

With the sponge, commence to fill in the remainder of the surface which should be from one-third to one-half of the area. Using a grey colour first, prepare a small amount on your palette board. At all times use a knife, do not mix with a brush. Soften frequently, as you proceed, with the hog hair softener.

Now prepare a few dull, deep pinks from light red, burnt sienna, and Indian red, apply them thinly with the sponge. This coarse red stipple should not be overdone as you cannot easily apply more grey over red.

Should the effect become too solid or opaque, take the sponge moistened with turps and open out the colour. Rag may be used at this stage to take off surplus paint and also to obtain the correct soft, transparent, marble effect down to the cream or grey background. The rag can be rolled, dabbed or twisted in a crushed pad, all to good effect.

The centres of the knots should now be given attention. Yellow should be laid on in a thin film. Vary the hue with grey or tint with white.

With the large sable pencil work in the large light veins which hold the work together. A number of finer veins may be worked in with the double pencils. The colour from the ground will work up into the white, but this is all to the good. It is possible to wipe out these large veins with clean soft rag moistened in turpentine. The finer ones can be cleaned to the ground with the wooden end of the fitch.

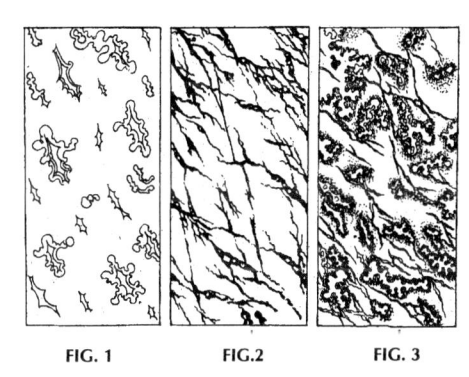

FIG. 1 **FIG. 2** **FIG. 3**

Fig. 1 shows the pattern of grey shapes, with which the work is started. Fig. 2 shows how the heavy white veins run; in some examples they cover much of the ground. Fig. 3 shows 1 and 2 combined. The remainder would be sponge work in grey or red

A splatter of turpentine from a fitch, to give a fine crinoid shell effect in parts, completes the operation.

Glazing: Most work calls only for a decorative suggestion of marble so that glazing is only carried out in exceptional circumstances where an exact reproduction of Nature is required.

Glazing is done with the same palette. Oil in the ground and lay on a thin stipple of white with the sponge. Give a second coat of white to the heavy veins, stipple on a little burnt sienna in parts. Continue with fitch or rigger on small areas with coloured glazes as required until the work is satisfactorily completed.

Continental Methods of Training – XXII

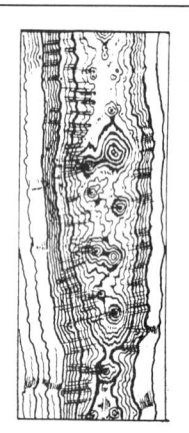

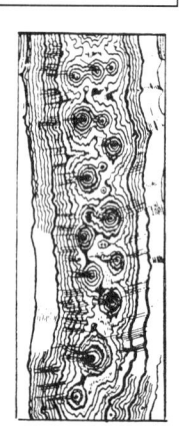

Curly Pine

ANY decorator who wishes to master the art of graining should spend some time on curly pine.

The "miniature" pattern of the wood is very interesting, and is splendid for improving brush technique.

Curly pine is to be found, for the most part, in chancel woodwork and the gallery fronts of churches and chapels built during the past eight years.

Its early botanical name was Pinis Australis, which signifies Southern Pine, but, as the term is sometimes mistaken as a reference to Australia, it is now abandoned in favour of Pinus Palustris. Curly pine is not found in Australia.

The ornamental curly pine grows on one side of the tree only; boards possessing this figure are in great demand. The wood, however, is not well suited for the important positions it is often given, as its shrinkage is great and long continued.

It is also difficult to obtain a good smooth surface, as the heartwood markings run in many directions, and the spring and summer growths of the annular rings shrink unequally.

The gradual exudation of the liquid resin from the rings makes it a difficult ground on which to paint or varnish.

This resinous fluid is a powerful and persistent solvent, and quickly destroys decorative finishes.

Description: The general colour of the ground is a rich, brown yellow. The markings, in raw and burnt sienna, are fine but clear.

The grain of curly pine consists mainly of a number of small heart shapes; two are often joined together side by side.

The whole centre of a panel is a complicated network ot small shapes. They are clean and hard; only a few are serrated, softened, or thinned out at the edges.

The veins are quite broad for their number, leaving less of the background showing than the width of the dark vein. No straight grain is found down the sides for every few inches a knot appears to attach itself to a vein; adjacent veins have to curl round it.

The cross shading of the glazing is very fine indeed; changing at every small knot, it shows up very well. Each knot radiates a shadow to the outside of the panel.

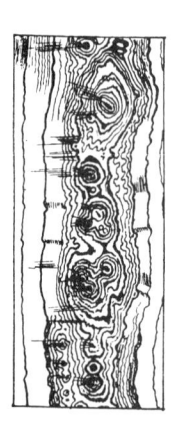

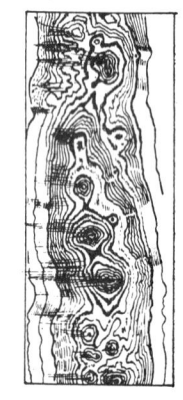

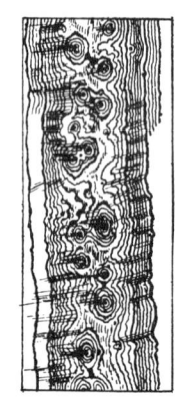

Drawings of Curly Pine by E. Dobson

Origin: Southern States of U.S.A.

Ground: Cream to buff colour.

Palette: Raw and burnt sienna, vandyke brown or burnt turkey umber and a little white.

Brushes: Sable pencils, a small fitch and hoghair softener.

In the Dipper: Equal parts of linseed oil and turpentine, with a few drops of terebine.

Method: Proceed as for pitch pine, by oiling in the ground and working with the sable pencil.

Commence near the centre of the panel with the drawing. This wood is mostly used for panels; it is comparatively weak for constructional work. It should not be used on stiles of doors or framework. The drawing being more involved than pitch pine it takes much more time to work.

The general colour of the veins is raw sienna. I often used a little white with it for the lighter parts; this prevents the thin colour from running on the oily ground and gives a pale tint without undue thinning. More burnt sienna and vandyke shaded lines are found about every third or fourth vein. In the smaller shapes the outer ring is usually dark, which brings the smaller knots out in apparent relief.

Glazing: The glazing is fairly complicated, but should be carried out in water colour, using raw and burnt sienna for the light coloured wood and vandyke and burnt sienna for the darker.

The waves are numerous, and you should attempt to get a light flash from every one. This is more important than getting a darker shadow. The centre portion, where most work is found, should be slightly darker than the plainer sides. A softer effect in glazing can always be obtained by keeping the mottler on the work all the time and not lifting it off in places, which always leaves a dark line. With this method glazing should be done much quicker; pressure makes a darker mark or shadow, whilst a lighter touch lifts the colour.

Where much time has been spent on the graining, it is always better to give a thin coat of varnish to make sure the colour is well fastened before glazing; a rub up may remove part of the delicate drawing.

Whilst adjudicating at a recent competition, however, I came across a panel that was much improved in colour by the varnish having acted as a semi-solvent and having removed almost one-third of the colour used in the graining.

Painted Example: My painted example this month is of bleached curly pine. The difference consists of changes of ground and graining colours only. The ground colour should be a grey-cream to white, whilst raw umber and green are added to the palette. My example was carried out with raw umber and white for three parts of the graining, with a little raw sienna and green in the remainder.

The glazing was done in water colour, using very thin black, a little titanium oxide, and a touch of raw sienna.

Drawings: These are from examples I have collected from public buildings in Lancashire, and should form a good basis for further study. Keep your notebook always handy to jot down good specimens. Drawing is the basis for advancement in graining.

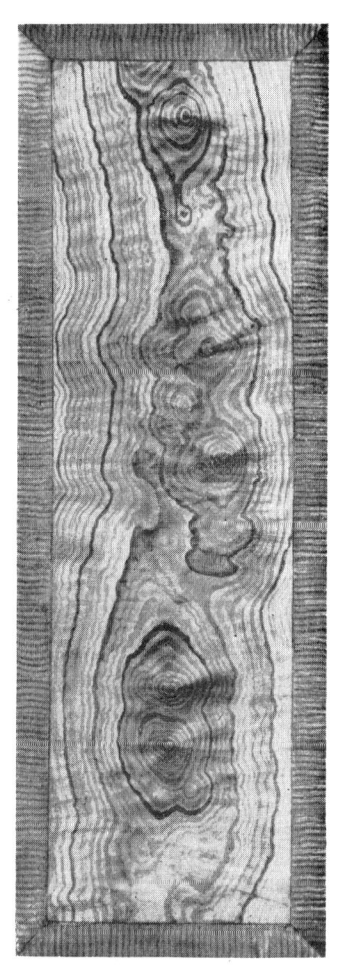

Bleached Curly Pine

Continental Methods of Training – XXIII

Granite Marbles

THE inclusion of Granite in a Painter and Decorator's training course is not new, though perhaps neglected in recent years.

Its inclusion in this year's Final Examination of the City and Guilds came as a blow to many who were excellent at other, more familiar, subjects.

Whilst travelling over the Pennine Range into Yorkshire a few days ago, I came across two fine examples of carnation pink, and blue-grey granite, laying by the road side.

I stopped to examine them. The colour was charming and the texture was even but much coarser than limestone.

For road-making or building, granite is a most valuable material because of its tenacity, durability and hardness.

In most large towns and cities in the British Isles, good examples are to be found.

The Liverpool Cotton Exchange contains some of the best coloured granites I know in England, including Ruby Red (Sweden), Emerald Pearl (Norway), Royal Blue (Norway) and the standard grey, close grained varieties from Aberdeen.

The largest and most valuable, however, is reputed to be the block of Scottish Red Granite purchased by Louls XIV when he built the Hotel des Invalides, Paris, and which contains the remains of Napoleon Bonapart. Around him rest the remains of his generals (mostly Irish) all interred in caskets of Grande Antique.

From the round gallery above, the light passing through the amber stained glass shows up in a most impressive manner and is one of the sights of Paris.

Description

The texture of Granite varies from a coarse rubber stippled effect, to a fine sponge or hair stipple. It is always sharp or clean cut, the particles never soften into each other.

The length of the particles of the essential minerals forming the granite is about one-eighth of an inch.

In the samples I have examined, the lighter colours were finest whilst the dark grey and red were coarser.

Pieces of hornblende and augite are frequently found up to one inch in length.

In decorative work, a small amount of open veining is found. In small examples this will not be noticed as the markings are only slightly darker than the ground.

To help with the decorative effect, the tone should be changed slightly on either side of the line.

The colours of Granite are a series of greys, pinks and reds. In the rough-cut state they appear light; after polishing they darken considerably.

The texture is often composed of many fine colours, in the Pearl Green variety, emerald, grey-green and pale blue-green dots are found.

The light grey Granite often has a blue or green cast or, sometimes, mauve or violet. It is not just a darker tone of grey.

The pink variety shows hues of blue in the darker splatter.

In the carnation red variety, the colour of the texture is mostly black, and of a coarser marking; a few white splashes are found.

As the granite was once a boiling mass, it gives a swirling, cloudy impression that is particularly noticeable in large areas, though not to the same extent as in onyx.

Composition

Granites are known as igneous rocks – they are composed of felspar, quartz, mica, hornblende and augite.

The igneous rock is of three varieties, the hardest, plutonic type, has solidified and slowly cooled deep down in the crust of the earth under heavy pressure.

Next there are the hypabyssal rocks that have cooled quicker and have less crystallisation or shiny sparkle.

Lastly, there are the volcanic rocks that have cooled rapidly on the surface, under less pressure.

A large block of the latter type, of which I have a photograph, weighs 2,738 tons. This was dislodged by blasting in a Scottish quarry using 110 lbs. of black powder.

Origin

Norway, Sweden, and other countries. In the British Isles granites abound from Cornwall to Aberdeen, and also the Channel Isles.

Whilst I am writing these notes a most unusual coincidence has occurred.

That ace broadcaster, Wilfrid Pickles, whilst visiting the rocky coast of Galloway in South West Scotland, interviewed a foreman at a granite quarry.

A large colony of jackdaws nesting on the rocky ledges of the quarry, had settled down to the local conditions.

The siren sounded, giving two minutes notice to take cover, for blasting was to take place!

Wilfrid was worried for the safety of the birds, but the foreman allayed all anxiety by explaining that they are used to it, they fly away when the alarm sounds and return when the all clear is sounded!

Palettes

Light Grey Variety – Black and white.

Carnation Pink – Black, white and Indian Red.

Medium Grey – Add Prussian Blue to above.

Pearl Green – Black, white and Brunswick Green.

Dark Red – Black, white, Burnt Sienna and Indian Red.

Grounds

For the first four, white to off white: the dark red requires a salmon pink ground made from Venetian Red and White.

Tools and Sundries

A two inch tool, sponges (or granite dotter), fitches and pencil. The flat, artificial sponges are quite suitable.

Method

For the light grey variety rub in a coat of pale grey thinned with equal parts of oil and turpentine or turpentine and flat varnish.

This coating gives a solid appearance, whilst saving much labour on stippling.

The tone should be a little lighter than the desired finished effect.

Mix a darker grey with a knife on your palette board; continue to stipple all over with this colour. Allow to dry, then oil or varnish in the previous work. Now stipple again with the sponge, using white.

Any small markings desirable should be put in with the pencil and the wavy effect should be considered whilst sponging.

As the particles of granite are hard and sharp no softening is required.

A fine rubber stipple will also make a good granite effect.

The colour should be laid on a little heavier than for the sponge stipple process; one coat of the grey glaze is quite satisfactory.

Dark Red Granite

Using glaze medium, oil and turpentine, rub in a semi-transparent glaze of black, stipple vigorously and allow to dry.

Oil in the stippled ground; proceed to sponge over in places with sienna and Indian Red.

When dry, a little white may be sponged on in places and a few small stones added.

As the above colours, when mixed together, would be muddy they must be kept separated.

Other coloured varieties can easily be carried out from the above instructions by simply changing or adding other tints and colours.

Granite is used extensively on the Continent for dados and pilasters.

73

Continental Methods of Training – XXIV

Figured Oak

TO grain English Oak really well is the ambition of most boys who enter the painting craft, and as important today as it was forty years ago. The demand may not be so great as it was in my early days, but oak figuring is still called for more than any other subject that we teach in our schools. Oak graining appears to be the one branch of our craft in which little alteration has taken place.

A few changes in colour, however, are worth noting. When I first started with my father, a warm sienna colour was preterred for the medium oak, then green on a buff or grey ground was popular. Dark oak, very dark oak, limed oak and cooled medium oak have all had their turn. Grey natural and bleached effects are popular at the present time. The principles remain the same, so that anyone who masters the fundamentals with which I shall deal, can readily adapt himself to smaller changes.

Varieties and Figure: I propose to deal with English, Austrian, Australian Silky, American, Pollard, Limed, Natural White, Bog Oak, Fumed Oak, Heartwood, and Feathered types of oak in this series.

The Continental method is to stress the importance of drawing on paper the many types of grain, so I shall continue to give full page drawings of figure, which can be used for class work and reference. I recommend the student grainer to draw them on a large scale. The cutting of timber will be dealt with, however briefly, for many errors occur through failure to understand the difference resulting from the way the timber is cut.

Constant patient study, a facility for drawing and much practice are all required before one becomes an accomplished grainer of this difficult and tricky wood.

The value of good figuring is such that many youths concentrate on it for many years, and then, unfortunately, regard themselves as accomplished craftsmen.

On the Continent however, all forms of graining and marbling are regarded as stepping stones to employment as decorators. Most of my fellow students at the College in Brussels had this outlook.

In Britain we start with Oak at an early stage of our training; on the Continent it is well down the list of subjects; this I consider all to the good. Most people are very disappointed with their early attempts, but drawing instruction and practice on other simple woods, sharpens their observation for the accurate placing of the figure in oak.

Oak is traditionally British, it grows well in our moist climate, has strength, long life, stability and decorative effect. In none of these does it take first place, but it makes a good showing in them all.

Figure in oak is, of course, made by the medullary rays which grow in radiating lines from the centre of the tree. The presence of large rays is a prominent feature of oak timber and, they hold the grain together. They are very prominent on true quartered surfaces.

Many different terms are given the rays in various parts of the country; painters refer to them as "figure" or "silver grain," whilst other trades use such terms as "flower," "chunk," "flash," etc.

English oak gives a fine display of unusually complicated figure; it contains many knots and darker streaks in the grain, with the rays radiating or winding about them.

The figure shows considerable variety in size on one board, and there is much open space between the heavy markings. These points are all accounted for by the bends and twists in the slowly grown timber of our cold, wet island. The American and Austrian varieties are both straighter and steadier in figure.

References: I often use figures from early Saxon and Norman churches or from country houses In the Midlands and North of England. Hampton Court Palace, built by

Cardinal Wolsley and enlarged by Henry VIII, contains much good oak from which I have collected some examples. Here King Henry VIII spent most of his married life, and the decoration of the rooms has not been materially altered since they were occupied by his many Queens, whose names they still bear, and whose tastes they still reflect.

Examples of painted oak are to be seen on the plaster walls. Others, of good quartered oak, are seen in the Hotel de Ville and Palace of Justice in Brussels.

The latter building was considered to be the finest example of the Grecian style of architecture built during the nineteenth century.

It stands on a low hill near the centre of the city; its outside walls enclose many acres of land and the high tower is a landmark.

The interior contains fine panelling of natural and painted examples of English oak.

The work was carried out by my old professor, Monsieur Alphonse Logelains, who, like my first teacher, Mr. W. Rhodes, of Batley, is still living – and teaching. Mr. James Dearden, of Huddersfield, met Mr. Logelaine at the recent International Convention in Paris.

The new Civic Hall in Leeds again contains some fine figured oak, which will be represented in my collection, and will repay a visit by anyone living within reach of it.

In early times much of the timber was cut indiscriminately, and so did not show the figure. It was only when the saw caught the quartering fair and square that a figured board was produced accidentally. Thus we find a preponderance of the straight or heartwood markings in early cabinet work.

Grainers have an advantage over craftsmen who use the actual wood, for we are able to produce the best figure possible for any position.

The Illustrations: The illustrations are all of timber about 400 years old. No. 2 is a fine example of English Oak grown in open country. It is from a 4 ft. wide trunk. My drawing was less than half of that width.

No. 3 is from a large and very straight trunk grown in a forest. It was cut well below the branches. The smaller side figure in the latter should be carefully followed. The direction, spacing and the varying lengths all lend much interest in contrast with plainer examples. No. 1 was cut to show both plain and heavy figure.

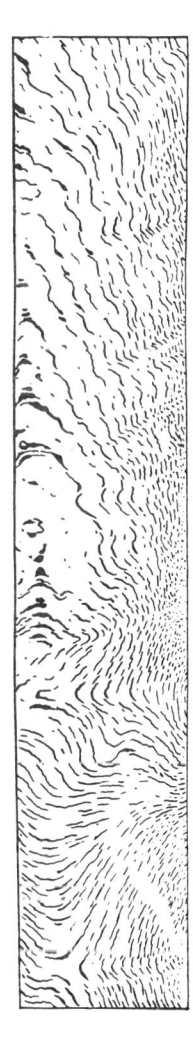

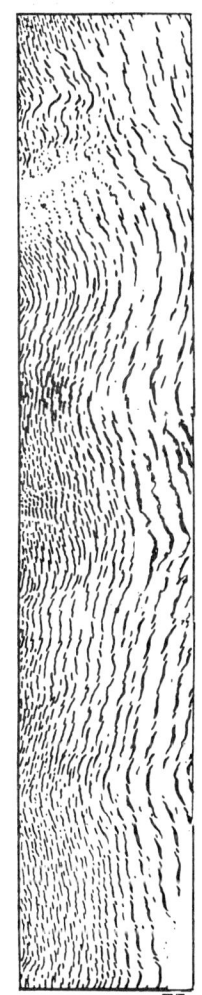

Continental Methods of Training – XXV

English Figured Oak

Grained example of English Oak

Ground
A medium cool buff colour, composed of white, golden ochre and burnt umber. The ground colour should be thoroughly hard before the figure is attempted. Thinners should consist of one-third oil and two-thirds turpentine, with a small amount of mixing varnish; this helps the gilp to bear up, to scumble or comb cleanly and the figure to wipe well.

Where much time is to be spent on the grained effect, 24 hours to several days should be allowed for drying. I prefer white lead for the ground, but other pigments are satisfactory if sufficient gum or oil is included to stop any absorbency and consequent feeding of the binder from the gilp. In Continental countries white lead is not used.

The darkening of lead paint in industrial towns is no detriment to its use, for this, together with the deepening of the sienna adds to the appearance of richness. Many rooms carried out in medium oak by my father are still giving good service. Prior to 1890, when he commenced on his own account, he was employed as the grainer to a large West Riding firm.

Tools and Brushes: A few worn brushes for rubbing in. Set of steel combs, 4in. brush grainer and a worn No. 2 writing pencil. A worn brush grainer must not be used for panel work, as it is liable to pick up the colour near the moulding, leaving a shady patch. Rags for wiping out should be well washed to remove starch, which does not allow the rag to pick up the paint cleanly. Chamois leather is used by some decorators, but its thickness causes difficulty in making sharp corners to the figure. Well worn green baize or billiard cloth is used regularly in Continental countries. It is torn into strips about 1in. wide. Owing to the difficulty of obtaining supplies most of us must be content with cotton rag nowadays.

The graining horn should have a good spring and be rounded at the end. For square figure, use one with a flat end and rounded corners.

Thin steel or perspex can be employed, so long as the edges are rounded and the material has a fair amount of spring. Some craftsmen prefer the thumb nail for wiping out the figure. This is quite convenient and never gets lost!

For continuous working on large surfaces, the graining horn is most satisfactory. It should be held on the inside of the thumb so that pressure can be kept up for a long period and the figure will be clean and sharp.

For roller overgraining two rollers are required, the cut disc type, for vertical rolling; the small check roller for use under the mouldings where the first roller will not reach. For glazing, a mottler and a badger hair softener are required.

Thinners: Turpentine (pure American if avail- able) two-thirds; raw linseed oil, one-third or slightly more; a few drops of terebine driers and a knife point of aluminium stearate glaze.

It will be found that too much turpentine causes the graining colour to flow and spoils the grained markings worse than does an excess of oil, so the proportions quoted must be strictly adhered to. The small amount of clear glaze helps the figure to "stay put."

Palette: Raw sienna, raw umber, black and Prussian blue.

For small work, or specially accurate reproduction, it is always better to use a palette with thinner separate; then many delicate, nearly related colours can be produced.

Where large, single coloured surfaces are required, prepare a kettle of colour on the previous day, and allow it to stand and settle. This ensures clean work. Any excess of thinners should be poured off.

All colours used should be finely ground. They are ground specially for graining by the manufacturers at a little extra cost. Keg stainers are heavy and may contain extenders which render them unsuitable for good grained work.

There are many satisfactory proprietary scumbles, but some have a tendency to set quickly, and may require slowing down with oil. This, however, should always be the subject of experiment.

Method: The gilp or scumble having been prepared, and the colour sample found to be satisfactory to all parties, proceed to rub in as follows.

Work the long way of any surface with the grain of the wood, stretching the colour well out without too much brushing. Streakiness, or shadiness with the grain, is desirable, but not across it. Crossing and laying off, when rubbing in, is permissible but not desirable on large areas.

The film must be sufficiently rubbed out to hold the colour and prevent running, and so endangering the fine markings that are to follow.

Extra brushing often forces too much oxygen into the wet surface, so that it becomes sticky or partly set, thus making it difficult to work.

Try to extend the gilp well without too much brushing and to get it right the first time, so that it is wet enough to work easily and to wipe out clean.

Combing: Steel combs are not so much used as formerly. They give very propronounced markings which have a tendency to detract from the figure.

The coarse comb, with teeth six to the inch, should be used first and should be drawn straight and firm down the panel.

Then take a finer comb, about 10 teeth to the inch, working in a wavy manner twice down the work to make the coarser marking.

This will produce a fairly naturalistic representation of the oak texture background, which may now be reduced by softening, using the finer comb very lightly, passing it quickly over the surface many times, or use the hog hair softener.

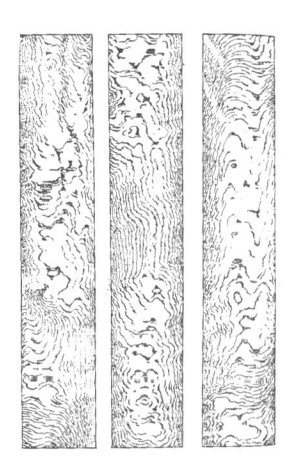

More drawings of English Oak by Mr Dobson. The original wood panels were about 18 inches wide

For other effects in combing, coarse cork or rubber, suitably cut, may be used. These, however, are too hard for use on a figured background. Strong contrasting lines are useful on stiles and rails where a lighter colour effect is desirable.

A small brush grainer may be used as an alternative tool for obtaining the background effect. Used in a gentle, wavy manner it gives a soft, suitable texture.

Too many students are satisfied with a carelessly executed background. They are so keen on the figuring operation that they leave the mouldings full of colour and "misses," and the joints are often not clean.

It should always be borne in mind that these defects cannot easily be corrected when the figuring is completed.

Continental Methods of Training – XXVI

English Figured Oak (continued)

English Figured Oak

Care of Small Details

Many factors other than the figuring contribute towards the success of good oak graining.

Colour in all woods is of paramount importance. In oak it should never be too warm; burnt Turkey umber and Sienna are both, in my opinion, too red.

These colours require cooling with a little blue, green, black or white or a mixture according to taste.

The tone of the gilp should never be much deeper than that of the ground; if it is, there is not only a tendency towards shady rubbing in, but the combing and the figure appear to jump off the ground in a startling and anything but pleasing manner.

The texture of the ground combing, or brushing, should never be too coarse for the size of the work in hand. I prefer the texture background to be always soft, never loud or showy.

The rubbing in should be clean; never allow colour from the mouldings to encroach on the stiles. After completing the panels, the stiles, rails, and muntins must be cleaned up with rag, or rubbed up extra well with the brush side to remove the half-dry gilp.

The gilp and the subsequent glazing must always be transparent. The laying on must be done in a clean, good, smart painter-like manner. The success of the finished effect is then more than half assured.

Figure Tones: In oak graining, the figure is often lighter than the ground, so of course, we work with a gilp darker than the ground colour. At times we find the figure darker than the ground; here two methods are open to us; we may add the figure in darker colour with a pencil or we may reverse the previous position and use a lighter gilp. This latter method I will enlarge upon at a later date.

In nature, looking from one side the figure often looks lighter, whilst in another position it appears darker. This quality we cannot yet introduce into our work.

The shapes of the figure vary considerably; yet, when joined, or interwoven with smaller shapes, they form a pattern that is unmistakably oak.

Figuring: The washed rag should be torn down to about 6in. x 12in.; no larger, for it is liable to get in the way, marking the work as it sways about. Should the rag be too thin, use it double, if that won't result in clumsy work.

Place the graining horn on the inside of the thumb, cover with the rag, the short end passing over the top into the grip of the left hand. The left hand should, of course, be held above the right, and a few inches behind, or nearer the body.

Both hands must be used, all the time, to hold the rag firmly, and as each figure is drawn slip the rag over the horn with a gentle pull from the left hand.

This changing of the rag is important; you should have almost as many small brown lines on your rag as there are figures on your panel.

Concentrating on the figuring, we are apt to forget

the slight movement of the rag; a hole is soon worn through it, resulting in scratching with the horn. A clean wipe out saves going back over the work and prevents a dark line of colour round the figure which may run back, leaving the figure smaller than desired. Commence with the large figure near the top of your panel; choose the most striking in shape and work round it, leaving plenty of space.

Draw carefully, paying particular attention to the sharpness of corners and cleanliness in wiping out.

Ease In Working: At all times be on top of your work, so that you can see quite clearly over your hands what you are attempting to do. Step ladders or other forms of light scaffold are required even for a door. Work downwards with your large and medium figure, completing the smaller work last. The smaller figure is always well filled towards the outer edge.

When the wiping out of the figure is completed, a quick glance over the work will often disclose places that can be improved. Select one or two larger figures and give them more weight, or broaden them. Others may require extending, or the points sharpening; others again may be too full and some may want removing.

At all times the figuring should be orderly, wrapping well over like slates on a roof; the ends should not cut into each other if extended. Above all avoid a 'snow storm' appearance.

There are several methods of approach to the pattern or design for the beginner, the most simple being to have a good example of the timber alongside and work from it. In Continental schools no natural example was ever used, the only help coming from the teacher and his graphs.

The next step is to make small drawings of the larger figure, and fix them by the side of your panel or door. This gives you confidence. Another method is to commit to memory some good, simple examples and use them, but there is a tendency with this method, to make your work too uniform.

With experience you will learn to design your own figure but don't attempt it too soon; the results may be disappointing and discourage you.

Wiping Off Between Figures: Between the large figures we find the background lighter in colour, at other times darker. To produce the lighter effect, fold the rag into a long pad, gently dabbing the combing space between the figures; this lifts part of the colour.

Continue until a satisfactory even effect is obtained. The same rag-pad can be used for removing unwanted figure; the small amount of colour removed from the combing will cover the unwanted figure quite easily.

On grained work that is to be glazed, it is quicker to leave the softening between the figure for the glazing process.

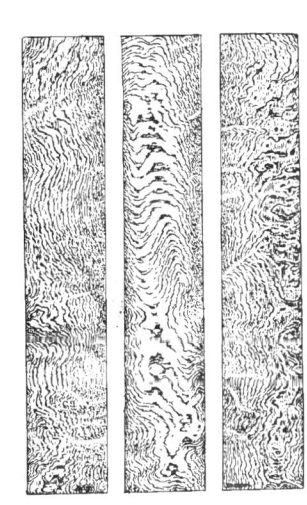

Drawings of English Figured Oak by Mr Dobson

Weight Under the Figure: An additional refinement to the work can be obtained by underlining in a darker tone under the figure. Take a worn sable pencil or fitch and work in a thin line of colour on the underside of the large figure. It may be carried out while the graining is wet with the fitch, or with the sable if the ground is dry. Soften the work with the hog hair softener.

The two painted examples reproduced in the September issue and this month were worked whilst the gilp was wet up to this stage. They have not been glazed or rolled with the overgrainer. Many other refinements can be worked and I will give details of many interesting processes in a future article. Figured oak will be continued next month.

Continental Methods of Training – XXVII

English Figured Oak (continued)

THE illustrations of the figure of oak are, I believe, so important a help towards good graining, that I am continuing with them whilst discussing other interesting matters about this wood. A little of the botany of oak is dealt with this month.

Origin of the Name

The name of Oak is derived from the Anglo-Saxon word "ac," and has distinctive versions in many dialects. The Scots use " aik," whilst "yak" comes from Hampshire. Oak with its twin vowels is, in origin, the East Midland form.

The Anglo-Saxon invasion took place in 449 A.D. so the word gradually developed from that date.

Many place names owe their origin to oak in some form or other, such as Ickornshaw, "the wood of acorns," and occur frequently on the map of England.

To-day the moors (Ickornshaw), between Colne in Lancashire, and Keighley in Yorkshire, are bare of trees and sheep graze where the forest stood.

Acid Nature of the Wood

Oak contains a large amount of acid, which enables it to resist salt-water.

I understand that oak piles, used under the old London Bridge, were taken from the River Thames in good condition after having been in use for six and a half centuries.

Oak is a difficult wood to paint upon, particularly for outside work. The acid is very liable to form blisters, even when many precautions have been taken.

To a maritime nation like the British, oak with its acid, salt resistant nature, was a great boon.

Most of the large forests in the country belonged to the Crown and many new trees were planted after each heavy naval engagement.

Patriotic noblemen and large landowners in the past have planted oak trees extensively, offering them to the King in times of emergency and sometimes to court favour.

I know of some avenues of large well matured trees in the Midlands that were refused by the reigning monarch of the time. They are still growing and stretch for miles, in many directions, and in double lines, amongst rich agricultural land.

A number of centuries ago this country was largely forest land. Much of the timber was oak and it was cut down for fuel and also to make room for the rapidly growing population.

Before the deep mining of coal, the oak trees were used as fuel for iron ore smelting.

Queen Elizabeth was greatly concerned about the rapid decrease in the number of oak trees and made a law forbidding their use for this purpose.

Varieties of Oak

There are many varieties of oak growing in Britain. The two varieties that are most widely distributed

Oak panel grained by Mr Dobson

and are considered as native are the Pendunculate Oak, Quercus Robur Liebe, and the Seselle or Durmast Oak, Quercus Patraia Liebe.

Unless otherwise stated, my remarks will apply to these two types. The grain markings are similar and it is impossible to tell the difference after the foliage is removed.

Both types are slow growing, taking life leisurely, growing, developing, then decaying.

Each process takes an average of three hundred years, nine hundred in all.

When fully developed on good soil they reach a height of 50-80 feet, with a trunk up to 15 feet in circumference.

Some old trees may be more, but they are often unsound.

The leaves, catkins and fruits are generally well known.

It may be noted that the Pendunculate Oak has very short leaf stalks, and the bases of the leaves are lobed, whilst the Durmast Oak has long leaf stalks.

The Pendunculate Oak bears its acorns on stalks, often two or more in number.

The acorns of the Durmast Oak are without stalks or have very short ones.

These two varieties grow in a number of European countries.

Botanical

The male flowers grow first, in great profusion, from axillary buds from the shoot of the preceding year: flowers are solitary, consisting of 5-7 segments and 6-12 short stamens.

Female flowers grow erect in the axils of the upper leaves of the shoot of the current year.

They occur as close petalled, solid flowers. Each flower is invested by a cupule, which at first is scarcely visible but is fully developed on the ripe acorn.

The flowers and stems vary slightly with each variety. Oak are the largest deciduous trees of European woods.

Oak trees, grown in open park land as specimen trees, develop huge spreading crowns with surmount stout, squat trunks. This type is a popular design motif.

Cork Oak

Coak oak, which is a species that has been introduced to this country, grows in good numbers in the Midlands and South.

The bark of this tree is the fine cork used in industry for bottle corks and decorative purposes.

Cork oak thrives well, producing cork of the finest texture after being stripped the seond time. Other trees often die if their bark is removed, even in small quantities. The timber is sound and useful after producing cork.

Turkey Oak

Turkey oak is a very hardy variety: it seems to revel in the high, wet, cold and stormy northern hills.

It is to be found singly or in groups blown over to one side by the wind, and often where there is thin clay soil.

Turkey oak is readily recognised by its twisted branches. They twist in a violent manner from the trunk almost to the tip of the thin leaf stems.

The markings of the timber it produces are, in turn, violent. The trees do not grow to any great height.

Evergreen Oak

It is most unusual for any species of tree to produce both a summer leafing variety and an evergreen; oak does both.

The evergreen oak, however, does not grow much in England but abroad its thick glassy leaves are frequently seen, often forming a dividing hedge or giving shelter along the highway.

I saw many miles of it this summer, growing 8-12 feet high, very strong and thick, with its new light yellow green leaves with curly edges.

The drawings this month are partly from the Hotel de Ville, Brussels, and the painted example is my own.

The illustrations are all of the two commonest varieties found in Great Britain.

Oak Trees

MY recent articles have digressed at times from the subject defined by the heading "Continental Methods of Training". Perhaps, therefore, it will be wise to drop a title which may not always be accurately descriptive of my subject matter.

Certainly it does not apply to this one, which is better described by the heading "Oak Trees."

On account of their stability and long life, oak trees have been much used to commemorate important events.

Recently, in the beautiful Valley Gardens, Harrogate, I found a new oak tree had been planted by the Mayoress on 26th February, 1949, to conunemorate the birth of Prince Charles.

The Yellow Bark Oak, Quercus Valuntina, has larger leaves than most varieties, but the indentations are not very deep. The bark is not the bright colour the name might lead one to expect, but is inclined to a greyish yellow.

Among my friends are two botanists and they have, over many years, taught me much about trees, timber and botany. One of them was responsible for the lay-out of the above gardens a long time ago.

When I was a pupil in North Yorkshire, he told me of the planting of two oaks by Edward VII, then Prince of Wales, and William II of Germany, in the grounds of a large country house. To commemorate the occasion, ten golden sovereigns were buried at the base of each tree, which greatly impressed the gardeners.

"United States of Europe": While in St. Peter Port, Guernsey, I once visited the former residence of Victor Hugo, the decoration of which was still as he had left it.

From Madame Moreau, the French curator, I had a brief but lucid description of his life and work, and learned that five days before the Franco-German war broke out (14th July, 1870) Victor Hugo planted an acorn in the grounds of Hautville House. The tree which grew from it now covers the lower lawn.

It was named "Oak Tree of the United States of Europe;" Hugo contended that there should be a United States after the Franco-German war, but it has required three German wars to bring much significance to the name of this oak tree.

Historical Specimens: Rambling recently in the Pendle district of East Lancashire, I was shown a fine old tree. Its age was probably 800 years; the circumference was 25 feet at three feet from the ground. Many of its large branches had been broken by reaching out too far or, perhaps, by the weight of snow. Five still remained and all were over two feet in diameter.

Years ago I was teaching in Wiltshire and paid many visits to the famous "Savernake" forest, where many remarkable specimens grow.

The long green drives into the depths of the woods are a source of pleasure to anyone interested in trees, many of which have metal plaques giving

A panel carried out by Mr Dobson in one operation on a brush grained ground. See note at end of article

their history and names, such as "King Oak," the "Decanter" and the "Duke's Vault." The latter is supposed to have taken its name from the protector, Somerset, who was the owner of Savernake some four hundred years ago, when the oak was in its prime. An account, in 1812, gave its circumference as 30 feet on the outside and 20 feet around the hollow within.

Savernake was well established as a forest in Saxon times. Later William the Conqueror took a great interest in it. The "Boscobel" oak which sheltered Charles II from his pursuers in 1660 is still growing.

One evening I was examining the large oak trees near Read Bridge, Lancashire, which were used as cover for the local Parliamentary forces on April 20th, 1643.

Most of the East Lancashire families were on Cromwell's side, and here they were met by Royalist troops from Preston, under the Earl of Derby. This battle was the turning point in the fortunes of the Roundheads; the Royalists lost 300 men killed and 40 prisoners, to one Roundhead killed.

I must mention the "Major" oak in Sherwood Forest, Nottinghamshire, which gave shelter and served as headquarters to Robin Hood and his merry men. This outlaw who "plundered the rich to give to the poor" is buried at Hartshead Moor, Yorks.

Returning North, after attending the Royal Jubilee in 1935, we passed through Sherwood. My small son filled his pockets with acorns and planted them all over the garden. Most of them germinated and we allowed one to grow. Of the Pendenculate variety, the tree is growing at the rate of one foot per year, being now 15 ft. high and 9½in. circumference at the base.

English Varieties: The illustrations this month are of the two English varieties. The three drawings are from parts culled from various bedrooms in Hampton Court Palace.

The two outer examples are rather heavy and would take quite a lot of plain figure work around them, while the centre one is a good example of the use of plainer figure with small work at the top, large figure drawn down the centre, and one radiating point down the right-hand side only.

The painted example is a panel 4 ft. x 1 ft. 6 in. which I carried out at one operation on a brush grained ground. A standard 4 in. brush of grey bristle and horse-hair was dragged down the panel quite heavily.

The figuring, which is original, was executed with a horn, after which light softening was done with a rag to lift a little colour from the background between the figures.

It still requires glazing but I have left this in order to aid reproduction.

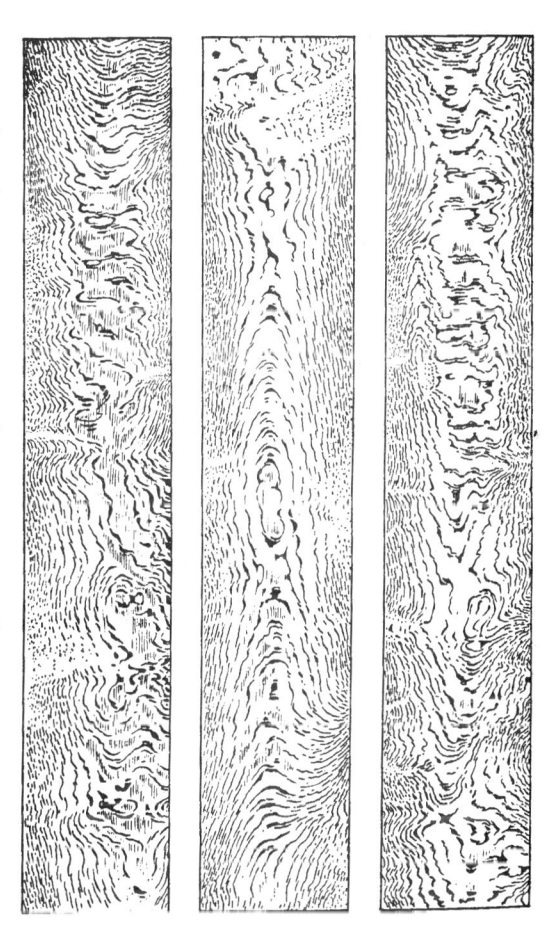

Drawings by Mr Dobson from oak in bedrooms at Hampton Court Palace. See reference in article

Marbling Vert Campan

DESCRIPTION: Green Campan belongs to a family of five marbles, of the same type, but differing in colour and scale of figure.

Green Campan marble is characterised by vertical bands of strong colour contrasting with the ground and of a darker tone.

It is covered with what are, in effect, lighter pebbles or small shells, giving an interesting, sparkling effect.

The shapes are so near together, however, that a broken colour effect is produced, such as we often obtain with a coarse rubber stippler. They are arranged in the same order from top to bottom of the slab; at no place are they larger than three-quarters of an inch.

The general colour effect is a light bronze green, though bands of blue green and dull red show through in places.

The whole is held together with veins of open crosswork in grey and off-white colour, as in Sienna marble.

Origin and Composition: Campan comes from a valley in the French Pyrenees mountains. The Campan marbles belong to the amygdaloidal group, which means they are built up largely of calcareous nodules, containing shells built up in a green matrix or cement.

Palette: White, yellow ochre, Brunswick green, Indian red, Prussian blue and black.

Ground: White.

Tools and Brushes: Double pencil, sponge, hog hair softener and two 2in. tools.

Coloured Ground: The marble is worked on a coloured shaded ground, the application of which is the first of three simple operations. This ground is of clean fairly bright colours, the second glaze being of darker, quieter shades of colour.

There are narrow bands of striking colour, pink to red, made from white and Indian red. They are separated by green bands of lighter tone (ochre, white and black).

The bands are usually tapering; the edges should be softened into each other. Narrow bands of tints of green, blue and violet are used; they are much lighter in tone than the red bands.

The reds and pinks work into the other colours while softening; it is most difficult to work clean with this combination of colours. The width of the darker tones tapers from 2in. to 3in, while the paler tints are 8in. to 9in.

The thinners may consist of one part oil, one part varnish or goldsize and two turpentine; this mixture will dry hard and glossy for the colour to open out upon later.

Method: The contents of the dipper are important and should be the subject of a little experiment before commencing work on a large surface, as the power to run, stay put and dry differs with different

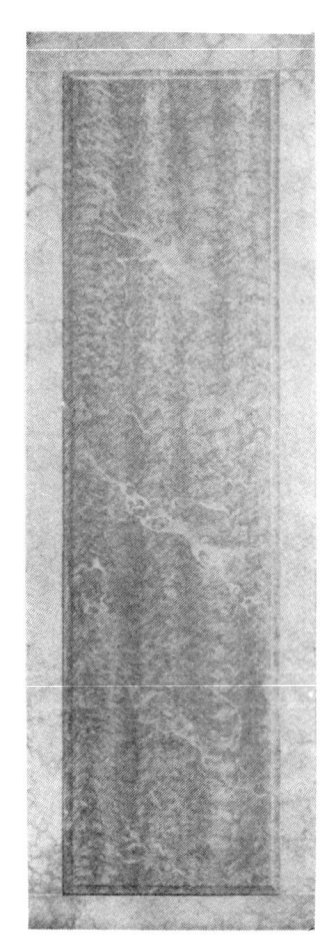

Panel of Campan Marble with a border of Sienna

samples. I have used recently one part flat varnish, one part linseed oil, one part copal varnish and two of turpentine.

One other very successful medium was prepared from equal parts of pure American turpentine and linseed oil with a little terebine. The medium should be well brushed out and allowed 10 to 15 minutes to set before being worked.

For the most part, the glaze should consist of two parts of green to one of black; smaller patches of other colours may be introduced sparingly from the palette to cover about one-tenth of the area; they should not be too far removed from the ground colours or the dull green glaze, which should be transparent to allow the ground to show through.

Take a piece of sponge, well squeezed out with turpentine substitute until almost dry, stipple with the pointed side of the sponge gently down a line of colour, using the same pressure all the way down.

A gentle sliding stipple may be attempted, slightly at an angle, giving a longer narrow shape of stone or shell. Do not twist as in wood grain.

The sponge should be rinsed frequently in the turps substitute. The texture should open out slowly and remain steady; it must not run. This fault, however, can often be checked by rolling lightly with clean rag.

A few of the larger shells may be worked round with a rigger and some darker green glaze, used almost dry.

Glazing: Soften the surface all over with oily rag, paint in with a light tone of grey the open chain as shown in the pen drawing, almost like an open type of black and gold marble. Roll the pencils to give a grey tone. Fill in some larger shells with a thin glaze of white and soften all the overglazing with the hog hair softener.

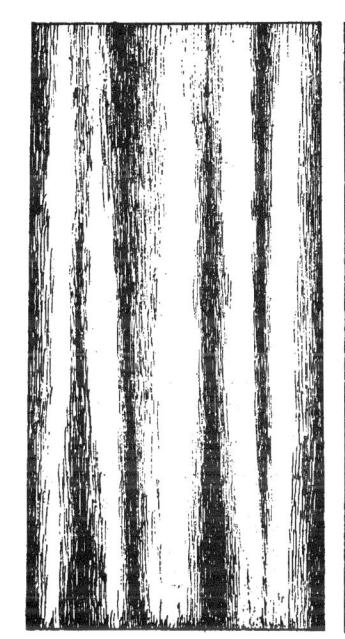

The first process of the coloured, shaded background

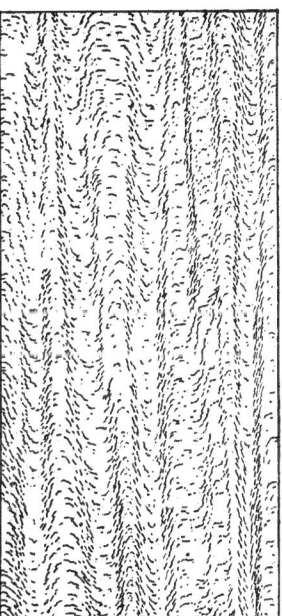

Lines of direction for the sponge stipple, over the first shaded ground

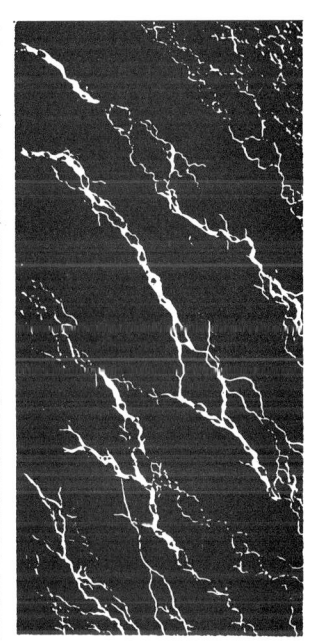

The third process of glazing, the veins are painted in light grey and white

Harmonies: Other marbles which will harmonise with Vert Campan are: Serancolin, Sienna, Bleu Flueri, Bleu Turquin, Pavanazzo, Rouge Royal and Skyros.

I have to thank many readers for suggestions for future chapters. They are all being prepared and will appear in due course. I am much gratified by the interest shown in these subjects.

85

Sandstone

AS I walk about our towns and cities I often see large buildings being cleaned by steam or scrubbing. Then, when the grime is removed, a charming soft yellow or cream emerges.

While in Liverpool Cathedral recently, I was impressed by the soft, gentle harmony of the warm red sandstone and the light oak wood work and the large areas of stained glass. The local stone had formed a suitable and pleasing background to the choir, congregation and furnishings.

From the time of Stonehenge onwards, more important shrines have been carved and built in stone than in all other materials combined, because stone is found abundantly in these islands in colour and quality suitable for many purposes.

I spent my young days in a stone quarrying district, my grandfather being a stone contractor.

It was a thrilling sight to see six large shire horses drawing a wagon with a block of stone measuring several cubic yards and weighing several tons. The arches of Liverpool Cathedral contain hundreds of such blocks.

Two of my friends were sons of exporting merchants and it was interesting to hear of stone blocks being shaped in Yorkshire and, without further cutting, used on buildings in New York, Rio-de-Janiero, or the Cape.

The work of the quarryman is arduous. He is exposed to the elements and works at dangerous heights, in deep cuttings or in the depths of the damp quarry, and often in freezing weather.

He has a tendency to develop silicosis or stone masters' disease.

Craftsmen are called upon to do unusual things; the representation of stone is one of them.

I have often assisted in this in both oil and water colour in slabs, blocks, and unusual shapes.

The Festival of Britain is focussing attention on the outsides of buildings, and a few notes on the subject might be helpful.

With Mr. James L. Brooke I saw some of the finest grain markings in building stones that I have ever seen, in Ripon Cathedral and Fountains Abbey.

The crypt of the cathedral contains a number of short, stout pillars, probably of the Saxon period.

They are cut from well marked yellow sandstone and are adorned with such prominent heartwood markings that they look almost like fossilised ash.

The painted example is from a drawing made on the spot.

Painted example of stone from Ripon Minster, Yorkshire, by Mr Dobson

Types: There are three main types of building stones; sandstone, limestone and granite. I have previously dealt with granite, although not completely. I now propose to say a little on sandstone.

Composition: Sandstone is formed by grains of sand cemented together by silica, carbonates of lime, magnesia, etc., in a liquid state. Sandstone is chemically perfect, the silica being imperishable.

The durability of stone depends entirely on the resistance to decomposition of the cement materials.

If a quantity of lime carbonate is present in stone it indicates the likelihood of rapid deterioration if the stone is used on the outside of a building.

The binding material, silica, forms the larger part of the mass. In the grey calfarious stone of Edinburgh, 98% of silica is found, while the Mount Charles stone from County Donegal contains only 76%.

The stone with which my family was concerned was the hard Yorkshire blue stone.

After being quarried it must be worked to the required shape within a few days for, on exposure to the free air, it hardens rapidly, becoming so hard that it cannot be worked economically.

Blue stone contains no lines of the grain or strata, but traces of waves or swirls can be seen which indicate that it was a boiling mass at some time.

Varieties of Sandstone: The names of the different variations are intriguing, often indicating places of origin, e.g., Bramley Fall, Casterton, Corncockle, Crow Hall, Darley Dale, Huddlestone, Pennant Stone, Scotgate, Ash and Shamrock.

The colours of these are light brown, warm cream, rich red, cool brown, whitish cream, slaty blue, brown blue, French grey.

In my drawings of ashlar hewn stone, there are four types of strata markings.

This form of buliding stone has always interested me, and I strongly recommend it for school work, as giving good practice and dexterity with the brush, and also in the mixing of colour tones, using school wall surfaces and thus economising in the use of panels.

In four of the blocks the lines are going off at a tangent. This is rare in building stone of the Huddlestone type, of which York Minster, Selby Abbey, Westminster Hall and Fountains Abbey were built. It was from the latter that I made my drawings; these are numbers one, two, six and eight.

Two of the blocks, numbers 3 and 4, consist of plain bands of colour as found in the Runcorn type, which is a dark red colour and cuts easily and weathers well.

Number 7 is a close grained hard sandstone of the gritstone type, such as Halifax Blue and Pink Hall. This is excellent building stone but hard to work.

Drawings by Mr Dobson of Ashlar carved stone, showing four different varieties

Number 5 is a warm yellow sandstone with wood grain markings, from Ripon Minster.

The vein markings are of a good raw sienna colour and probably fossilised from wood. The cream yellow to red markings are due to the presence of iron.

Turkey Oak

I PROPOSE to deal from time to time with the lesser known varieties of Oak, all of which are valuable to a painter.

Some grainers confine themselves to one type of figure to the exclusion of others, and many develop a good style but some go a bit astray.

Turkey Oak, however, finds many keen exponents, particularly among the really fine craftsmen.

This can be accounted for in many ways. Most men start with a simple and easy figure and then, after they have mastered it, other more intricate types are attempted. Eventually the most elaborate and complicated types are found and practised.

Most schools possess some fine examples of Turkey Oak among their wood specimens and no grainer is satisfied until he has mastered it.

Turkey Oak is not considered native to this country but was imported from the shores of the Mediterranean Sea.

The tree of this oak is a weary looking one, considered by many to be a poor specimen on account of its weather-beaten appearance; this is, however, a sign of its health.

The trees of this variety are very common in the North, where they very well withstand the cold. They are readily indentified by the violent twists and turns of the branches.

Description

This variety is easy to distinguish by the complicated manoeuvring of its figure and heartwood.

Its figure is never steady or flowing as it is always changing its direction and size, with large open spaces and clusters of small figure quite near.

I have examined many trees in my friend's timber yard and all were true to the above description. The colour is of a medium to light yellow brown. The foundation grain is fine and soft, such as can be obtained by brush graining, and is never coarse or hard.

The right effect is obtained by softening or wiping out either between the figures or even when no figuring exists. The figure is never large, even when cut across the centre of the tree.

In all the specimens I have examined the figure was much lighter than the ground.

Palette

The colours required are raw sienna, raw turkey umber and white.

In the Dipper

Two parts of oil, one part of clear glaze, three parts of turpentines and a small amount of terebine driers are required as thinners.

A specimen of Turkey Oak

Method

Many grainers for convenience use prepared scumbles, but others mix their own in a kettle.

I find, when working by the latter method, that it is better to prepare the thinners to the above formula first and then add the stainers gradually until the desired colour is obtained.

To prevent a stronger colour rising from the kettle bottom it should be strained before use.

For the lighter tone I use equal quantities of white, sienna, and raw umber, while for the darker tone I use one part of raw sienna to two parts of raw umber.

The amount of thinners used also has a bearing on the colour.

Many interesting tones can be obtained between the light and the dark, remembering that sienna is a warm colour and raw umber a cooler one.

For small work I prefer to work my colours from the palette, preparing in the centre sufficient at one mixing, say, for a door, with the colour in a round state. I thin it from the dipper as I rub in.

Working with the grain a number of colours may be used in a most natural manner if they are related, and also a little shadiness is desirable, but brushed with the grain with no crossing.

The wiping out of the figure should be bright and sharp with good corners and finish to all sizes of figure, well wrapped over each other and the ends pointing in the right direction.

The soft brush grained effect of the background grain will be noticed in my painted example.

The grey bristle brush was drawn down once only, lightly at the sides and heavier towards the centre, though never very heavily.

I have seen many occasions good work spoiled by too vigorous an application of the dragger. Gentle quiet figuring cannot show up against this.

The figure on my specimen starts at the top in a double row, works into three and finishes at the bottom in one row, thus showing the violence of the changes.

The three lines of figure can often be seen in this oak. Many of the shapes are made by using surrounds of small figure.

The wipe out or softening between the figure should be carried out with a pad of clean graining rag.

A dabbing motion is to be preferred to a sliding one as the latter will remove too much colour.

If overdone this is liable to ruin all the effect after much time has been spent in the figuring process.

OAK
See also:
Figured Oak 74
English Figured Oak 76
English Figured Oak (cont.) 78
English Figured Oak (cont.) 80
Oak Trees 82
Oak Graining:
The Heavy Figure 110
Oak Graining:
Heartwood Markings 116
Graining of Brown Oak 134
Heartwood Markings
of English Oak 142
Graining of Pollard Oak 148
Graining of Pollard Oak (cont.) .. 150
Oak Graining: Larger Figures 154
Graining of "Natural" Oak 178
Knots in Oak Heartwood 184
Light Oak and Linen Fold 206
Brown Oak 234
Bleached Heartwood Markings
of English Oak 253
Feather of Oak 262
Limed Oak 273
Oak Heartwood 280
Pencilled Figure of Oak 287
Australian Silky Oak 296
Bog Oak 311

Verde Antique

VERDE ANTIQUE is a green marble found in tones of medium and dark green; the darker varieties often contain black. The matrix always has a sparkle of green inclined to blue and white.

This marble is classed as a Brecciated Serpentine; the background or matrix is a serpentine marble, filled in with broken or brecciated parts of dark green or black in sharp, angular fragments. Small white patches of calcite are present which give it life, and are quite pleasing.

Occasionally the amount of calcite is considerable, forming a cloud-like combination of delicate colour which adds much to the beauty of this decorative marble. The varying amount of calcite makes the difference between the light and dark varieties. Although this marble is quarried extensively in Greece, the Greeks used it sparingly, preferring stone rather than marble.

The Romans were very fond of it, and it has been used in many fine Italian churches.

Verde Antique is used on the large 25 ft. columns on each side of the nave of the famous Church of St. Sophia, Constantinople. A large cross of it is laid in the floor of the nave, while the walls are lined in horizontal bands of White Marble and Verde Antique, which has also been used to adorn many English banks, theatres, churches, and offices.

Origin: Small amounts are found in the U.S.A., Turkey and the Swiss Alps, but the largest quarries are at Thessaly, Greece.

Palette: The colours required are white to a yellow grey for the ground, and white, yellow-chrome, Oxford ochre, deep Brunswick green, Prussian blue, black and Venetian red.

Dipper: One part of oil, two parts of turpentine, and a small amount of terebine driers are required for thinners.

Brushes and Sundries: These consist of sponge, fitches, pencils, feathers, and hog hair softener.

Method: In all marbling, the method and appreciation of colour strength must be studied and mastered before good results can be obtained.

The colours are considerably affected by their shapes, area and proximity to other colours.

In this marble the large amounts of black, white, grey green and sage green are surprising in what appears to be a bright green marble.

With your tool, work a glaze of green-grey for the medium toned marble; for the light tone use a pale green glaze, while for the dark tone use a green grey – almost black – leaving spaces for the lightest stones.

For the middle-toned marble, the glaze should be prepared from white, green, ochre and black, with a tone of each of these colours predominating in different parts. Sponge in parts a lighter grey-green tone, similar to the ground, and, in other parts, a tone darker. Make a definite job of the sponging, as much of it will show on the finished panel.

A specimen of Verde Antique

Decide where the largest dark stones are to be placed, and here stipple with almost pure black, limiting this to only a few parts. As you are working on a fairly wet ground, sparkles of light will show every time you stipple colour on with the sponge.

Turpentine can be sponged on quite freely in parts, but must be kept in a running stage. With your feather, work in the criss-cross lines of the serpentine veins in light green and arrange the markings around the spaces allotted to light or dark stone shapes.

With a fitch proceed to paint the broken shapes of the larger stones in a darker tone than the ground. The largest of the stones, which are few in number, may now be painted and they should not differ much from the general tone of the ground; certainly they must not be too dark, or they will appear to jump from the ground.

Leave spaces for the many smaller stones that surround the larger ones. With the double pencil charged with green, work in the fine veins around the stones, adding red and black to the green for variety.

Using a moist rag, remove the background colour to form the lighter stones. A graining horn, thumb, or a flat piece of wood may be used for making a firm pad to clean out the smaller stones. The small amount of colour left on the ground may be softened into a thin glaze. Continue to wipe out, paint in the small darker stones, and pencil in the veins until a satisfactory arrangement has been developed.

Care must be taken not to destroy by too much work the bright green marking of the sponged matrix. After the sharpening of the light calcite shapes, a few more bright green lines should be painted in with the double writing pencil.

These initial operations can be carried out on the bright, contrasting side and it is much better if you can maintain a good transparencey all the time. In continental work, however, much reliance is placed on the glazing to obtain this.

A few splashes of turpentine from a springy fitch, to open out the matrix and give a texture to the wiped-out stones, completes the first marbling process.

Glazing: When the marbling is thoroughly hard, soften the surface with a rag containing thinners from the dipper. Sponge all over the surface with broken colour in a grey-green, and in places pure green, but chiefly on the half tones and finer stones, keeping it thin and transparent but not running.

This sponging can be made to intensify or reduce the groundwork as desired.

With the fitch continue to put in more stones and darken others; in places lighten with thin white. Restraint must exercised or the light patches will appear to jump from the surface. All work should be near in tone to the general colour of the ground and should not be too contrasting or colourful, or the result will not be harmonious.

A drawing by Mr Dobson showing how variety of distribution can be obtained on a large surface

With glazes of colour continue to work on the stone shapes for a long time, in tones of greens and greys, until you produce an almost perfect reproduction of Verde Antique marble.

The double and single pencil should be used to complete the bright green lines in the background, and to finish off the outline on a few of the larger stones. The drawing shows variety of texture and stone distribution on a large surface of 6ft. x 8ft.

Other marbles that harmonise with Verde Antique are Sienna, Rouge Royal, Pavanazzo, Skyros, Golden Onyx, Breche Caroline and Levanto.

Reproduction of Stone of the British Isles

Tools and Sundries: One or two tools of varying widths, a few fitches, a small stippler, hog hair fantail grainer, sponge and clean rags.

Palette: Black, white, raw sienna, burnt or raw umber; these may be ground in oil or water according to the method of working.

In the Dipper: Equal parts oil and turpentine, a touch of clear glaze, a few drops of terebine driers.

Method: The setting out of the stone shapes should be carried out before the final coat of paint has been applied, checking the horizontal lines with the spirit level, and the vertical lines with the plumb line.

Line over the struck lines with a stout black lead pencil using a straight-edge. The firm black lines will show through the final coat of paint sufficiently to enable the run lines to be executed and thus avoid the necessity of setting out by chalk lines, which always tend to dry up the colour in the lining fitch, leaving rough edges to the line.

Commence by coating, with a clean tool in the prepared medium, a square on which to work some good strata markings.

With another tool, charged with raw sienna and white from the palette board, draw in a series of almost parallel lines of pale colour, very little pressure being required to give the stone effect.

The fantail brush, charged with a tint of umber, may be used to give clearly marked

Painted example of squared rubble stone bonding

lines, usings caution to avoid too hard an effect.

Continue until a good clean reproduction of stone is obtained, the lines being formed at the first attempt. If the colour is too dirty or heavy, run a handful of rag through the work, following the lines of the grain to produce a cleaner effect.

A sponge, lightly charged with turpentine, will often assist both to lay on the colour and to remove it, but avoid a dabbling or stippling motion.

Most building stones are plain, but others show the strata grain, which varies between a freehand straight line and a slight wave, with layer upon layer of slightly different tints running parallel to each other.

Often, in the plain stones, four different tints are found in one type, and this necessitates different mixings of colour. The only treatment required in the self-coloured blocks is neat cutting and light stippling.

The more complicated grain markings shown in my drawings are found only in a few stones, about one in ten, and are carried out with the tool and fantail as previously described. They should be set out (not too many of them) among the plainer ones.

In places a fitch on its side may be used with a scrubbing motion to strengthen a line. Much of the plainer stone background should show, with the grain markings light and wide apart.

I always leave the working of the stronger markings until the last, when all the tools are in good working order and the heavier colour can be well gauged. Restraint is very necessary in the use of curly grained stone.

Colour plays a most important part in the success of stone painting, and the painter who excels in the mixing of delicate tints will find great pleasure in this type of work.

On close examination it will be found that all forms of sandstone have an even distribution of small dots of grain, of brighter or darker tone.

Splashing on colour from a hog hair fitch may be resorted to, though it is a rather dirty process.

A spray gun can be brought into service by partially closing the air supply to the gun, to prevent good atomisation; the spatter produced will give just the size of markings required.

The spraying will soften the previous grain markings, but it should not be over-done.

In Distemper: The tools and colour are as for oil colour.

In the Dipper: Thin with equal parts of warm water and petrifying liquid in a small kettle.

Method: When working in distemper, body up in cream oil-bound water paint to a solid finish.

It should be thoroughly hardened by the use of sufficient petrifying liquid allowing, say, two days for the oxidation of the oil content.

Set out the stone blocks with a chalk line, avoiding pencil lines, as the mortar lines will probably be lined out in white.

Neatness in this type of work is of paramount importance, and a dark line is more difficult to cover in distemper.

Coat in a shape with the medium from the dipper, take the sponge, with a little colour from the palette board, and draw it lightly over the glaze.

Continue to use the sponge, without recharging it until the last of the stain is exhausted, leaving space for work with other colours. No other tool is required for the grain markings.

Working in distemper is more tricky than in oil colours, the vein markings in stone being on the soft side and, as we cannot soften the colours in the ordinary way, we must rely on the flow of the wet ground, which very soon sets.

The water paint reproduction of stone, with the joints drawn in white or pale grey, is very successful in Gothic churches of halls of Jacobean or Elizabethan character.

I have carried out many jobs of this kind with entire satisfaction.

I am, of course, writing of inside work only and not about painting old coarse sandstone surfaces.

A very fine effect can be obtained on a smooth plastered surface using a suitably prepared ground.

Afterwards the surface should have a coat of pale outside varnish.

Drawings:
The drawings of stone are from some of my early studies, taken from large facings of

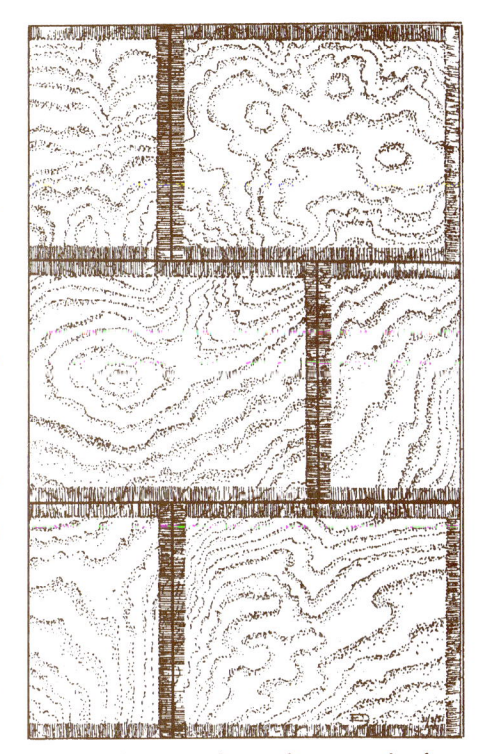

Drawings by Mr Dobson of stone grain, from blocks 3ft x 4ft

yellow sandstone, four feet by three.

The grain had been attacked by industrial grime on the softer parts, while the harder parts were still light, leaving the design quite clear after perhaps one hundred years of exposure.

The Graining of Walnut (1)

WALNUT is a wood of great beauty, from a tree that has been grown in Britain for centuries. It has fine foliage, handsome habit and delicious fruit.

I have been examining a tree this morning in the well-laid out grounds of Townley Hall, Lancashire.

This mansion, which was built almost a thousand years ago, now belongs to the Burnley Corporation, is used as a Museum and Art Gallery and its acres of forest and park land are open to the public.

My special interest this morning was a walnut tree that still produces fruit; it appears to have been planted when the grounds were remodelled about two hundred years ago.

I learnt from the park superintendant that its fruit-bearing qualities are irregular, but it commands great interest from the younger generation.

Walnut trees are not prolific in Britain; they are slow growing like other hard woods, perhaps preferring a warmer climate.

They thrive in a rich, deep soil.

From the time of Queen Elizabeth they have been planted in the parklands of the "Stately homes of England," more perhaps for the trim shape and beautiful foliage than for their fruit.

Walnut is native to Western Asia, including the Western Himalayas, Kashmir and Persia.

It has, however, been cultivated outside its natural habitat for many centuries, for its nuts, in addition to their food value, yield an oil which is much in demand.

With mahogany and oak, walnut has always been a keen favourite for pride of place in a good grainers' repertoire.

It is well worth the time necessary to master this beautiful rich wood.

The markings of the soft heartwood shapes should be used (as in nature) with restraint.

The colour is generally cool, often appearing to be coated with a thin glaze of black; the grain markings vary in colour in many types from a pale brown to black, with sprinklings of purple or Indian red.

The plainer types have single lines of stronger colour every two or three inches apart, whilst others have the lines almost touching each other, with others crossing over and under.

The striking beauty of the well marked, darker, complicated pieces is a joy to behold, it can be grained by a good craftsman to give a remarkable likeness.

There are great possibilities in quartering in these dark well marked faces, giving fine decorative shapes both with veneer and in painted examples.

The burr in walnut is a prominent feature; quite

American Walnut grained by Mr Dobson

large pieces are to be found in most British and Italian varieties.

Often the burr is in small pieces worked in with the heartwood markings, at others with the heavy winding grain; sometimes nothing but the knotty burr shows.

More skill is required in the reproduction of the burr than the heartwood markings; it is all individual handwork.

A good grainer aims at reproducing the glitter and sparkle of the glazing from the groups of knots in the burr.

Burrs only form on old trees, of course, and these and stumps, butts, and crotches which contain well figured wood are valuable.

Painters are never handicapped for want of good material in examples of walnut, for fine furniture and panelling have been made in this wood for a few generations.

I propose to deal from time to time with several varieties of walnut, commencing with American.

AMERICAN WALNUT

Description

American walnut is a dark coloured wood, varying from a grey-brown to a purple brown, which is often relieved by lighter streaks.

A marked texture of a darker colour is found in the background; this is almost as coarse as if the horse hair dust brush had been used for the flogging operation.

The markings of the heartwood show good clear drawing; they are wide apart, and many oval shapes are included.

The extreme ends are more rounded than pointed, the insides are sharp and clear, whilst the outsides are shaded away.

The colour of the veins is a warm chocolate brown.

There is very little mottling, and it should be on one side only; the general tone is deeper down the centre of the tree.

I have been asked many times to describe American walnut, and to explain why it should be different from any other type.

North America produces no less than six varieties of walnut.

Whilst I was writing these notes a master painter friend from Wembley called on me and discussed the lively Burnt Walnut of Canada, from which he had recently been working.

The grain of American walnut being open and easy to produce is suitable for early practice in walnut graining.

Nothing is startling; the wood is dark, and the flogging, graining and glazing are near in tone.

The butt of the short Lea Enfield I carried for years, was made from this hard wood.

Latin

Juglans Migra, which means Black Walnut.

Ground

A medium to dark, cool, buff colour, composed of umber, ochre, venetian red and a little white; for the darker variety omit the white. For the dark purple brown coloured wood add a little blue to the ground.

Brushes and tools required

Tools, overgrainer, pencil, fitches, flogger, clean rag and hog hair softener.

For glazing

Tools, sponge, mottlers, leather and badger hair softener.

Palette

Vandyke brown, black, burnt umber and burnt sienna ground in oil or turpentine.

For glazing

Vandyke brown in water.

Method

In a small kettle prepare a scumble composed of burnt umber and a touch of black, thinned with three parts of turpentine to one part of raw linseed oil, adding a small amount of clear glaze medium.

On the painted example that I illustrate, burnt umber only was used as a base for the scumble.

95

More depends on the ground colour than on the scumble for the final effect in graining; should a particular shade be required, it will readily be obtained from the given palette.

Coat the work in sparingly with the scumble, placing your heartwood markings in the centre or to one side.

Clean off a little of the colour down the sides of your panel with rag or with the brush sides, to leave your flanks lighter and drier.

With your overgrainer charged with a little umber or vandyke, or sienna in turns for variety draw in the heartwood shape.

This drawing is not to give a strong finished grain, but just to add a little colour and to form an idea about the size or general appearance.

At all times this variety of walnut is simple and open; care must be taken not to make the drawing too large for its position on the door or panel.

Those I illustrate are perhaps too full and ornate; that is only because I want to show as much as possible for the benefit of readers.

Drawings of American Walnut by Mr Dobson: Heartwood

Heartwood

He pauses, backwards steps his work to view
Is pleased with compostion, tone and hue
He closer draws, examines every part;
Is sure he had produced a work of art.
A youth just poised between the man and child
A shade of doubt fleets o'er his features mild
But 'ere a pensive hand had left his chin
He knows that he can call the critics in.
Hey Mum and Susan!
Can you come in now?
But doubt again must corrugate his brow,
And did aspiring R.A. ever wait
An academic judgement on his fate
So anxiously?
But doubt is soon awing
They've come and paeans of praise around him ring.
Much older now, a sea of paint has flown
From off his brush since then, and mother's gone;
Yet in their parlour keeping mem'ry green
A panelled door grained oak can be seen.
It's not as good, if he must tell the truth
As work more lately done.
But part of youth
Is there on paint, and who would have the heart
To paint out that which is of youth a part?

Alabaster: Marble Limestone

ALABASTER is a fine decorative limestone, too soft to claim the title of marble, though its colour and markings give it a splendid marble appearance. As a mineral it is very useful in the manufacture of plaster.

Its use in decoration dates back to biblical times, when it was used for rich, carved boxes and vases.

According to some authorities it takes its name from the town of Alabastron, in Egypt, where it was first found.

The slender-necked water vessels carried by Orientals on their shoulders and called alabastron may have given the material its name.

The alabaster of earlier times is thought to be the Onyx of the present day, often referred to as Oriental Alabaster.

The name, however, has passed from the original stalagmite carbonate of lime to the fine granular varieties of gypsum which are employed for decorative purposes.

It readily takes paint, and is often partly painted and gilded for decorative effect. Alabaster is suitable only for interior use, on account of its solubility in water.

The limestone, when first quarried, is soft and can be carved easily; it later hardens to take a high polish.

From the Mddle Ages up to the present time Alabaster has been popular in the interior decoration of churches, particularly for memorials, screens and balustrades.

In the fourteenth century a huge reredos, erected in St. George's Chapel, Windsor, was made from Alabaster quarried in Nottingham. A few days ago I was admiring some fine examples of this marble at Haworth, Yorkshire, in the church of St. Michael, where the Bronte family are buried.

The reredos in Ely Cathedral, designed by Sir Gilbert Scott, is of Alabaster. My drawing this month is from a vault in the chancel in Mitton Church, Lancashire, which is over three hundred years old; it is in a splendid state of preservation.

Bright colours were originally painted on it in places and, although the paint has almost worn away with centuries of cleaning, the colour of the alabaster remains bright.

My painted example is from a wall plaque in Bradford Cathedral.

Colour: The general colour of Alabaster consists of patches of a tint of burnt sienna with orange-red markings and grey patches with grey and, sometimes, red markings.

All examples are transparent. In some samples tints of orange, olive green and ochre are to be found. Some examples are covered with red, while others are almost grey. The red veins are less conspicuous, being near the ground in tone, while the grey veins are sometimes almost black.

Alabaster, Marble Limestone

Composition: The composition of Alabaster is a fine variety of hydrous sulphate of lime. The purest form is white and translucent, showing great depth of marking.

Some Alabaster is suitable only for the manufacture of gypsum; this type is found in great abundance in or near the red sandstone formations which come to the surface in many districts.

Origin: The finer varieties of Alabaster are to be found in South East Derbyshire, where the material is also known as Derbyshire Spar, but it has no connection with Fluor Spar, which is also found in the district.

This variety shows the reddish brown markings of the Kempar Marls, caused by oxide of iron and also shows green markings produced by sulphides of iron.

Westmorland and Cumberland deposits are only suitable for the manufacture of plaster of Paris.

Tools and sundries: The painted example is worked in water colour, the tools employed being leather, badger softener, and sable pencils.

Ground colour: Off white.

Palette: Blue black and burnt sienna ground in water.

Method: Rub in with a thin glaze of black, producing a pale grey on the light ground.

With a dabbing motion of the soft wet leather, take out part of the colour to represent the pearl grey broken ground.

With the side of your tool apply more grey colour, a little darker, in a gentle painting motion, without disturbing the delicate glaze underneath, again breaking the colour with the leather.

This second application will only be applied in limited areas with a marbling technique. With the burnt sienna, rub in a thin glaze of the orange-red tint.

Rinse out your leather or piece of rag, proceed to wipe out the red surface with a dabbing motion, and soften well.

In all these operations try to avoid working up the surface with heavy brushing.

Any edges of colour can be dealt with by the leather, and much of the colour thus picked up can be applied to other parts.

The areas of red and grey are usually separate, perfaps merged on the top edges, but not in the same tone all over.

With the sable pencil, charged with thin red or black, paint in the delicate veins; I often use oil colour for this operation.

Glazing: My example is not glazed. If, however, an accurate representation is required, glazing is necessary.

After binding with thinned varnish I should glaze in oil colour.

White, orange and raw sienna should be added to the palette, working on an oiled ground.

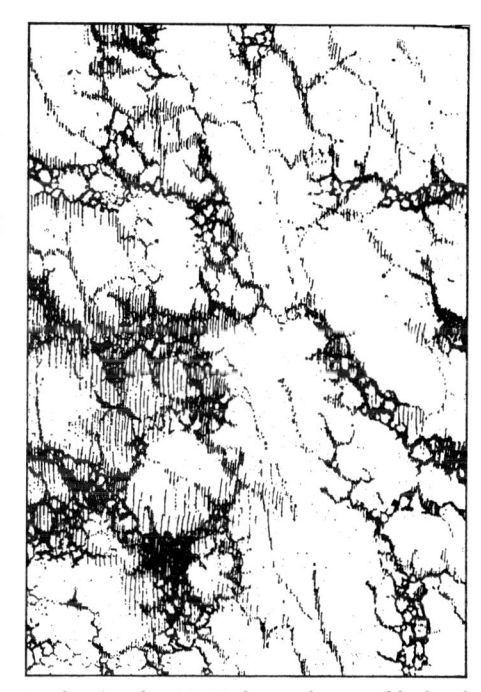

A drawing by Mr Dobson, from a block of Alabaster Marble found in a church in the Ribble Valley, Lancashire. Before carving, the size was 6ft x 4ft x 1ft 6in

The centres of the lights can be heightened, and the red strengthened or subdued.

In the two examples I have studied for this article the reds, over the years, have gone slightly deeper, while the greys and whites are more transparent.

The Graining of Walnut (2)

Golden Walnut
The name given to this medium toned wood, Golden Walnut, is a fair description of its general appearance. It is a humble type of wood, very suitable for a background.

The ribbon grain shows light and dark zones, divided from the sapwood by a narrow transitional part. This is most pleasing, and gives opportunities to the grainer to show his skill.

The grain markings of the heartwood are very handsome and attractive. The ripple marks (mottle to painters) are thin and pale in colour and wide apart. Where they are found a little heavier, the mottle is cut about every half inch.

In the large number of panels that I have examined recently, none of the grain markings was strong or the mottling very pronounced.

Golden Walnut is known by many names, often taken from the country where it has been grown. A good tree grows to a height of 75 feet or more, with a diameter of five feet. This fine wood has been used extensively for furniture and panelling.

The colour is several tones lighter than that of American Walnut – light nut brown instead of deep chocolate.

The grain is finer, the veins being much closer together, and of a tone very little deeper than the ground. The texture of the background is well defined, but much finer than in American Walnut.

There are many plain areas relieved by just a few grained shapes, which make demands on skill, for they must have clean edges, and the cutting in of the mitres must be accurate to prevent little waves from the stile running over the mould or down the door edge.

The drawings
In Fig.1 I show many heartwood shapes. The cut was taken near the centre of the tree, which was bent, and probably had a number of branches growing out near this point. Well marked pieces of this quality are rare, but they give much scope in graining.

The centre panel is typical of many The centre panel is typical of many examples of which I have made sketches. The long, unusual centre is very pleasing and the tricky typical Walnut markings near the bottom are worthy of note.

In the third panel, the plainer part at the top contrasts with the heavier and wider knot from the middle downwards. The lower half is unusual; it is rare for a heartwood shape to widen to this extent without lengthening. This drawing, taken from one of my sketch books, was, I remember, from an outstanding piece of Walnut with fine mottling covering the lower portion.

In some districts we find this close mottled work grained all over a door as a decorative effect. My father was a past master at this type of work, carried out with a feather.

Golden Walnut

Latin Name: Lovoa kiaineana. (French, Noyer d'or).

Ground Colour: A medium buff, composed of yellow ochre, a touch of umber and a little white, mixed to dry hard.

Brushes and Tools: Tools, fantail grainer, fitches, hog hair softener and flogger. For glazing; tools. mottlers. leather and badger softener.

Palette: Raw sienna, burnt sienna, burnt Turkey umber, and black.

For Glazing
Raw sienna and vandyke in water.

Method of Graining
Prepare the glip from raw sienna, umber and a touch of black, using a medium of one part linseed oil and two parts turpentine, with a few drops of terebine driers and a knife point of glaze medium. Prepare on the thin side, and apply liberally at just running consistency.

With a worn fitch, commence to draw the wood design of the more prominent lines with the colour on the dry side. With the fantail, charged with the same colour, fill in between the darker drawing, and the markings should hold quite well on the wet ground.

Continue thus until all the shapes are filled in and a good representation has been obtained. In places add a little burnt sienna to the umber, in others use thin black only, leaving the yellow-brown veins the most prominent.

Now the side portion may be dealt with. Wipe out lightly in parts with the rag, or scrub off with the brush side. Shades of umber or black may be added in places. The fantail. lightly charged with colour, may be run down in places, and a narrow fitch line used to divide the tones of brown.

The fitch may be used to lift out some of the colour between the veins, while, in other places, a little colour may be added. It is fatal to attempt to remove any colour with the rag at this stage.

When the graining is satisfactorily completed, soften with the hog hair. lightly down the centre, but firmly down the sides. Now apply the flogger lightly in places, following the grain or wave of the wood carefully. The flogging softens a grained panel and, therefore, cannot be carried too far.

Glazing
Rub in a thin glaze of Vandyke and sienna, and pass the mottler over to give a wide undulating effect over three parts of the panel. Soften across the grain and inwards in the case of the knot centres. The star shaped centres can be cut out with the leather.

Drawings of Golden Walnut by Mr Dobson: the size of each panel 6ft x 18in

A Grainer of 1851

CRAFTSMEN of the stature and ability of James Bradley, who was a master painter and decorator at Exeter during the middle of the last century, were rare even in that age of fine craftsmanship.

His descendents, the Bradley-Rowes, have carried on the tradition of fine, public spirited citizenship to this day.

His work, which was awarded the highest award at the Great Exhibition of 1851, may be seen in the Royal Albert Museum at Exeter.

A small, neatly framed tablet over the work reads: "Examples of woods, and Devonshire Marbles, executed by J. Bradley, Esq., of Exeter, that won the Gold Medal at the Great Exhibition of 1851, Also another award at the Devonshire County Exhibition of 1892".

These amazing panels were painted by a veritable genius, and even after one hundred years, such is the standard of the preparation, the grounds, and the finish that they are still faultless.

You can count on the fingers of one hand the men of to-day who could approach the quality of this work.

At the hotel where I stayed before reaching Exeter, I learned that it was "Lammas Fair," and a public holiday – a great week in the city.

One symbol of this event was a great arm protruding from over the balcony of the third floor of the historic Guildhall, in the busy London to Lands End road. It indicated, I suppose, a friendly welcome to all.

I felt too, that the arm symbolised the help of all who assisted me to bring this work before my fellow craftsmen.

The Bradley collection consists of ten panels, worked on slabs of slate 60in. by 24in., and about one inch in thickness.

This non-absorbent ground has contributed much in their preservation, for the binder has remained in the film, not being drawn away into porous wood.

The panels cover the whole of one side of a ground floor room, which houses also smiths' work, also stained glass, old plaster work, and stone and wood carving.

These collections are still being enlarged by Dr. Blackie, the enthusiastic Director, and the Governing Board.

A panel of Root Oak firsty caught my eye – and held it. Next came a numberof coloured marbles, striking in their beauty.

To view this great work for the first time was, to me, a breathtaking experience. The examples are so beautiful that one is entirely carried away.

The specimens were well chosen, both for their design and colour, which does not appear to have faded. Even more remarkable, the paint and varnish films have remained stable.

The panels were, I believe, hand polished with an abrasive, for they are now semi-flat.

With the slight shrinking or settling down of the film, all the methods of working and brush strokes can be detected.

The masterly use of the fitch and pencil; the strong colour running out to a thin edge; glazes delicately used; the gentle use of the hog hair and badger softeners – all are eloquent of high skill and vast experience.

Any work to be given a National Gold Medal must be of exceptionally high standard, but to win the 1851 Exhibition award, given when craftsmanship was at its best, is unique.

There is no doubt that Bradley was one of the finest European grainers and marblers of the past 150 years, and the re-discovery of these panels in Festival year, 1951, is highly opportune.

The four grained wood panels are nearest

the entrance, and so are the first to be noticed, though they are quieter than the bright coloured marbles.

With the lessened demand for marbling, we have fewer men who can even approach work of this standard.

The work was carried out in transparent colour, mostly on white or light grey grounds, the black and dark grey being put in last with a fitch.

They are not the varieties in use to-day, but are of local origin; Sienna, Breche Violette and Carrara are missing.

But they show the careful use of harmonious and complementary colour.

They mostly contain red veining on grey grounds, indicating that they have been thrown up by volcanic action from deep strata near the granite bed.

No.1 contains a large amount of pale, yellow tinted limestone amongst the grey black granite.

The lighter part has been opened out with turpentine, which can be seen in the photograph; the vigorous lines of the fitch work is to be noted.

No.2 is of the St.Ann's type, and shows a great amount of patience in the faithful reproduction of the fine network of veins, which are carried out in bright orange red on a very stony grey ground.

No.3 shows the stalactite formation that we find in so many marbles.

Bright reds are again used in a masterly manner; they are concentrated to good advantage on one half of the panel.

No.4 contains much limestone formation, which has been carried out in glazes on the red ground; here again a small amount of grey is to be found.

The colours are still bright, and a credit to the colour maker of 100 years ago, as well as to the clever hands that blended them into the Medal Winning Panels of 1851.

(to be continued)

Sections of marbled panels by the late James Bradley, from the Royal Albert Memorial Museum, Exeter

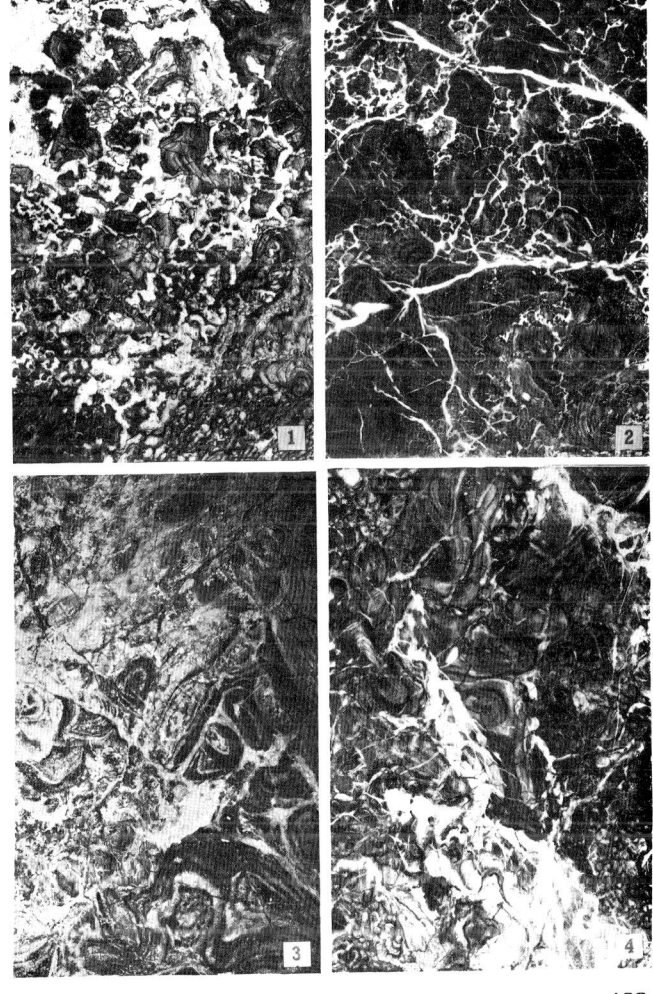

A Grainer of 1851 (continued)

THIS month I have more to say about the work of the late James Bradley, of Exeter, awarded a Gold Medal for the best examples of graining at the Great Exhibition of 1851. Four large panels, painted and grained on thin slabs of slate, are fixed in heavy wooden frames, and displayed in a vertical, position next to the marbled panels described last month.

The Royal Albert Memorial Museum and the College of Arts at Exeter are accommodated in one building, which gives students a fine opportunity to study this and other rare work.

The building, erected in the early part of the last century, is of local stone containing much veining.

Though the stone is roughly hewn, the veining looks almost like marble.

Carving on the bosses, capitals and string coarses is the work of Henry Hems, the famous Devonshire designer and carver.

This was his first commission when he settled in Exeter.

A collection of his work, recently purchased for the Nation by the Victoria and Albert Museum, was presented to the city for safe keeping.

It rests near to Bradley's work, and is considered so valuable that the public are only admitted by special permission, but no interested person is refused.

Root Oak

The panel, about half of which is illustrated here, is a masterly piece of work, the best I have ever seen and possibly the finest in existence.

The knots, figure and heartwood markings over the whole panel are well displayed, though the illustration shows the portion most heavily knotted, the plainer parts being omitted.

The buff ground was of a medium to light colour; the graining was carried out in a straightforward manner in oil colour, glazed in water colour, varnished, cut down and hand polished.

The graining of the knots is the main feature of the panel. They are on the strong side as compared with the remainder, but they are well shaped and show good drawing.

Most of them have been put in with a sponge, cleaned out in the centre with a splash of turpentine and then strengthened on the outside with a writing pencil. The colour was probably terre-de-cassel, or Vandyke brown.

The small pointed shape given to the knots on the outside is most interesting, being different from the rounder ones of burr walnut.

The glazing of the knots is very well carried

A section of a grained panel of Burr Walnut by the late James Bradley

out; the cutting with the mottler is still quite clearly visible and not over-done.

Sweeping and intertwining heartwood markings have been grained with both fitch and crayon.

The last touch of the grainers' art is to be found in the reproduction of the crack in the wood which is clearly painted towards the bottom left hand corner of the part illustrated.

The small amount of figure on the left is interesting, working in with the knots, following the grain, changing direction several times, and showing much variety in a small compass.

Burr Walnut

The panel of Burr Walnut reproduced is taken from near the bottom of a large tree.

The colour is a cool, black-brown, worked on a ground of medium yellow buff which sparkles through in many parts of the graining.

A textured ground appears to have been prepared in water colour, using the sponge to work in delicate markings, and fastened with a coat of varnish.

The graining was then carried out in oil colour in thin black from a palette board, using plenty of turpentine on the pencil overgrainer or thin flat fitch divided with a coarse comb.

The wavy lines were first started with fine, light, thin colour and continued stronger and stronger. The darker markings were worked in with a sable pencil.

The knots and heartwood markings are fairly evenly distributed, and the knots have been simply ringed round with the darker colour.

The glazing was carried out in water colour, using a mottler and badger.

To show up the grain markings to the best advantage, a colour filter was used by the photographers, but it has, perhaps, done its work too well by detaching the grain too much, and thus making the ground appear too light.

This panel, the darkest in the collection, is still well preserved without blemish or scratch, and might well have been grained only some five years ago.

(to be continued)

A section of a grained panel of root oak by the late James Bradley, from the Royal Albert Memorial Museum, Exeter

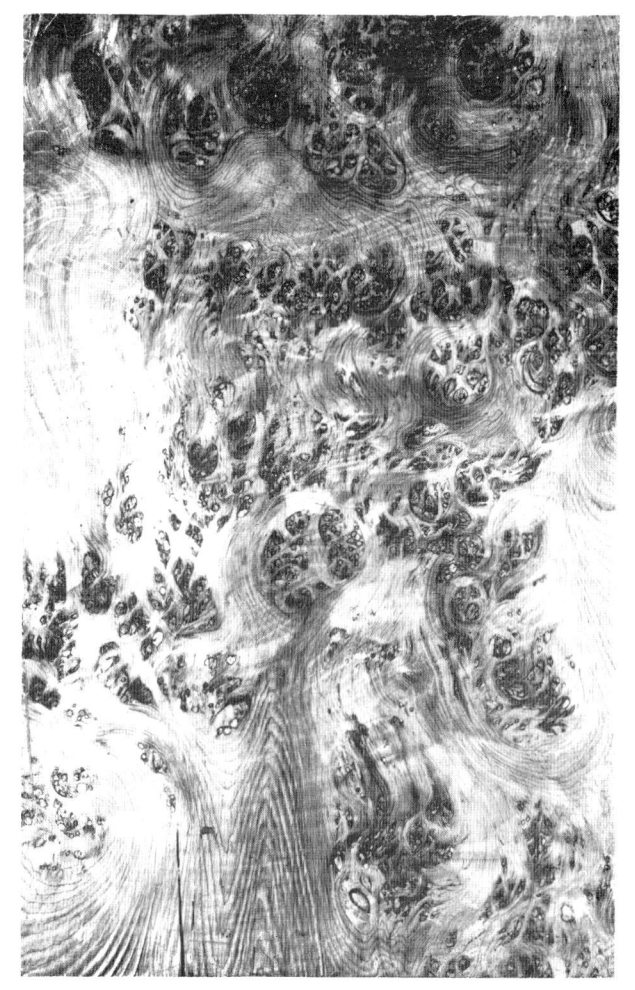

A Grainer of 1851: (continued)

THE graining of Mahogany in 1851 was no half-hearted affair, the large feather standing erect over four feet in height is the largest that I have seen.

In nature they occur even larger, but it is rare to find one much over three feet in height.

The size might give one the impression that this panel was grained in a loose, free manner, but that is not so.

The feather of mahogany was another decorative wood with which James Bradley was well acquainted; the panel illustrated would be one of his best, though less than half of it is seen in the photograph.

The colour is that of a new cut mahogany – just a simple cool toned burnt sienna, with a little crimson.

The panel does not appear to have developed or faded in colour; it was grained in transparent glazes which show all the stages of working.

Although great care was taken in the graining and overgraining, a few lines crossing over each other can be detected in the photograph.

The drawing is excellent, the radiating lines flowing smoothly from the centre of the feather, whilst the shape of the darker portion starts wide at the base, and narrows towards the top in a gentle sweeping curve.

Quiet wavy lines of grain can be seen on the right hand side of the feather.

The dark centre is on the hard side, even by to-day's standards, though this is useful for the purpose of reproduction.

The Ground: The ground colour is of a light warm buff; a light tone would be necessary on account of the three graining processes used, which soon tend to make the work dark on a medium or heavy ground.

Method of Graining: A thin glaze of Vandyke brown was first flogged on the clean ground; this process would be continued until the grain markings were fine and almost dry.

The second process was to rub in very gently, in oil colour, a glaze of burnt sienna with a touch of black. With a very sharp, round ended graining horn, the narrow lines of the shape of the feather, and the clever heartwood markings were next wiped out.

In the painted example I have prepared to show the method of working; the narrow lines are represented as they would appear behind the feather; in the heartwood the edges on one side would be shaded away with hard scrubby fitch.

In the finished work these lines are almost lost, but they would act as a guide for the later stages of the feather. In most of the panels Bradley kept well to the guide lines but, on the left, we find that he has gone astray with his side grain on the bottom half of the feather.

I am impressed with the good, careful workmanship that was put into these preparatory stages of the graining. The fine lines were all put in singly, and can be seen to good effect on the large panel.

A section of a grained panel of feathered mahogany by the late James Bradley, from the Royal Albert Museum, Exeter

Heartwood Drawing: In the heartwood these narrow lines are particularly pleasing; the variety used in the distances, the good shape at the ends of the markings and the gradual change of direction, all contribute to the success of the finished work.

The good, accurate drawing of the shape itself gives the heartwood a most natural appearance.

Using probably the same colour and a fitch, the drawing of the lines was strengthened on the inside with a narrow band of darker colour; it was carried out whilst the ground glaze was still wet.

The work was now softened, in places gently, in others more vigorously, almost submerging the lines into the ground.

Graining the Feather: This process was carried out in water colour, using vandyke brown and black. A moderate amount of colour was applied down the centre of the feather, whilst a thinner glaze was used for the sides.

The cutting out of the colour was carried out with the mottler and softened with the badger hair softener.

This cutting is very clean, and the contrast, which was toned down later, was very marked at this stage of the work.

Most of the colour on the sides would be wiped off at this stage; a few patches of wavy, slightly darker colour would be allowed to remain, however. The badger was now drawn down the sides, and it would be at this time when he went over the guide lines. The graining was next fastened with thin varnish.

Overgraining: This process was probably carried out in oil colour; the surface was softened with an oily rag; and the overgrainer charged with thin colour drawn gently over.

These lines are still to be seen over the centre of the feather, in a few wavy dark lines. Evidence of the overgrain is found in a few places on the heartwood shape.

Glazing: This was carried out in water colour, very softly, with vandyke and a little crimson.

The efficient use of glazing was a strong point of all Mr. Bradley's work; his mottle marks are very dainty, never in long straight lines, but passing from one dark edge to another. These mottle markings being so delicate, little or no softening took place on the side grain or the heartwood.

Down the centre of the feather the glaze of colour was fairly heavy; a short bristled, long handled cutter would be used.

This brush was very clean in its work, and would quickly sharpen up the close radiating lines down the centre of the feather.

One can notice that the work of this brush is particularly good down the right hand side of the panel, which shows the Mr. Bradley was not left handed. There is evidence that a

Mr Dobson's illustrations above are designed to demonstrate the procedure followed by the late James Bradley

sable was used to bring the sharp lines of the feather further into relief.

Though the time taken in all these processes would be rather long, the final result made it worth while.

In my two painted examples the five processes are shown in their correct order, and should be of value for any one attempting really ambitious reproductions of Mahogany.

The final article on the Exeter work will be on Australian Oak.

A Grainer of 1851: (continued)

THE most popular form of graining today is figured oak, but it was not so popular in 1851. The panel of Austrian Oak, grained by James Bradley and exhibited at Exeter, is a fine piece of craftsmanship, which time has mellowed but has not impaired.

The types of graining previously described were more popular one hundred years ago. Graining was a comparatively new craft process in those days, and few men were conversant with it.

It was originally used to adorn poorly marked wood with a representation of a more decorative, scarce and often costly cabinet hardwood, and the more ostentatious types were apparently in greater demand in the West Country.

The panel of light yellow Austrian Oak appeared to have been well used and exposed to strong sunlight at some time or other.

Originally of a pale delicate colour, the figured portion of the oak had merged into the combed ground and, as it would be difficult to photograph clearly, I decided to make a drawing on the spot, and carry out the graining myself, as faithfully as possible to the original. Mr. Dixon of the College Staff assisted in this task.

For some reason that I cannot understand the panel had a title painted in black block letters, which were far from delicate. They show up conspicuously on the light ground, and are of a type often seen on the sides of railway waggons, and in common use 100 years ago. It may be that Mr. Bradley, being a very honest man, did not want to claim this wood as a Devonshire variety, as all the other panels were without painted titles of any kind.

This panel of oak had another distinction. It was divided into two parts; there was a joining down one side, showing that he considered twenty-four inches too wide for a good piece of figure.

The important board was eighteen inches wide, and the narrow one six inches. It may have been so divided for effect, or it may have been to show his skill in working a long clean joint; this he certainly accomplished. The two boards were probably worked separately.

To help with the display, the narrow board was combed at an angle all the way down, and marked with fine, small figure.

Graining

The method of working was straightforward, the colour cool, and not obtained with sienna but by a thin scrumble of Italian ochre, killed with a touch of black, well brushed out on the light cream yellow ground. This was combed about four times with a fine comb, twice straight, and twice wavy, to make small heartwood shapes.

The wiping out of the figure was done with rag and probably, the thumb nail, the weight and width being quite small for such a large area. The painted example includes all the figure found in

A painted example of Austrian Oak by Mr Dobson, copied from a panel by James Bradley

the large division of the panel so the figuring is quite open in the original five feet high panel.

A little softening was carried out between the figures, with a rag folded into a pad, which removed some of the combing and left the space lighter. There is a great difference in type of figure on the two boards, the whole of the graining being confined to figuring only. The figure was underlined with a sable pencil, using the same colour of gilp, but this is now hardly discernible. The hog hair softener was used to soften the sharp edges of the figure, and the hard lines of the combing.

This panel was well ahead of most examples of its day, and was indeed a remarkable piece of work. It cannot be claimed that any progress has been made in the graining of woods previously mentioned in this series, but there has been an advance in the graining of figured oak. The quartering or scientific cutting of the oak tree had not been practised in 1851, and few large examples would be available; any old prints of the grain would be very crude.

Glazing

In the Bradley panel there are traces of glazing in water colour, a thin wash of Vandyke brown having been used and drawn through lightly with the badger, leaving the fine lines of grain showing over the top of the figure.

With the finding of Mr. Bradley's prize collection I have, to a certain extent, solved a minor mystery of the 1851 Exhibition.

Thomas Kershaw, the reowned Lancashire grainer of that day, did not compete for the medal owing to a difference with the master painters who were running the competition.

He did, however, exhibit in the Geological section, and was therefore not in competition with James Bradley. His work, however, was much admired by those who saw it

Up to the time of his arrival in London as a journeyman, Mr. Kershaw was a grainer; afterwards, he turned to decoration and marbling, in both of which he was great success. I cannot imagine what the result would have been if Kershaw had been able to fulfil the conditions of the competition and the two great craftsmen had been in competition with each other. As it was James Bradley was the winner of the Gold Medal of 1851, and certainly he was one of the finest exponents of the craft in the British Isles.

• **Mr Dobson thought he had solved the mystery of the Kershaw and Bradley prizes. However, the Council Medal was the top award in every section of the ehibition and only one was awarded to each section. The prize medal was awarded for good work and in graining and marbling three were awarded: to Kershaw, Moxon and Holland.**

Bradley? James Bradley had a shop in Fore Street, Exeter and did a John Bradley.

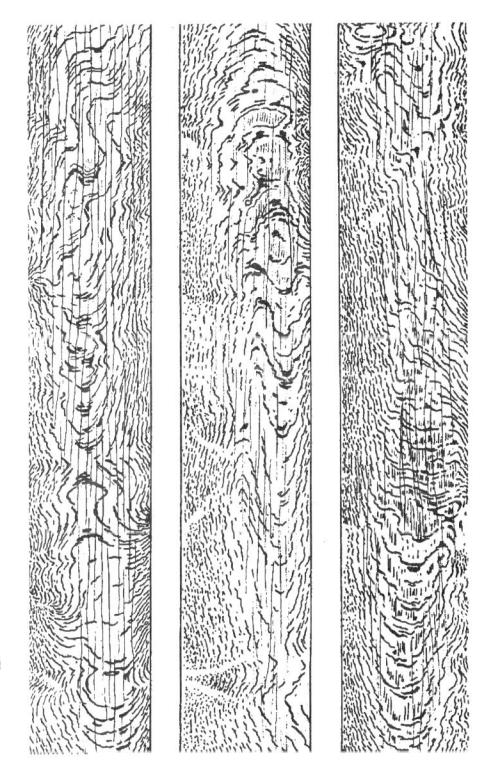

Mr Dobson's drawings of Austrian Figured Oak

The reason no Council Medal was given was that Prince Albert who supervised the exhibition said the medal was only to be awarded to new innovations and given that graining and marbling was not new no medal was awarded. Perhaps some reader can solve the mystery?

Oak Graining: The Heavy Figure

FROM my early student days I have made a habit of sketching the figure of oak with separate small drawings of interesting side figure, handsome or peculiarly shaped larger figure and also complete, well designed panels.

The many drawings that I have collected are all different.

This month I am dealing with the coloured growths that are found on oak trees at this time of the year, and I include some drawings of the larger figure.

A well known writer and craftsman recently told me that he had enjoyed my articles on oak, but that I had finished them too early.

I assured him that I had not yet finished with oak but that there were other interesting subjects I wanted to deal with, and many requests, for others which I could not delay too long. Similarly, I still have more to say about mahogany and walnut.

Figure in oak is produced in many ways, such as wiping out with clean rag, washing out with turpentine, pushing to one side with a rubber, drawing in with crayon and painting in with writing pencil. All have value in differing circumstances.

Figuring has, however, a habit of developing a sameness unless we constantly try to vary it.

When producing figure at speed there is a tendency to grain in a straight or only slightly curved line.

Using a few newer shapes for the larger figure can effect a great improvement, and while it calls for a little more study, should not take much more time.

Often variety can be obtained in graining the large figure by a few slight movements of the wrist.

I prefer to grain the most prominent figure first, but sometimes I return to it when the rest of the graining is completed, making slight enlargements or additions.

My drawings are all taken from the true British oaks, Pendunculate and Dermast.

It would be possible to get larger and a squarer figure if I were to adopt another type, but those I have noted are the more decorative, more suitable for painters' work.

Large figure should never be used alone, but with a fair amount of plainer straight figure, one or two areas of heavy figure on one panel are ample.

The scale, size and weight should be the same on all the heavy figure, or the general effect on completion will be too wild. Small and medium figure may be varied.

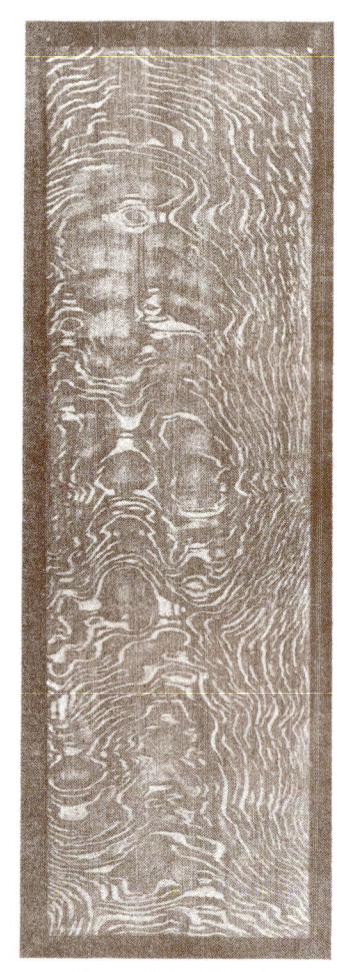

Figure of English Oak

I try to produce a few useful motifs that can be used as central panel figures.

Oak Apples

Last summer, while collecting the foliage of various species of oak trees at Broad Clyst, a Devon village, to compare them with the species found in Lancashire, I was attracted by a number of coloured, growing attachments.

The leaves of the oak were well advanced, having changed their colour from a red-yellow to a summer green; the bright yellow male flowers had shrivelled, and the pollen had dispersed.

In Devon I found that the flowers had changed to a cluster of red berries, due to the work of the gall-wasps which were very numerous and of many differing species; they lay their eggs on the leaves, twigs or flowers.

The spongy, leathery little balls that grow on the twigs are now about half size, and will change to yellow and then red as the autumn advances.

They remain on the tree until the spring, when a clean hole can be seen that has been cut by the wasp while escaping to freedom.

Each wasp appears to have a special kind of irritant with which it covers its eggs; this compels the oak cells to provide the kind of nursery she requires.

The gall-wasps are tiny black creatures with no bright yellow stripes like the ones that I used to fear as a boy.

It is a most amazing thing that gall-wasps have alternate generations.

Coming out of the oakapple the wasp has wings, and flying to the tree, it forms a gall on to its root.

From the root gall a crawling, ant-like wasp appears without wings. it is this creature which lays its eggs on the upper twigs of the tree to start the cycle all over again.

Each wasp is thus different from its parent but like its grandparent.

The wasp which emerges from the gall of the yellow flowers evenually forms the spangle gall on the leaves, while the pale green blister gall is formed by the insect from the silk button gall.

The bright cherry-red gall we see is paired with the violet egg, and vice-versa, and the hairy catkin with the artichoke gall. These and many other interesting botanical features are prolific on our oaks in summer.

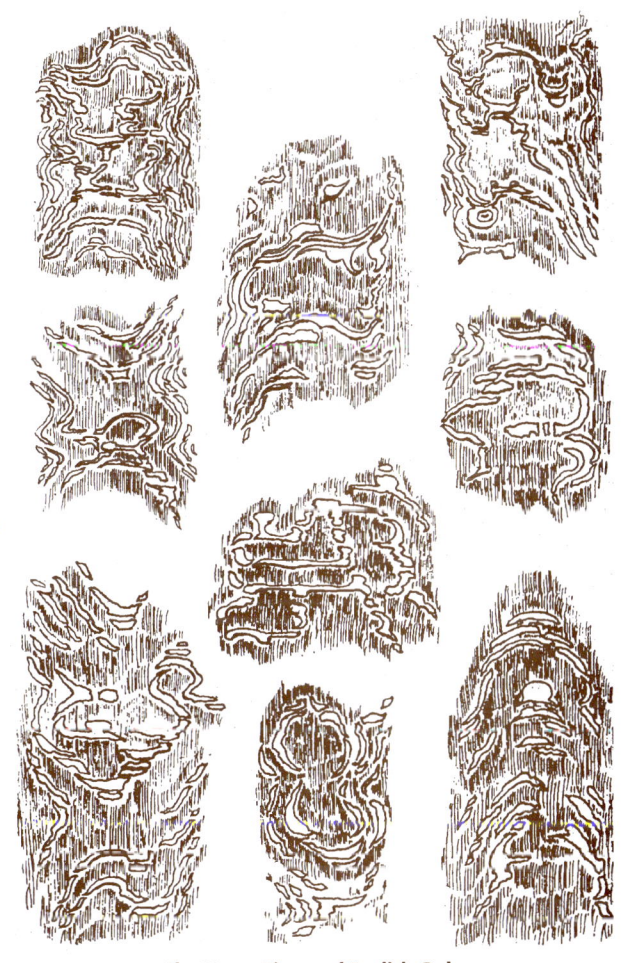

The Heavy Figure of English Oak

The Graining of Walnut

No. 3: Walnut Burr

THERE is often misunderstanding about what constitutes the Burr of Walnut. Burr is the knotted, knarled portion found near the root or the bole of the tree, with nothing else included. This knotted portion is often found at a depth of only a few inches from the outside of the trunk, but sometimes it goes very deep, even through the bole.

Large pieces are rare and, therefore, the wood is always cut to the best advantage. There are, however, many examples which contain flowery heartwood markings.

My drawings give three examples which show the development of the growth found higher up the tree. The top panel, with the smallest amount of burr, would be cut from the portion between six and ten feet from the ground.

My drawings could be described as Walnut with 80% of Burr. This grouping of both heartwood and burr in one panel can look very handsome as each gains from the contrast.

Many of the unusual shapes we see in fine cabinet wood are obtained by cutting the wood by a rotary cutter. The effect is often enhanced by reversing or quartering the veneer.

Larger pieces can be obtained by a rotary cutter if the Burr extends all round the tree at a depth of only a few inches. The Burr markings are not distorted in the cutting as are heartwood markings, because the many small knots are globular.

Frequently the centre of a piece of walnut heartwood is very violent in its markings. Where lines of veining cross over each other in a startling manner small circular openings of light background are exposed among the dark lines of the grain. This can easily be mistaken for walnut burr.

Having established that Burr Walnut consists of knots only and no veining whatever, let us note that some of the knots are grouped most effectively, while others are widely dispersed.

In all cases there is mottling amongst the knots and on the almost clear background.

In the days when light walnut piano cases were popular they were often made of most beautiful Burr, which, when fashion favoured darker woods, was almost obliterated by glazing.

Colour: Burr Walnut varies from light yellow brown, through green to purple brown. The knots are always darker than the background, but there should not be too much tone contrast or they will seem to jump off the ground. As opposed to Pollard Oak, the knots contain very little red but lean more towards cool vandyke or shades of grey.

Origin: Africa is the main source of supply; boles often weigh up to twenty tons. Burr is not found of adequate size in English Walnut and the Burr of American walnut is, of a very unusual shape. The Italian variety, however, provides some very beautifully marked examples.

Burr Walnut

Ground Colour: This should be of a cool buff, similar to the ground for Walnut graining; it is prepared from ochre, umber, white, and a touch of black, in diminishing amounts. Use two parts of turpentine to one part of oil and a little mixing varnish or gold-size for hardening.

Tools and Sundries: Fitches, sash tools, hog hair softener, sponges, and a piece of grease proof paper. For glazing in water colour; sash tools, leather, sponge, cutter, mottlers and badger hair softener.

Palette: Black, burnt sienna, and vandyke brown or burnt umber, ground in oil. The black may be ground in turpentine, as good oil black is not readily obtainable except in tubes and there is also the drying difficulty. The same applies to varldyke brown. For glazing the same three colours ground in water are required.

In the Dippers: Two dippers are required, one containing an oily mixture of two parts of turpentine to one of oil, and another containing turpentine only. Both should have a few drops of terebine driers added.

Method: Rub in sparingly an oily glaze of vandyke or umber. With a sash tool, rub in thin glazes of burnt sienna or, in some places, black.

The brush should be twisted or dabbed and, in some parts, a scraping motion may be employed to remove part of the colour. In fact, an uneven distribution of the coloured scrumble should be aimed at from the first.

Crush the grease proof paper into a ball and proceed to break up the colour still further in the areas where the lightest toned knots are to be placed. Soften lightly and, with the sponge, stiff colour may now be added from the palette. Spread the colour out to its fullest extent, using very little black.

As the number of knots is increased the tone value of the ground must be retained by keeping the light areas plain and adding mostly to the dark ones.

Skill is required at this stage in making some of the knots slightly larger, either in groups or singly, and in using the sponge more lightly in places. Variety must be the aim. If the work is laboured too much there is a tendency for the shapes and colour to appear too flat.

With a fitch a few drops of turpentine may be added to the sponge, which should not be soaked by dipping into a vessel. The effect to be aimed at is a transparent, bright piece of work.

Take a dry fitch and open out some of the centres of the knots; if the colour is stubborn, a spot of turpentine may be used. With another fitch a small amount of colour may be added to some of the Burrs.

Restraint, however, must be exercised in making heavy rings, or a very mechanical effect will result as compared with the small broken marks left by the sponge. If the work is getting too dark, the rag may be used in a dabbing motion, or even rolled in places.

The paper may again be used on the lighter parts, where it is not desirable to add further colour. Soften well in places, and lightly in others where the knots are the thickest and darkest; otherwise a smudgy effect will result.

With a worn mottler, take out a few cuts across the work in places, but do not over-emphasise the mottling at this stage. Later, more mottling can be carried out in water colour.

Drawings of Burr and Figured African Walnut

Glazing: This can be carried out in vandyke, in black or burnt sienna, which should not, however, be intermixed.

The groups of Burrs should be slightly shaded with the leather, and the cutting left to the odd markings that stand alone. Finally, soften lightly.

Skyros Marble

SKYROS, a beautiful coloured marble from the Aegean Sea is of the Breccia type. It is cream with red veins. It contains quite good sized oval shapes, often connected by fine veins.

The darker and broader breccia markings are grouped well together and richly coloured. Shades of reds and purples are much in evidence, while black is found in some examples.

The markings are round rather than angular, and include shapes almost like wood grain.

The background colours of the marble are a cream-yellow with a fair amount of pink, well softened into it in patches, with smaller amounts of grey and stronger yellow.

Up to eight varieties of slightly differing weight of colour are used in England to adorn banks and other fine buildings.

Cararra type veins are to be found in yellow and orange tints breaking up the larger stones. Some large stones are found with an ultramarine tinted background. In many robust examples quite a lot of the cream background is covered with red, broad markings.

The painting of the veins should be kept as transparent as possible, but the shaded back ground should be quite solid.

Where pink and yellow are used the work should be very soft, while in the case of the reds little or no softening is required.

Another handsome member of the Skyros family is Skyros Alpha, which has a white ground.

Origin
A rocky island in the Aegean Sea a hundred miles north of Athens. It is about thirty miles long.

Ground Colour
Broken white to cream according to the variety.

Tools
Fitches, tools, hog and sable pencils, sponge and softener.

Palette
White, chrome yellow, yellow lake, vermilion, Indian red, crimson lake, light red, black and ultramarine blue.

In the Dipper
One part oil and three parts turps.

Method
Rub in a thin glaze of cream, made up of white, chrome and ochre and leaving patches of the yellow. Soften well with the hog hair.

With the hog hair pencil commence to draw in the large shapes, allowing for the open spaces and the areas to be tightly packed with breecia markings.

Take the sponge, charged with a grey inclined towards blue, and stipple on in places, particularly where there is to be heavy work.

Continue to apply both gold colour (ochre and

Skyros Marble

chrome) and rose colour (vermilion and lake) in the same manner. The whole should be softened lightly, forming a bright, broken coloured background for the fitch-work.

Two fitches can now be used to put in the stronger veins.

A mixture of grey red on the palette, composed of light red, vermilion, black, white, and a touch of crimson lake, will provide a useful general colour.

Most of the veining can be carried out with this, the brushes being charged with other colours from the palette in turn to give a little variety.

It is best to darken the colours progressively, using the purer colours on the smaller areas. Very little of the Indian red should be used, while a little added blue will give the brown markings required.

Continue to soften at intervals, stopping before the work gets dirty through mixing colours together.

Thin yellow lake and chrome should be used cautiously at this stage to complete the veining.

Now proceed to fill in with dull deep red, grey-yellow and dull pink, some of the stones amongst the smaller breccia.

All must be slightly darker than the ground colour, though not as heavy in tone as the vein markings.

Now with a clean fitch, break up the interior of the larger stones with thin crack-like markings in yellow-red and warm grey, slightly darker in tone as required. These lines should be vigorously softened.

Finish at this stage if the work is to be glazed.

If, however, a first-class job is not required, proceed to clean up some of the small stones with a rag, and with a fine fitch or pencil put in some fine lines of grey to black over the heavier breccia markings.

The use of bright colours in marbling is difficult, and demands much study and practice if the result is not to be disappointing.

Glazing

This is carried out with the same tools and palette. Rub over with the oil medium from the dipper. The preliminary work can thus be brightened up considerably, or subdued in places as desired.

Charge the sponge with thin white, stipple over the lighter parts, but, on the darker parts, use the sponge sparingly. Continue next with a tone of light grey in places and then soften gently.

With a fitch intensify the red in some places and the crimson in others. Keep the fitch on the dry side or the colour will soon spread. When you are satisfied with the sharpness of the dark colours, soften lightly.

Proceed to fill in the centres of the lighter stones with white to pale chrome, shaded in

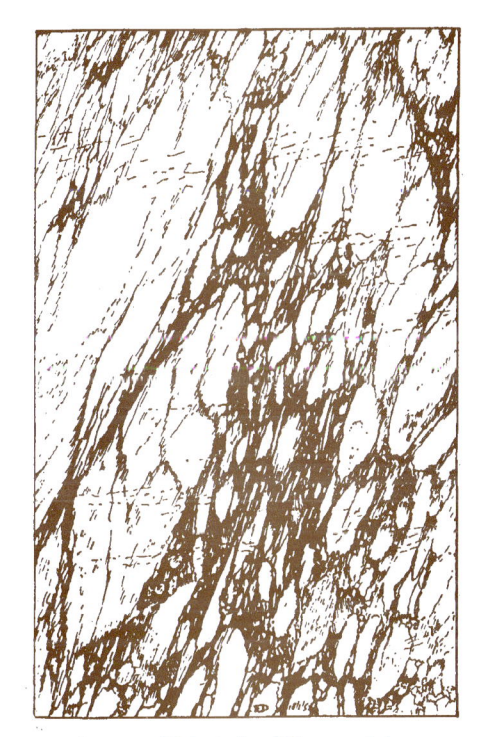

A pen and ink study of Skyros veining

places with a touch of vermilion or pale grey.

Other marbles which harmonize with Skyros are: Blue Fleuri, Blue Turquin, Comblanchien, Grand Antique, Vert-de-Mer, Sienna, Vert Campan, St. Ann's Black and Gold, Rouge Royal, Vert Antique and Onyx Vert.

Oak Graining: The Heartwood Markings

THE Heartwood markings of oak have many easily distinguishable features.

Note first, the many dark lines of which they are composed, which are compact on the inside (that is nearest the centre of the heartwood shape).

Here they are so close that they form a dark line, whilst they are shaded away on the outside simply by spreading further apart. The almost clear background of lighter colour occupies about three times the width of the darker portion.

At a recent lecture and demonstration it was pointed out that I had not yet dealt with this very useful variety of oak in the J.D.A. I will try to make amends.

During the winter I spent several weeks in Hampshire, where I examined many specimens of oak, I found that two-thirds contained quite pleasant heartwood markings, most of it choice and only two per cent coarse; the remainder was either plain or figured.

In large public buildings, good residences and even for gates and fencing, oak has been used freely; this beautifully marked timber has probably been grown in the county.

Large oak trees are growing today in vast number over the land bordering on Southampton Water; they would have been more plentiful some fifty or a hundred years ago.

A local worthy told me that on one estate alone over £5,000 of timber is cut annually, chiefly oak, and the gaps were scarcely discernible.

Whilst the air was still, the pleasant smell of burning logs in the hearth could be enjoyed all day. The twisted small branches are cut up for burning; oak logs warm me as I write.

The drawing of oak closely resembles that of ash, and at times they are hard to distinguish, though generally speaking the markings are not as coarse.

The spoon-shaped end in the drawing of oak is quite a feature, followed by ten or more ringed markings with dull to rounded points.

A small knot or other interesting shape occurs to one side, followed by another series of plainer markings, with perhaps another size of spoon shape.

Oak is a slow-growing timber; thus most of its markings are fine. The annular rings are close

A study of Heartwood

together, which keeps the spaces between the heartwood markings narrow.

Most slow-growing trees have wide boles, thus giving a quick taper to the trunk; the cutting is done largely parallel to the centre of the trunk, which gives the heartwood markings.

The branches of a tree have an important bearing on the markings of the heartwood, forming a complete set of annular rings of their own, which may be almost as old as the tree itself.

My 16-year-old oak has now six permanent branches; they will probably live as long as the tree.

The branches produce a large heart down the side of the trunk nearest the branch, and sometimes a feather in an old, mature tree.

The figure has also the habit of pointing towards the branch from long distances up or down the trunk.

The drawings I show this month are from sketches of Hampshire oak; they will be followed later by others from the same place.

In the first drawing a number of small knots are to be seen near the centre, giving an interesting joining arrangement.

On the bottom portion the two side markings are unusual in not being opposite the centre.

In number two we find several good features; near the top the winding grain crosses over the centre, winding round the smaller knots.

The left-hand side of the top shape is dealt with quite differently; the bottom one is very wide and runs clean off the edge of the panel.

More grain is shown in all three examples than would be desirable on actual work. Each would be improved with a little more side grain.

The third drawing is composed of straight grain, and three of the spoon-shaped ends are used, variety being obtained by slight changes of direction in the plainer markings.

The straightforward wipe-out method of graining heartwood has declined somewhat; pencilling in has become popular.

Perhaps the best work is done in this kind of graining by the use of cutting tools, the grain markings being incised into the surface.

One can produce oak with a minimum of effort and moderate skill that is pleasing and looks natural, using heartwood markings as opposed to figure.

In a dark, ill-lit position, the striking use of a wipe-out clean heartwood looks well.

The painted example has been carried out in one colour, in a thin glaze of raw sienna.

The markings were painted in with a fitch, and lightly dragged towards the centre with the hog hair softener.

The glazing was done lightly with Vandyke brown in water, marked with the mottler and lightly softened.

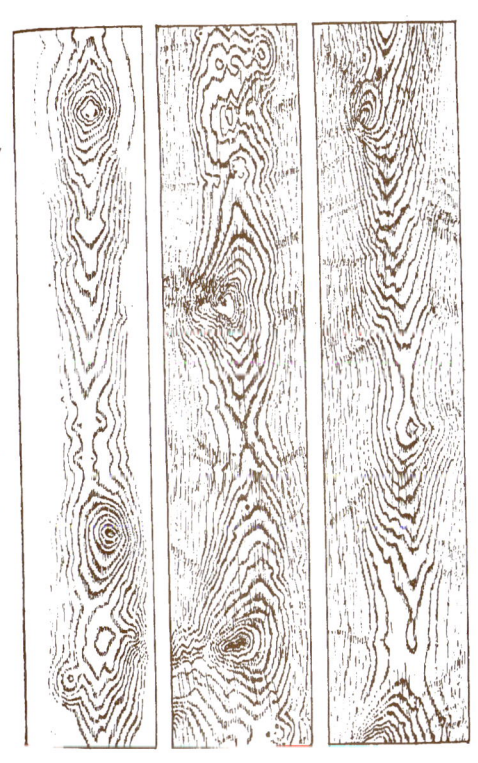

**Oak: Heartwood Markings
Drawings by Mr Dobson**

(To be continued)

Italian Walnut

I HAVE always regarded Italian Walnut as among the choicest of woods. In design, colour, knots, grain, texture and depth it has no equal.

The grain is often vigorous but there are never coarse knots and burrs intermingled with the heartwood markings.

The light and shade from the knots sparkles strikingly, and the veins around and between cross over each other in a very charming way.

Origin

Italy is a country of varying climates, and the growth of timber is affected by wind on the mountain slopes.

The summer sunshine is warmer than ours, but the evenings and winters are cold.

This makes for good heartwood markings, as the seasons of growth are well defined.

Owing to the sheltering range of the Alps and the semi-insular nature of the country, the summer mean temperature falls between 70' and 80', whilst the winter average is between 35' and 50'.

The greatest extremes occur in the region of the Po basin, at the head of the Adriatic Sea, where the scorching, drying wind known as the sirocco blows at all seasons of the year.

In the spring, the sirocco visits the southern parts of the peninsula and Sicily.

These climatic conditions have a bearing on the growth of the beautiful figure of Italian Walnut.

Most of the mountains of Italy, varying in height from 600 to 6000 ft., running the whole length of the country from Switzerland to Sicily, are densely wooded.

In the lower reaches the straight timber is found, while the well marked varieties grow well up the slopes.

Colour

The colour of the wood is largely a green-brown, while the knots and vein markings range from vandyke to transparent black-brown.

The old burrs are cool and darker in colour, while the younger growths are straighter in the grain and also lighter in colour.

Ground

Italian Walnut of a medium tone should be worked from a cool buff ground, consisting of ochre, umber, orange chrome and white.

This should dry hard with the assistance of gold-size or terebine.

A knife point of black should be substituted for the umber where the coolest ground is desired.

Tools

The tools required are: tools, fitches, flogger, hog hair softener, mottler, badger and sable over grainer.

My examples were grained with a home-made overgrainer made from two medium sized camel hair water-colour brushes, first divided into two halves with silk down the centre of the bristle, which is then wrapped round a few times and touched with knotting to secure it.

The two brushes are then bound together with a 1in. block of cork or wood between and near the bristle, the ends of the handle being bound and forming a "V" shape.

The four points of soft bristle are in use every time you apply the brush, while the soft hair holds the turpentine well.

Method

There are several methods of graining Italian Walnut, all of which I will deal with in turn.

The first method which I have used in my examples this month came from the Continent. It is rather laboured though not difficult. A flogged water colour ground is followed by the graining in turpentine colour in several stages.

The Painted Examples

The reproduced painted examples show the method of working in progressive stages.

In the first can be seen the flogging of the background, covered with a thin glaze of umber, while the first red lines of the drawing are clearly visible.

Canvas has been used down the sides to give the lighter tone in places.

The drawing in the first example is very simple; a few places are left for the knots, but they have not been developed.

In example No. 2 all the working from No. 1 has been carried forward, while the first of the black lines have been added.

A few knots have been painted in and the sides have had a thin glaze of turpy black in a broad mass.

While there is no attempt to make a finished job of the graining, the tone has been developed, the differentiation of the design of each panel also adds interest.

In example No. 3 the Walnut type of grain now begins to show, and was obtained by working forward with the black and turps, using the camel hair or sable brushes.

In the lighter parts the same number of processes has been carried out, using less colour and more turpentine.

All the stages of the graining have been worked wet on wet, which is quite simple as the turps colour soon sets giving the softness from the slightly running colour which is very desirable in walnut graining. No pencils or fitches were used up to this stage.

Additional black was added with the overgrainer to the heartwood grain in example No. 4. A fitch was used to sharpen the edges of the lines dividing the tones of brown.

The knots were strengthened with black, and a small piece of canvas was used with a slight twist of the wrist to give character to the inside of the small burrs.

One half of this panel was glazed with vandyke.

(To be continued)

Painted examples of the progressive stages in graining Italian Walnut by Mr Dobson

Italian Walnut (continued)

IN the May issue I gave a description and botanical notes on Italian Walnut and led up to the growth of this remarkable and decorative wood.

I shall now describe the ground and the tools required and the methods employed in graining the examples illustrated in May and on this page.

Palette

Colours ground in oil; black, Indian red and burnt umber. If there is any difficulty in obtaining good tube black ground in oil, any fine stainers ground in turpentine will be satisfactory.

Vandyke brown and blue black ground in water, are required for glazing and flogging.

In the Dippers

Two dippers are required:

(a) One part of linseed oil to two parts of turpentine, with a few drops of terebine,

(b) Pure turpentine only; this becomes greasy as the work proceeds, and must be changed at intervals or the colour may run more than is desired.

Method

For the flogged ground spread with a tool a thin glaze of vandyke brown reasonably well bound. Using the flogger or badger, flog upwards until a fine texture is obtained, and allow to dry for twelve hours.

The flogged ground should not be fastened with thinned varnish, as part of the colour will be cleaned off later in the graining, giving a soft appearance to the side grain.

Oiling the Ground

Rub in very lightly a thin glaze of the oily medium and burnt umber, working with and not across the grain, keeping the glaze on the dry side, with the umber scarcely visible.

Success depends on the amount of oil on the surface. If there is any sign of running, a little should be wiped off with a rag, following the direction of the grain. If some of the flogging is removed it won't matter.

Drawing the Grain

From this stage turpentine only is used to charge the brushes, with red and black used separately.

The drawing of the grain is first done with the red and in a delicate outline every few inches.

The small amount of oil on the surface is pushed to one side by the turpentine, while the red gets a firm grip on the flogged ground.

Care must be taken to get good shapes with these first few lines; no rubbing out is permissible.

The lines, however, can be crossed over with no serious harm to the finished work.

About a quarter of the surface may be covered with the red lines, most of which will be covered later, though some will remain untouched. This process is intended primarily for the drawing.

Burr in oil

Graining

The over-graining of the brown lines is now commenced, the colour used being black only, worked in turpentine up to the completion of the graining. Start with almost a clean brush dipped into the turps and just stained with black, use all the four points of the brush and cover more than half of the plain brown glaze.

Strengthen the tone of black for the next part of the work; at the same time use less turps, and continue to grain the heavy parts of the walnut. Of course, this portion of the grain will be allowed to run over lighter portions.

As the work proceeds, use darker and narrower bands of colour. Should the general appearance become painty or muddy, discontinue with the colour and use turps only. The opening out process being the best of this method and giving a most natural appearance, most of the work must be amongst the darker part of the graining only.

Should any part of the work run too much, dab with a rag and allow to set for a few minutes before working on the same place again. There is a danger of putting too much detail into the walnut.

All the different stages of working should show in places when the panel is completed. The side grain is much lighter than the heavy centre figure; here it is necessary to run down the various tones of colour to give a wavy effect.

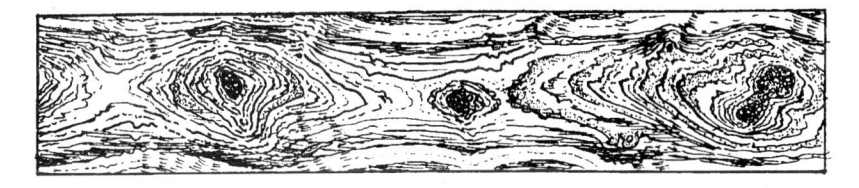

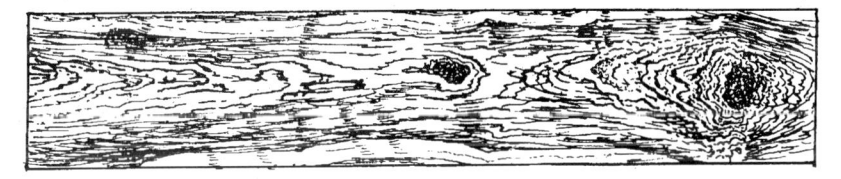

To clean up the graining a small piece of hessian is used, folded carefully into a pad, the edges being used just like a comb. It will be noted that it only draws the colour together in lines, and does not remove it, which is an advantage.

For the small groups of knots use a fitch and a touch of black; here again the canvas may be used as a point with a twist of the wrist.

The quality in walnut graining bears no relation to the amount of time spent; accuracy in the drawing and skill in using the correct amount of turpentine and colour are what count. Drawing may be developed with long and diligent application, imagination and practice.

A fitch is used to sharpen up the outlines; it should be lightly charged with black in a dry state and scrubbed on with the side of the brush. Soften with the hog hair softener in the direction of the grain.

Glazing: Glazing is carried out in water colour with black and brown, the centre being the darkest. The side grain shows just a little water-wave mottle.

Three studies of Italian Walnut by Mr Dobson

Cipollina Marble

CIPOLLINA is a handsome green marble, composed of wavy bands or laminations of colour in tones of green alternating with white and grey.

Small patches of dark green are embedded in the light grey, with white to pale grey stones in the darker grey portions.

The large half diaper-shaped waves of colour are divided by narrow soft lines of grey, which vary considerably in width. These bands of colour are not as well defined in the Swiss and American varieties as in the Greek.

There is also a scarce and valuable red variety obtained from Asia Minor with pink and white waves on a red matrix. Much interest has also been focused lately on the early Greek marble of Carystus.

Recently the name of Cipollina has been applied as a generic term to all marbles which include alternate bands of pale green and white mica. The name is derived from cipola (onion), the shape of which is suggested by some of its markings.

Composition
The matrix consists chiefly of grains of calcite, serpentine and a madder coloured mineral, possibly a serpentined hornblende with an occasional granule of pyrite or flake of biotite.

The green colour is also attributed to a fibrous muscovite, which is rendered brighter by the association of epidote and chlorite.

Origin
Greece, Italy, Switzerland, U.S.A. and Canada.

The Greek quarries are situated on the island of Eubocea; the town of Carystus lies in the south of the island, from which huge consignments have been exported during the past century.

Considerable quantities have been used in England.

The Greek quarries were lost sight of for many centuries, during which supplies were derived solely from ancient buildings.

The Italian quarries are to be found on the island of Elba.

Swiss Cipollina is blasted from the Rhone valley beds (over six thousand feet deep), the Canadian from Quebec, and the American from the State of Vermont.

Brushes and Tools
Two 2in. tools, a few fitches, a well worn sable pencil, sponge, clean rag, a small fine rubber stippler and a hog hair softener.

Palette
Brunswick green, vandyke brown, black and a little zinc white. For the finest work, Prussian blue, crimson and yellow lake may be added.

In the Dipper
A mixture of one part of oil and glaze to three parts of turpentine.

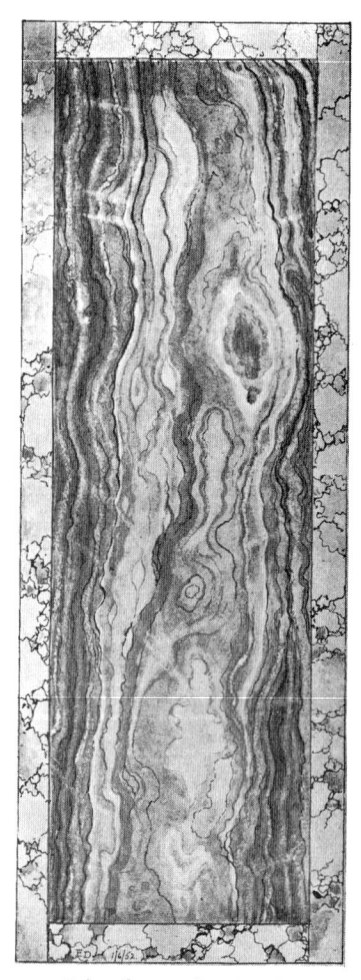

Painted example 6ft x 2ft

Drawing

On a sheet of cartridge paper draw to scale the panel to be worked with the lines in the colour you propose to use, and include any stones.

Method

With a rag or tool, oil in the ground fairly liberally.

Draw in the main lines in places with a fitch charged with green and grey.

Charge a tool with a very pale glaze of green, and scrub in the widest ribbons of colour and, with a fitch, put in a few stone shapes.

In places grey should be used, prepared from pale green and a touch of black and white or pale green and red.

For delicacy of colour a few tints of grey may be used.

If you are able to work very cleanly the white may be omitted but, on account of the oil in the glaze, and to allow more black and red to be used, a proportion of white is almost a necessity.

Apply all colours with a broken or wavy fringe down the edge.

Try to place all the colours correctly at the first attempt, they soon lose their brightness with too much brushing, crossing or stippling.

Work all the widest waves in light colour with dark edges, and the narrow waves in deeper tones of blue-green and grey-green. Vandyke and Prussian blue make a suitable colour for the dark portions.

The stones which run with the laminations are few, and most of them are white.

Wipe out the white parts with a rag on the ball of the thumb.

Soften lightly with the hog hair softener, taking care to run with the waves.

In order to obtain a small amount of texture, one colour may be stippled with a fine rubber stippler, another with the end of the hog hair, while others may be splashed with turps.

No glazing should be necessary.

Uses

The Greeks used Cipollina as a building stone from the earliest times.

Craftsmen were taken as slaves to Rome, where there are over five hundred columns of this marble in classical buildings today.

The famous Byzantine Mosque of St. Sophia, Constantinople, is lined with broad bands of it.

Because its wavy pattern resembled the sea it was used also in the Temple dedicated to Neptune and built by Agrippa in 420 B.C.

It is rather surprising to find that this marble has been used for the columns of the new vestibule of the Royal College of Art, for its wavy pattern is not easy to incorporate into any scheme of interior decoration.

The exterior of the Palace of Justice, Brussels, considered to be the finest building erected in Europe during the nineteenth century, was adorned with it.

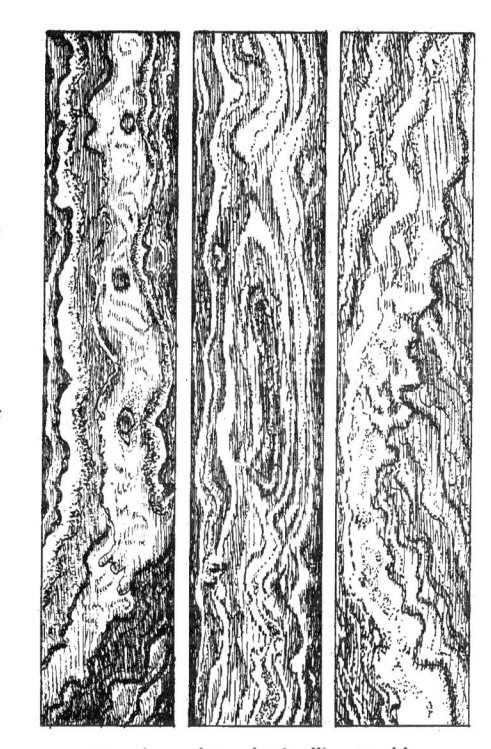

Drawings of Greek Cipollina Marble, by Mr Dobson, representing slabs, 8ft x 2ft

Italian Walnut (continued)

THERE are many methods of graining walnut, the most accurate, and the one I have always preferred being that in which a turpentine medium is used on a water flogged ground, which I have recently described.

At a well known Lancashire coast resort I recently came across a heavy moulded front door, grained in walnut. The effect was arresting and rather showy – just the note for a young master painter after more business.

Upon enquiry I was given an account of how it was produced – by means of a feather. Many other doors in the same district were of the same pattern by the same craftsman, who was the manager of a firm of decorators in the town.

He took a lively interest in the graining of his front doors. The work was clean and crisp, showing a mastery of his craft. I was invited to inspect other examples of graining which were equally good.

I live in the country, and on my rambles I collect any large feathers I see, even from domestic fowl, so that I am always prepared for the many jobs on which feathers can be used.

This interesting method of graining Italian walnut I have used many times; I start by cutting about one inch of the thin end of the feather away. The feather must, of course, come from a large bird, so that it will be strong and about 8 or 9in. inches in length.

Feathers are quite simple to handle, and easy enough to use, but to control the marks they make, and get the same effect with another feather on another door is not such an easy matter.

A feather must be used damp to wet; it should be worked briskly, with a fair amount of swing if we are to produce a good wood graining effect. A dry feather used with a firm hand, slowly, will actually pick up colour, leaving a series of light lines.

Do not apply the colour with the feather, or it will probably come off in a blob, or at the best show a large dark patch.

The method that I have found best is to rub on all the colour that you require with your tool, and use the feather to draw the colour together in lines. To carry this out successfully, keep your ground moist, indeed almost "running."

Vandyke brown is a most efficient colour for feather graining; with a slight variation of the ground colour it will satisfy most needs for graining walnut.

I have used the siennas and black, the binding of which wants well watching, but they are not really satisfactory with the feather as a graining method, though they may be used to get a little variation from the colour of the Vandyke.

Description
I propose to work to the description of Italian walnut that I have given previously, and to aim more at a decorative rendering than a slavish reproduction of the wood grain.

Ground
This should be hard and smooth; for some reason water colour has a tendency to hold up, and not soften out well if the ground is not well papered down. The colour may be anywhere between oft-white for the bleached variety and a green buff for the darker toned cool walnut.

Tools and Sundries
A one and two inch tool, and good stout feather from a goose, turkey or domestic fowl, badger softener, and sponge for keeping all mould edges well under control.

Palette
Vandyke brown in water is satisfactory alone; blue black for use where a deeper or cooler effect is desired and a touch of burnt sienna.

Method of Working
Rub in your panel with your tool, add the colour slowly as desired until all cissing and fretting has settled. Use slightly more colour than is required for your finished effect; some of it is always lost in the graining.

Brush marks must be reasonably well lost in the shapes and grain of the wood; the light and dark tones should now be put in their correct positions, shapes and areas. Don't rely on the feather to move the colour during the graining process.

The correct placing of the colour will count a lot towards the finished effect; the door or other work should look half completed before it is touched with the feather.

Charge the feather with water, rub it lightly on the palette board on the long side, when all the fine fur edge will draw together like uneven pencils.

Draw in the shape of the heartwood markings, keeping your feather vertical all the time, or nearly so.

Commence at one of the knotted centres near the bottom of the panel.

A slightly shaky or trembling motion should be developed, which should be more marked down the centre of the panel.

Continue to work quickly and cleanly until the whole door is covered, this being a matter almost of seconds.

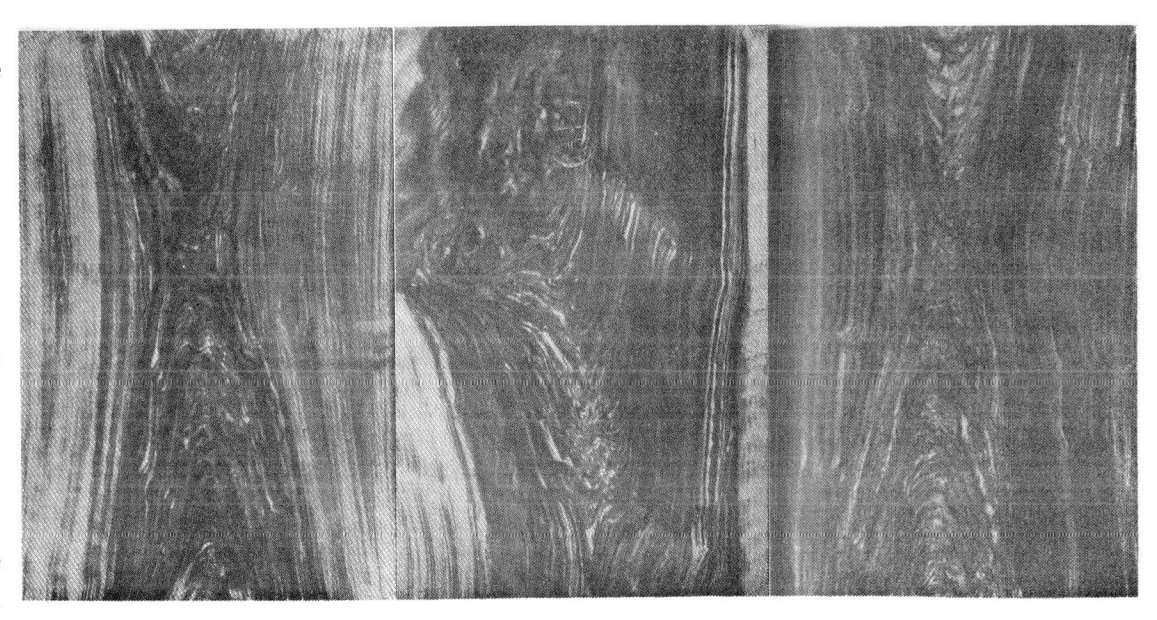

The part of the side grain adjoining the central heartwood must be worked in a vertical direction, but on the side grain proper, the feather should be held in a horizontal position.

Softening with the badger should be carried out away from the centre; in parts it is better omitted.

Glazing

Glazing can be carried out in oil colour if desired; the colour may be self prepared, but proprietary scumbles are very satisfactory, thinned with turpentine.

Painted Examples

The illustrations have been painted to show three types of effect. One has dark centre grain, and is well softened all over.

The second panel had the colour laid on evenly, and was then grained all over with the feather. The softening was carried out only in places where the graining was straight; on the curly parts it was left hard, thus having a lighter appearance because more of the ground showed.

The last example has been grained with a light central grain and dark side grain.

Graining of Obeche

OBECHE is one of the lighter woods that has recently sprung into prominence owing to the demand for newer effects both in decoration and panelling.

The soft waterwave markings, the delicate colouring, and the absence of hard grain or texture markings satisfy present day requirements in decoration. Her Majesty Queen Elizabeth II likes Obeche; it was recently used for the panelling of her boudoir.

The almost complete absence of resin in this wood accounts for its lightness both in colour and in weight, and also makes it easier to cut. It is, therefore, much favoured for handicraft work.

I understand that it was first used in the Far East as a wall covering, mounted on a thin cotton scrim. As veneer it is easy to apply by a paper-hanger.

Instead of relying on brush graining or cream painting the craftsman, with a little practice, can obtain a much better effect by an elementary form of graining which the reproduction of Oteche involves. The process is simple and can be completed in one operation in water or oil medium.

In the graining of these lighter woods the ground must be kept lighter than the traditional light buff ground. A medium coloured gilp cannot be used to cover up the painting faults; a minimum of three coats of paint must be given to obtain a satisfactory ground colour.

Origin
Obeche is one of the newer African woods to be imported and is grown in the provinces of Cameroon, Nigeria, Benin and Onda. This wood was greatly admired at the Empire Exhibition held in Scotland in 1938, when an effort was made to popularise some of the lesser known Empire woods.

The forests of Nigeria are situated near the coast and are penetrated by deep waterways, by which ocean-going vessels can carry the timber direct to the markets of the world. In Nigeria the area of available forest land extends from 50,000 to 60,000 square miles. In fact British West Africa possesses over 12% of the forests of the Empire.

Description
The absence of usual figure or grain is of particular interest to the grainer. Instead, Obeche possesses a soft water waved mottle in bands from two to four inches wide, which are not too clearly defined. The grain is interlocked, similar to that of grape vine and rosewood, which causes the surface to tear up when sandpapered or scraped. This can present difficulty when thin veneers are being applied.

The colour varies from a green cream to a pale orange, but in each case there is the same light tone.

The waterwaved mottle often runs in bands spaced at one to three inches. The slope or angle of the mottle, even on a board five feet wide, will be the same. Small, short dark lines of pith are distributed fairly evenly over the surface, about double the quantity of those found in oak.

Tools and Brushes
One and two inch tools, a flogger, a badger hair softener, and a cutter or mottler. As the cutter is the most important brush in this particular graining process, I will give a detailed description of the one I used for the painted examples. It is of standard British make, three inches wide, $1/4$ inch thick and made of white lily bristle which protrudes $3/4$ of an inch from the metal sides and has a wooden core.

A small piece of sponge was used to keep the work clean and to remove surplus colour from the brushes.

Ground Colour
A good solid off-white.

Palette
Raw and burnt sienna ground in water, but oil colour may be used if desired.

Method of Working
Rub in a thin glaze of raw sienna, or a mixture of both siennas according to the colour required. Flog the surface upwards,

keeping the ground as wet as possible just within a running condition. Wet the cutter, adding a little colour to make it as near as possible to the glaze already laid on or it will leave a light patch when the brush is applied.

Hold the wrist slightly at an angle, right or left, and proceed to mottle a width the full length of the panel. Keep the brush on the work all the time, while releasing and pressing alternately all the way down, and continue from top to bottom until the door or panel is covered.

Soften gently at an angle and in the direction of the mottling. The badger may be used on its side to lightly flog the work in places. If time and circumstances permit, the graining can be fastened with goldsize and turpentine, and lightly flogged all over as a separate operation.

Example No. 1
This shows the flogged ground with three lines of mottling, the first being worked with one finger held on the bristle near the tip. It will be seen that a line of mottle is prominent down the centre, with brush lines showing down each side.

In the centre line of mottling the mottled portion is slightly wider and the lines narrower, and in this case two fingers were held on the brush. In the third line four fingers were held firmly on the bristle near the tip. My fingers were not quite as wide as the bristle so that a small narrow brush line

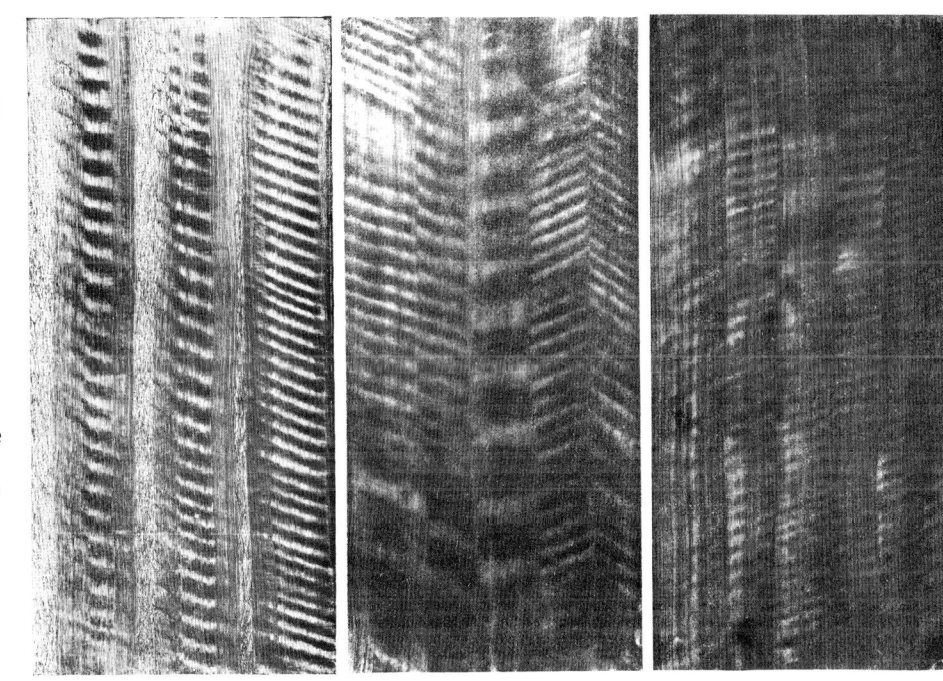

Fig.1

shows. With a wide brush a thin piece of wood or cardboard can be held near the tip of the brush.

Examples 2 and 3
These show further stages of working up to the completed panel. It will be noted how the mottling slopes to the left and to the right, being affected by holding the wrist to either side; caution is required in making too

Fig.2

many changes of direction. I prefer only one change on each panel, though, in nature, the grain is more boisterous.

Variety has been obtained by bringing the waves nearer together in some lines of mottle, whilst in others they are left wider apart. After softening with the badger, the final panel was slightly flogged in places to give texture.

Fig.3

Napoleon Marble Limestone

THE attractive stone, Napoleon, known also as Corsite, always reminds me of my happy student days as the dadoes in the flat and estaminet which I used while studying abroad were decorated with this light marble.

In the October J.D.A., W. W. Davidson told of some experiments with this stone which produced some fine results.

Here I deal with a straightforward method of reproduction.

It is strange that this quiet subdued marble-limestone should be associated with the name of the once vigorous Marshal of France, Napoleon.

Just as figured oak is popular with British grainers, so Napoleon and Henrietta marbles have been with continental marblers, who have been highly skilled in its execution and have used it more than any other marble.

Its small texture, quiet colour, and the fact that it will withstand knocks without disfigurement make it suitable for use on a dado.

It also adds dignity to the wall filling and harmonizes well with other marbles and with woods and wall hangings.

It requires a fair amount of skill in its execution, the scope of the marbler being limited by its very restricted colours.

Origin

France in the neighbourhood of Boulogne, in some of the Mediterranean islands, in smaller outcrops of other European countries and near Kansas City, U.S.A.

Composition

Lumps of diorite, ranging from one to two inches in diameter, are found in a grey matrix which covers seventy per cent of the area, and show well defined concentric circles of crystal.

The centre of the spheroid is usually white to pale grey, consisting mainly of felspar, while the darker parts are rich in hornblende and pyroxene. Other small shapes are composed of plagioclose, separated by areas of diorite.

Description

My first impression, on recently seeing a bank lined with Napoleon, was that it was a fine example of broken colour which could easily be reproduced by using three grades of rubber stippler.

The colour is a soft grey fawn, in some places faintly pink, and in others a greenish hue.

The slender veins of brown shades cut across at intervals ranging from inches up to two feet. They have a trembling effect, are never steady and always wild in direction. Pink and white lines run through the mass, and in some specimens all the three colours are found, but the brown lines predominate.

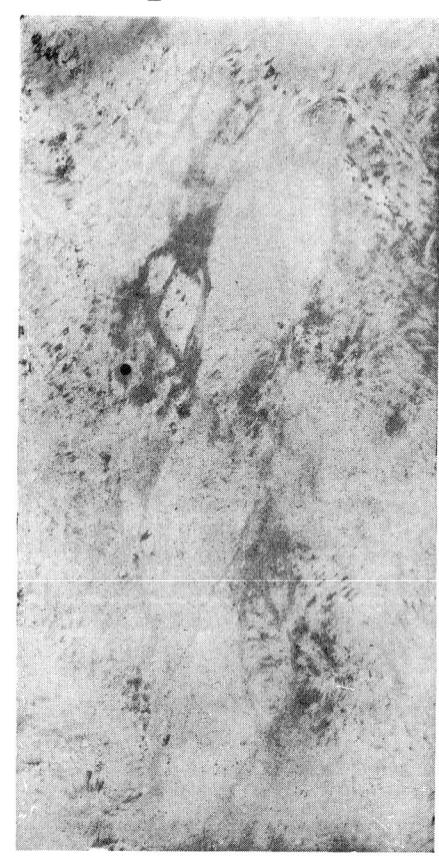

Fig. 1

The texture is perhaps the main attraction of this marble; the ground is entirely broken by different sizes of shells and crinoids.

Emphasis is given to the line dividing the veining by more open or closer texture on different sides.

A small portion of the broken surface contains the outline of the smaller stones grouped together; this area is more violent in tone contrast.

This portion is often omitted from painted samples but is desirable when used in narrow borders for framing other types of marble.

Ground Colour
White.

Palette
Black, white, burnt umber and ochre.

In the Dipper
Three parts turpentine, two parts linseed oil and a few drops of terebine.

Method
On the palette board prepare tints of pale grey and umber. Paint in a shaded ground largely using the umber tint with spaces of grey, and a tint of ochre.

Soften well with the hog hair softener.

In the broken parts of the marble, where violent changes of colour are found, a little fitch work may be introduced using stronger tints of umber on the light background.

With slightly stronger tints of grey umber proceed to stipple inside the larger shapes straight on to the wet painted surface.

Cover most of the area with a sponge stipple.

In the painted example, Fig. 1, the preliminary fitch and sponge work is clearly visible. Sponging must be continued until a satisfactory arrangement is obtained, all the colour being picked up from the palette in a prepared state.

At no time must the sponge be dipped into the dipper, only a fitch being used to pick up the thinners. A soggy sponge applied to the surface causes the spots of colour to run out the moment the softener is applied.

Glazing
The same palette is used for the glazing when the panel is first oiled in. Commence sponge stippling in pure zinc white, covering most of the surface, and apply more to some stones than others, thus slightly helping the tone values.

A fitch charged with cream or stone may next be used to strengthen the veining in places, gradually working up to a medium toned colour.

Often the marbling is completed at one operation, but transparency is better obtained by using the two processes.

Fig. 2 shows a rather elaborately finished example.

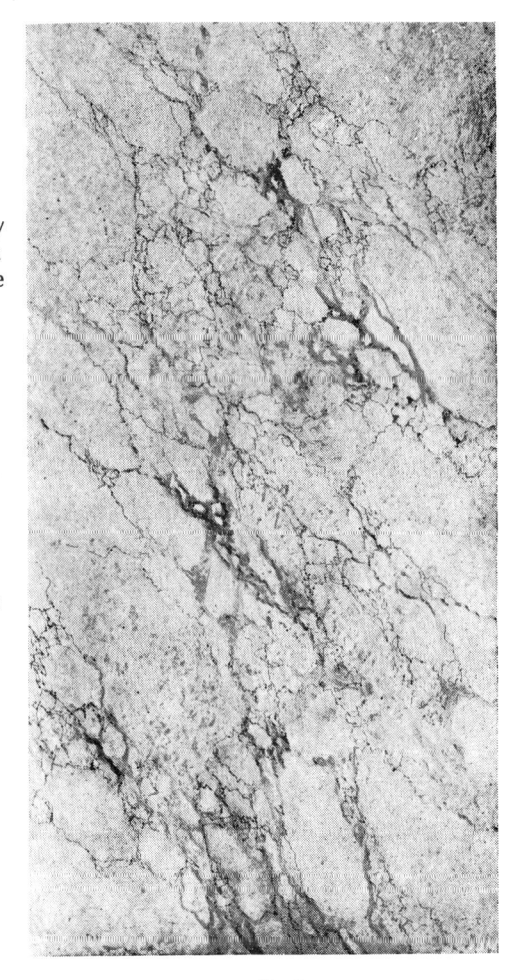

Fig. 2

The Graining of Sycamore

ORIGINATING in Europe and North America, sycamore is a tree that flourishes in the moist climate of Great Britain. It grows in great profusion in the West Riding, is fond of moisture and is found near the banks of rivers.

Sycamore is closely related to maple, the plain, straight grained types of both woods being very similar. The five lobes on the large leaf are not quite as pointed in the sycamore as in the smaller maple leaf.

The tree itself is very handsome, with a straight trunk, smooth bark, large spreading, billowing branches, thickly covered with leaves possessing crimson stems. In early Spring the greenish flowers appear in long, drooping clusters, and later these develop into winged seeds of a reddish-green colour.

Although classed as a slow growing hardwood, sycamore grows much quicker than oak. A tree, planted by my father some 50 years ago in our garden at home, had grown to 40 feet in height with a trunk 50 inches in circumference when it was cut down some three years ago.

This light coloured wood is popular today in decoration and for the manufacture of small domestic utensils. For centuries printing rollers, bread cutting boards and hard serviceable table-tops have been made from sycamore.

Description: The colour of sycamore is a light orange cream, delicate and transparent, with markings only slightly stronger than the ground. In places the markings are very interesting; they run around the few small knots, found up the sides, and have narrow fine lines of grain close together. These are rounded at the ends and the light markings are often comparatively wide.

Frequently secondary smaller shapes grow up the sides of larger ones.

A fine water-wave mottle runs over the well marked grain, while the plainer examples are mottled quite vigorously. The centre of the panel, like the under side of the knots, is darker in colour than the rest of the surface.

Ground Colour: Off-white with a touch of ochre.

Tools and Sundries: Tool, fitches, one and two inch mottlers a quarter of an inch thick, palette board, coarse hair comb.

In the Dippers: Turpentine only in the first, and a mixture of two parts linseed oil and one part turpentine with a few drops of terebine in the second.

Palette: Burnt and raw sienna, burnt umber, black and white.

Method: Rub in a bare glaze composed of a touch of sienna, umber and a little white sufficient to hold the glaze firm. With a fitch, lightly charged with sienna, set out the skeleton outline of the shape of the veining only, as a guide to subsequent graining. I have found that most

Painted example of sycamore

grained work has a tendency to spread too large for its situation if worked freely without guide lines; the operator gets so interested in his work that he keeps on adding to it.

The milky glaze colour does not show the brush marks which often help so greatly with the drawing of the grain shapes; thus reliance must be placed on the fitch outline.

Charge the one inch mottler with a spot of turpentine and raw sienna. Rub and dab it lightly on the palette to remove any excess of colour or thinners; pass the bristle through the comb to divide the bristle, hold the mottler lightly and commence to draw the grain.

It should now be found that the turpentine stain on the mottler will disperse the glaze and adhere well to the ground.

Continue with each brush of colour until it is exhausted, though without undue pressure, for this will crush out the combed division in the brush.

It will be found that the colour gets lighter as the work continues with an almost dry brush, and this must be turned to advantage in giving tone variations in different places on the heartwood.

A yellow-grey may be used in places by using a little black with the sienna, or a tint of umber and burnt sienna over the small narrow bands.

The finished effect to be aimed at will be the orange cream from raw and burnt sienna, the strongest colour being near the centre of the heartwood shapes.

After the narrow mottler has been used in separate places and with many colours, the wider one should be brought into use. For the side grain and the broader flat parts, which are worked in a fairly even tone, the wider mottler is the better tool.

It is better not to work over a second time on the still wet fine grained lines, as they are liable to run. With a little practice, it will be found quite easy to get a pleasing representation. The aim must be to put the correct colour in place at the first attempt.

For any wiping out, lifting, removing runs, and so forth, use clean jute or hessian.

When a fine and suitable effect has been obtained, take a short scrubby fitch and clean up the drawing in places with a stronger tone of sienna and umber.

Add a few burnt sienna knots, particularly down the side grain. With the wooden end of the fitch mark these on the outer edge and, perhaps, with a small cross in the centre. The graining is now complete.

Glazing: This is usually carried out in water colour, a good palette being raw and burnt sienna and black. Almost any sycamore colour may be produced from these, and the transparent effect is obtained largely by the glazing process.

Rub in the surface with thin raw sienna, slowly adding the other colours as desired.

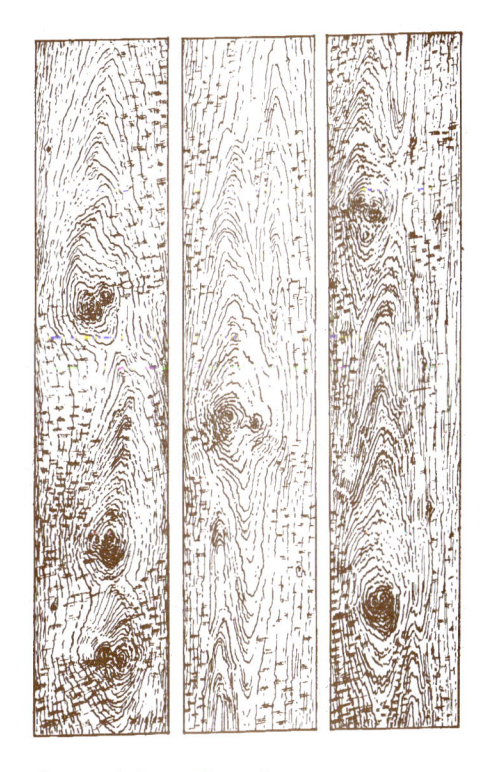

The gentle lines of mottling are near together and should not be too strong to hide the delicate grain.

Some specimens are almost covered with mottle, while others are mottled to a less extent, say one-third, and the remainder fairly plain. In all cases the beauty of colour depends on the glaze.

131

The Marbling of Breche Violette

IN the study of marbles Breche Violette is often the last to be considered, on account of its complicated markings and its brilliant contrasting colours. Though bright, the colours are pleasant, and give the impression that the marble is violet, though it is not.

The broken coloured vein markings contain some violet; three times as much of the veining consists of grey, interspersed with purple brown, a little red and some orange.

The ground is even more misleading; much of it is pure white and tints of orange cream, grey and dull pink are also to be found.

The veining is not confined to the heavy matrix and breccia markings, but a considerable amount of the narrow Cararra type may be found, and there is some likeness to the grain of Walnut.

Some five-sixths of the stone shapes are left empty; others are filled in with medium toned colour, while a few, in the knotted parts, are darker than the veining.

Many of the stone shapes are small. The medium and larger ones are all narrow.

The colouring of the markings, the tinting of the ground and the filling in of the stones are all related in colour; the similarity can be traced in bands almost from top to bottom of the panel.

Many fine examples of Breche Violette are to be seen in this country. The main staircase of the Guildhall in Hull is lined with this beautiful marble. The Royal Hall at Harrogate is decorated extensively with it, and the War Office in Whitehall contains some fine columns in the main entrance.

Origin: Italy, where it is quarried at Seravezza in Tuscany.

Composition: Breche Violette is a double limestone breccia, formed by faults and veins below the surface. A fissure, probably formed by a movement of the earth's crust, is later filled in by water-carried deposits.

Very often displacement takes place again, and the infilling is torn apart and brecciated. It is then cemented together by the introduction of further oxides of copper, iron and felspar. Some of the colouring is due to chemical reaction.

Ground: White to a yellow cream.

Palette: White, lemon chrome, yellow ochre, vermilion, crimson lake, Prussian blue, a prepared tone of grey made from black, white and a touch of ochre.

In the Dipper: One part of oil to two parts of turpentine, with a few drops of terebine driers.

Brushes and Tools: A few hog hair fitches and pencils, small pieces of sponge, sable pencils, clean washed rags, a 2 in. tool, and hog hair softener.

Drawing of Breche Violette Marble

Method: Rub in a thin glaze of yellow-cream, using a rag for small spaces, and for areas over a few square feet, a tool.

This glaze may be applied in a shady, uneven manner, running in the general direction of the marble.

With the sponge, charged with a little ochre and a touch of lemon chrome, sponge and stipple in a band of stronger yellow-cream, followed by other bands of pale tints of lake and vermilion, of blue and grey, and of orange.

Probably all the ground will now be covered, and so remove some colour.

With one or two hog hair fitches charged with a medium tone of grey, commence painting in the larger, more important central markings.

It is best, while the brushes are in one colour, to move away to another place and complete the grey colour.

Nos. 4 and 6 fitches are most suitable; they rub up the ground glaze, adhering to the white ground with a good broken colour effect on the narrow bands and small angular surfaces.

The hog hair pencils may now be charged with pale blue and crimson to paint in a few medium sized shapes, to be followed by orange, and orange and crimson.

Two pointed pencils (size No. 2) should now be used for the finer veins, the colour range being the same as previously used with the fitches. The finer veining will be found down the side of the earlier heavy work.

Stones forming Breche Violette marble are all on the narrow side; the longer ones are from two to three feet long, being no more than seven inches wide at the widest part.

Two or three such stones form the basis of each square of marble.

Using a sponge and clean turpentine, the work may be opened out in places by light stippling among the finest work, or near the centre of the largest stones, but not on the heavier colour, which must be dealt with in the glazing process.

Rag, wrapped over the thumb, may now be used to wipe the colour from the inside of some of the smaller stones, a few of which may be only lightly cleaned. Rag rolling may be resorted to on some parts.

A few of the stones may now be filled in with a colour resembling the breche markings near them, but slightly darker in tone.

With a dry fitch, a little pure colour – crimson, vermilion, violet, pale blue and orange – may be used on the darker markings.

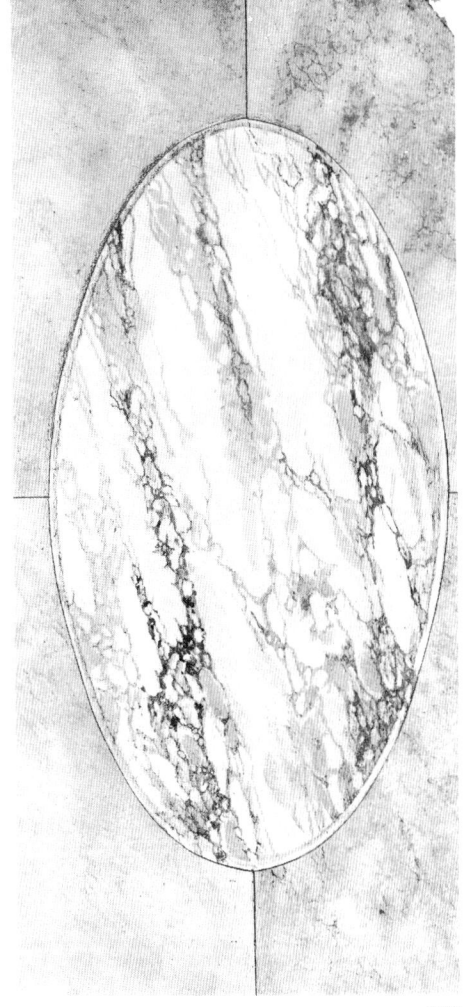

Painted example of Breche Violette by Mr Dobson.
Size of oval shape 5ft x 2ft 6in.
Border of Napoleon

Graining of Brown Oak

BROWN OAK has a distinctive type of figure. Only the timber from trees that are centuries old changes its colour to brown; younger timber is of a cream yellow colour.

To produce the figure of Brown Oak the tree must have many branches near the ground which, in turn, have been broken with the wind, cut or damaged, thus creating large polls.

The growth of the figure inside the tree, and even in the root, is materially affected by such outward changes.

Pollard Oak is found growing on the outer edges of the Brown Oak, while Root of Oak grows below it; thus a very large cut, some six feet from the base of the trunk, would include all three.

This portion is one of the first to decay in mature trees; therefore many fine examples become casualties while the other parts remain sound.

Origin: Great Britain and Southern Europe. Slow growing, it requires a moderately damp climate and a sheltered position.

Description: It is a medium toned grey brown with a well textured ground, a few knots and swirling figures.

As the texture, knots, and figure are of a similar tone, it is much quieter in appearance than the description may suggest.

The textured ground is most interesting, containing fairly prominent lines of grain, coupled with streaks of brown, similar to those we associate with Pollard Oak.

On close examination, green, burnt sienna and a touch of Prussian blue are found in the soft grey brown background, running in bands of about two inches wide and shaded into the background.

Waves of swinging texture are quite a feature of Brown Oak and never do we find the ground-work straight. The waves down the panel almost form lines across from three to nine inches apart creating pockets for the figure.

Knots are few in number; the smaller ones are arranged down one side and are the stray ones from the Pollard Oak. The larger knots are different in both shape and type; inside they are usually light in colour and shaded darker on the outside.

The figure is well defined, covering some 80% of the surface area. It is fine, close and compact, often following the shape of the knots down the side and in harmony with the large cross knots.

In the pockets formed by the waves and knots, the figure sweeps and twists, finishing with small figure on all the four sides. This gives prominence to the large figure in the centre. This dividing of the figured area makes it more interesting and, perhaps, easier to grain.

The colour of the figure is usually lighter than the ground, although there are darker examples.

Painted example of Brown Oak

Ground: A grey buff of medium tone, prepared to dry with a semi-gloss.

Tools and Sundries: Two tools (one well worn), fitches, steel graining combs, fantail overgrainer, hog hair softener, graining horn, and clean rags.

Palette: Raw umber, white, green, burnt sienna, Prussian blue and black.

Method: Rub in a thin glaze prepared from raw umber and a little white and, with the worn tool, draw or scrub in the waves of the grain.

Next carry out the combing with the steel comb, following the lines of the waves previously formed.

The comb should be run over a few times, using less pressure each time. Quite a varied effect can be obtained by the combing.

With the fantail, charged with gilp and a little dry or stiff colour, rub in a little green, black, and Prussian blue.

The application of a small amount of colour has the effect of softening the combing, which is helpful so long as it is not overdone.

If the ground combing becomes almost obliterated, put in more with the same comb and then soften across with the hog hair softener. Only one coarse comb was used for the painted example illustrated.

With a fitch, proceed to draw a few knots down one side of the panel, keeping them small and not very dark in colour.

With a pad of rag soften out the shape of the large knots in the curve of some of the waves, but not those in all of them.

With the fitch, paint in a brown shadow on one side. The longer knots are often eight or nine inches in length and, therefore, they must be made interesting or they will look monstrous.

Before figuring, the sides of the panel should be well softened to a quiet texture.

Commence to wipe out the figure. Much of the work is fine, so that it is best to keep the rag thin and to use a narrow fine horn.

Wipe out or soften with the rag between the large figuring; this helps to quieten down its striking effect.

Glazing: Glazing is necessary only if a perfect reproduction is desired. Vandyke brown in water makes a satisfactory glaze.

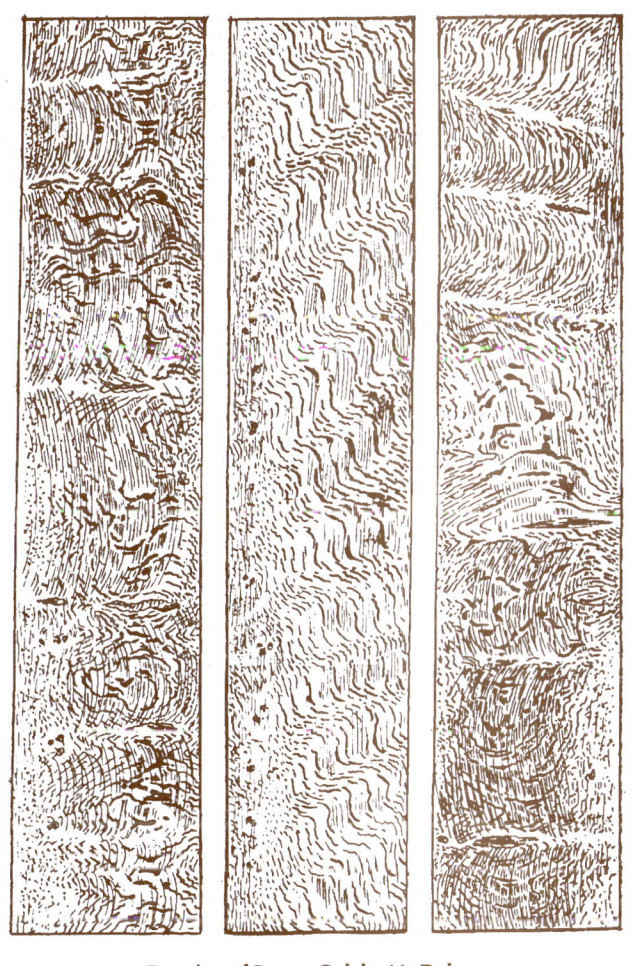

Drawing of Brown Oak by Mr Dobson

Blue Fleuri Marble

THIS medium-toned, blue-grey marble is often found in schemes where a number of coloured marbles have been grouped together.

Being inclined towards ultramarine, Blue Fleuri combines pleasingly with warm yellow, and shows up to advantage any marbles of a brighter colour than itself.

Its ribbon-like veining makes it suitable for quartering or cross banding and, having an even ground, it contrasts with marbles that have a textured background.

The light centres of the long shapes give the effect of a dark streak running under the veining. This simple effect can be reproduced by a capable marbler with just a few strokes of the brush.

In Blue Fleuri all the dark trembling lines of the vein ing are narrow, sometimes almost broken and with little variation in thickness. White is found in the form of lines and splashes, so minute that they are of little importance.

All examples of Blue Fleuri that I have examined have been very similar.

Grey or blue marbles are rare and, as the use of neutral colour in any form of decoration is often an advantage, Blue Fleuri is most useful. Simply and quickly reproduced, Blue Fleuri is suitable for use on large-scale work such as wall fillings and dados in public buildings.

Other Grey Marbles: Dove marble and Bardilla are in the same class as Blue Fleuri, with only slight variations in the colour or veining. They fulfil the same purpose in decorative marbling.

Origin: France, Spain and Italy.

Ground: Off white to light grey, prepared from white and touches of black and ultra-marine.

Palette: Black, white and ultramarine.

In the Dipper: One part of oil to two parts of turpentine, with a few drops of terebine.

Brushes and Tools: Tools, fitches, pencils (either hog or sable) and the hog-hair softener.

Method: Rub in a thin glaze of medium-toned grey, prepared from white, black, a touch of ultramarine and thinners from the dipper.

Using the sponge, stipple in places a slightly darker tone of grey; this will partly mix into the thin coat of paint and, although submerged, it will spread out when softened in a later process and show up a little stronger.

The stippling should be carried out in the same direction as the flow of the marble lines. Using the side of the brush or a piece of rag take out some colour almost to the background where the larger shapes are to fall.

Charge your pencil with a darker grey than was used for the stipple and commence to put in the darker veins. I often use two pencils held about three inches apart in one hand, but this should not

Blue Fleuri in three stages

be attempted until the use of one is completely mastered.

Commence to draw in the top right-hand corner and work a broad band of veins downwards and continue until the panel is covered.

Keep the stone shapes narrow, from a half to two inches wide and from two to seven inches long.

Work carefully and make variations of tone and colour in the veining.

Also, vary the size of the stones, drawing carefully and making trembling and broken rather than clean-cut lines.

The slope of both vertical and horizontal lines should be in the same direction, slightly left to right or right to left, all angles going off at a tangent and never at right angles.

By putting in some points of dark grey just at the junctions of the cross veins a brighter, sharper appearance is obtained.

Soften vigorously in the same direction as the long veins, but only soften lightly across. This tends to give a woolly appearance.

With a fitch, fill in some of the stones with a lighter grey, paint others in with a darker colour and soften to take out the brush marks. Your work should then be complete.

Should an accurate representation be desired, it will be best to allow time for the work to dry before filling in the stones, when more detail can be put into the work.

Before glazing, the surface should be softened with an oily rag.

Common Errors: Filling the space with too much veining with lines too wide and too dark.

Other Marbles which Harmonise: White-veined marbles, Sienna Marble, Vert Campan, Breche Violette, Jaune-Larmartine, Golden Onyx, Rouge Royal, Skyros and Paonazzo.

The Painted Examples: Three stages of working are shown.

In No. 1 the grey glaze has been applied and slightly shaded with a darker grey.

No. 2 shows the sponge stipple effect with the veins painted but not softened. The thick, heavy lines of colour can be clearly recognised.

In No. 3 the hog-hair softener has been used vigorously and a slight overglaze of colour applied after the first surface was hard and dry.

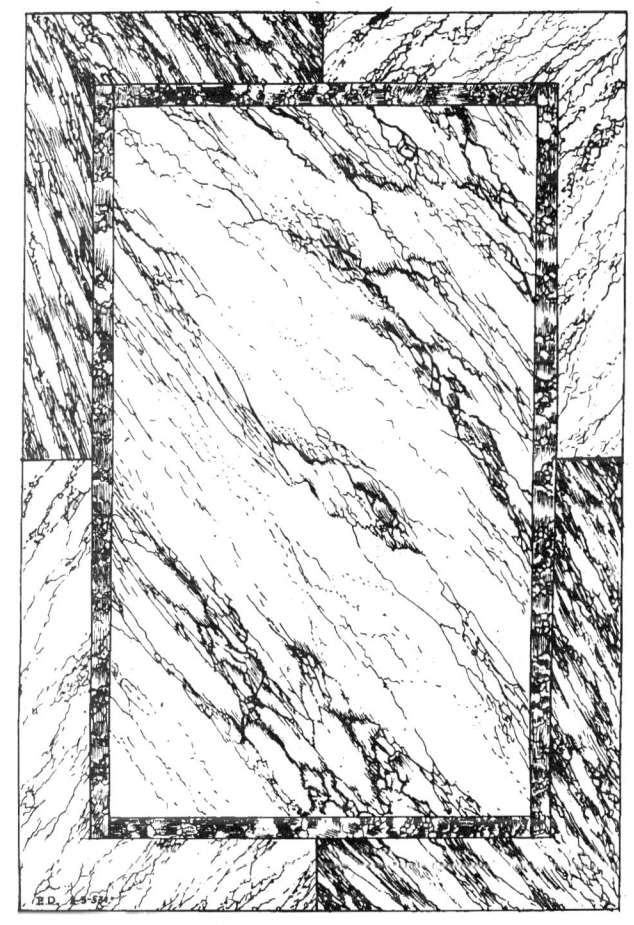

Drawing of Blue Fleuri by Mr Dobson. The border is of Carrara, and the inlay of Convent Sienna Marble

The Graining of Teak

THE graining of teak is a comparatively lazy process, much of the work consisting of a plain flogged ground. The heartwood drawing is not very complicated and can be soon mastered.

Used in the exterior construction of railway passenger coaches, teak has been also a popular wood in shipbuilding.

It has great strength and durability; thus, any position that calls for these qualities is suitable for its reproduction in paint.

Teak was used in building more than 2,000 years ago in the Persian Gulf, where whole townships were entirely built of it.

During the dry season the tree is leafless; in hot localities the leaves fall in January and the tree remains leafless until the monsoon rains arrive.

The leaves are large, up to two feet in length and twelve inches wide, resembling those of the tobacco plant, but they are hard and the surface rough.

The wood is heavy, often 46 lb. per cubic foot when seasoned, and, when freshly cut, will not even float in water.

The leaves of teak are used by the natives to dye silk and cotton red.

They are also used for wrapping parcels, thatching roofs and for culinary purposes.

The trees are quick growing at first, and will survive up to 200 years, but they do not grow to a great height, even under favourable conditions.

Over the past century several thousand square miles have been devoted to the cultivation of this useful tree.

Description: Teak is a rather coarse grained wood, and contains quite a large number of short grain markings, such as we associate with oak.

Its colour is a light golden brown when freshly cut, darkening with age to a red mahogany colour. The heartwood markings are a deeper tone.

The grain markings are fairly stable, containing a number of oval centre shapes, at all times quiet and plain. They are spaced from one to four or five inches apart, showing a background of flat tone with a flogged texture.

The timber has a strong aromatic fragrance which it retains to a great age.

A little shading is noticed across the curved side grain, but only in a few examples is it prominent.

Origin: Teak requires a tropical climate and the most prolific teak forests are found in the monsoon countries of Burma, India, Java and the Philippine Islands.

Painted example of Teak

Tools: Tools, fitches and flogger.

Ground: A warm medium buff colour, composed of white, Italian ochre, orange chrome and a touch of umber.

Palette: Burnt umber and burnt sienna.

In the Dipper: One part of linseed oil, one of clear glaze, two parts of turpentine, and a few drops of terebine driers.

Method: There are several methods that can be employed in the graining of Teak.

I will, however, describe the one I used to produce the painted illustration to this article.

A small amount of scumble was prepared in a kettle, using the medium from the dipper and a knife point of burnt sienna and burnt umber.

This was applied sparingly, to hold the subsequent flogging and to receive the grain markings.

Having studied the positions where the heartwood markings were to be placed, slightly darker colour was worked around these areas.

The rubbing-in almost amounted to the first drawing of the grain, the lightest part being where the markings or centres were being placed.

The side of the rubbing-in brush helped much in this preliminary operation.

With a fitch, charged with burnt umber in a fairly dry state, the markings were carried out.

Recently I examined teak in preparation for this article, and found only about one panel in every ten was well marked.

Therefore a large amount of straight grain and very little figure is required in graining teak.

The end of a fitch was used on the scumbled surface to make the narrow light line in the heartwood marking which adjoins the dark line; both are very narrow and nowhere more than a quarter of an inch wide.

The flogger was then carefully used in general all over the panel.

This has a softening effect on all the previous work, but it must only be used once or the dark sharp line will spread out too wide.

A good stiff dry mottler was used to bring out some light before the work had set. No further softening was necessary.

Drawing of Burma Teak by Mr Dobson

Breche Blanche

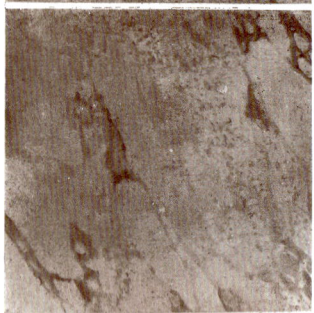

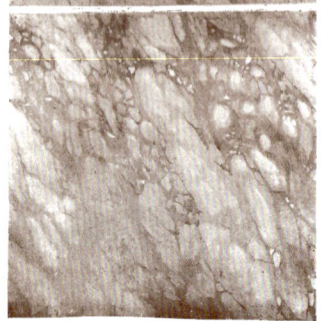

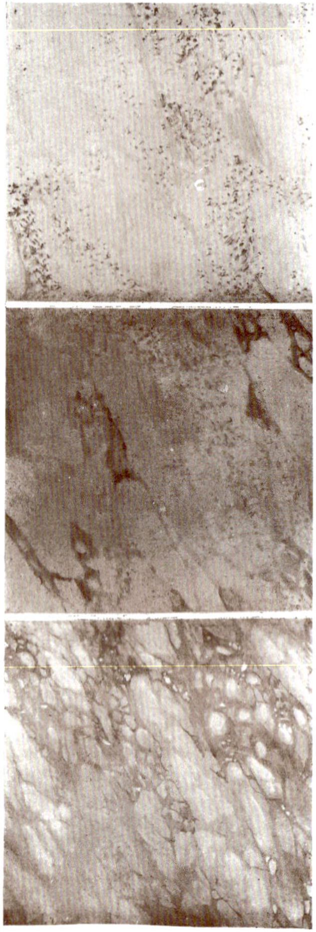

THE French name Breche Blanche means broken white. The painted marble so named is used extensively in French and Belgium cities.

It has long been popular for the decoration of the large staircases of blocks of flats and large apartment houses, probably because it is cheerful and reflects light well.

Breche Blanche is one of the key marbles, from which many others can be worked by simply adding other colours.

In using it as a basis of study, all our efforts should be concentrated on the drawing of the markings and the shapes of the stones.

The word brescia, as applied to marble, has been so important to Italy that a northern province has been given the name of Bresciano.

One-third of the province is occupied by the great chain of Alps above the fertile plains of Lombardy, which produce heavy crops of fruit and corn.

The foothills are covered with orchards, and the mountainous parts yield iron, copper, marble, alabastine and granite.

The capital town, Brescia, had a population of 80,000 some hundred years ago.

It contains many fine collections of antiques, notably pottery and Roman monuments of great historical interest, still in good condition.

The Temple of Hercules (God of Strength), which was built by Vespasian, was excavated in 1802, and is a masterpiece of classic art.

Brescia marbles are most frequently found near volcanoes; underground explosions of steam and molten lava have been responsible for the breaking or shattering of the rock in these mountainous areas.

Hence the sharp fragments of rock that form into groups in Brescia marbles, as opposed to the rounded, water-worn conglomerates that have been transported some distance, and have, in the process, lost their sharp edges.

Composition: The soft grey-white which forms the background of Breche Blanche is a crystalline limestone of great age. Above this layer of hard limestone lay beds of carbon and iron.

After the shattering by explosion, and later subsidence, the yellow grey vegetable matter has been water-carried down into the fissures, filling them with sediment.

Heavy pressure over millions of years has hardened the mass sufficiently to form a marble that takes a good polish with friction.

Description: Breche Blanche is a vigorously marked marble in light tones of grey. The fragments of near-white which form the stone shapes are angular, varying in length from 3 inches to about 3 feet.

The smaller shapes are usually grouped together,

Breche Blanche in three stages

but do not run evenly around the larger stones.

One pleasant feature is a long soft line of grey, which sometimes forms the side of a stone, at other times running alone across perhaps three large open shapes.

Small, fine, soft lines of veining are to be found in the larger stones. The grey matrix is of broken texture, like a sponge stipple effect.

Origin: The Italian Alps.

Palette: Black, white, yellow ochre and ultramarine blue.

Ground: White.

In the Dipper: One part oil to two of turps.

Tools and Sundries: Sponge, tool, fitches, hog hair pencils and hog hair softener.

Method: Rub in a thin steady coat of white and pale grey, the shady streaks following the line of the marble. Charge the sponge with pale grey and stipple in parts, heavier where the smaller stones are to be placed.

Soften lightly with the hog hair softener, brushing vertically or in line with the marble.

With your pencils charged with a medium to light tone of grey, proceed to paint in the outlines of your largest stones. Next tackle the medium sized shapes, working round them but not with an even line.

The drawing is at all times sharp and angular, taking perhaps a heavy line down one side and a broken line on the other. Continue with the remaining areas, filling them with smaller work; the sponge will complete much of this.

In the sponge stippling, however, care must be exercised or dark grey masses will emerge.

Soften gently on the areas where the smaller work is placed and vigorously over the remainder.

Glazing: For a satisfactory finish, glazing is always necessary; it will be observed that the work has dried much darker than was anticipated. This is often due to the spreading of the grey with the softener.

If the time factor, however, does not justify glazing as a separate operation, something can be done at the end of the marbling operation before the surface is dry, though this method is not desirable.

Oil in the surface – sparingly – with medium from the dipper and a rag.

Charge the sponge with white zinc or titanium, but no lead, because lead soon turns yellow when used as a glaze. Then stipple out well, to give an effect like snow-flakes all over the surface.

With your fitch proceed to paint in the centres of most of the larger stones. Soften lightly, particularly over the snow-flakes.

Sharpen up a few lines with stronger grey in places, when your work should be complete.

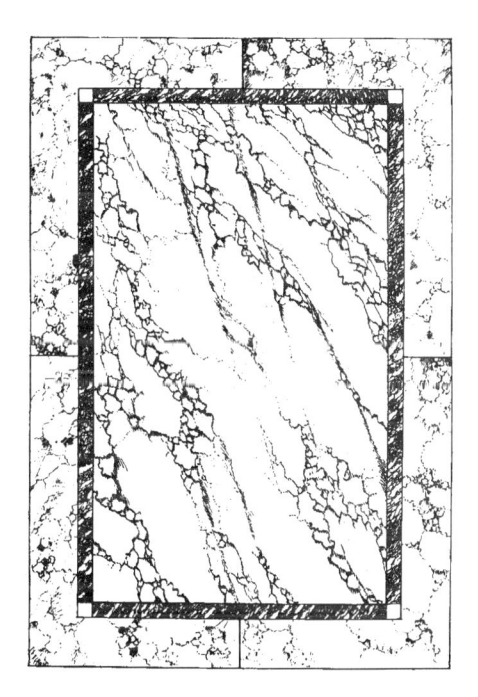

Other Harmonising Marbles: Sienna, Jaune Lamartine, Napoleon, Serancolin, Blue Fleuri, and Breche Caroline.

Illustrations: Three stages of progress are shown in the painted examples. The sponge stipple and preliminary setting out are shown in No.1. No. 2 shows more and heavier work, along with vigorous softening with the hog hair. In No. 3 there is more fitch work and the glazing has been carried out.

Heartwood Markings of English Oak

Painted example of Oak Heartwood by Mr Dobson

GOOD examples of the figure of oak are not easy to find; most of them are plain, small, dull and uninteresting. But this does not apply to heartwood markings which are more plentiful and of a much better quality.

A young tree of, say, two centuries of age, with a trunk of some thirty feet in height, produces a total of four hundred half ring markings. Branches have the same number of rings as their years of age.

On a twenty year old sapling that I have examined I found twelve branches; three or four of these will live to full maturity of the tree while the others may be lost by storm damage or trimmed off by the forester.

In any event, they will be represented by a knot when the tree has fully grown.

Thus, when the number of rings runs into thousands, oak becomes well adorned with heartwood markings.

At the saw mills most of the heavy trunks are cut into straight consecutive one inch boards. Thus, only five of the centre planks show figure of any description but all, however, may show some heartwood markings.

The upper arched terminal of every annulation will produce a heartwood marking down the centre of the tree. These markings are not equally spaced but depend on the quickness of growth, which is much slower as the tree gets older. A dry or wet season seriously affects the width of the dark or light spaces.

The bending of the trunk in growth, due to wind pressure, and the growth of the branches have a marked influence on the beauty of the heartwood markings.

In cutting, quite a large number of annulations are crossed due to the taper of the trunk from the base to the top.

The most interesting markings are to be found half-way towards the centre of the trunk, opposite a large branch, and running parellel to the bark.

Markings on the outer side of this point are inclined to be coarse, while nearer the centre they start to include the figure.

With grainers, heartwood markings have never been as popular as figured or quartered oak. Many reasons could be put forward for this, one being that figure graining is neater in appearance.

Here I wish to deal with heartwood grained by the 'paint-on' rather than the 'wipe-out' method which I described in the J.D.A. last October.

In some circles the 'wipe-out' method has long

been considered as an out-of-date process and only suitable for cottages and kitchens.

Possibly its unpopularity is due to the fact that grainers of moderate skill find it a difficult method. In the 'paint-on' method the chances of success are far greater for the average painter.

There are a few grainers who can produce a satisfactory and pleasing effect by either method.

During my early youth in the West Riding the 'wipe-out' method was popular but later, on the Continent, the 'paint-on' method only was used.

Description
It should be noted that the lighter coloured portions are three to four times wider than the darker portions.

Ground
The ground may range from a pale cream to a dark buff according to the type of oak to be grained.

Tools and Sundries
Brushes for rubbing in, brush grainer, flogger, hog hair softener, hog hair fitches, steel graining combs, and clean washed rags.

Method
Prepare a small amount of thin scumble glaze in a kettle, only a tone darker than the ground. Apply sparingly, scrub off with a rag down the centre of the panels or any place where you intend to paint in the markings.

If a very sharp contrast is required, the rag may be used in places to wipe the background almost dry.

With the small fitch or worn writing pencil commence to paint in the heartwood markings; the colour should be a little rounder than the scumble glaze.

I have always got the best results by using keg colour. If, however, a soft effect is desired, the thinned colour from the bottom of the kettle should suffice.

It is much easier to paint in a narrow line than a wide one. The pencilled markings should fade gently away into the side grain, which may be helped by dabbing with rag.

Proceed to brush-grain the side grain; flogging or combing may be introduced according to the finished effect desired.

Allow to stand for anything up to thirty minutes, when the hog hair softener may be drawn inwards towards the centre of the principal knots. If the effect is still too hard, the flogger may be used lightly.

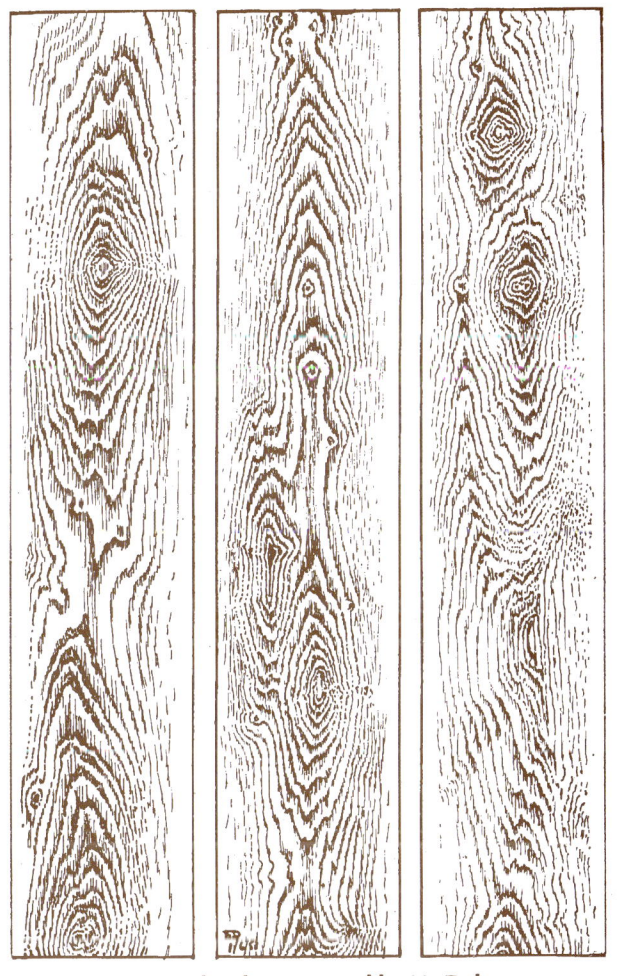

Drawing of Oak Heartwood by Mr Dobson

Walnut

THE home of the walnut tree is on the sunny mountains of Greece and Asia Minor. It was introduced into England in the fifteenth century for the sake of its nuts as well as its timber. The leaf buds are arranged spirally on the twig. The buds are round and the olive-green under-casing bursts through the two outer (and darker) scales. When the leaves first appear they have a fine orange colour. At the same time, the long male catkins are conspicuous, while the small female flowers at the ends of the same twig have to be looked for more carefully. The large leaves are made up of from five to nine smooth-edged, oval leaflets. The hard shelled walnuts have a thick fleshy covering which splits and dries when the nut is ripe. In winter the walnut tree is easily mistaken for an oak, until the rough silver grey trunk and the smooth thick twigs are noticed.

Walnut is one of the most valuable timbers grown in Britain, yet only a few trees are to be found. It is greyish brown in colour with streaks running through it and is light and tough. Though not as plentiful as the conifer or sycamore, there is compensation in its quality and value. Unlike many British timbers, it takes a fine polish. Because of the figuring, especially in the burrs, it is much used for fine furniture.

The golden age of walnut was in the reign of Queen Anne, when tapestry seated chairs and grandfather clocks were made out of the solid walnut; since then, however, it has been mostly used as a veneer on pine-made furniture.

Description: The walnut of Greece has always appealed to me. The colour is a cool pale brown, less inclined to green than is Italian, and less elaborate in detail in the heartwood markings. It has a quiet rich dignity in both design and colour, and a softer texture in the veining. This effect is comparatively easy to obtain with painters' materials, though it involves an amount of labour which would be justified only under the best conditions. Grainers like to give of their best, but they can do so only by adopting the correct sequence of processes.

Ground: A medium to light, cool buff colour prepared from ochre, white, black and a touch of orange.

Palette: Black in turpentine, Indian or Venetian red, and burnt Turkey umber.

In the Dippers: One with turpentine only, another with equal parts raw linseed and turpentine with a touch of terebine.

Tools and Sundries: A few one and two inch tools (for rubbing in both oil and water colour), flogger, badger, hog-hair softener, a few fitches, sable pencil overgrainer, hog hair fantail, rag and a small piece of hessian. My example was grained with a tool of my own make. Two squirrel water colour brushes were each divided and bound with thread into two parts. An inch block of wood was then attached to the two brushes, near the ferrule, and secured with rose wire. This gave me four "accidental" lines of colour.

Method: For a medium or dark example, the most natural effect is obtained from a flogged ground, which must be very thin and is obtained from a glaze made solely of vandyke brown. In the lighter examples this glaze can be dispensed with, though the finer texture will be lost.

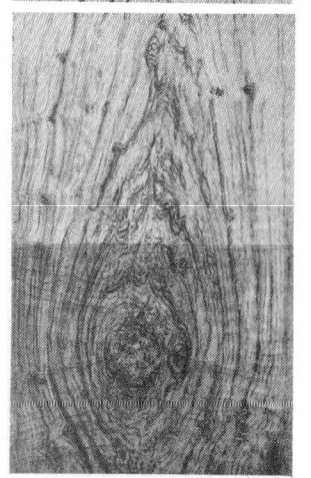

Examples 1 to 4

When the flogging is hard and bone dry, rub in a glaze of the oily thinners with just a touch of burnt umber. Care should be taken not to disturb the flogging. Rub as little as possible, and work the same way as the grain. A little shadiness in this direction is desirable however; no crossing should be attempted. I prefer a soft effect using an amount of thinners that is on the liberal side, but just avoiding the running stage. For a hard contrasting effect the glaze must be kept dry, the surplus being removed with rag in the direction of the grain. Should a little of the flogging be removed it is often all to the good.

With the overgrainer charged with red and turpentine, proceed to draw in the grain markings; red will be found at intervals of three or four inches showing very light in the background of the grain.

In a few examples traces of blue or green are to be found, but I have omitted these from the palette because of their rarity. We could, however, include them at this stage in place of the red, before the darker veins are put in.

The main lines of grain are all executed in thin black. Turpentine is the only thinner used here. The small amount of umber in the glaze will give a warmer effect.

Starting near the centre of a heart, proceed to draw in the shapes with the over-grainer. If the effect is too solid, turpentine only can be used to open out the grain. Should the work get too wet, a rag may be dabbed on to remove the surplus, but do not rub over the surface.

When a good general effect is obtained, a short fitch charged with black may be gently scrubbed down a few of the main lines of grain.

The canvas, wrapped in a square pod, should be drawn down the side grain, or in places amongst the complicated drawing. It will be noticed that every movement of the canvas is valuable in the making of fine grain and texture; it is almost a substitute for mottling.

When the grain is complete, soften gently with the hog-hair softener. A few small knots should be added with a fitch, and fine lines drawn around them with the end of the wood handle.

Glazing: Very little glazing is required. It should be carried out with vandyke and blue-black, ground in water.

The Drawings: These show three planks of Greek walnut each eight feet high.

Painted Examples: Example One shows a flogged ground of fine texture. There was no varnishing or fixing of any kind. It is clearly visible in the other stages.

Example Two shows the thin glaze of burnt umber with the preliminary drawing of the red lines, which were carried out with my squirrel hair pencils. Part of the flogging was rubbed away during the application of the ground glaze but the effect did not suffer.

In Example Three, the black and turpentine have been worked in, the knots have been added and the side grain run down with the hessian. A fitch has sharpened up the grain.

Glazing in Example Four completes the processes. It was carried out in water colour and softened with the badger. A little mottling is to be seen.

Black and Gold Marble

Painted example of Black & Gold, Border Egyptian Green Marble

IN my early days I was fortunate to be placed under a great craft teacher of the old school, who had collected a large number of marble samples to help us with our marbling.

The heavy slabs of marble were strongly framed in oak and are still doing yeoman service after half a century of use.

Among this fine collection was a large, well veined panel of Black and Gold, which made a lasting impression on my mind, for good examples are rare.

Its correct name, "Portor", is a corruption of the Italian "Porto d'Oro."

Only in Great Britain is it referred to as Black and Gold.

In rich schemes of decoration in which marbles are employed, Black and Gold is very useful.

Many cafe and hotel dining rooms have been lined with it, providing a pleasing contrast to the dazzling whiteness of the table linen and the shimmer of the cutlery.

On the Institute's outing to Lyme Hall, Cheshire, an exceptional piece was seen in the form of a table top, measuring eight feet by five, and three inches in thickness.

It was a rich blue black in colour, smooth, well polished and preserved.

Origin
Most of it is quarried at Porto Venere, Liguria, Italy, but it is also found in Algiers and Corsica.

Composition
The black parts were originally carboniferous limestone and the white veins were chalk, now stained with iron to yellows, dull reds and light browns.

Description
The general impression is one of dull yellow chains of veining running, about a foot apart, more or less in the same direction, with a background of black, clouded over with tones of dark greys and blue black.

Careful examination reveals reds, brown and white, flecked and shaded into the narrow veins. On the upper side of the yellow a thin line of white is to be found.

Palette
White, pale yellow ochre, raw sienna, chrome yellow, burnt sienna, burnt turkey umber and black.

Tools and Brushes
Sable pencil, double pencils, fitch, sponge and hog hair softener.

Ground
Black.

In the Dipper
One part of linseed oil to two parts of turpentine, with a few drops of terebine added.

Method

Take a piece of clean rag, soaked lightly in liquid from the dipper, and oil in the ground.

With a fitch, place well thinned white on the palette, and from this charge the sponge.

Proceed to stipple the white on the black background to produce a cold transparent effect.

The white should be placed unevenly to give a crystalline effect. Soften lightly.

With a fitch apply grey, prepared from umber and black, in the form of stone shapes.

With the sable pencil, charged with ochre, raw sienna and white, slightly touch the other colours on the palette, turning the brush after touching each colour.

Ensure that each of the colours is of the same consistency; any hard colour should be broken down with the palette knife.

Proceed to sketch in the principal chains by making a fine stroke with the point of the pencil, then applying more pressure and rolling the side of the brush by a slight twist of the wrist which will blend all the colours.

Take care not to make a heavy line around any one stone.

When a couple of feet of the chain have been completed, the double pencil may be used.

All the finer work may be carried out with it, the one disadvantage being that it cannot be rolled as easily as a single brush.

A portion of the work should be done in a lighter tone of yellow than the remainder, preferably near the centre line, about one-third from the top of the panel.

With a fitch apply a little more yellow, brown or dull red in places on the chain. Line some edges with white or light yellow.

Fill in some of the stone shapes with more tones of grey. Soften lightly with the hog hair softener.

Glazing

This is only required for a very accurate representation.

Oil in with a rag, tinted with black. This glaze of black over the yellow gives a very rich effect, especially when warm yellows or a little orange are added in places.

The stone shapes may need a little more grey, until a satisfactory effect is produced.

Black and Gold Marble Panel, 6ft x 4ft, by Mr Dobson

Graining of Pollard Oak

ON account of its sound, practical value, the demand for Pollard Oak graining continues.

Contributing factors to its popularity are its bright cheerful colour, its ability to take knocks without being disfigured and the ease with which it can be rejuvenated by a coat of varnish.

The art of pollarding appears to be peculiar to the British Isles.

The graining of Pollard Oak was not included in the curriculum of the graining classes at the three European colleges which I attended, and perhaps I was unfortunate, but I never came across any painted examples in the many countries that I visited.

Pollarding

Pollarding calls for great skill and is carried out in many species of trees, but mainly in Oak, Willow and Vine.

The Vine is pollarded to kill the excessive growth and to guide the strength into the fruit-bearing branches.

In Oak, the pollarding is carried out for the purpose of producing fine marked timber for cabinet making or decoration.

Willow, growing along the edges of dykes, is pollarded to produce canes for basket making, and stumpy trunks for cricket bats.

Fine Pollard Oak is scarce and costly at the present time. Two main varieties of Oak, Pendunculate and Durmast, respond well to pollarding which is carried out when the trees have almost reached maturity.

The first operation is to cut out the top or leading branch. Small branches then soon grow around the cut and, when these are subsequently removed, more new branches are formed.

Where pollarding is done several times the production of successive crops of new branches, each producing a knot, causes the timber near the branches to resemble that of a burr on the trunk.

Burrs on the outside of the trunk found in Ash, Walnut, Redwood, etc., are, however, the result of irritation in the tree itself and not of pollarding.

Large Knots Undesirable

Large knots are not desirable in Pollard Oak, as they are the result of an interval of too many years between cuts.

The best grain markings are obtained from trees that have been pollarded regularly.

The more attractively marked pieces of Pollard Oak are always structurally weak. To-day, they are used in the form of veneer.

The constant exposure of freshly cut surfaces encourages attack by fungi; these travel quickly down the centre of the branch, spreading outwards from the knot. Few good examples of

Painted example of bleached Pollard Oak Burr by Mr Dobson

Pollard Oak are found which do not need to have these knots replaced.

Description

Pollard Oak is of a cheerful orange. buff colour and usually of medium tone. The various types of grain markings with which it is always well covered are in a warm burnt umber, varying from soft faint transparent short lines to heavy solid markings.

Most of the grain softens from umber to raw sienna on both edges of the line markings.

The main features of Pollard Oak Burr are knots connected together by a series of broken wavy lines. The knots are found in large groups, mixed with a few that are very fine in texture, giving almost a sponged effect.

Others are found as hollow oval shapes spread about among the wavy lines and are open in character.

A small amount of figure is found among the wavy lines of grain In general, Pollard Oak is wild in appearance and so the figure should not be emphasised.

In the heavily marked wood, heartwood markings are found scattered about.

(To be continued)

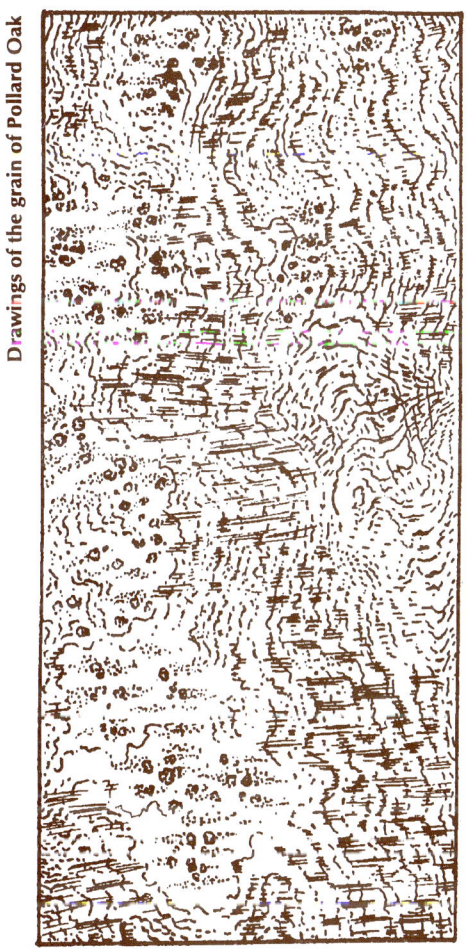

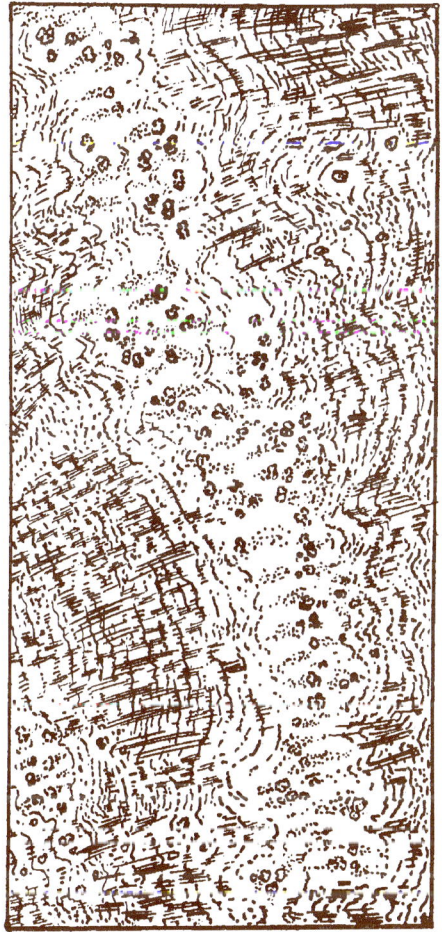

Drawings of the grain of Pollard Oak

Graining of Pollard Oak

(Continued)

DRAWINGS: The drawings in this issue are of the plainer type of Pollard Oak markings, taken from timber cut from planks deep in the trunk. The effect of the pollarding is not as marked as it is on the outer sides of the tree, with which we dealt in the last issue. Both the mottle and the knots are fewer and quieter.

Pollard Oak of the plainer type, with its long, soft, wavy lines, is well suited to modern tests in graining, as on large flat doors. The three examples have been drawn for this purpose in response to the many requests from readers. I hope to deal with other requests from time to time.

In the first drawing the door is quartered with the grain running slightly diagonally. The few knots arranged near the centre make an interesting shape when reversed four times. This idea is simple to carry out, and is a popular method of dealing with large surface.

The central door is divided in half by line running from top to bottom. Both halves are alike, but the most interesting work is reversed down the middle of the door. To emphasise the division, part of the work near the line is made darker on one side than on the other.

The third drawing is much heavier, and again is quartered, though no particular interest is given to the central meeting of the four quarters. The two heavier lines running with the grain, one near the centre, the other on the outer edge, give the door a massive, almost clumsy appearance. This I have drawn to demonstrate the neatness of this method of arranging the interest near the centre.

When quartering or halving, I prefer to work one half or two quarters at a time, allowing this to dry or at least to set before completing the rest. This should present very little difficulty today, with our fast setting materials. On a small job the first two hours in a morning and the last in the afternoon will give at least a set, though I prefer to wait overnight. I should continue on a large job doing all the first halves even if this entailed several days' work to allow perfect hardening; working is so much cleaner when the surface is really hard.

For cleaning the edges a damp rag or one slightly softened with linseed oil is desirable. Never use turpentine, however. Some grainers use adhesive tape. This, however, requires just as much cleaning after use to remove all the sticky gum; thus little time is saved, if any.

In using rag for cleaning down a line, fold it into a small pad with a square edge. Press on this square edge with the ball of the thumb and run it down the edge of the line; but do not wrap the rag around the thumb. If cross bands are used, grain them always first, as a little colour on the usually darker surface of this work will not greatly matter.

In graining the second half of the door, do not remove all the colour in the wiping-out process. A

Painted example of Pollard Oak

very clean cut edge will show with the first line, which will be emphasised with a little additional colour, just softened away at the edge.

Ground Colour: Medium orange, buff colour.

Tools and Sundries: A well worn two inch tool, hog hair fantail overgrainer, sponge, fitches, rag, worn writing pencil and hog hair softener.

Palette: Raw sienna, burnt sienna and burnt turkey umber.

In the Dippers: Oil one part, turpentine two parts, a few drops of terebine. Second dipper, turpentine only.

Method: Rub in a thin glaze of raw sienna and burnt umber well thinned with the oil medium. In the drawing the rubbing-in brush can be very helpful, and should follow the lines of grain. A dabbing and shaded effect should be obtained as a background to the knotted parts.

I often use newsprint, rolled into a ball, to prepare the ground before graining. This must be done carefully just where the lines of grain are to be followed. These will show through the completed work even after glazing. A twisting motion should be used for the arrangement of the knots, and no colour should be added with the paper.

Should a very light coloured example be required a handful of clean rag is the best, as the rags pick up some colour, whilst the paper pushes it on to one side. Soften with the hog hair softener. Charge the fantail overgrainer with turpentine and burnt umber. A worn tool cut down into a series of teeth gives a more accidental look than the fantail. Amongst my graining kit I have several of these tools of varying widths, which are very useful.

Commence with the short wavy grain about the knots near the centre of the panel. The lines are at all times broken – simply by lifting the brush. A secondary number of short lines run across the main ones; they should be put in at the same time.

Variety in the grain is the main feature of Pollard Oak. At all times leave plenty of space for both the groups and the isolated single knots, which have almost a clear ring of plain background around them.

Stop the line drawing in good time, returning to fill in afterwards.

With a small piece of sponge charged with umber colour dab in a few fine points of dark brown; the larger knots may also be put in with the sponge, using a small point between two fingers. To give prominence leave some space around the larger knot.

With a dry fantail proceed to rub across the grain in places, to break up the markings that are too strong or too even.

A little colour may be applied also across the run of the grain.

If a wet dirty appearance has developed in places, this can be removed by rag rolling.

A worn fitch should be used to complete the knots, whilst a pencil is useful in final work near them.

A little figuring, winding about near the knots, completes the work. The whole should be carefully softened with the hog hair.

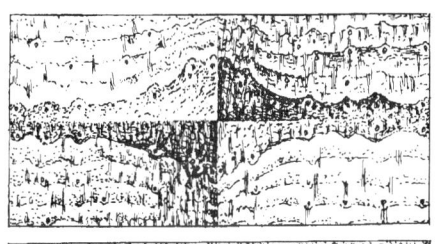

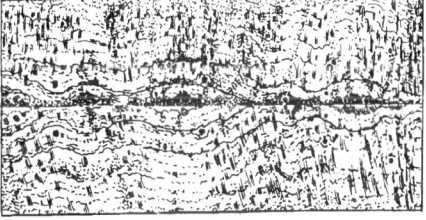

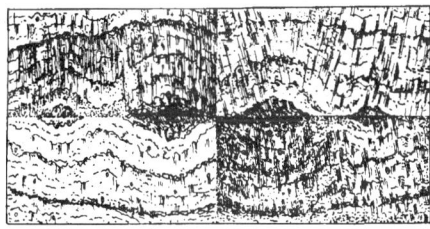

Drawings of Pollard Oak on flat panel doors

151

Serancolin Marble

THIS fine, gaily coloured marble may well have inspired many of the schemes of interior decoration or the daring examples of heraldry that were on view at the Apprentices' Exhibition at Harrogate.

The marble has a duck egg blue ground, which emphasises the vermilion streaky veins in a most striking way.

It is most suitable for pillars or pilasters in large rooms with painted walls.

We find the spelling of the word 'Serancolin' is changed slightly in many books and "sar-" or "serr-" is used.

Origin

France, the valley of the Adour in the Pyrenees, an area of volcanic rocks, hot springs and mines of copper, lead, silver, cobalt and iron.

The existence of these metals in the rock has given the bright colours to Serancolin marble.

Description

The general appearance of the marble is of a blue grey, medium to light in tone.

About a quarter of the coloured ground is covered with a sponge texture effect of grey and pink.

The remainder is glazed with a deeper cool grey and thin yellow glaze. Veining is in pink, grey and red with a small amount of yellow, all of which are darker than the ground.

Quite a lot of white is used in the glazing, as well as stronger lines of yellow and white in the cross veining.

Brocatelle markings are found even inside the larger stones; most of these lines are pale grey, white and ochre yellow.

Heavy breccia markings are largely red, varying from almost Indian to salmon pink, with a little green-yellow.

The larger stone shapes are square or angular, running in bands and often resembling wood grain.

Good distinct streaks of pink are found in places running alongside the divisions of blue-grey veining.

Ground Colour:
White.

Palette
White, lemon chrome, yellow ochre, vermilion, Venetian red, ultramarine blue, black and a light tint composed of white, yellow ochre and Venetian red; a second colour composed of white, black and a touch of ochre.

Example of Serancolin Marble by Mr Dobson

Brushes and Sundries
Sponge, fitches, sable and hog hair pencils, and hog hair softener.

Method
Rub in a thin, fairly wet glaze composed of white and black, with a touch of ultramarine.

Charge the large hog hair pencil and the sponge with a grey slightly darker than that used for the rubbing in.

With these proceed to put in the drawing.

The larger stones may be defined and placed accurately, though the sponge work may be used down one side to avoid soiling the reds which will be used later.

The smaller work must only be carried out where it is to be left in grey.

It is important that the longer wavy line dividing the areas should be carefully put in with the same colour; some sponging down one side perhaps will help with the definition.

Charge the sponge with a pink composed of a tint of Venetian red, and stipple in a texture in some of the larger stone shapes, and among the breecia, according to taste.

With the large hog hair pencil, continue to draw in the coloured veinings with the pinky reds, followed by some smaller areas in lemon chrome darkened in places with yellow ochre and vermilion.

Care must be taken to keep the brushes and palette clean or everything on the panel soon becomes brown. Keep the bright colours separate. Rinse out the pencil.

Always dry the brush with the rag before making changes in colour.

Pink, yellow or grey fine pencilled veins occur in many of the larger stones where the sponge texture is not prominent. They must not be overdone.

The breccia marking on the finer, closer parts resembles that of Grand Antique, while the colouring is similar to Breche Violet.

Next, paint in the large cross veining which runs partly alongside some stones and cuts across others.

Use a sable for this work as it does not disturb the colour underneath quite as much as the hog hair.

The cross lines are in clear deliberate colour composed of white ochre and vermilion, to give prominence.

The whole should be well but carefully softened to give a transparent effect.

Glazing
Soften the whole panel sparingly with oil from the dipper, using the piece of rag.

With a large fitch, rub in a glaze of thin black mixed with yellow ochre over some areas, and clear thin vermilion on others.

Using a small short bristled fitch, sharpen with slightly darker colour some of the breccia markings; others may be treated with lighter colour.

The sponge should now be used with a tone of lighter colour on the close work, with very little on the masses. Soften lightly.

With the fitch, put in a glaze of white and chrome on a few of the smaller stones.

The same colour should be used to strengthen the yellow cross veining, which will have been subdued by the glazing.

Continue the process until all the colours are reasonably balanced. Soften lightly again.

Common Faults
The use of too much red; a small amount on a complementary ground makes a good display.

The masses being too large or too compact; they require a fair amount of semi-plain areas.

Insufficient variety of tone and colour.

The excessive use of opaque white.

Other Varieties That Harmonise
Vert Campon,
Rouge Royal,
Grand Antique,
Comblanchin,
Napoleon,
Vert-de-Mer,
Levante,
and all white marbles.

153

Oak Graining: Larger Figures

GOOD examples of oak graining consist of three distinct groups of figures.

The large figures are few in number, the medium figures cover more than half of the ground, and the small close figures are found in the side grain.

While recently investigating the use of figure sizes, I examined the front doors of a number of terrace houses built in a city suburb about 1910.

Ninety per cent were grained, and more than half were in figured oak.

On a number of the best grained doors all three sizes of figures had been used, while on others appeared only the medium figure.

Most grainers had used two sizes only, either the large and the medium, or the medium and the small.

It is usual for the beginner to use the medium sized figure first and then to adopt one of the other sizes according to taste.

Only when he becomes an accomplished grainer does he use all three types.

The large figure is the centre of attraction in a panel of graining, the medium figure running from and around it.

In many cases, the heavy figure is built up of a number of sections forming a small design.

This requires careful attention, not just a flick of the thumb. It must have good sharp points in places and a clear curve in others.

In general, the larger figures are congregated in two or three groups in a panel or, alternatively, they are arranged in rows down the centre or the edge.

Before placing any figure I make a mental note of what I propose to do, and keep carefully to it.

I start with the important large figures near the top of the moulding or architrave and then work the medium figures near them.

The outside small figures are brought along at the same time.

If the panel is not being glazed I proceed to soften out the secondary figure.

The effect is much improved by glazing however in either water or oil colour.

I fold the rag into a square edged pad to soften between the larger figures, or a few of the medium figures if they are sufficiently widely spaced to allow for softening.

The pad may be gently dabbed, or lightly slid, just

Figured oak by Mr Dobson

to take off a little colour, thus giving the effect of further secondary figure. This brings out the larger figure in relief.

As the larger figures are important they should be touched up with a fine graining horn and clean thin rag. Two tones of figure colour can be obtained by accurate draughtsmanship, keeping a thin clear line on the top edge.

In looking over the work, unwanted medium sized figures are often found; these can be easily removed by dapping with the pad.

After lifting the colour from one place the rag will deposit it in another.

With a small fitch or worn sable, a line of darker colour should be put in under the important figures.

For this purpose, the colour in the bottom of the paint kettle is strong enough, provided that it is not too thin.

The fitch will, of course, scrub it on, while the pencil will lightly apply it.

A few minutes afterwards the work should be examined to see that the colour has not run.

My illustration and painted example are from the Bolling Hall Museum, Bradford, Yorkshire, and are taken from specimens 600 to 800 years old.

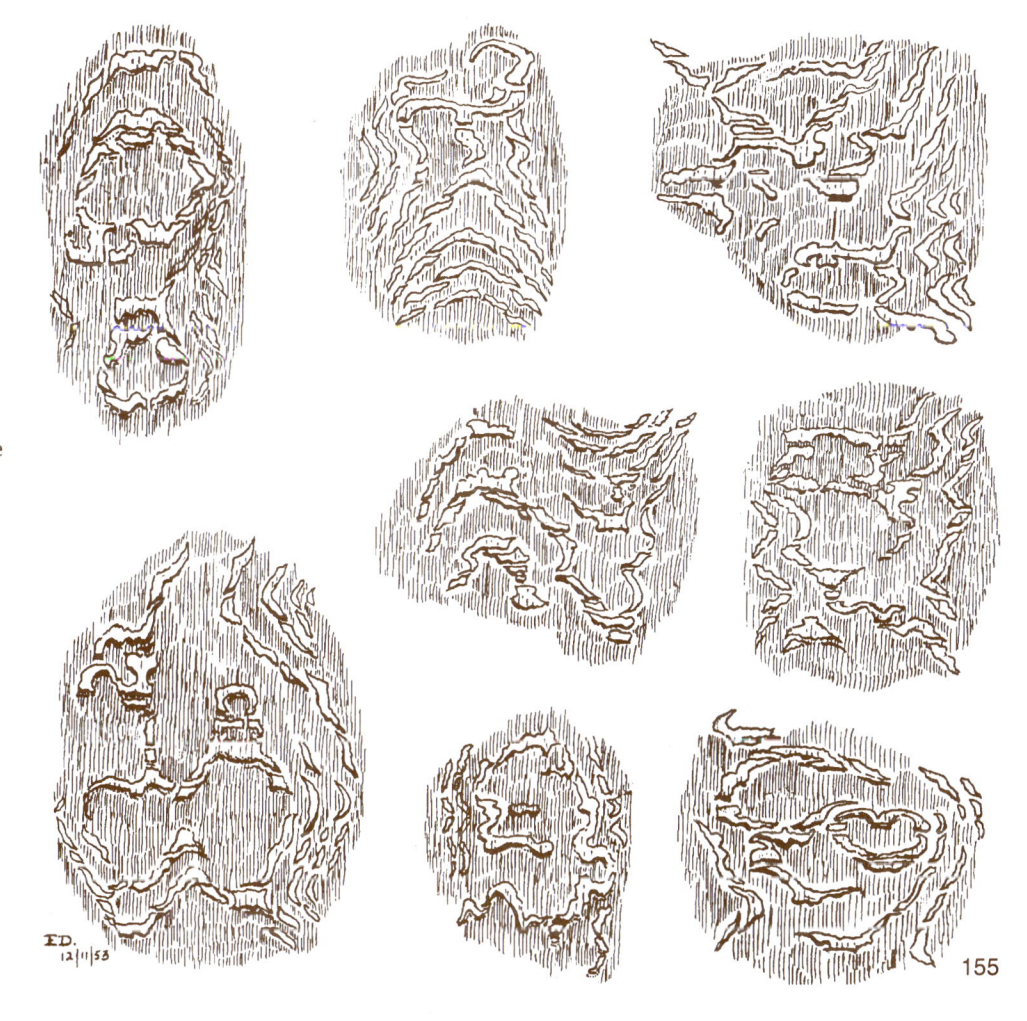

The Mottled Graining of Teak

THE mottled grain of teak, like the bird's eye in maple, is a rare type of an otherwise common wood.

Teak is not selected for its beauty of grain, but for its strength and durability. It is not cut, therefore, with the skill and care employed in the case of more decorative woods.

Drawings: The drawings this month are of teak heartwood, an interesting but simple wood, similar in its markings to American walnut.

The mottled portion is found down the side grain of the heartwood although all examples of heartwood do not contain mottle. The reproduction of mottle is better illustrated in the painted example.

I strongly recommend teak as a suitable wood for study and practise by the beginner.

The graining of mottled teak is far less complicated than that of mahogany, having a more evenly coloured ground glaze and also larger cuts with the mottler.

My drawings and painted panel are reproduced from the large entrance doors of a new Lancashire college of engineering.

The rails, panels and moulds were all constructed from timber with the familiar heartwood markings, while the styles were covered with mottle.

Origin: Teak is a timber commonly associated with Burma, but it is also native to India, and the best quality comes from Maulmain.

Teak contains a non-drying oil which makes it very durable, prevents the darkening of the wood and also the rusting of holdfasts or iron bolts used in framing it together.

The annular rings are near together, but regular and straight grown.

For outside use teak will last half-a-century without paint protection and will bleach to a beautiful light grey-brown colour.

Growth: Teak grows into a large spreading tree, with a life of two hundred years, but never attains a great height.

Its growth requires a high annual rainfall of upwards of fifty inches with an average temperature of not less than 75F.

Description: Mottled teak has mahogany-like markings, but from four to six inches wide.

In tone they are very similar to the ground, the average cuts being two inches deep, with quite a number of smaller ones dispersed at irregular intervals.

They taper away to a point on either side, giving variety to the mottle in both width and area.

The mottled grain appears to change from light to dark when viewed from a different angle, a quality that we cannot reproduce in graining.

No background streaks of darker colour are to be found as in mahogany, and the cuts of mottle are

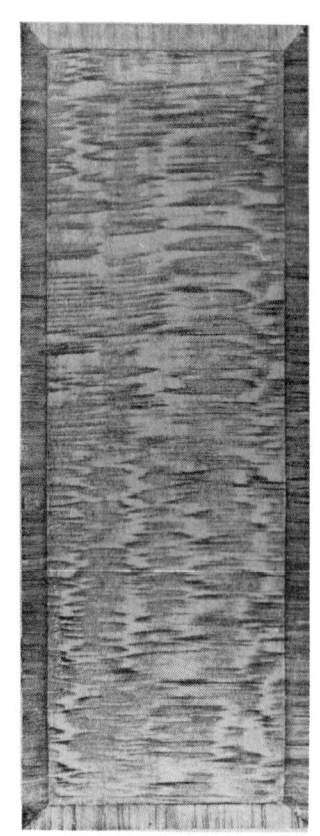

Painted example of mottled teak

made in broken lines down the pale glaze and are delicate and soft in appearance.

As in other varieties of teak, the ground is of a coarse texture made up of a number of short grain markings.

Tools: Two 2in. tools, flogger, hog hair pencil overgrainer, mottlers or cutters and badger.

Ground: A warm medium buff colour, composed of white, Italian ochre, orange chrome and a touch of umber.

Palette: Vandyke brown in water; or burnt umber and burnt sienna in oil.

In the Dipper: One part of linseed oil, one part of clear glaze, two parts of turpentine, and a few drops of terebine.

Beware of the searching qualities of white spirit on water colour graining.

Method: Rub in a thin coat of well-bound Vandyke brown in water, keeping it fairly wet.

Then flog with the flogger in an upward direction. A new horsehair dust brush is quite good for this purpose. Flog vigorously and allow at least four hours for drying.

The glaze for the mottling, using medium from the dipper and a small amount of colour from the palette, is now rubbed in.

For a cool effect use only the burnt umber, but the burnt sienna, rubbed in gently without crossing, may be added for a warmer colour.

With a small amount of the colour from the palette run down a few lines with the pencil overgrainer.

It they appear too hard, soften them by a few strokes with the flogger.

Mottling: The mottling, or cutting process, is carried over the grain markings while they are still wet.

In the painted example a rubber cutter was used, but other tools which may be used are a metal bound bristle cutter or a piece of cardboard with a slightly convex surface.

All are capable of producing good mottling with slightly different qualities.

The painted panel was carried out with four runs of the mottler from top to bottom of the panel.

Finally soften in a horizontal direction until a soft, pleasant effect is obtained.

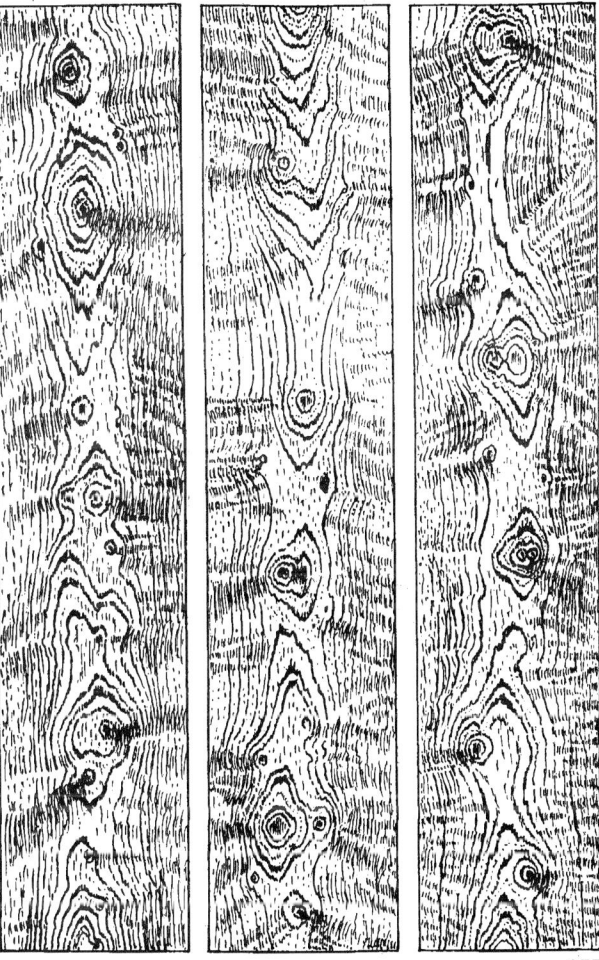

Convent Sienna Marble

THE reproduction of Convent Sienna marble, the most popular of the Sienna group, brought fame to many decorators in Britain during the last century.

In fact, during the past few months I have seen three remarkable examples; one at Sheffield by Mr. Zeph Carr, one at Manchester by the late Mr. W.G. Sutherland, and the other at Wakefield College of Art by the late Mr. Scott of Darlington.

They are masterpieces and well worthy of visits to the p. and d. departments of the local colleges where they can be seen on request.

Origin
Sienna Marble is quarried in Tuscany, a Northern province of Italy.

The name Convent originates from the Convent of Monterenti on whose land the quarries are found, situated on the upper slopes of a hill some three hours journey from Sienna.

The blocks of marble are first moved on skids and then wagons to Empoli, and from there to Leghorn for shipment abroad.

Description
Convent Sienna is a large scale marble with large chain formation markings, well suited for the decoration of important public buildings.

The general colouring is a rather dull tint of Oxford ochre or raw sienna, but traces of almost every other colour are to be found, either in the backgroung tints or with the burnt sienna vein markings.

Purple and black are found in the richest parts, and sometimes with orange as a background.

A milky-white glaze covers most of the lighter parts, with a heavy cross veining over the darker parts of a green-white to white.

Ground
White to cream.

Palette
White, lemon chrome, yellow ochre, black, raw sienna, Prussian blue and crimson lake.

Tools required
Tools, fitches, sponge, hog hair softener, rag, and worn pencils.

In the Dipper
Two parts of turpentine, one part of oil, and a few drops of terebine.

Method
As this marble is very colourful I shall give the Continental method, working on a wet painted ground of thin white from the palette instead of an oiled ground.

A considerable amount of bright colour applied in

Painted example by Mr Dobson

a transparent glaze on a white ground is difficult to control or place where required.

All light tints used should be mixed with a little white, while the general tone should be half the strength of the final colour required, thus allowing for the transparent coloured glaze.

Sketch the marbling, then lay in glazes of ochre and chrome, with some parts in orange, and soften well into the background colour.

The stone shapes can be further worked on with the sponge and fitches.

Texture may be given to some shapes, while others may have the edges darkened.

To obtain good results, all the principles in the use of colour must be observed.

Small areas of rich cream and warm sienna are later separated by a fine outline.

To keep the surface reasonably dry, a fitch should be used for the stronger tints of raw and burnt sienna, crimson lake and purple.

A sponge used on these heavier colours fairly soon breaks up and spreads the deeper, brighter colours where the heavy matrix markings are to be placed.

The background glazes will give a clear picture of the finished work, but be careful not to harm the good work already done while striving to improve it.

Soften the sponged work lightly, and the remainder vigorously.

Preliminary work may be carried out in water colour, and the veining with one or two pencils held near together in the same hand.

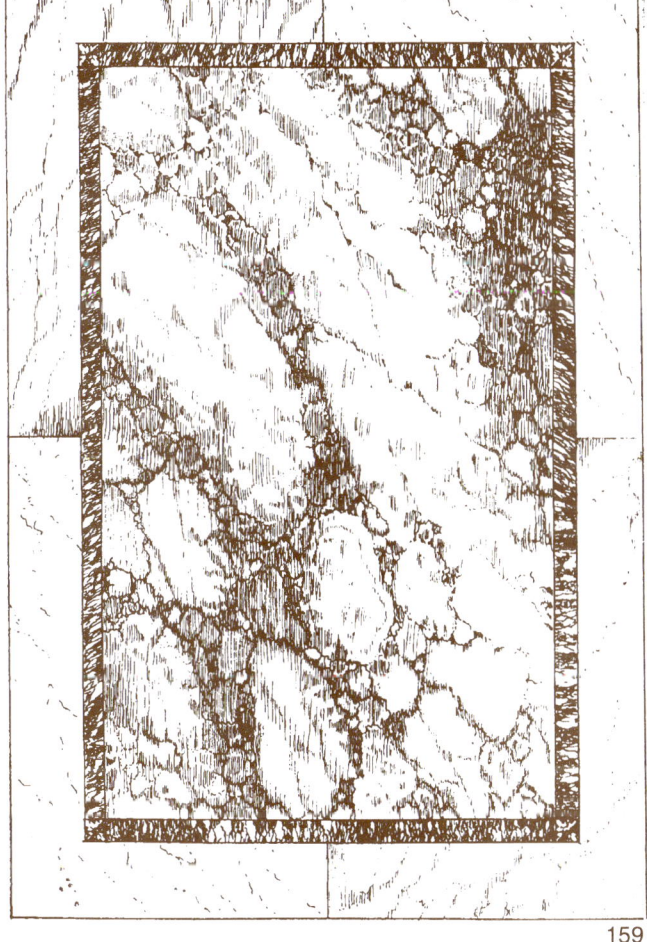

Drawing of Convent Sienna Marble by Mr Dobson

Satin Walnut

A FEW years ago wood carving, fretwork, and cabinet-making were hobbies of mine and the knowledge thus gained of the nature of the wood that I worked in has since been of great value to me.

Satin walnut was one of my favourite woods for it took on a good polish, had no hard annular rings, was free from splitting and cracking, and was, compared with such hardwoods as maple, oak or ash, easy to carve.

It is a light brown colour with very little grain markings and, though classed as a hardwood, is on the soft side.

In Britain it is also known as hazel pine, while abroad it goes by the names of sweet or red gum.

Although satin walnut is grown for its timber, it also produces some very decorative foliage.

In the inset in the drawing of the wood grain, is a sketch of the foliage.

In many cities where the tree will grow, avenues are lined with it because of its brilliant colouring.

Origin
In Southern Asia and the U.S.A. vast forests of the witch hazel family are found.

The tree grows a straight trunk often five feet in diameter and up to one hundred and fifty feet high, with a rough bark, corky winged branches and large deeply lobed leaves.

Botanical Name
Liquidamber styraciflua; the words "liquid amber" well describe the colour of our subject, the light varieties being of a milky yellow amber.

Balsam
The walnut tree produces copal-balsam, a fragrant gum resin, in a semi-liquid state.

This sticky substance is known locally as sweet gum, and is used for perfuming soaps, hair cream and tobacco.

Value
The importance of satin walnut in the world market may be assessed by the fact that in 1930 the cut of lumber in the U.S.A. alone amounted to 660 million cubic feet.

Description
Generally, satin walnut is a quietly marked, lightbrown to light-yellow wood.

The grain markings are of three distinct types; all are delicate and may be found in one piece of wood.

Ground
A light, cool, buff colour, composed of white, ochre, orange chrome and a touch of black.

The ochre and orange may be varied according to the yellowness required.

Palette
Raw umber, burnt and raw sienna, and black.

Painted example of Satin Walnut

Brushes and Tools

Fitches, tools, hog hair softener and fantail or equivalent brush. Clean washed rag.

In the Dippers

Two parts turpentine to one of linseed oil, and a few drops of terebine driers.

Method

Two methods may be adopted in oil colour, an oiled ground giving better representation.

The other method is to prepare a small amount of gilp coating for the surface, later wiping out the lighter portions and adding the darker ones.

Should a lighter effect be required or the minimum of work desired, I recommend the latter method.

With the first method the surface should be oiled with a rag, using the mixture from the dipper.

This must be applied freely but not too freely.

A glaze of umber should be worked in with a large fitch or one inch tool where required, and in the same manner add raw sienna, burnt sienna and lastly black.

As burnt sienna and black are the strongest colours, one can work over the previous glazes and they will still show.

Colour should be added with an almost dry brush, but some shapes should be left clear.

The hog hair softener may be used to test the colour for spreading; if too wet it will spread too easily but some may be taken off with a rag.

If no glaze is used, softening can be carried out most vigorously.

Prominent lines can be put in with the smaller fitch and the heartwood markings with the fantail.

Work with the fitch until a satisfactory effect is obtained, and then soften with the grain to complete the work.

Drawing of Satin Walnut and foliage by Mr Dobson

Black and Gold Marble

BLACK and gold marble may be worked on a black, grey or white ground.

This article outlines the method to be used on a white ground and when a first class effect is required on a small area.

A little time may be saved by using darker grounds, however, and by giving the veining only one coat of colour.

The late Mr. Will Cantrill of Manchester was a strong advocate of the use of light ground which is particularly suitable when marbling on stone, the numerous coats of paint, well rubbed down with punice block and water, thus acting as a filler of the coarse surface.

Origin: The name "Portor", by which the marble is known outside Great Britain, is dersived from the name of the Italian port – "Port d'Oro".

The marble was originally formed when a bed of white siliceous limestone was turned black by vegetable matter carried by water.

Later deposits of lime coloured with carbonates of iron, again carried by water, filled in the cracks opened by volcanic vibrations, thus forming the yellow veins.

Black and gold marble is attributed by many geologists to the Devonian Period when great changes took place in the formation of the earth's crust. Four great belts of the strata run across these islands.

The Devonian formation stretches fron Russia across Europe to the North American continent. It is a most valuable strata as it contains oil and gases derived from the organic matter trapped in the strata below.

Description: Black and gold marble consists of chain-like formations of yellow veining upon a field of broken black and greys.

Ground Colour: White to pale grey.

Palette: Black, pale yellow ochre, raw sienna, chrome yellow, burnt sienna, burnt turkey umber and white.

Tools and Brushes: Sable pencil, double pencils, fitch, sponge and hog hair softener.

In the Dipper: Three parts turpentine to one of linseed oil, with a few drops of terebine driers.

Method: Oil in the ground with medium from the dipper, thus allowing the pencils to work smoothly and with less wear.

Charge the large sable with colours from the palette, mainly yellows, and proceed to paint in the heavy portions of the marble in the traditional manner.

Turn the brush in the fingers to allow a blending of the colour as the work proceeds. Too much of the finer veining should not be put in at this stage.

Using a large fitch, begin to fill in the stone shaped openings with blacks and greys. This will

Painted example by Mr Dobson

take up a fair amount of time but should be done gently.

Do not attempt to fill in every little corner, a brighter and more sparkling efect is obtained when portions of the white background show.

For larger stones, run the fitch round the edges and fill in well with the sponge.

Tones of grey are obtained by using thinner colour, either darker or lighter, from the palette.

Shapes can also be varied by using a comparatively dry brush, the lines from the bristles remaining visible.

Again, texture can be reproduced by stippling with a sponge moistened with medium from the dipper. Care must be taken not to make the effect too severe.

Soften lightly with the hog hair softener, then touch up the yellow veining.

The end of the fitch handle may be used to make a few of the finer lines, little pressure being required but, to avoid the lines becoming submerged by the colour running over them, this work should be left until the medium is partly set.

No glazing or second coating is required.

Painted Example: Here the yellow veins can be seen running through a circle of the white background.

The black and grey filling of the stone shapes has been omitted to show more clearly the method of working.

Line drawing: This shows some of my tools and brushes, part of my marbling kit.

A number of these may be used, of course, for both graining and marbling.

They are:

1, glazing brush;

2, hog hair fitches;

3, palette knife;

4, sponge;

5, palette board and dipper;

6, chiqueter;

7, feather;

8, twin mops;

9, hog hair softener;

10, sable pencils;

11, twin sable pencils.

All, with the exception of Nos. 1, 6, 7 and 8, were used in the painting of the black and gold illustration.

The Graining of Mahogany

GOOD graining of mahogany is recognised by four qualities – colour, texture, mottling and design.

It is the mottling process I want to stress in this article. Mottle can be produced quickly with our present day materials by most craftsmen with a delicate touch. A quick responsive wrist movement is desirable, almost as light as the wings of a butterfly.

Graining at Blackpool: I am prompted to write on mahogany by recollections of the exhibition of the North Western Region at Blackpool, on which the committee are to be congratulated; it was a splendid show.

In a short report by "Jaybee," mention was made of a leather pattern, most skilfully designed by some "old master," and possibly the great Kershaw himself.

Mr. R. Barnett, of Bolton, had used it to produce mahogany graining which was unusually fine, even for Mr. Barnett, who, as a grainer of mahogany, has few equals. I recall a fine mahogany feather he showed in the Grundy Gallery some two years ago, which was a substantial advance on most of the panels grained during this generation.

The coach party of teachers and students from Burnley with which I travelled, was delighted with these studies and, like others, paid much attention to them.

Other Exhibition Work: Mahogany graining in public exhibitions and examinations over the past few years has left much to be desired. A few in the competition class at Harrogate showed that it is well taught in some colleges, which was refreshing and to be encouraged.

I seriously commend all students of graining to attend exhibitions where good work is on view. The stimulus it gives cannot be over-estimated, for it shows a goal that is attainable. With fine wood examples one is apt to despair, as no amount of study or practice will ever equal them.

One has greater confidence, however, on seeing work that has been done by a craftsman and which demonstrates that with guidance, study, a certain amount of ability and hard work, good results are obtainable.

Origins of Mahogany: Mahogany is grown in Africa, the West Indian Islands and to a small extent in South Europe.

Mottling is associated with all varieties, but in Cherry Mahogany it is more profuse than in the others; this variety was introduced into England about two hundred years ago.

Colour: This may be a light burnt sienna red to a deep blue crimson.

Tools and Sundries: Tools – overgrainer, sponge, badger hair softener, mottler and cutter.

The mottler should always have a good square edge; it must never be used for rubbing in or crossing of the colour, as, when the corners are rounded, the centre hollow and the bristle "V" shaped, its usefulness as an efficient tool is over.

The cutter is a thinner, shorter, bristled version of the mottler; for cutting in it is more efficient than the mottler.

Few of us are tempted to use it for rubbing in. Most grainers prefer the mottler, though it is more difficult to use.

A piece of cardboard or rubber with a concave edge may also be used; both are keen and very clean to use, and in water colour they cut deep, but in oil they are at their best.

Description: Mottle in mahogany depends on the sharp play of light and shade running at right angles to the vertical grain, the ends of which have sharp stabbing points, running in lines with the grain, something like a double-edged saw – that is, one with serrations on both sides.

Though the points are often near together they are uneven both in length and width.

We find mottle in many other woods –

Satinwood and Maple, for instance – but to a lesser extent than in mahogany. In each wood it forms its own type of pattern.

In Satinwood it is the main feature of the pattern of the timber, swinging and radiating.

In Maple the mottle is a good all-over pattern in most plain work, with a little more demonstrative vigour in the bird's eye variety.

In the darker, blue-crimson Spanish Mahogany, the mottle is wide, obtained simply by using a wider cutter, while the contrast between the ground and glaze colour is near in tone.

In newly cut, medium coloured wood, the contrast is often very violent, varying from dark bands of grain to extremely light streaks. This contrast of tone is often greatly accentuated by treatment.

I have a bedroom suite which I designed some twenty-five years ago the work being carried out in our own workshops.

Before filling it was treated with oxalic acid; the wet acid worked violently on the darker parts of the wood, intensifying them, and bleaching out the lighter parts.

Each portion of mottled grain is produced by a wavy direction of the vertical grain, which is cut with the straight machining of the timber, reflecting or absorbing rays of light, and in turn producing the light or darker parts of mottle.

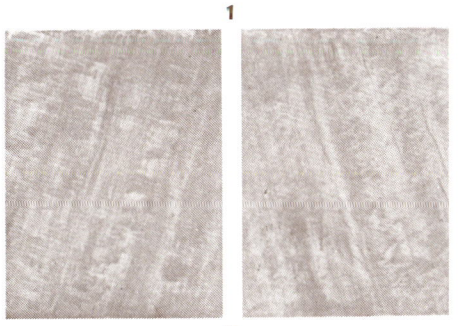

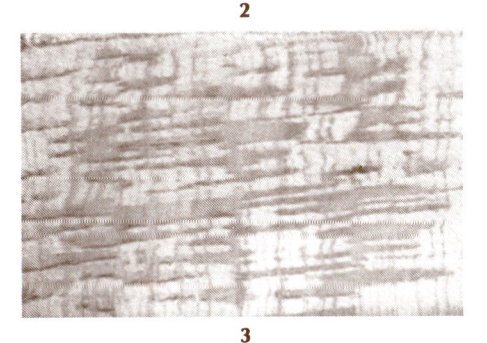

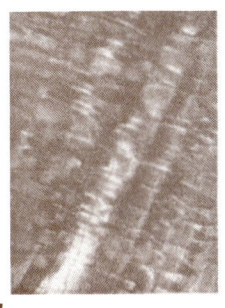

1. **Example of mottling worked in oil colour with a cardboard cutter**
2. **Mottling in oil colour over a water colour ground using a rubber cutter**
3. **Effect created by using a wide continental mottler & thin water colour**
4. **Water colour mottling produced by the use of a narrow cutter**
5. **Another example of mottling in water colour but using a heavy duty mottler**

Drawings of Brushes

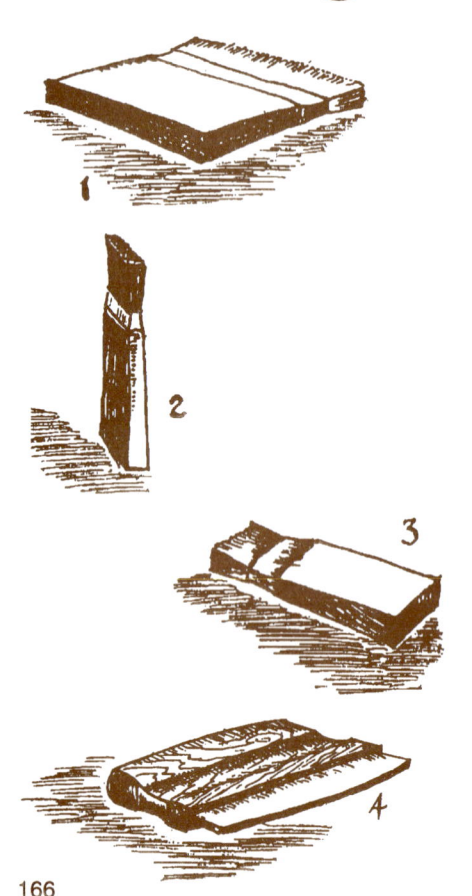

THE brushes and tools illustrated are concerned with the mottling and overgraining processes.

These are duplicated in so much as one hog hair cutter would be satisfactory for most grained examples.

I show no less than six that I use for special purposes, each giving slightly different effects.

No. 1. Three inch hog hair cutter. Thickness of bristle, one quarter of an inch.

No. 2. One inch ox hair. No. 3. Squirrel. Both of one-quarter inch type cutters.

No. 4. Rubber cutter four inches wide.

Nos. 5 and 6. Thin two inch and three inch hog overgrainers, about one-eighth inch thickness.

No. 7. Continental type of mottler four inches wide, one quarter of an inch thick. Can be used for both mottling and overgraining. The long handle is much easier to control for steady accurate work.

No. 8. Sable pencil overgrainer. Works well in both turpentine and water colour.

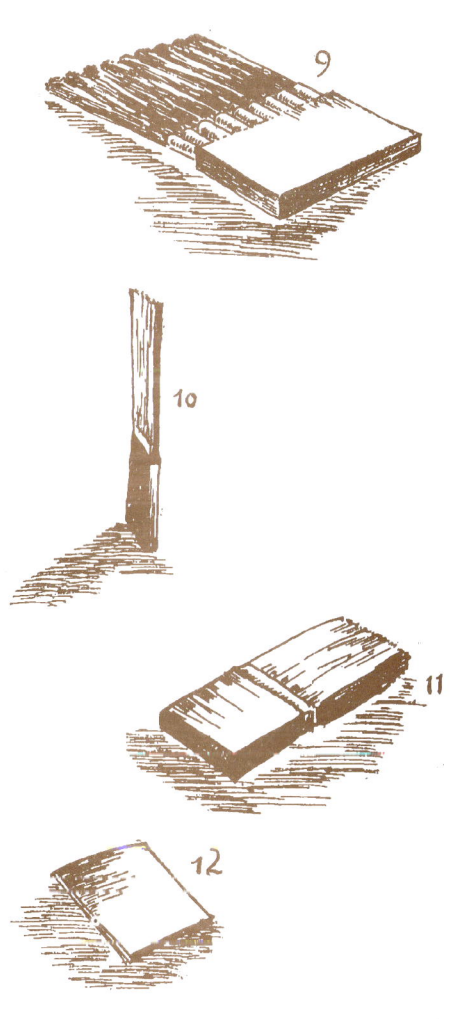

No. 9. Hog hair pencil overgrainer, suitable for oil colour in stiff pigment form on not too smooth a surface.

No. 10. Edge view of hog overgrainer.

No. 11. One and a half inch wide, one quarter inch thick, lily bristle mottler; note, the longer bristle compared with the cutter.

No. 12. Small square of oiled cardboard; note the slightly rounded edge.

Nos. 13 and 14. Heavy duty mottlers. Three inch and one and a half inch hog hair, half inch in thickness, suitable for mottling only; not for sharp cutting.

No. 15. A four inch bone, or plastic, hair comb, used for separating the bristles of the overgrainers when a lined effect is desired.

Please note that my brushes are not all new. They have been collected over nearly fifty years in the trade.

Neither myself nor the J.D.A. can put you in touch with the manufacturers of them.

Most manufacturers have the equivalent tools, however, and will be pleased to supply you.

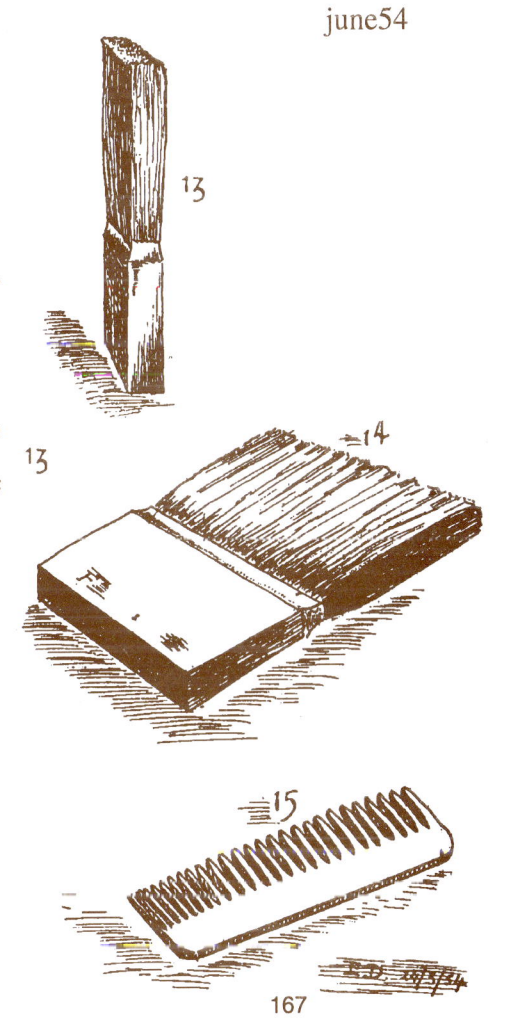

St. Anne Marble

ST. ANNE marble comes from Belgium, a country rich in coloured, but not white, marbles.

This carbonaceous black marble is found in the quarries on both sides of the Meuse and the Sambre. It is a fossilferous rock, but the organic remains are not easily detected.

On the north bank of the Sambre, a short distance from the mining and engineering town of Charleroi, is a bed of marble extending some six miles in length.

Name: This useful marble was named after St. Anne, the mother of the Virgin Mary.

Description: St. Anne marble is a medium grey with white markings on a black background. The ground is so well covered that only about one-eighth shows.

Tones of grey in the many small stone shapes, which are irregular both in size and shape, cover half the total area. Many are about three-quaters of an inch, and only a few up to four inches, in diameter. They are mainly angular in shape.

The veining, very light grey to white, is quite similar to Black and Gold marble in shape and character, but the white markings are much closer together.

They are numerous and have heavy and broad portions of white down one side. Only very small areas are pure white.

Most of the white appears to have a thin glaze of black scumbled over it, which gives a rich effect.

Flecks of white are found alone among the grey shells and there are only a few narrow connecting veins, none of which is very long.

Ground Colour: Dark grey to black.

Tools and Sundries.: Sponge, rag, fitches and double pencil.

Palette: Black and white with a touch of ochre to slightly yellow the greys. Mix three separate tones of grey.

In the Dipper: One of oil to two parts of turpentine with a few drops of terebine driers.

Method: Oil in the ground sparingly with rag and thinners from the dipper. Take the sponge, charged with a medium grey colour, and cover the whole surface using stippling, sliding and twisting motions.

This preliminary ground work should bear some relation to the subsequent direction and situation of the stone shapes and the veining.

The stippling, carried out where the veining will be placed, should be well softened to even out the colour into a thin film.

With a fitch, put in some of the heavy white patches that are found among the veining.

Using the double pencil, continue to draw in the finer veining with white; the broader shapes can

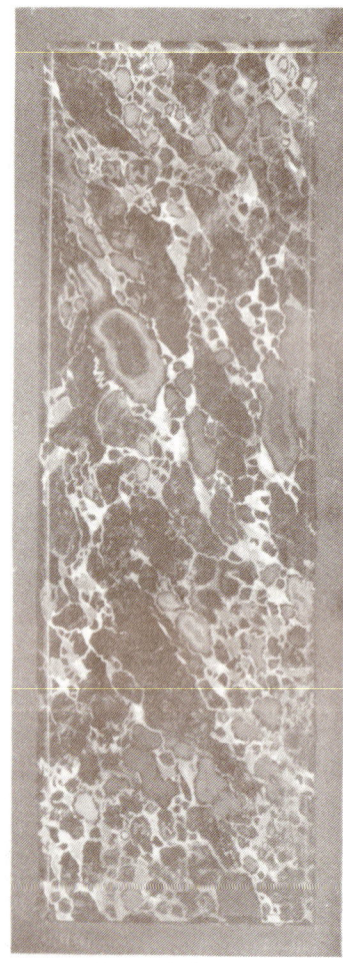

Painted example by Mr Dobson

best be made by using the sides of the pencil held flat to the surface instead of using pressure to open out the bristle.

Double pencils speed up execution but are not very selective, until one is proficient in their use.

It is better therefore to use a single pencil for the completion of the painting of either fine lines or heavier marks, by rolling the pencil on its side.

In charging the pencil with colour from the palette board, turn it round, touching one side with light grey.

This gives a splendid blended effect when the sides of the brush are turned on the work.

The veining, done rather loosely, is not connected with fine lines as in Black and Gold marble.

The inside of the stone shapes may now be filled in with dark tones of grey, using a small fitch and keeping well clear of the edge near the white, thus leaving a black margin.

Many of the insides of the stone shapes should be left with the earlier sponging exposed but just a few may be filled in with a fairly light grey.

To complete the work soften gently to remove the raw edges of colour only.

Glazing: Glazing should be carried out with the same colours if an accurate representation is desired.

The method is to oil in the ground and at the same time rub in a small amount of black.

The black "knocks back" the white but has little effect on the greys.

Turpentine may be splashed on to open out the black and give a little more texture to the whole.

Strengthen the white in a few places with a second coat, using zinc or titanium for extra whiteness, and soften lightly.

This Month's Drawing

1. Combs cut from flat cork.
2. Maple dotter brush.
3. Maple dotter paper tube.
4. Steel graining combs.
5, 6 and 7. Graining horns.
8. Grey bristle flogger.
8a. Grey bristle brush grainer.
9. Badger hair softener.
10. Check roller for oak texture.

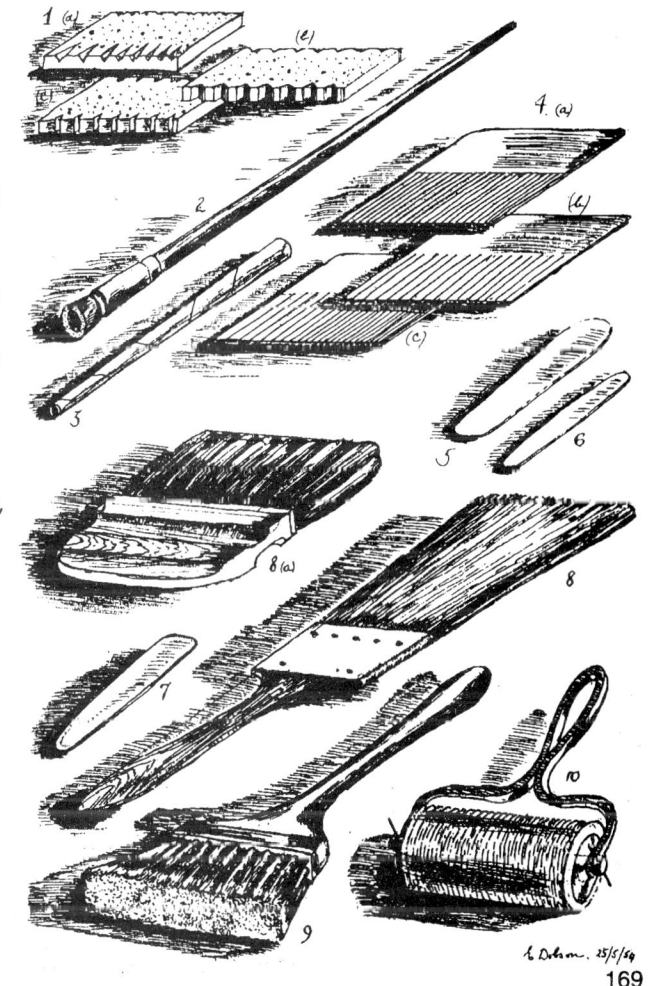

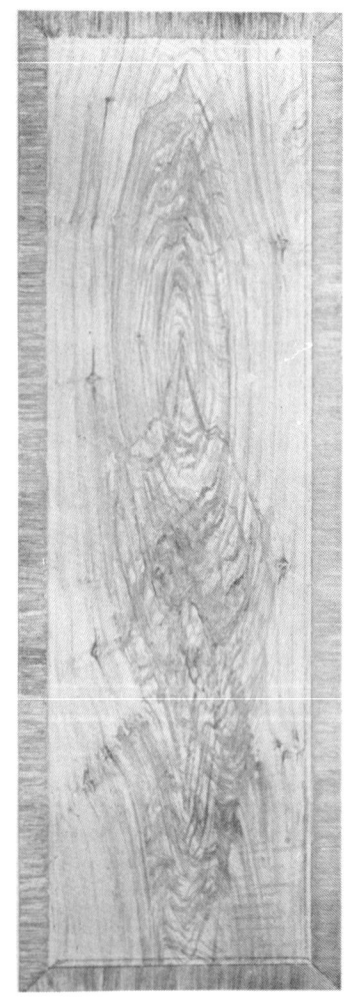

Bleached Walnut

THE craftsman must adapt himself to changing conditions, and, in the reproduction of wood grain, must ensure that it is in keeping with colour trends in decoration and the type of furniture in popular use.

A few days ago I was attracted to a beautiful window display in a Bradford shopping centre, the backround being in bleached walnut.

The beauty of the delicate colours of the large panels was a real delight; they fitted perfectly into the new scheme of decoration.

It was not a painted example, but genuine bleached golden walnut.

The bleaching of any decorative wood is a simple treatment by a chemical solution to lighten the tone of the grain markings.

Colour in timber reacts to bleaching in a peculiar way; yellow almost disappears and becomes an off-white, reds change to a lighter grey-green, dark reds to grey-pink, while brown changes to a greenish-grey.

The bleaching out of yellow and red from walnut results in a delicate blue effect.

Lime treatment of oak and pine led to the discovery of wood bleaching in the early part of this century.

Bleaching of wood to-day is not confined to antique or used furniture, but is carried out on new timber, such as maple, in order to lighten it.

White lac in polish from which yellow has been bleached out or cellulose lacquer provides a very pale protective coat to bleached timber.

Most of the chemicals used for the bleaching of woods burn the skin and, therefore, require to be used carefully. No form of bleach will act on paint, varnish or polish, which should first be carefully removed with a paint solvent. Prepared bleaches are available.

Description: Bleached walnut may be either golden, English, Italian or burr. American and satin walnut do not bleach satisfactorily. Italian walnut yields a tint of a grey-green colour with grain markings of raw umber.

In places black and burnt umber are found where the bleach has not worked too well or penetrated deeply enough. In no place do grain markings show prominently, and they would be invisible from fifteen feet.

Ground Colour: White.

Palette: White, raw umber, burnt umber, black and ultramarine.

In the Dipper: Three parts of turpentine to one of raw linseed oil, and a few drops of terebine driers.

In a second dipper or small kettle prepare a small amount of scumble glaze by pouring in a small quantity of thinners from the first dipper, adding about one-sixth in bulk of good quality white undercoating containing titanium oxide but no lead. Stain this with raw umber, then take a trial sample.

If the colour is too warm, cool off with black, or, if too cool, warm up with burnt umber. The mixture should be no stronger than a cream colour. A small amount of clear glaze may be added to hold it.

Tools and Sundries: Tools for "rubbing-in," fitches for working into corners and finishing off stronger grain markings, overgrainers or fantails, hog hair softener, coarse hair-comb, palette board and knife, and a piece of hessian.

Method: With the prepared scumble from the second kettle or dipper, rub in the panel.

If the panel is a large or important one, first make a sketch on paper of the outline of the grain. Do not work haphazardly, or rely on accidental effect; no good work is produced that way.

Should it not be convenient to make a sketch, form a mental picture of what you wish to carry out and stick to it.

In rubbing in the scumble glaze, work in the direction of the grain so as to form a complete drawing in colour of the heartwood shape.

The brushing-in must not be crossed, and a reasonable amount of colour should be applied.

If it is too wet, the subsequent grain markings will spread too much when softened; if too dry, they will stay on the top and be too prominent, not merging into the ground scumble. The correct amount of pigment and driers, and the quantity applied, are important.

Before overgraining, any excess of scumble may be removed or an alteration to the drawing may be made, either with a piece of rag or with the side of the rubbing-in brush.

Add four parts by bulk of white to each of the colours on the palette; then, with the overgrainer touched with thinners, apply your colour.

The choice of colour is left to your own discretion, although I would use three-quarters raw umber and the remainder from the other colours.

In working, I find one gets greater variety by moving all over a door rather than finishing one part at a time, providing, of course, that the drawing has been carried out first.

It is surprising how far one charge of colour in the overgrainer will go; three or four should suffice for a whole door.

The comb should be drawn through the bristle after the overgrainer has been charged with colour, but, of course, this is not necessary if the fantail is used instead.

After graining, the work should be sharpened with a fitch, a little darker colour added down the sides of the most important shapes, and a few knots placed here and there.

Drawing of a door grained in bleached walnut

The whole should be lightly softened in the direction of the grain and more vigorously down the sides. No glazing is necessary if a little mottling is carried out while the graining is still wet. This may be done either with an old, strong hog hair mottler or with a piece of rag folded into a pad.

Knots in Graining

EVERYONE is aware of the hard, dark, resinous spots in timber that we call knots; they have, from the earliest times, caused much trouble to painters.

In graining, however, knots have a decorative value.

Knots form an integral part of the display in the fine panels of various woods grained by Mr. Z. Carr, of Sheffield, which he presented to the Painting Craft Teachers in 1951.

When suitably placed down the side grain or in the centre of the heart, a few knots give an emphasis that is well worth the effort in most forms of graining.

In well-figured English Oak, however, we find only a few small knots; these play an important role in determining the direction of the figure. They are at their best when painted in outline only, as a broken ring, with lines radiating from the centre.

In Pollard, Brown Knotted Oak, and in Root of Oak, knots cover a large part of the grained surface. When small knots are few in number, they gain their prominence with the glaze shading, as shown in a previous painted example of Cedar.

Growth of the Knot: A knot may be described as a section of the branch which has been embedded in the wood by the natural growth of the tree.

A branch starts as a small green bud on the side of a young plant's leading shoot; it develops by covering itself with active growth cells, which are part of the layer of cells covering the trunk and all other branches of the tree. Each year a new layer of wood cells is added to the trunk and branches alike; they all increase in girth at the same time.

The covering bark is gradually stretched to form a protective barrier over the whole tree.

Generally speaking, the branches begin in the centre of the tree, though should they be destroyed through storm or by accident, often others will grow out near the missing limb.

It can, therefore, be readily understood that when later a tree is cut up into usable boards the saw must pass through some knots which have formed in the centre of the embedded portion of the branches.

Drawings: The first drawing shows a small Sycamore which I am growing from the familiar winged seed. This small tree is now five months old, and has four pairs of leaves, along with the seedling leaves, which, it will be noticed, are different in shape.

The knots will form later down the centre of the eight branches, which will now have grown the spring sections of their first rings.

The second drawing shows its progress ten years hence, when more branches will have grown and the tree will be twenty-five to thirty feet high. The relative positions of the branches will not change though they will be thicker and higher up the tree.

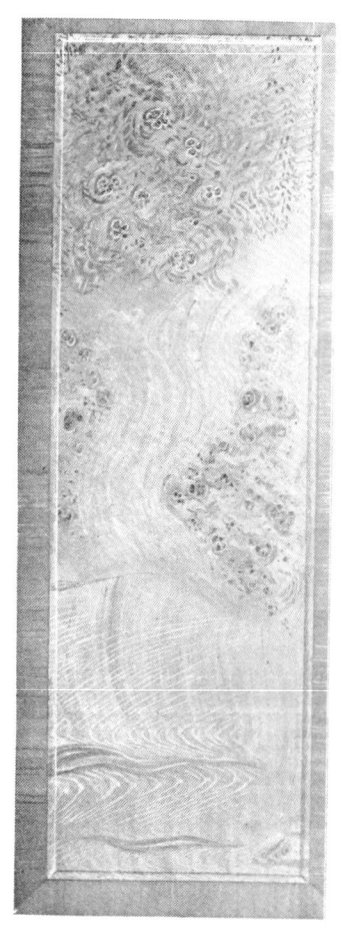

Painted example of three types of knots in graining

Drawing number three shows a log cut from the same portion at forty years; good knots will have grown whilst the trunk is getting fairly solid.

The branches are only half their final thickness, as most of the growing strength has gone into the central part of the tree, with its three 'leaders' that have developed to form the crown of the Sycamore.

It would take it a hundred years to grow as in the fourth drawing. On top of the log the three centres of the annular rings are prominent whilst the outer ones have developed into full circles.

In the drawing the log has been cleaned up with the adze, a cutting tool with a curved blade set at right angles. Eight of the knots from the ten branches are showing; the three on the left are drawn a little to the front. Coarse grain is showing around the outside vertical section, giving the same effect as we get in a radial cut when there are only a few rings.

Number 5 shows the grain and knots as they would appear from the third log, the cut being taken down the centres of three knots each down either side and through the pith in the centre of the tree as well. Little development has taken place down the centre; the ends of the grain in front and out at the back can be seen. Down the side grain, however, the cut sections of the six trumpet-like knots are prominent.

In the last drawing, where the cut is taken slightly away from the centre, the knots are now smaller, having been severely crushed by the growth of the wood.

The centre heartwood markings are well developed, whilst the knots down the side have been cut through.

The Painted Example:
The knots in the Pollard Oak were worked with the fantail overgrainer, using umber on a middle-oak scumble.

One or two twists of the wrist being given with the corner of the brush, which was used lightly, and was kept on the dry side.

A space of light has been left round each knot, and the line of light again cleaned up.

The second group of knots was made with the same materials and medium as number one, but the sponge only was used for both the grain and the knots; the outline was drawn with the brush end.

In many woods we often find a big contrast between the knots and the short grain, giving pleasant emphasis to the knots.

The long knots in the brown oak at the foot were painted in with a fitch, whilst the textured background was just drawn down with a fairly dry fantail.

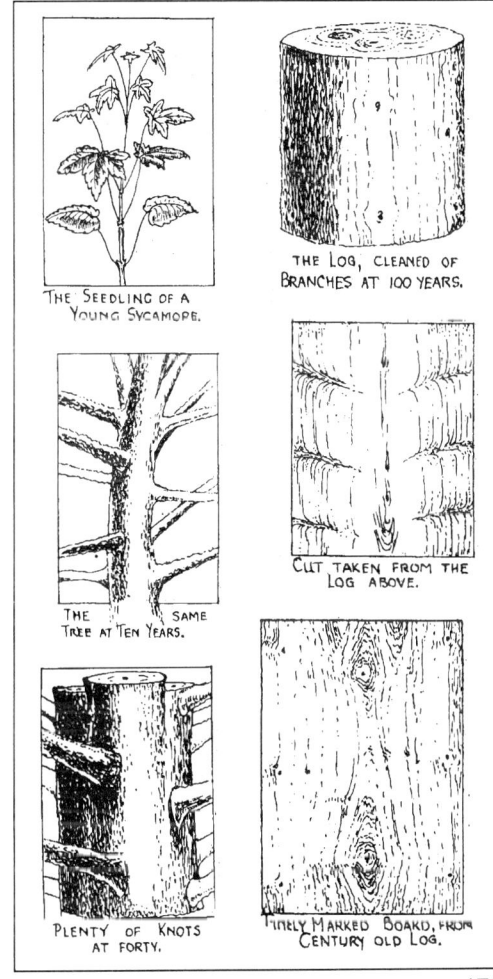

THE SEEDLING OF A YOUNG SYCAMORE.

THE SAME TREE AT TEN YEARS.

PLENTY OF KNOTS AT FORTY.

THE LOG, CLEANED OF BRANCHES AT 100 YEARS.

CUT TAKEN FROM THE LOG ABOVE.

FINELY MARKED BOARD, FROM CENTURY OLD LOG.

Dark Dove Marble

IN the past few years this quiet, attractive marble has been very prominent in the trade tests for apprentices in England. It is a very suitable subject, being comparatively easy to reproduce in oil colour.

The ability to assess accurately the drying time required, the amount of oil that can be used without running, and the vigorous softening that can be done without the colour spreading too far, can be judged in the finished work.

In a scheme of decoration, Dove Marble can form a splendid background for furniture and fitments because of its quiet colour. Its soft texture and almost neutral lines of veining give an interesting and steady effect compared with most other marbles.

Its colour is a good medium blue grey, which goes particularly well with rich Spanish mahogany.

Dove Marble is found in upper beds of crystalline limestone existing in mountainous areas and, owing to its very hard nature and freedom from faults, it can be cut into large sheets. It is mainly used in architectural work and is frequently employed with white marble in decorative panelling.

Origin: France, Italy, Greece and Ireland. Irish Dove is quarried at Formay in County Cork.

Ground: Light grey, prepared from white and touches of black and ultramarine.

Description: Dove Marble has a soft appearance of a medium grey colour. The veins are more like soft ribbons of darker grey, or white, than the narrow cracks that we associate with a normal marble vein. The lighter splashes or ribbons of white are more prominent than the darker ones, which, on the other hand, are more evenly distributed, roughly two inches apart, and run in the same direction.

Palette: White, black, ultramarine blue and raw umber. With this palette a considerable range of greys can be produced; raw umber, blue and white make a splendid dove colour.

Brushes and Tools: Pencils, tools, fitches, sponge and hog hair softener.

In the Dipper: One part of oil to two parts of turpentine, with a few drops of terebine.

Method: In a small paint kettle prepare a medium grey glaze, much darker than the ground, using white and colours from the palette. Great care must be taken to get the exact shade required, as most of it will show unaltered in the finished marbling.

Use more ultramarine for a cold effect and more umber for a warmer, with black as a stabilizer. Keeping it on the thin side with thinners from the dipper, rub in a liberal coating, working in one direction without crossing.

As little brushing as possible is important, as the drying is hastened with brushing, often causing tackiness before the subsequent softening is complete.

The width of a panel in a wall filling should be limited to thirty inches. In order to have a clean

Three progressive stages in the painting of Dark Dove Marble

working edge, marble alternate panels, allowing a day before filling in the rest, and wipe the edges after rubbing in the ground scumble, touching them again with a rag when the veining and softening are completed.

With the side of a tool, scrub off part of the ground scumble in streaks, following the direction of the marble. A piece of clean rag may be used to help to shade the ground, but care is required to avoid wiping it too clean.

Prepare on your palette two tones of grey colour, both darker than the ground scumble.

Charge a fitch with the lighter grey and paint in the long streaky veins. These should be two or three inches apart and six to eighteen inches long, following, of course, the basic design of the marble.

With another fitch paint in about a third of the veins with the slightly darker grey; leave some spaces plain without any broad marking.

For several minutes soften with care in the direction of the marble, then a little across the panel watching carefully that the lines do not spread too widely, and then finish in a vertical direction.

With a pencil charged with the darkest tone of grey, paint in a few narrow clear veins, covering about one-tenth of the area. After adding the last few dark lines, again soften in the direction of the marble.

Glazing: When quite hard, glazing may be carded out with colours from the palette.

Oil in the ground sparingly with rag, using thinners from the dipper. With the sponge charged with very thin white proceed to stipple over most of the area.

Take a fairly large fitch or clean tool and soften the stipple marks out down the centre of the large stones.

Using a fitch, draw in the broader white markings and small stone shapes.

Soften the whole lightly and the last white markings fairly heavily, but be extra careful with the fine sponge stippling.

Now charge the pencil with white and draw in the finer white veins; these are intermittent and all run in the general direction, and over most of the surface.

Drawing of quartered Dark Dove Marble, with inlaid border of Jaune Lamartine, by Mr Dobson

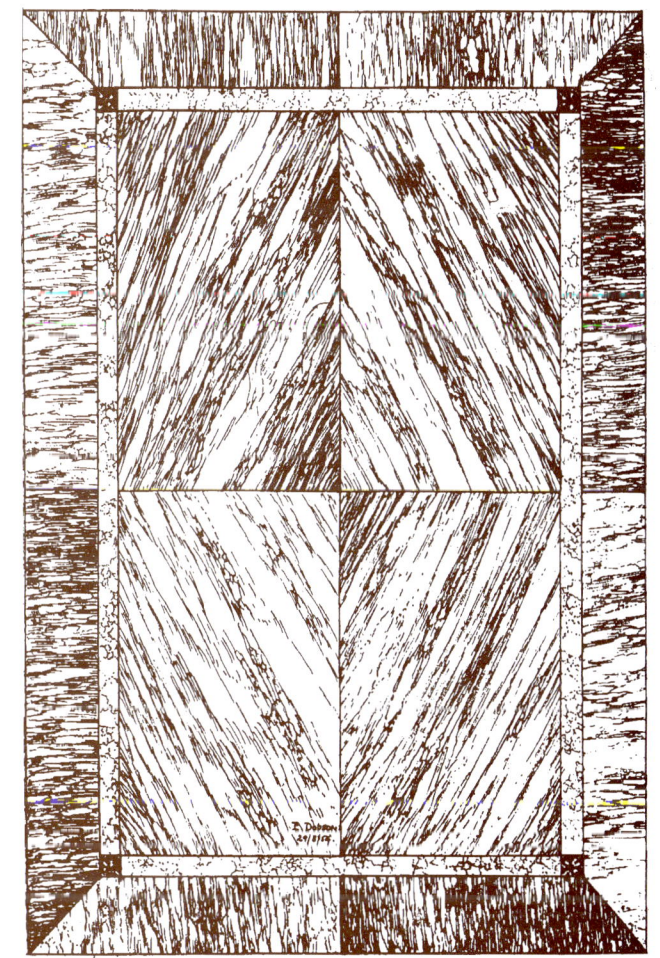

175

Knots in Graining (continued)

KNOTS are slightly darker in colour than the surrounding grain. This is because a dark resinous fluid fills the cells, and also the cells are compressed into a small area. In the pine family the contrast of tone between the knot and the surrounding wood is most marked.

Medullary Rays: In the grained example in the September issue, two large trumpet-like knots appear towards the bottom of the panel. Sweeping towards the knots were a large number of fine figure markings (medullary rays).

The resinous sap which fills the dark cells of the knot flows down the tree between the bark and the sapwood, and from outside it is guided inwards by the medullary rays and delivered to the knots. Knots are, of course, much longer and wider in section than the rays, which are very thin indeed.

Knot Shapes: Knots take on the outside shape of the branch that contained them – round or oval. In a few cases they are double or triple, depending on the number of branches converging into the trunk at the same point.

Dead or Alive Knots: A dead knot has a thin light line separating it from the surrounding timber, indicating that the branch was severed sometime before cutting, the sap no longer flowing through its cells. An alive knot is tight and more even in colour, having been active up to the tree being felled.

Spike and Splay Knots: The spike knot is one that has been cut in a longitudinal section, such as in brown oak.

Since each branch begins as a small twig on the leading shoot and increases in girth each year, it follows that a cut through the centre of the branch will produce a knot which develops from a pin point to a much wider diameter near the outer edge of the trunk.

The Pine Knot: Pine knots have a high decorative value, particularly in limed or bleached panelling. An example I have before me is interesting, and I have had it cut carefully for examination purposes. The knot is almost a full circle, being cut at right-angles near the outside of the trunk. Measuring half an inch in diameter at eleven years of age, the rings are only visible through a strong magnifing glass.

The heartwood lines in the timber adjoining the knot measure four inches for eleven rings, being eight times wider than the rings in the knot.

This variation in width is due to severe compression and to the fact that the rings in the knot were produced many years earlier when there was very much less sap flowing in the tree.

The colour in the knot is interesting, starting with a burnt sienna tinted centre, shaded first lighter then darker towards the outside edge, it is cooled with grey. The changes of tone and colour indicate that the roots have penetrated to different minerals. The difference of colour from the knot and the surrounding wood is cream to a cool sienna.

Painted example of knots in Walnut, Ash and Birch

The Drawings: The first drawing is of knots in Knotted Oak with fine close figuring down one side.

Prominence is given to the knots by a fair amount of plain space around them. They are of an oval shape with a rough edge, the centres being crossed with radiating lines and ornamented with darker markings.

The pleasing effect obtained by the drawing of a bold line near or around the knots of the central area should be noted.

The second drawing is of knots of Hungarian Ash; this lesser known wood is famous for its curly grain.

The knots of Ash are large than those in Oak, of a good oval shape and well supported with curved lines of grain.

Another feature of Hungarian Ash knots is that thay are well and evenly distributed over good sized boards.

The third and central example is of Pollard Oak, and here we find knots of all sizes and of a broad oval shape. The edges are broken and uneven, the centres are dark and well marked.

Grouping of the knots is a feature of Pollard Oak. New branches grow out from where the original branch was cut, and thus the knots form at the base of a group of branches.

A small amount of intricate figure is associated with Pollard Oak. The way the grain closes together when it surrounds the knots is interesting.

The fourth drawing is on knots found in the burr of Redwood.

The knots are small dark patches, a little darker than the red brown of the wood; they are arranged in rather long groups of five to thirty knots.

Between the groups there is a thin wavy line of grain. I find the sponge the best means of reproducing these knots.

Drawing number five is of Elm, a piece having been selected that was full of knots.

This strong hard timber produces some beautifull knots, arranged in circular groups, and a few lines of grain not unlike curly pine.

Quite a lot of plainer grain was present as indicated at the top of the drawing.

All the knots are of a good round shape of varying sixes up to two inches in diameter.

Drawing by Mr Dobson of knots used in graining

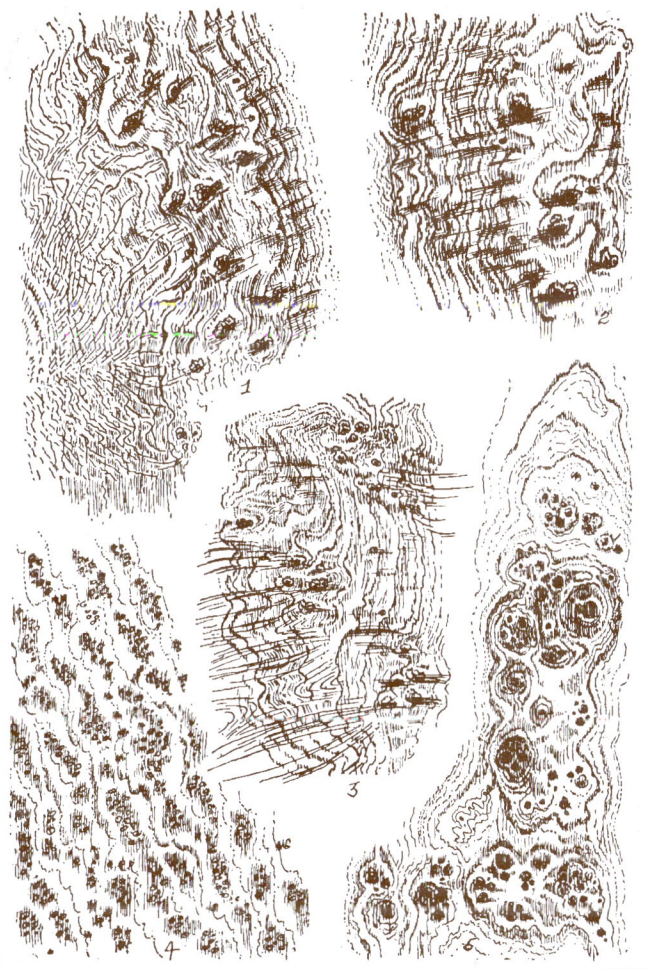

Graining of 'Natural' Oak

SINCE my youth I have experimented to try and accomplish something practical in the graining of "natural" oak.

The process that I describe is that one which I consider the best.

Description
The process consists of a delicate brush grained texture with a slighty more vigorous figure, darker in tone.

To attain this would at first appear most difficult, yet it is really simple if a few guiding principles are adhered to.

Ground colour
This should be of a medium to light medium buff. It may be an orange buff or of greenish golden ochre colour.

Tools and Brushes
Tools for rubbing in the gilp and glaze: brushgrainer, graining horn and washed rags.

Tools needed if water glazing is adopted: leather, motter, sponge and badger.

Palette
A small kettle of white paint consisting of undercoating thinned with oil and turpentine, or equal parts lead and zinc thinned with equal parts oil and turpentine.

Titanium should not be used as its covering or obliterating power is too great, making it difficult to wipe the figure out clean. Raw umber, raw sienna, burnt umber and black, ground in oil. Raw sienna, Vandyke brown, black and titanium, ground in water.

In the Dipper
Linseed oil one part, clear glaze one part, turpentine two parts and a few drops of terebine.

Method
With the white paint rub in a moderate coat to act as the ground gilp, and lay off evenly in the direction of the grain.

It should not be shady but a few brush marks are not amiss. Try to avoid showing the marks caused by the brush being laid on at the top or bottom of a panel.

On rails and styles, the white gilp should be rubbed-in in the same direction as the painted undercoatings.

No combing, brush graining or other texturing should be done at this stage.

The figure should be next grained on the wet paint. This will look rather strange, but it must be left without any further treatment until it is dry.

It is difficult for most grainers to leave the figure alone in the first stage, and allow it to dry without a bit of flogging or brush graining.

Overgraining
The overgraining may be carried out in either water or oil colour. Watercolour has the advantage

Painted example of "natural" oak

of drying quicker, which is often important on small jobs.

The colour of the glaze is one of personal taste; thin Vandyke with a touch of white gives a suitable mushroom tint, but a touch of raw sienna will warm it up.

Raw sienna and black, well thinned down to a dull green, make a suitable colour, while mixtures of raw sienna and Vandyke, well thinned, are suitable if a warm effect is desired.

After a suitable colour has been decided upon, rub in a thin pale glaze until all cissing has ceased; then draw the badger lightly down the work.

The colour cannot be too pale, but it can easily be too strong and obliterate the figure.

With a well-worn, small mottler take out some colour between the heavy open figure, and touch lightly with the badger.

Glazing in Oil Colour

Where conditions allow, I prefer to glaze in oil colour; it gives greater freedom and much easier control in all temperatures.

The colour mixture would be the same except that raw umber would replace the Vandyke brown, which is a bad drier in oil colour and rarely available to us.

Prepare a small amount of coloured glaze and lay it on in direction of the grain.

Avoid shadiness, but streaks of tone running with the grain are drawn down gently with the brush grainer.

Fold the rag into a hard square pad and soften between the figure.

Oil colour is a more reliable medium for softening out than water-colour; it is easy to rub it up and make a second attempt without damage to the figure underneath.

Mention must be made of the fine effects that can be obtained with tools which cut the surface of soft woods; in the hands of a skilled grainer they produce a most natural effect.

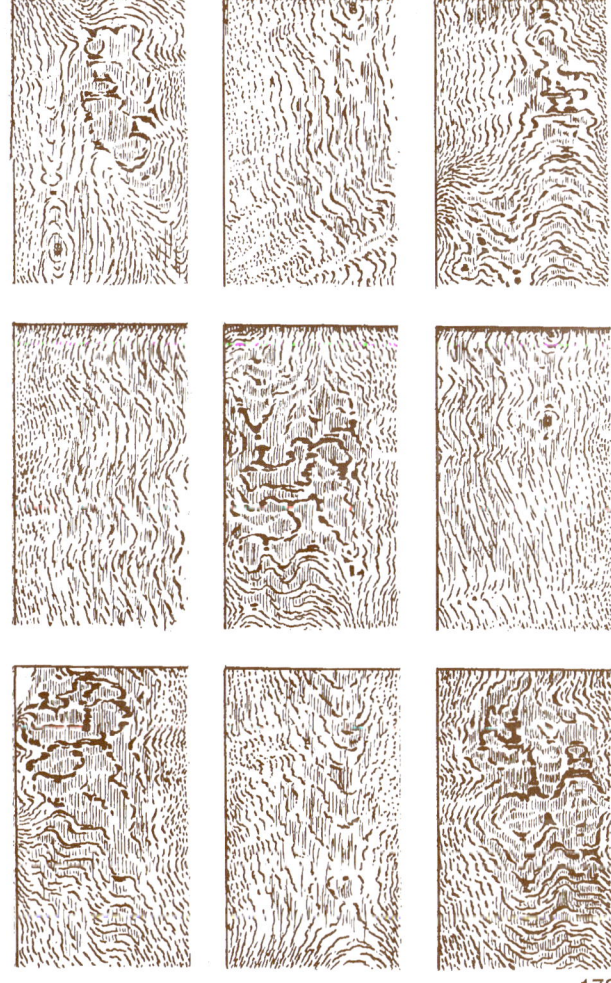

Drawings of the figure of Oak, by Mr Dobson

Waulsort Marble

WAULSORT is a good example of a breccia marble. It contains more broken fragments of marble than any of the examples which I have previously described, and it is an inspiration for broken colour effects. Its general colour is a quiet, dignified purple brown, and its interesting textures give it a highly decorative value which makes it suitable for use on large plain surfaces.

As in the case of timber, the cutting of marble can affect the markings. It either diminishes or accentuates the breccia markings.

Origin: The Hastieres Quarries, Namur, Belgium. These quarries are near the village of Waulsort. Many other brecciated and variegated marbles are obtained from this area, both by quarrying and from the many caves.

Composition: A specimen I have before me is composed of white, grey, pink, black, red and brown stones or angular fragments set in a purple brown matrix. These crystalline fragments are again stained and crossed with irregular lines of oxides of iron, carbon and grey matter. About one third of the medium purple brown of the matrix contains fine grey markings along with a few of yellow brown and some almost pure Indian red in colour. Like many red marbles it is referred to as of the lower carboniferous system.

Several varieties of Waulsort marble are found in the Namur Province, all of slightly differing colours and names.

Ground Colour: White, to obtain good transparency when turpentine is used to open out the colour, and the white stone shapes are produced by the wipe-out method.

Palette: White, yellow ochre, orange chrome, Indian red, violet and black. If unavailable, violet may be prepared from crimson lake and ultramarine.

In the Dippers: (1) Turpentine only. (2) One part linseed oil, two parts of turpentine and a few drops of terebine. A small amount of clear glaze may be added, which helps to keep the colour in place and assists in cleanly wiping out the stones.

Tools and Sundries: A one-inch tool, fitches, double sable pencil, sponge, hog hair softener, graining horn and clean rags. The condition of the fitches is important; they should be sharp, square and not too long in the bristle. Some should be well worn.

Method: The method here described is for the medium to dark purple brown variety.

Using a rag, oil in the ground with medium from the dipper.

With the tool and a large fitch paint in the first glaze colour, working round the larger stones as in the painted example No. 1. The principal colour of the glaze should be a warm grey to dull violet, composed of white, violet and a touch of black.

Painted example No. 2 shows the addition of the second process, carried out while the first was still wet.

It consists of sponging a black stipple coat on the matrix between the stones. I find the best way to charge the sponge is to prepare thin turpsey black on the palette and pick it up with the sponge – this keeps the colour on the projections outside the sponge.

Variety can be obtained in the stippling by using more turpentine and less black. Some black may be stippled on a few of the selected stone shapes.

When satisfied with the amount of black stipple, change over to red but cover less area, keeping clear of the stones and covering about half of the small matrix area.

By using the same sponge, the surplus black in it causes the red to incline towards brown. Prepare the thin red from orange and Indian red.

Continue, while the remainder is wet, to fill in some stone shapes with medium grey, as in example No. 3, reserving the largest shapes for white and black. Work a lighter grey into some shapes until white is reached.

Only a few of the largest stones are white.

A sharp scrubby fitch is best for this purpose; even the line texture of the brush marks is of value.

Now work other stones with darker grey to black. Soften the whole gently with the hog hair softener.

Do very little softening in the area of the matrix and smaller stones or the result will be a blur of soft colour. A small amount of stippling with the end of the hog hair softener may be tried in these places.

The softening is useful when adding a small amount of red to the white stone shapes. With a sharp fitch paint in a few red, brown and pink stone shapes.

From example No. 4 it will be seen that a few stones have been wiped clean to the ground colour.

This was done with a piece of rag wrapped over the graining horn. Part of this wiping out should be carried out in straight lines across the stones. The end of the fitch may be used to draw lines across other shapes.

Glazing: Four distinct processes have been carried out while the colour was wet, to obtain good depth.

Glazing is required, however, and should be carried out, of course, on the following day when the rest is hard and dry.

Touch down with sand paper to take off the many points produced by stippling and sponging, and oil-in the ground with rag. Sponge stipple thin black and Indian red in places and also thin white on the white stones and here and there among the matrix. Lightly soften with the hog hair softener.

A few lines of black and red may be drawn with the sable pencil round some stone shapes, among the finer work and across the stones.

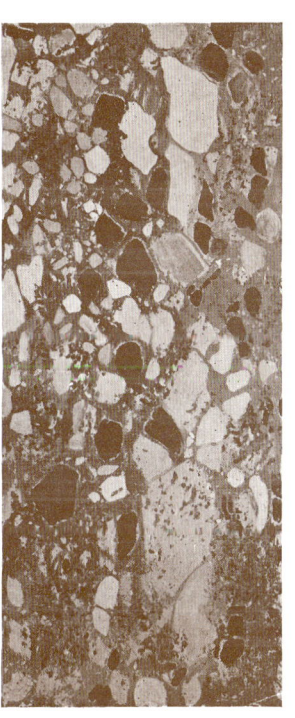

Example 1

Example 2

Example 3

With a short fitch sharpen up both white and black stones.

There is no limit to the amount of work one can put into the glazing of the stones and the fine effect that can be obtained. Cost is often the governing factor, however, and sometimes glazing has to be left out completely.

Graining of Bleached Rosewood

IN its natural state, Rosewood is a deep transparent brown to crimson and of great beauty in colour and markings. All the vein markings are black, narrow and often complicated.

Glazing plays an important part in the success of the finished work as the shapes have many tones, the heavier ones being down the centre.

A few lighter shapes peep through, but are mostly located down the outer edges.

In Britain during the past century much furniture has been made from this sweet smelling wood, and specimen pieces are now being bleached.

By this process the full beauty of the grain is brought out, whereas a few years ago it was partly hidden by a glaze of crimson lake.

Origin: The finest specimens come from India, and others in smaller quantities come from Jamaica, New South Wales and Burma.

Ground Colour: From white to pale buff, prepared from white and Oxford ochre, but for the "natural" Rosewood use a strong buff ground.

Palette: Vandyke brown, black, raw sienna and titanium white, ground in water. For the "natural" Rosewood, Vandyke brown, crimson lake and blue-black, all ground in water.

Tools and Sundries: Flogger, tools, mottlers, hog hair and badger softeners, and black crayon.

Flogging: A flogged ground provides a key and gives texture to the subsequent graining, although for very light bleached work it may be omitted.

For a medium tone, thin Vandyke with a touch of titanium white should be used. Flog until almost dry to obtain a fine texture, but make sure the colour is well bound.

Method: With medium from the dipper, composed of one part linseed oil to two parts of turpentine and a few drops of terebine, gently oil in the ground. As the turps. sub. is very searching, a dabbing motion is preferable.

This oiled ground is later to act as a lubricant and spreading agent to the subsequent graining, and also as a binder. No colour should be added to the medium.

With black conte crayon or pencil, starting at a knot near the centre of the panel, draw in the first shape; continue upwards and downwards completing the centre of the panel. The sides are often made plainer, working out to straight grain towards the edges. The shapes are all contained in rather strong outlines, produced by running the crayon over the work a few times.

It will be observed from the drawings that the outside shapes are the most important, the inside short grain often being filled in almost at random.

The painted example has been worked with two crayons held side by side, which not only speeded up the work, but gave twice the amount

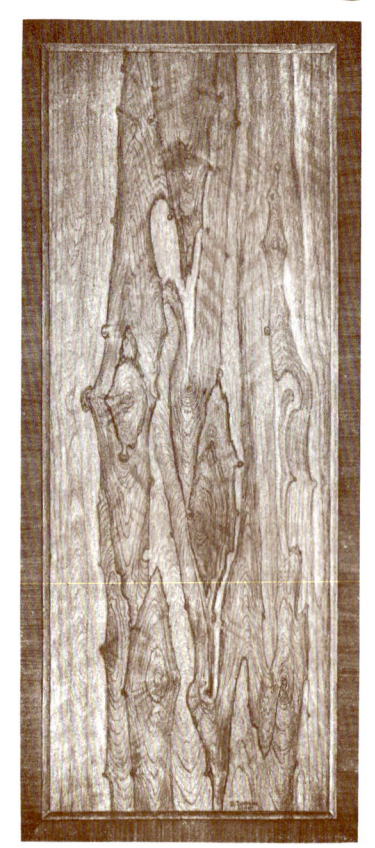

Printed example Bleached Rosewood

of colour on the heavier lines, one crayon following the track of the other. The silhouette down the edge of the larger heartwood shapes is important. Small knots protrude at intervals.

There are portions of plain grain among the knots, outlined with dark conte crayon. Other shapes are clothed in very pale grain markings.

Both the drawing and the painted example include the maximum amount of grain shapes likely to be encountered in this wood.

Softening should be carried out with great care towards the centre of the knot and with the grain, using the hog hair softener.

To preserve the sharpness of the drawing, very little softening should be done down the centre, but it can be more vigorous down the sides.

Glazing: In the accurate matching of colour or effect, glazing is important. At all times it hides or submerges the hard lines, making the final effect softer and more like the wood.

Thin white paint, nothing added, is often satisfactory, and may be partly taken out with the mottler and softened with the hog hair softener.

Should the colour permit the use of strong contrasts, blue-black, a touch of Vandyke and a small amount of titanium white should be added, all of course thinned with water. It

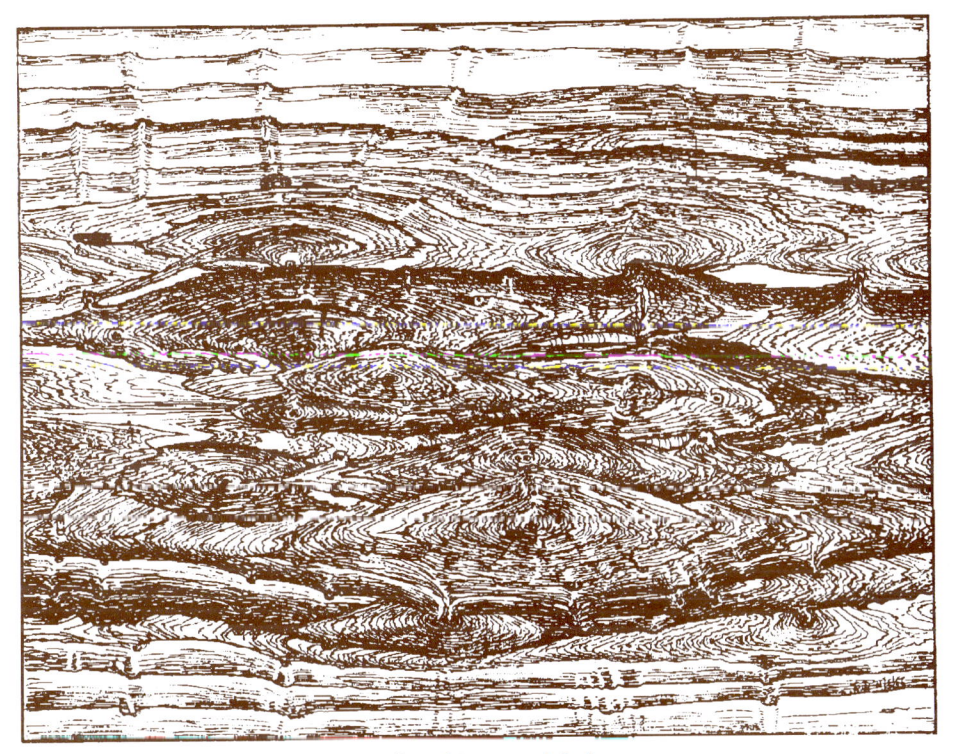

Drawing of Rosewood Grain

will be noticed that there are at least three separate tones of colour.

In applying the final colours it is best to start with the darkest first and keep the lighter parts clean with sponge and water. Should the area being grained be a large one, work the centre first from top to bottom later completing the sides. Joining can often be carried out down the heavy markings of grain without being noticed. Soften quickly with the badger and fasten with thin varnish.

A flat finish is preferable for bleached wood.

Knots in Oak Heartwood

THE graining of oak heartwood is greatly improved by the addition of a few knots carefully placed down the centre or in the outer field of the panel, amongst the side grain.

All the important focal points, from which lines radiate in the heartwood markings of oak, spring from branches, and all contain knots in some shape or form and many hold a few clustered together.

One often finds a beautifully bleached or weathered gatepost of oak most delicately marked, displaying charming groups of small knots.

Gate-posts, garden fences, screens and wind shields form a splendid hunting ground for fine examples of oak heartwood markings.

Many wind breaks were built in the pre-war era and are now in a weathered condition, with the markings almost exaggerated. The softer portions of the wood have changed from a yellow brown to a silver grey, while the harder parts have bleached to a reflective off-white.

Training, or observation, has made me prefer all the centres of the heartwood markings to be filled in, either with a cluster of knots or with slightly darker colour.

Drawings: The drawings of oak heartwood are from wood that has been grown in a warmer climate. It is selected from a large number of planks, as knots are not generally prolific in oak.

Most of the centre shapes are double; otherwise they are similar to the ones that I have drawn previously. The knots are small and unobtrusive, only the shading giving them prominence.

Their position is interesting; most of the centres of heartwood have one or two, and the majority of the remainder occur in the tenth to the fifteenth rings.

The well-marked and knotted examples selected are cut from large branches and not from the trunk of the tree.

Painted Example: This has been carried out with a crayon worked on an oiled ground, a method with many advantages, the most important being that you can see the work better than with the wipe-out method; also, a crayon is more easy to control than a soft sable pencil, and gives a cleaner line than the hog hair fitch.

Ground Colour: This should be from off-white to buff, according to the type of finish desired.

Palette: Raw and burnt sienna, and a touch of black or burnt umber.

In the Dipper: Equal parts of oil and turpentine, and a few drops of terebine.

Tools and Sundries: Crayons (assorted colours from medium brown to black), tool, sponge, fitches, rag, hog hair softener, mottlers, and badger.

Method: Oil in the ground from the medium in the dipper; should a medium or dark coloured effect be desired, rub in a small amount of colour with the tool. The ground should be wet, not just tacky, as crayons of any description do not work well on a dry ground.

More colour should be used on the sides than where the drawing is to be carried out. Place this colour with the tool or sponge; avoid wiping the centre part out with rag, which would leave the ground starved of oil. The oil must act as a binder to the crayon, as well as a vehicle where softening can be effective.

Give the ground and crayons a trial before starting in earnest on the finished work.

In the painted example the ground was oiled in, and all colour was put in with a sponge, which was drawn down the sides about three times, shaped to where the subsequent drawing was to fall.

Some craftsmen draw a straight line of light across the panel.

This is to be deprecated, but, when the work is completed and the crayon marking all put in, run along the edges again with the sponge, canvas, or graining comb to fit the drawing accurately.

The drawing should be started near the centre of each shape, working outwards until the area is covered, and leaving spaces for the small knots.

These should be put in with a fitch, using a touch of burnt sienna and umber. A twist with a small pad or rag on the wet knot often gives a pleasing, natural appearance.

All the skill of the grainer must be brought into play, both in the drawing and the execution of the knots.

I used two colours of crayon, drew some lines closer together than others, and added a few short lines of grain to the side grain over the sponge drawn lines. The length of the short grain may be varied.

Glazing: A limited amount of glazing can be carried out, using a well worn mottler in a dry state.

Extreme caution is, however, necessary, or much of the previous work may be lost.

Also, a pad of rag will serve to remove a few of the high lights; if, however, you wish to add dark shadows a separate process must be resorted to, details of which have been given in previous articles in 1954.

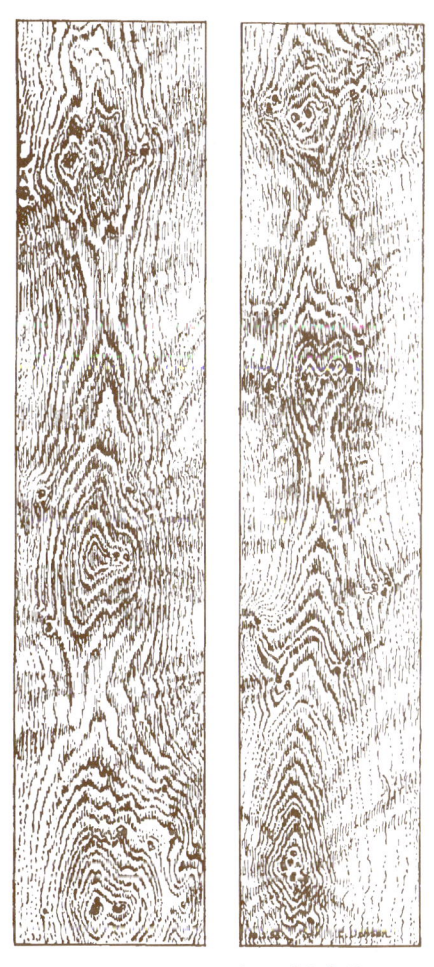

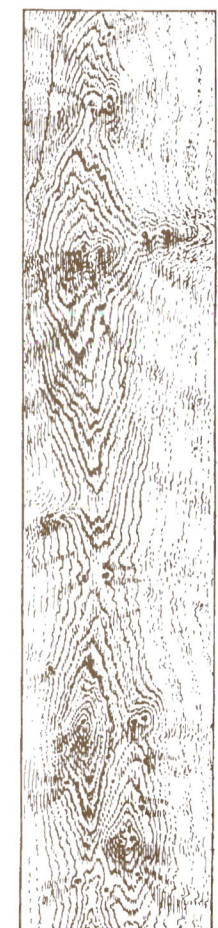

Drawings of Oak Heartwood

Painted example of Australian Walnut

Australian Walnut

ONE hardly expects to find inspiration for graining while travelling by British Railways.

Stranded for two hours at a country station in a snow storm, I evenually boarded a train, the coaches of which had been lined with different woods, neatly named on small plaques which also gave the country of growth.

In the one in which I travelled Australian walnut had been used. I brought out my sketch-book and quickly forgot my troubles, taking notes and marking sketches, and reached my destination far too soon.

Colour: Australian walnut is of a cool medium brown tone, with quite a lot of the plain ground showing.

Texture: A fine texture, whicb can be easily obtained with a flogger, covers the whole surface. It is, however, more prominent in the lighter parts, while in the darker bands the grain and mottling overpower the interlocking pith or fibre.

The sapwood is several tones lighter than the heartwood. Great play is made of this in cabinet making, and it offers scope to the grainer to use two tones on one panel.

Mottle: The most striking feature of the wood is the mottle, which covers the whole of the surface. It cannot be compared with that of any other wood as it is a distinctive type of its own; starting from the centre of the tree it falls gently at an angle of about 15 degrees.

The finest of the mottle is near the centre, where the waves are three quarters to one inch apart, sloping downwards towards both sides where the lines of mottle may be up to two inches apart.

Scattered here and there towards the outer edges a little cutting of the mottle may be discerned.

All the edges are soft, changing from dark to light both at the top and bottom, a feature that can be obtained by the correct use of the mottler and careful use of the badger softener.

Grain: The lines of grain are very simple and of a darker tone of brown, particularly when the specimen has been cut from the straight portion of the trunk below the branches.

Just a slight wave or point can be observed in the otherwise straight lines, which vary from one quarter of an inch apart down the middle to one inch apart near the outside edge.

Perhaps every four inches or so a stronger line of colour occurs, while the width of the line itself is nearly one eighth in, or a little more.

Another interesting point is the softness of the lines of grain.

Origin: Australia. This valuable cabinet wood is

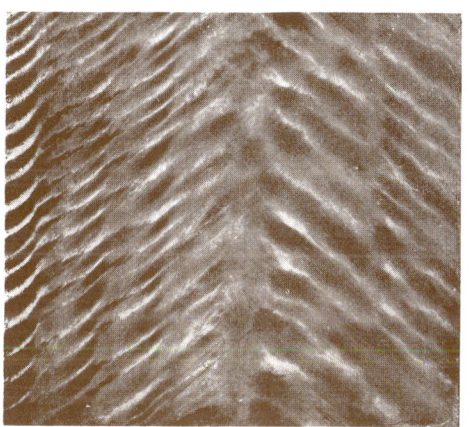

Far Left: This painted example shows, top: the flogging on the ground colour, centre: the oil glaze applied, and bottom: the graining carried out

Centre left: The ripples of the glazing on a plain painted ground

Left: A drawing of the grain of Australian Walnut

grown extensively on the Northern Peninsular in the Province of Queensland, between the Coral Sea and the Gulf of Carpentaria.

Ground: A light grey buff, composed of white, a touch of black, and Italian ochre.

Tools and Sundries: Tools, hog hair pencil overgrainers, hog hair softener, fitches, mottlers, flogger, badger hair softener, clean washed rags.

Palette: Colours ground in oil-raw umber, black and burnt sienna; in water-Vandyke brown.

In the Dipper: Three parts turpentine, one part linseed oil, one part clear glaze medium, and a few drops of terebine.

Method: Lay in a thin glaze of well-bound Vandyke, flogging the water-colour to a fine texture.

Prepare a gilp from raw umber and thinners from the dipper; this should be dark enough for the darker tone. The lighter tone may be produced by cleaning off with rag or by manipulation with the side of the brush.

It should be well wetted, however, to take the lines of grain and allow them to be knocked down with the hog hair softener. Rub in the gilp and arrange the colour tone, taking great pains not to disturb the flogged ground unduly.

A small amount of black or burnt sienna may be introduced into the work with a clean tool, using the gilp and a little colour from the palette.

With a short scrubby fitch lay in the strongest dividing lines of grain. Fill in the spaces between with pencil overgrainers, taking advantage of the different types and widths available to obtain variety.

The grained lines require careful softening with the hog hair softener or a smudgy effect will be obtained; I find it expedient to delay this operation for an hour or so to allow the graining partly to set. Work with the grain; a flogging stroke is very suitable if the gilp is half set, and gives a very natural effect.

Glazing: This is carried out in the traditional manner with Vandyke brown in water rubbed in as a thin glaze. Mottle with a three or four inch mottler, keeping the brush on the work all the time and varying the pressure as you draw the brush down.

Swedish Green Marble

SWEDISH Green, a quiet sage green marble, is one of the varieties lesser known among the painting fraternity. It is a serpentine marble, with green wavy bands in tones of medium sage to light green.

White bands of calcite often divide the tones of green, some of them being beautifully reduced by a small addition of vermilion, which just takes off the brightness of the green.

There is some confusion in the naming of this marble; three examples in the Sedgwick Museum, Cambridge, are exhibited under the name of Ringborg Green (G) and (N Y).

Last year the annual summer outing of the Institute of British Decorators was to Cambridge, and the members were delighted with the large display of marbles.

It is little wonder that a reader who recently wrote to Painting and Decorating had difficulty in tracing this marble, for other names by which it is known are Kolmard or Nyvert.

Cutting: As in the case of timber, the cutting of marble affects both the pattern and colour.

At present it will suffice to say that this marble cut with the grain will show up the wavy bands typical of the serpentine variety. Cutting in another direction will produce a light green face with flecks of white, while another cut will reveal a ribbon faced marble with plenty of flecks.

Origin: Sweden only. The Marmorbruket Quarries, Norrkoping in the Province of Ostergotland. These quarries have been worked intermittently for the past three hundred years, although more actively during the present century. The workings are 200 feet above sea level, on the slopes of the Bravic Fjord.

This variegated marble is much used in Sweden, while in the British Isles it can be seen used decoratively at the London Coliseum, the Strand Palace Hotel, Liverpool Cathedral, and several Manchester office buildings.

Ground Colour: White.

Palette: White, Brunswick green, yellow lake, ultra-marine blue and black.

In the Dipper: One part linseed oil and one part glaze medium to three parts turpentine.

Brushes and Tools: Two 2 in. tools, a few fitches, a small hog hair stippler, softener, sponge, rags and worn sable pencil.

Method: With a piece of rag and medium from the dipper, oil in the ground. It should not be too dry, but considerably inside the running stage. With a good sized fitch, charged with light green, draw in the principal lines, taking pains not to fill in much space with any particular tone of green. Next work in a few lines of dark green, leaving some of the ground showing between each wavy band. Other bands of grey green and yellow green should be worked, using all the colours from the palette. The use of ultramarine blue with the Brunswick green will produce a suitable grey green. The yellow lake is a very transparent colour and not too strong for our requirements, though very little of it is found in Swedish Green.

Continue to fill in with colour until a pleasing arrangement is obtained; wide bands of white and very pale green should be included.

Draw a dry sponge carefully down a few of the coloured bands, gently dividing the colour with a series of fine lines running through it.

I find the sponge, with the small amount of colour that it has picked up, very good for obtaining a most delicate effect by running it down some of the white or background bands. If they now have become too green or slightly soiled, they may be cleaned up by running the rag carefully down them.

The tool or fitch should be charged with white and worked down the line, when it may be followed by the sponge stained with green. The whole may now be carefully softened. Take the small stippler and run down some of the bands to make a fine hair stippled texture. The hog hair softener also may be used on some of the narrow bands.

It will be noted that stippling reduces the contrast and, in effect, quietens all colours a little towards the ground colour. In practice, therefore, allowance should be made for

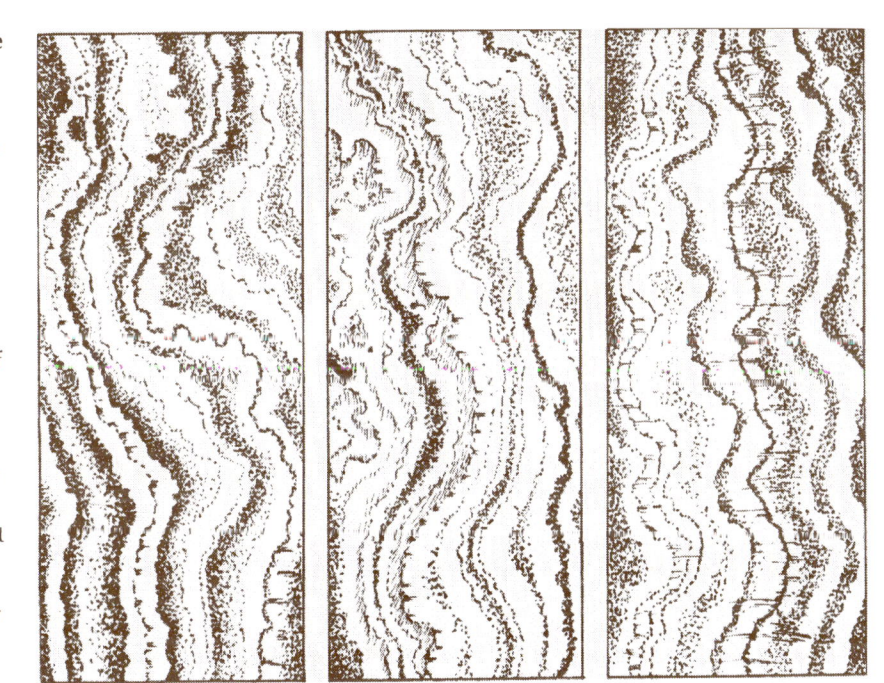

this. The sponge, if of a fine texture, may also be brought into action on the darker edges. A piece of strong drawing paper can be used as a mask to obtain a sharp edge to a dark band. No softening is required after stippling, but a fitch or pencil can be used to sharpen up the lines of veining.

Glazing: For a special finish, glazing should be carried out in the same colours and with the same brushes. Again, first oil in the ground, then with a fine sponge thinly stipple on different bands with white or a shade of green. Some deepening and sharpening with various greens may be done carefully with fitches, keeping the colour transparent.

Painted Example: This was carried out in one operation without glazing. Light and shade was obtained by cleaning up with a turpsy rag. All the four examples are of 6 ft. slabs.

189

Painted example of Beechwood

Graining of Beechwood

BEECHWOOD is one of the lighter woods which are very popular today in interior schemes.

The Beech tree grows to a great height – 90 to 120 feet. The bole is often clear of branches up to 50 to 70 feet, and when cut into straight boards the grain is usually straight and lacking in character, but it has a distinctive and rather attractive silver grain when cut on the quarter.

In England the fruit of the Beech was formerly known as "buck," and Buckinghamshire was so named because it was famous as a Beech growing county.

Description

Beechwood is of a pinky cream colour, with quiet grain markings. Beechwood darkens rapidly if left exposed without sealing after cutting.

A very pleasant feature is the slight variation of colour of the ground from, say, a pinky to a yellow cream.

The grain or vein markings are all of one colour, a light pinky brown, not much darker than the textured ground.

The width of the dark lines is about one-eighth to a quarter of an inch, with three-quarters of an inch to one inch space between each.

The darkest part is on the outside of the curve of the grain, and it gently shades lighter until it reaches the next wave of grain. A texture of flecks of dark colour is spread evenly over both the ground and the grain; these flecks are pointed at both ends as opposed to the straight and square ended pith in oak.

Ground Colour

White on cream.

Tools and Brushes

Fitches, fantail, tools and flogger.

Palette

White, burnt sienna, vermilion and raw umber.

In the Dippers

(1) Turpentine only.

(2) One part oil, two parts glaze, two parts turpentine, and one part flat white or undercoating.

With the white glaze from the second dipper rub in a thin coat over the panel. Tint the centre portion with burnt sienna and a touch of umber, working evenly where the heartwood markings will fall.

Later some of this pinky colour will be carried on to the flanks by the flogging.

Work quickly before the glaze sets and do not undertake too large an area.

Charge the fantail overgrainer with a slightly darker colour than the glaze and proceed to paint in the pale heartwood markings.

If it is found that the fantail gives results which are too regular and mechanical, a one inch overgrainer, drawn through a course comb, may be substituted. If a very open type of grain is selected it should be drawn in with a fitch.

Proceed with the painting of the grain until the panel is covered.

Colour stronger than the finished work should be used as more than half of it will be dispersed by the flogging.

This process should be carried out smartly before the ground glaze starts to set; each place should be touched once only or the delicate grain will be lost.

Use only one side of the flogger in order to distribute the dark parts of colour over on to the lighter ones. If, however, some parts are too dark and smudgy a few touches with the flogger will soon remove them.

A short, scrubby fitch charged with a spot of umber may be used for putting in a few knots or cleaning up the lines of grain. The knots are small in size and few in number, and are found both in the heartwood and the outer field. No flogging should be done to these.

The whole should present a flat, even appearance; no glazing is required.

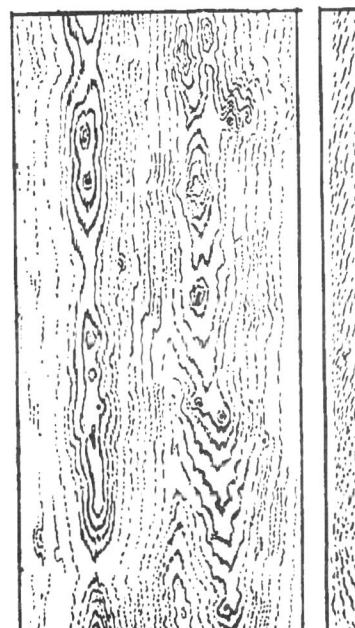

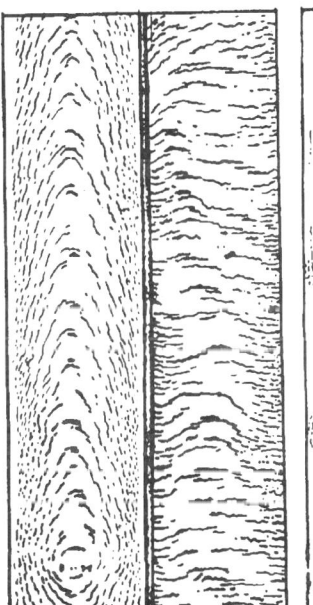

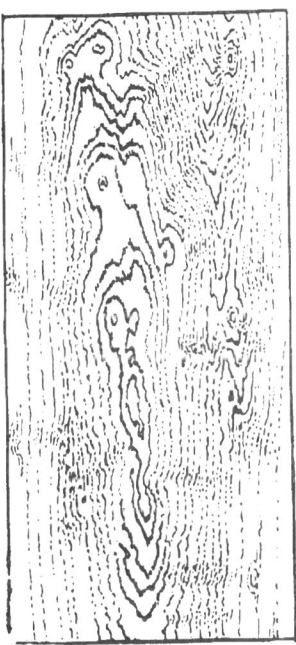

Examples

Most Beechwood is very little different from a textured ground, but the drawings are of wood cut either tangentially or radially. They might be described as good painters' examples, being a little on the ornate side.

The two double heartwood drawings are of examples of nearly four feet in height, whilst the figure in the centre was only one quarter of the size.

An interesting point is that, cut with a straight face, most of the small figure simply runs from side to side. When cut with a curved face the figure droops quickly down both sides.

The painted example was taken from a large plank cut at a tangent near to the outside of the tree and near a large branch and a few minor ones. The small brown knots from the centre of the branches give additional interest.

National Master Painter

43 articles between

July 1956

to

July 1960

A drawing made from an example of Juniper found near Cartmel Priory, showing the female flowers

Juniper

PAINTERS and decorators are a conservative and suspicious set of craftsmen when anything new threatens to upset the theories and practices of years.

Few of us can claim that we are very progressive, with a mind that is always open to try anything new, and graining today still uses many methods devised by earlier generations.

I was trained by my father in a busy industrial city in the West Riding of Yorkshire, attending the local school of art and later completing my studies in Europe.

Often I took home some new point that I had learned and my father was pleased and interested to listen.

Few were different from what he had used years before, and he would enlarge upon many of them pointing out the advantages and disadvantages.

Graining in Britain has been of a good standard for the past two generations.

I well remember as a boy seeing panels worked as classwork winning first-prize awards in the National Competition. It was with great regret that I learned of the death of my first teacher, Mr. William Rhodes of Batley, a well known master in the West Riding.

In this series, work of the past will be confined to comparison only. Grainers as a rule are proud of their achievement but are retiring people, and so few get into print that they may be counted on the fingers of one hand.

Prepared Scumbles

One change that has taken place in this century is the almost universal use of prepared scumbles; they are quick, finely ground, easily prepared, clean and convenient. Before retiring from active business I used them exclusively.

In the early days they had a decided tendency to crack through the use of too much drier, too little oil and the inclusion of wax, but all these drawbacks have now been overcome.

Although I shall describe the basic

colours used in any glaze, and also the tone, tint, or shade desired, readers may use any maker's scumble that will fit my colour description. I cannot mention the many proprietary brands produced by more than two hundred paint manufacturers.

The subject matter of these articles will be taken from any interesting graining that has been carried out recently.

Sketches, drawings and painted examples will all be specially prepared; no photographs of wood grain will be included.

Frequently I am consulted on both graining and marbling problems, some of a most unusual nature, and I shall mention some of these where appropriate.

To make the series more useful, I shall welcome any problems from members which can be dealt with in print.

Juniper
Juniper is a light red-brown wood with narrow red markings, the knots are small, found singly, both in the heartwood and the side grain, and similiar in colour to the grain markings.

The whole is well glazed, and light and shade play an important part in the beauty of this wood. It is being used in modern schemes of interior decoration in the most striking manner.

The examples that I have just received from Canada where this warm coloured wood is popular are fixed to a fabric backing; decorators apply this with a paste adhesive so that the open joints of wood and other imperfections are covered at one operation.

The narrow lines of grain are best carried out by the crayon method, which is simple and clean.

Most wood grain papers this year are in full colour, with careful representation of fine grain and texture. Juniper, being one of the fine grain varieties, is in keeping with what appears to be the new trend in wood grain, and this was one of the reasons I chose it as the subject of this first article.

The ground colour should be a pale buff composed of white, a touch of raw umber and ochre.

The tools and appliances required are rubbing-in brushes for both oil and water colour, mottlers, overgrainer, badger and hog hair softeners, rags, hessian canvas, and a few crayons of medium to dark red colour.

Botanical
Juniper is found growing throughout the cold northern hemisphere; there are some twenty-five different species, growing as large bushy shrubs or small trees up to 50 feet in height. The finest specimens are found in Canada.

The leaves are needle-like in form, arranged in groups of three; in some species the leaves are minute, adhering to the branches with the apex only.

They are furnished with oil glands at the back. The oil glands are important, for the oil when extracted forms the scent in many disinfectants with a pine odour and is also used in polishes and for other domestic needs.

The female flowers which are shown on the drawing are produced on trees other than those on which the male flowers appear; they are cream in colour and consist of two or three whorls of scales.

The male flowers are developed at the end of short lateral branches.

With its succulent scales fused together, the cone is fleshy, forming a fruit-like structure or berry. These berries are red or purple in colour, varying in size from a pea to a nut.

They differ considerably from the cones of other members of the conifer family to which they belong. Some varieties are poisonous.

The fragrant red hearted wood takes on a light polish, and is now popular in good class cabinet work.

My drawing was made from an example

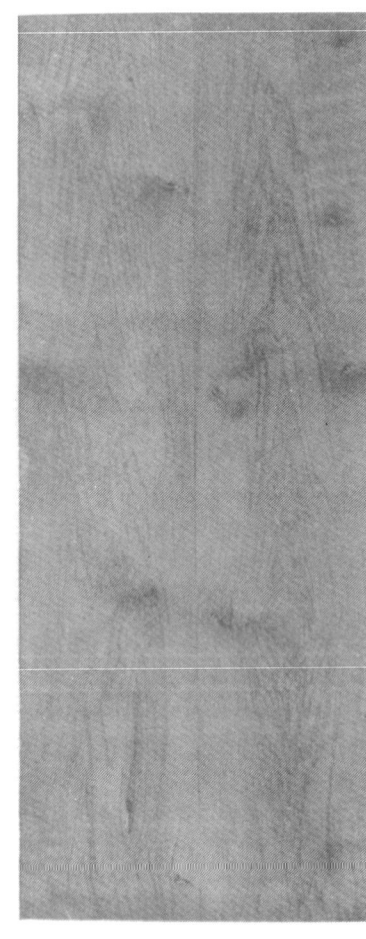

A painted example of Juniper

found near Cartmel. Priory. This fine old priory, which was founded in 1188 by the Earl of Pembroke, is one of the few that escaped destruction at the dissolution of the monasteries.

As Juniper grows to a great age, my example may have been planted by the monks of Cartmel. I know of many interesting trees of this variety, and Juniper is mentioned several times in the bible.

One particular tree I know well is now growing in the "Buttertubs" near Buttertubs Pass, the western-most highway between Swaledale and Wensleydale. It can be found down the hoar channelled flutings of the deep pit shafts that have been washed out with water from the limestone.

Painted Example

The example illustrated was painted by rubbing in a thin glaze of colour composed of burnt sienna with a touch of umber, thinned with oil turps and terebene.

The surplus colour was removed by using a handful of loose rags, and the centre where the drawing was to be placed was left a little drier than the remainder.

Drawing was commenced near the base of the panel at one of the centres of a knot. One, two or three crayons may be held together to make as many lines of drawing; this not only completes the operation quicker but makes the result look more natural. The ability to draw well, incidentally, has a decided influence on the quality of the graining.

An overgrainer should be used down the plainer side grain. This is charged with a little stiffer colour from a palette, passed through a coarse hair comb and drawn gently down the panel.

After a few knots have been painted with a fitch, the whole should be drawn together with hessian canvas folded into a pad shape. This canvas pad acts as a graining comb, making fine lines and altering shapes without removing much colour. A few minutes subsequently spent on the finish of the graining is well worthwhile.

Glazing

Glazing carried out in water colour is both quicker and more effective than other methods. Vandyke brown is all that is required.

It should be rubbed in a little darker around the knots, the shading worked in as shown in the painted example – light in one top quarter and well softened away to almost nothing at the edges.

A little of the narrow mottling is used down the side grain and this is softened in an horizontal direction. The washleather can be used for sharpening up the lights in the glazing; the colour should be made very hard and clean cut and softened well in the direction of the cut.

If the colour dries too soon it will have to be softened and another start made.

English Walnut

THE ability to use to the best advantage all the many materials available for decoration today is enjoyed by only a few people.

Pattern, colour, ornament, woodgrain, lincrusta, plastic paint, all have their places, and finding the right medium for a particular purpose makes exciting work for the craftsman decorator.

A jeweller and silversmith I know is a very enterprising craftsman from Coventry who appreciates the sales value of well decorated shop premises.

I was particularly interested to see when I visited him recently that he had had his display rooms redecorated.

The effect was pleasant and eminently suitable for the display of goods.

The door was grained in English Walnut, the remainder of the woodwork was brush-grained in the same colour to match, and the plastered surfaces were suitably papered in wood-grain papers.

Many of us will have used the same walnut paper that constituted the basis of the scheme; it was of medium quality and the whole scheme would be moderate in price. It was an excellent example of the correct choice of medium for the job and the decorator is to be commended on his skill in the graining of the woodwork and the client on his taste.

The graining of the door is of course the important part of my story, but I mention the wallpaper because it was an integral part of the scheme.

Walnut may be grained by several methods and mediums according to the detail required or the specimen being worked.

The subject of this article had been carried out in turpentine colour on a flogged water colour ground.

Country of Origin

Walnut is grown in the Northern Hemisphere, the principal producing countries being France, Italy, Roumania, Turkey, Bulgaria and Hungary.

Our British variety Juglans Regia is one that was imported from Turkey, probably by the Romans, A.D. 43 to 410, but it was not seriously developed until the sixteenth century.

There are some seventeen varieties of walnut in the family (Juglandaceae) all of which are popular in both furniture and interior decoration.

Though it grows well in Britain it cannot be said to be popular.

I live in a well wooded part yet I only know of one within walking distance, and I am probably right in thinking it is the only one, for the boys who come for the walnuts in the autumn do not appear to have found any more. The fruit is not grown every year, but only once every seven years.

I am looking for a bumper crop this year. In the spring I saw the long male single catkin hanging from the twigs and the females in groups at the end of the young shoots, which is a sure sign of fruit later.

The forester on the estate at Townley Hall estimates the tree to be about 200 years old; as other trees in the park are much older and the hall goes back almost to the time of the Conqueror one can assume this to be correct.

Walnut, like oak, is a slow growing wood and cannot appeal to anyone who desires a quick return on his outlay.

In small orchards however when grown for fruit or oil bearing qualities a yield may be obtained in thirty years; some interesting names have been given to the cultivated types: Adams, Cresco, Myers, Tasterite, Weard, etc.

In good fertile parts the tree will continue to bear fruit and grow to a height of 100 ft. with a trunk of 6 ft. diameter.

Colours and Tools

The ground colour should be a light, cool, buff colour composed of white, ochre, and a little black. As three glazes of colour are used, the ground must be kept light, and the glazes thin and transparent, otherwise too dark an effect will be obtained.

The other colours are vandyke brown, ground in water, raw and burnt sienna, ground in linseed oil, and drop black ground in turps. Prepared scumbles may be used.

The tools required are flogger, hoghair softener, filches, mottlers, sponge and fantail overgrainer.

Method of Working

The work is executed as follows. Rub in a thin glaze of water colour, flog the vandyke well, letting the brush travel forward to avoid cross markings with the end of the flogger.

See that the colour is suitably bound before much has been carried out and allow a little time to harden.

Two kettles may be used for the thinners; one should be prepared with one part linseed oil, two parts turpentine and a few drops of terebene, and a second with turpentine only.

If pure spirits of turpentine is available it is worth the extra money as only a small quantity is used and it is much easier to control and manipulate. White spirit is very searching, opening out the work violently every time the mottlers are recharged with colour.

Rub in a thin glaze of oil colour over the

flogged ground with a small amount of black and burnt sienna; raw sienna should be used in the glaze only for the side grain. If the surface is too wet, remove part of it with a soft rag, working downwards in the direction of the grain to avoid shadiness.

Draw in the grain markings with a short worn overgrainer charged with turps and a little black. A few places should be worked together so that advantage can be taken of the wetness of the overgrainer.

Where the brush overlaps the last brush stroke a darker line will result; this will have a graduated edge in a most natural manner, and a few lighter cross markings should be made at the same time simply by halting the brush.

Once a part has been grained it should not be touched again. A fitch side should be used for the centre of the shapes as the one or two-inch overgrainer is on the large side.

It is, of course, usual to make the best drawing down the centre of the panel, working with the thin black practically all the time. The general colour is a light brown but the overgrainer will leave a slightly darker tone of brown down both edges which will form the drawing of the grain.

A tool may be used for laying on the colour down the outer sides of the shapes, for it is much easier to spread the glaze with this than with the mottler. Here advantage should be taken of the three colours on the palette and a slight distinction made every few inches; a green-brown can also be readily made with the black and raw sienna. A ribbon of olive green is often found in walnut and it is a most natural and useful addition to a plain brown.

After the whole has been grained with the mottler, you should change over to the fantail for further detail in the grain. Charge the brush with turps only and work with the grain, and this should open out the colour slightly.

Watch carefully for running and clean the brush on rags or with the sponge for it becomes greasy from the glaze. Black may be added with the fantail in places where it is thought to be too light in colour. The whole should be kept wet, almost to the point of running, and a few small knots touched in with a fitch.

The use of the sponge down the side grain gives a good grain effect without adding more colour, and work should be continued with the sponge and fitch until a satisfactory effect has been obtained. A little softening with the hog-hair may be required, working outwards from the centre up and down only.

Glazing and Varnishing

Glazing may be worked in water colour using black and vandyke brown suitably bound. Light and shade may easily be produced in the first stages of the graining, but where a particularly quiet effect or a very realistic example is required glazing is desirable.

Two coats of varnish are required for a good sound job, using eggshell flat for the final one.

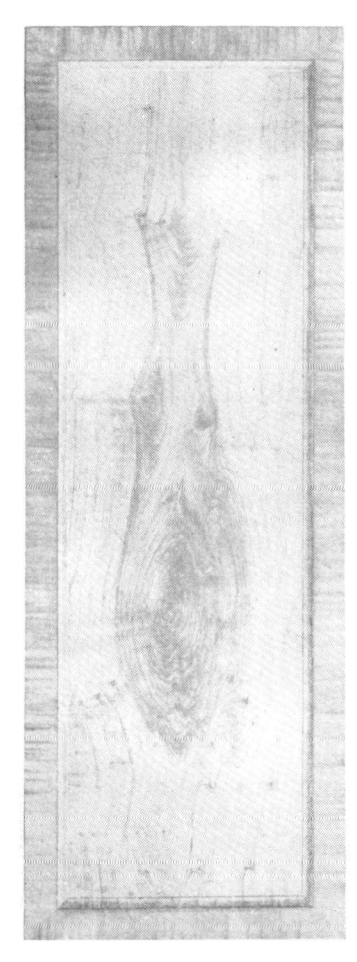

An example of English Walnut

Sandstones of Britain

A Church Interior

RECENTLY I was asked to view the fine Catholic Church in York that had been decorated by a well-known firm of that City.

The work was superb; the greater part of it comprised painted examples of sandstone, but the craftsmanship was so good that it was impossible to tell which was painted and which was natural stone without actually touching it.

Before the redecoration, parts of the church were painted white, some parts were distempered, others painted red, and a few arches were of natural yellow sandstone.

Now the whole of the interior is sandstone. The large blocks of stone have been set out and carefully treated in separate colours and arches have been struck. The lining effect of the mortar is another feature showing the fine skill of the craftsmen.

Although this work was carried out a few years ago it is still the finest example of stone painting that I know.

I understand incidentally that the work was much admired by the ecclesiastic authorities and attracted more new business than the firm was prepared to carry out.

> **The decorator is often called upon to reproduce stone effects on the inside plastered walls of public buildings and sometimes in smaller domestic interiors. In this article, Mr. Dobson deals with the handpainted method of imitating sandstone.**

Painted Examples

Painted examples have advantages over building stone inasmuch as they are easier to clean; dust, dirt and soot do not easily adhere to a smooth well painted surface.

Facing stones have been used in interiors since the Saxon times, whilst marble and granite were used even earlier.

As painted decoration however, stone on a lime plaster surface is comparatively recent. Stone treatment has been found effective in wallpaper both in simple outline and in elaborately shaded examples.

Paint manufacturers also prepare with fine ground stone remarkably useful products that give a very clean effect with little trouble to the decorator.

In this article however, I shall confine myself to the hand-painted method introducing several colours and also a little grain or wavy bands of colour.

Composition and Colours

As their name implies, sandstones are composed of grains of sand cemented together by colloidal silica, carbonates of lime and magnesia.

Chemically the sandstone is perfect, the silica being imperishable, and the durability depends on the cement materials.

The colour of sandstone is usually determined by the presence of iron, thus we get a predominance of reds and yellows. Blue and grey stone are also found, and my ancestors were closely connected with the Yorkshire blue stone.

The names of the various sandstones include Pink Hall, Darley Dale, Corncockle, Corsehill, Runcorn, Crow Hall, Heworth Burn, Pennant Stone, Scotgate Ash and Mountcharles.

There is a wide variation in the colours to be found in sandstone, but in painted examples it is best not to use many colours that are far apart but to confine the work to no more than two varieties with only a slight variance of tone.

As mentioned above, iron-tinted colours predominate, but the colours include warm cream, light brown, rich red, white, grey, whitish grey, pink, brown, hard blue, light blue, yellowish-white, light yellow, light grey and dull green.

A painted example of stone masonry

Markings

Stone possesses both grain and texture, but neither feature is as prominent as in wood or marble. These features appear to develop with age however and in some examples they show up well.

The yellow brown from iron stains or deposit develops into a stronger brighter colour, usually on the edge of a wavy band, whilst some of the white or cream from the silver sand bleaches out.

Builders and stone-masons frown upon marked and wavy bands of grain, preferring the blocks of even texture without any grain markings, whilst the decorator can secure the best effects with stones having good clear grain markings.

In the medium-toned varieties of stone, the grain markings are not visible, and the decorator must rely for his effect on the accuracy of the colour.

The interior of the new Cathedral at Liverpool contains many thousands of tons of red sandstone and no grain is showing because of the depth of colour.

Methods of Working

Several methods may be used to obtain a stone effect, and one involving the use of glazes of colour, semi opaque to transparent, gives good results.

Stone is limited in its size according to the thickness of the bed in which it is found, its weight, and difficulties of transport. We rarely find blocks of more than two feet by

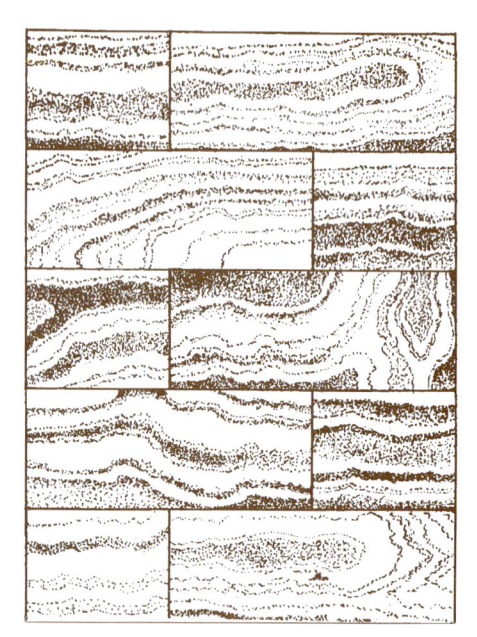

A drawing of smooth-cut masonry with Ashlar bond

four feet, and therefore the wall to be decorated must be set out in small shapes.

There are a few traditional shapes. Ashlar and Random Rubble are the most popular ones; Ashlar must be measured out, levelled and plumbed with great accuracy, whilst the Random walling involves the use of uneven stone shapes without dressing simply filled by a surround of cement-the painted stone, having the appearance of garden crazy paving with interchange of colours, is very effective for a painted dado.

After using the chalk line to denote the lines of the bond, a good solid black pencil can be used to make a firm line of division, and this if painted over will show faintly through one or possibly two coats.

Four to six tints of colour should be prepared in kettles according to the amount of ground being covered and the number of varieties of stone to be introduced.

On large flat surfaces a very small amount of difference in colour or tone will often show up more clearly than is anticipated.

The line of white or grey used for dividing the stone helps to give contrast to the colours and it is therefore best to err on the side of quiet harmony.

Most of the shapes should be painted in with the main colour, which may be light brown, cream, light yellow, yellowish white or dull green, with a few painted in the other colours. Two colours only may be used and the effect obtained with the marking or the outline.

Glazing

The glazing is carried out in oil colour using paint of a semi-transparent nature.

The skill of the craftsman is now brought into play both in the preparation of the colour and in its application and manipulation.

It must be borne in mind that a flat or egg shell gloss only is required, and there is a tendency for the colour to flash with too much working or through uneven brushing.

Thinners may consist of four parts turpentine, one part glaze medium, one part linseed, and one part pale varnish.

For the basic white, one containing a large proportion of zinc or titanium should be used.

The staining colours should be kept as simple as possible but I do commend the use of raw umber.

In working, the glaze should be laid on a little lighter or darker than the dry ground colour; many of the markings may be carried out with the rubbing brush and others with the fantail overgrainer.

All should be carefully stippled with the fine hair stippler. If a very clean division of colour is desired, one or more stipplers may be used. Several at a time may be worked in the same colour, wiping the edges between the stone shapes.

With a little care and a lot of skill a very fine effect can be obtained.

THIS article describes a three-process method of representing Willow.

Willow

WILLOW, one of the lighter woods, grows in most countries of the world with a temperate climate and also in the colder reigons of both hemispheres. It is not found in the South Sea Islands or in Australia.

Willows grow best in moist ground on the banks of streams and dykes. and in Great Britain East Anglia is the "Willow country." The trees there looked beautiful a few months ago as I passed many miles of them swaying gently in the summer breeze.

My first attempt at propagation was with a cutting of willow taken from a tree at Bent Ing, a brook in the Bronte country.

This small shoot I placed in a vessel of water with a sprinkling of sand; roots appeared in less than two weeks when the young plant was taken to more permanent quarters. A few years ago it had grown to massive proportions.

Description

The use of Willow is not new for it was used by the Romans. To-day it is popular for the manufacture of contemporary furniture.

Its general effect is of a quietly marked wood of a light pink brown colour, with heartwood markings comparatively straight grained.

The main lines of construction are lighter than the ground, whilst a thinner line of a slightly darker colour is found running round the inside.

If a cut were made at right angles to the annular rings, the heartwood markings would be found to be three-quarters to one inch apart, this large width being indicative of the rapid growth of the tree.

Knots are very small, and only slightly darker in colour than the grain, so that they have little influence on the direction of the grain.

In an example that had been pollarded for basket making, I found many knots grouped together.

The shading near the knot is quite important- even more so than the knot itself for it helps to give the knot a little prominence.

Overgraining is found down the centre of the tree, the drawing of which bears no relation to the grain and is similar in type to that we find in walnut, haphazard and striking.

Mottling, which covers the whole of the surface, is prominent, slightly wavy and growing at right angles to the lines of grain.

The cuts of mottle are near together, but uneven in tones of colour. To compensate for their nearness they are almost six inches in width; few are narrow.

All the knots appear to have two flashes of light radiating from the sides and a well defined shadow underneath.

The glazing, which is more vigorous down the centre of the panel, appears to bear no relationship to the overgraining.

The texture of the ground is fine such as can be produced with a good hair stippler, or by flogging with a quality paint brush.

Colours

The ground colour should be prepared in hard, smooth white, primarily because it is simple and convenient, but also because it is easier to secure a lighter effect by adding colour to the glaze, than by trying to keep a light effect with the ground on the dark side.

A gilp or scumble should be prepared from orange chrome, raw umber, white, and crimson lake, the colours being balanced with discretion and according to the sample

The three processes used in the graining of Willow: Left: Graining. Centre: Overgraining. Right: Glazing

being worked.

These colours, ground in oil of the decorator's tube quality, will be satisfactory for all the grain markings, knots and overgraining.

The glazing, however, should be carried out in water colour, vandyke brown for the bulk of the area, with a small amount of raw sienna where a little yellow is desired, or crimson lake for additional pink.

Method of Working

To obtain a fine representation of Willow, a three-process graining system is required, i.e., grain, overgrain, and glaze. This is carried out as follows.

(i) Graining
Rub in the prepared glaze, which should be very thin and pale, consisting of, say, one part colour to twenty of medium, the latter comprising one part linseed oil, two of clear

A painted example by Mr Dobson

glaze and three of turpentine, with the addition of a few drops of terebine.

The colour should be just strong enough to show on the white ground, whilst the quantity laid on should be easy, but bare enough to hold the flogging without running.

Flog to a fine texture or stipple as desired (stippling of course giving the finest texture); this helps to lay the colour on more evenly and dries up the excess thinners.

Using a narrow graining horn or a piece of hard India rubber, commence the wiping out of the grain markings, work upwards from the bottom centre.

Work up on both sides of the panel, and not one up and one down as is frequently done.

The line that you are making should be less than a quarter of one inch in width, and you should try to deposit a fine line of dark colour on the inside.

The side grain markings should be worked with a coarse steel comb, possibly with some of the teeth removed.

The lines must not be too prominent, so that too much colour should not be added to the medium in the first place.

If the dark line has been produced in the combing as desired, the work should be allowed to set for an hour or so before softening; if the dark line cannot be seen, a thin line should first be added with a thin worn sable.

Softening should be done in one direction only:- upwards; if the dark line starts to run the work should be left until it sets a little more.

(ii) Overgraining

For the overgraining, soften the surface of the parts to be grained with an oily rag.

The colour should be on the brown side and worked in with a fitch.

A narrow overgrainer should then be brought into action, working about the heavier lines.

The hog-hair softener is used to soften the work until a woolly appearance is produced.

(iii) Glazing

The cross lines of glaze, which are perhaps the most striking, are easily produced in water colour with the aid of a broad mottler.

Skilful mottling is done with a delicate movemen of the wrist.

The lines should be varied slightly in width, kept near together and softened gently in a horizontal direction.

Light Oak and Linen Fold

Linen fold was used on the walls in conjunction with light oak grained woodwork in the scheme described here. Mr. Dobson suggests that the treatment is ideally suited to premises which must necessarily stand up to a great deal of wear and tear and still look attractive.

A Merchant's Premises

THE main purpose of these articles is to describe examples of good work that is being carried out today.

I had a find recently whilst visiting Derby, in the Midlands. Amongst the material used to illustrate a lecture I was giving on "The Lighter Woods", was a large panel of "Linen Fold" lincrusta, supplied by the manufacturers.

Mr. S. F. Raley, the enthusiastic manager of W. Robinson (Nottingham) Ltd., was in attendance, and cordially invited me to see two rooms his company had recently had decorated with this material, one a display room, the other the sales department.

Both rooms were lofty and presented many difficulties for the decorator; the key-note of one was light oak, and of the other St. Anne's marble.

Many interesting decorative materials were used in the display; the results were excellent and Mr. Raley was justly proud of them.

Premises used by merchants are subjected to much heavy wear and tear, but at all times they must be immaculate.

Graining, however, will stand up to wear better than any other form of painted surface, provided the standard of craftsmanship is high, and that is why graining continues in use to-day.

At the same time, however well done, our painted examples cannot compete with the texture produced by the fine engraving and the heavy presses used in the manufactures of lincrusta.

My attention was directed to the fine light oak graining of the woodwork, which had been well prepared, grained in the fine traditional manner and twice varnished, flat finished.

The wall filling in the sales department had been hung with linen fold. After hanging, the surface had been painted, lightly scumbled and flat varnished.

Mr. Booth of Messrs. Wilkinson and Buntings was the grainer who carried out the work; he is an exceptionally fine man and, as a grainer, has few equals in Derbyshire.

The illustrations that I have made are similar to those used on the woodwork; for this no direct copy had been taken from the linen fold from the figure of the chestnut leaved oak.

A painted example of light oak graining by Mr Dobson taken from the panelling of the State Bedroom, Fountains Hall, Nr. Ripon, Yorks

The Tree

Though not the best known of British oaks, chestnut leaved is well distributed throughout our islands and is one of our most beautiful trees.

The leaves are large and glossy, long and sharply indented, and give an elegance to the tree for three seasons of the year.

The broad handsome tree seldom grows to any great height, the trunk is large and produces good vigorous figure.

The leaves in autumn are unusual, they change to a yellow hue in place of the copper red.

The bark is rough, whitish and rather scaly.

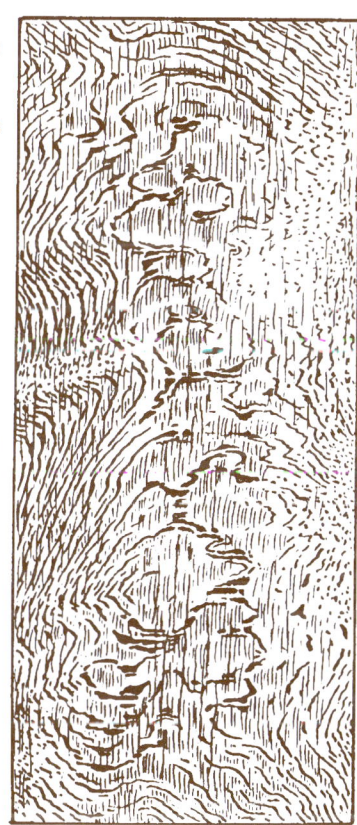

Execution

In colour the ground and the scumble were the same as were used on the wall filling of the lincrusta, so that the effect was identical.

It is always advisable to apply a coat of paint, well brushed out, on new fixed lincrusta, and it should contain a fair proportion of mixing varnish or oil and goldsize.

This helps to harden the surface for the wiping off of the scumble; it enables stopping to be used and fixes any thin paste film still on the surface after washing.

Graining combs were used on the

Figure of Light Oak by Mr Dobson

207

woodwork for a background for the figure, a coarser one first and then a finer one, and two wavy strokes were worked over the first straight one.

The fine grain was the most prominent as it was the last to be worked.

A number of mottle-like crosslines are also produced with this method of working.

The wiping-out of the figure was done with a piece of clean washed rag and the thumb nail, the whole being gently softened with the hog hair softener.

Between the larger principal figures some of the ground combing had been removed with a pad of the graining rag.

Care and neatness were the main characteristic, and the whole effect was pleasing, suitable and practical.

The Charm of Linen Fold

A large part of the charm of linen fold is that the reproduction is exactly as we find it in natural light oak, where the short grain is used to obtain the effect.

The short grain in lincrusta forms the background, leaving the figure smooth, and the wiping of the scumble from the surface makes the smooth figure appear lighter.

The short grain of the background, by catching most of the wiped colour, appears darker than the applied scumble.

In the heartwood, the broad bands are smooth and light, whilst the narrow grain markings are the darkest.

An alluring and inviting glazed effect is obtained on the wall filling by giving several tones of colour from the same kettle (three of which are visible from a short distance) varying from two to ten inches in width.

The effect is produced by the varying widths of the grain on different mould spaces, but much depends on the skill of the craftsman.

The band containing the figure is the closest in its texture and therefore comes up the darkest.

In a very large area, with a good high wall filling, this quality is marked and shows up well when the viewer is a good way from the surface.

Where a quiet effect is desired with the scumble, it is best to finish with a fine hair stippler to give a softened appearance.

Running the brush grainer down the applied colour also gives a quiet effect.

Wiping with a rag or scrubbing with the brush side gives the most vigorous effect.

The straight architectural lines used in the linen fold are based on the Gothic panel decoration, but in order to simplify the hanging the scroll work on the top and bottom is omitted.

When the source of light catches the edge of the moulding to form a shadow down one side, the grain becomes of minor importance.

The surface is entirely covered with mouldings – cyma, beads, fillets, etc., being incorporated.

Figure and heartwood grain are also based on chestnut oak, being reproduced in a bold and vigorous manner.

They are separated from each other by being allotted separate bands which cover them completely.

In graining generally I prefer to use the two types on separate boards or panels, for one distracts attention from the other.

A bead moulding run down the centre of the band containing the heartwood, with the grain running through it unbroken, gives additional interest to the surface.

The opportunity to examine a room carried out in linen fold with grained woodwork is one not to he missed. The actual thing is far more convincing than drawings or sketches.

Mahogany (Sapele Variety)

A painted example of Mahogany by Mr Dobson

Three Examples

THREE good examples of mahogany graining come readily to my mind. All are worthy of detailed description, but I must be content with a brief survey of each followed by a fuller description of the Sapele variety of mahogany.

The first example I found on the doors of a station hotel; the grainer and the contractor were unknown to me. The work had been carried out on the best prepared surface that I have seen outside a coach painter's establishment (National Competition work apart). The graining was of the Sapele type and of a very high order.

The second was a modern example in a public hall, the doors of which had been grained in a pale blue grey by a friend of mine. They were striking, even flamboyant, and well grained in the style of Spanish mahogany.

I am in favour of graining being carried out in colours other than the natural ones, and part of my collection consists of mahogany in colours ranging from dull gold to a pale crimson pink on white.

The third example was a fine piece of Spanish mahogany graining in a dining room, where the frieze, lock, and plinth rails of the door were all grained with portions of feather. This example I found in Kettering, the Northamptonshire shoe manufacturing town.

Botanical

Most varieties of timber known to man are to be found growing in some part of the British Empire, but only nine examples of mahogany are known.

Four of these are of importance to the decorator; they are Cherry, Feather, Sapele, and Heartwood. All the others can be accommodated merely by altering the colour, style and size of these four types.

The Sapele mahogany tree grows to a large size in the forests of West Africa in the region of high rainfall. The leaves are similar to other mahogany leaves, not unlike large beech leaves in spray formation. Flowers are of a pale green colour; they are followed by long seed pods, which in turn produce winged seeds. The bark is thick and smooth on the surface.

A large tree will grow to a height of about 170 feet; the girth or circumference may be anything from 12 to 30 feet, while the straight cylindrical bole often attains 100 feet. One tree of this type possessing blister figure has produced four logs which together sold for more than £3,200.

The wood is one of those used in the lounge and other rooms on the R.M.S. "Queen Mary."

The heartwood of the Sapele is of a pink to light red when first cut, which soon darkens to a red brown on exposure. It is characterised by interlocking grain which occurs at intervals, showing a ribbon grain when cut in quarter.

This quarter grain is the most valuable – wood with a narrow striped figure being preferred to that in which the stripes are broader.

When the stripe is confused and runs in curves and arcs, the stripe or ribbon figure is replaced by a plum or blister figure, and the decorative effect is much enhanced. These centres are darker and richer in colour and make the wood strikingly beautiful.

There is a touch of maple about the soft lines of grain, which are narrow and lighter than the ground and run round the blisters.

Mottle is round, small and well softened; all the surface is covered, but because the wood is on the dark side this does not show up prominently.

Graining

The ground for graining should be of a red buff colour, prepared from venetian red, ochre, orange chrome and a little white. This should be thinned with three of turps, one of oil, and one of copal or mixing varnish (which is better for drying with a semi-gloss).

The colours required are crimson lake, black, and burnt sienna ground in linseed oil, vandyke and lake ground in water.

As the colour is rich and transparent, it is better to work in glazes than to apply all the colour at one coating, for the latter method is sure to produce a solid and muddy surface.

I prefer to work on a flogged ground of vandyke, well bound by any of the standard binders, and, by the time one has gone round the room with the flogging, the surface will be hard enough for the oil glaze.

A prepared rosewood scumble. suitably thinned, will be satisfactory in most instances, but for a slightly shaded ground a little burnt sienna may be brushed on in places.

A grainer who prefers to work from his own separate colours should use the three previously mentioned, rubbing them in with the grain in a shaded manner, the general colour required being a crimson brown.

Thinner for the prepared scumble should be in accordance with the maker's instructions, and as driers and glaze are included turpentine only will suffice. For the grainer's own colour however, three of turps, two of oil and a little clear glaze may be used, along with a few drops of terebine.

Where the knots, plums or dark places are to be placed, the surface should be rag-rolled with a handful of clean rag, part of the surface being left plain.

On a large panel or flush door it is best to arrange the rolling down the centre, covering almost two thirds of the area, and an occasional rail or style can be mottled to take the plums.

The surface should be softened with a hog hair soften before the plums are put in.

The fitch charged with black and a touch of one of the reds may be used for the plums, many of which are double jointed in the centre.

The tone of the plums should be only a little darker than the ground glaze colour, and should be softened in as each few are painted in order to prevent the colour from setting and leaving a hard edge.

They should be worked in an irregular manner as is done in knotted oak – a few single, others double and some in groups.

From this stage onwards the general effect will be altered very little; in fact for a quick job the surface may be left as it is after this operation.

For further operations a narrow graining horn can be used to work in a few heartwood markings, as shown in the drawing, after the manner of bird's-eye maple.

Some of the curly ends in the graining

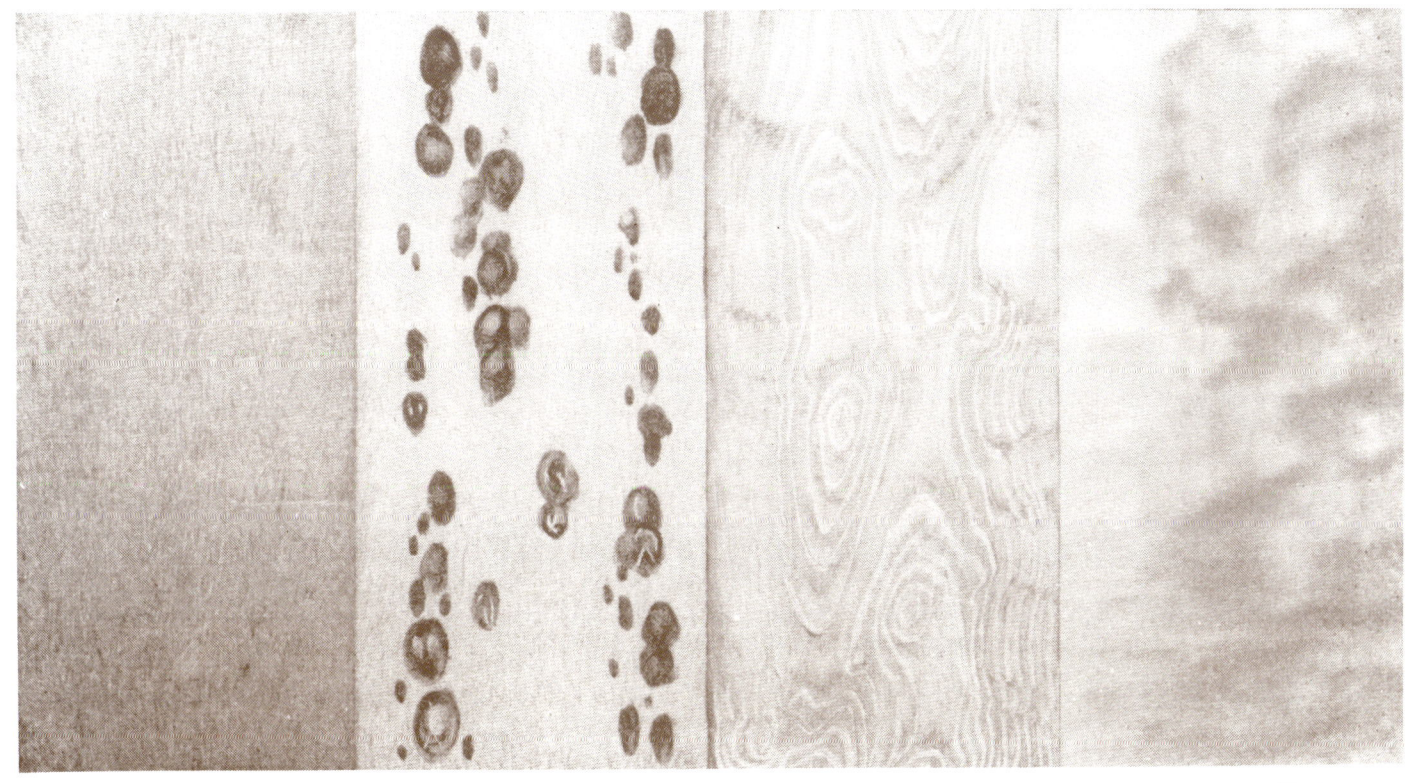

No.1   **No.2**   **No.3**   **No.4**

Methods of graining Sapele Mahogany. Nos. 1, 2 & 3 are worked on the wet scumble and No. 4 after the others are dry

should be attached to the ends of the plums.

The surface should be softened lightly with the hog hair softener, but without the lines of grain being lost in the ground.

Glazing
The glazing should be carried out in water colour, using thin crimson, slightly reduced in some places with black and in others with burnt sienna.

The plum blisters and the small areas near them are glazed a little darker in colour, with the light wave or line a short distance away from them. In the plainer parts, an effect similar to sand ripples should be aimed at.

211

St. Anne Marble

Few decorators, Mr. Dobson says, have the ability or the courage to use a marble fireplace as a leading piece of decoration. The painted reproduction of St. Anne marble, however, can be used to advantage in many schemes and may be found the ideal background for display purposes.

THE decoration of a room should be regarded primarily as a background for the display of furniture, carpets, objects of art and the dress of the occupants. In most apartments the focal point is the fireplace and the breast above it. How often, even when a room is centrally heated, do we find a fire burning and most of the occupants facing it; the heat is not required for personal comfort but only the spectacle of the fire and fireplace.

In the days of plenty a great deal of marble was imported from Europe, for fireplaces and many other uses, and marble could be purchased for as little as 3/- per foot, polished; today the cost is extremely high. Marble can still be enjoyed as a decoration however through the skill of the decorator.

In an earlier article I referred to a display room on the premises of W. Robinson (Nottingham) Ltd., the keynote of which was a fine marble surround in St. Anne marble. When the premises were adapted for their present use, the existing mantle was retained and fitted with an electric interior; the black, white, and grey of the St. Anne marble, just manage to predominate, and thereby hold the busy scheme together. One reason for the attraction of this marble is the combination of the three neutral colours, black, grey, and white, but few of us have the ability, or the courage, to use a marble fireplace as a leading piece of decoration.

Origin and Description

Belgium is the only country where this type of marble is quarried. It is a rock of fossiliferous origin found on both sides of the rivers Meuse and Sambre, but the organic remains are not easily detected.

Saint Anne, incidentally, from whom the marble takes its name was the wife of Joachin; they belonged to the tribe of Judah and were the parents of the Virgin Mary.

The general effect of St. Anne marble is a sparkling white on a black ground; the ground is well covered, only about one eighth of it showing. The many tones of grey pebbles inside the veining cover half the total area; a few are up to four inches in length but most are only about one inch in diameter.

The veining is similar to Black and Gold marble in shape and character, but the white markings are nearer together. Only small areas are pure white in colour; most of the white appears to have a glaze of black over it. Flecks of white are found amongst the grey shells and there are a few connecting veins of light grey.

A finished example of St Anne Marble painted by Mr Dobson

                    No.1   No.2   No.3

ABOVE:
Painted examples showing the stages in the reproduction of St Anne Marble:

No.1 – the sponge texture

No.2 – the pencilled veining

No.3 – the filling of the open stone shapes

Method of Working
Pencils, tool, rags, fitches and sponge are the implements required for this work. Two of turps to one of oil are used for thinners, and the colours required are black, white and ochre.

The ground colour should be dark grey to black. The ground should first be oiled in with the prepared thinners and a piece of rag. The sponge, charged with a medium grey colour, should then be used to cover the whole of the surface, using stippling, sliding, twisting and other motions.

This preliminary ground work should bear

some relation to the subsequent direction and situation of the stone shapes and the veining.

The stippling, carried out where the veining will be placed, should be well softened, and some of the white patches that are found amongst the veining worked in with a fitch.

The light veining is worked in by the use of two sable pencils held or fixed about one inch apart; light grey to white should be used for this purpose.

The broader markings are best painted by using the side rather than the point of the pencil.

Double pencils speed up execution but are not very selective until one is proficient in their use.

It is better therefore to use a single pencil for the completion of the fine lines, rolling it on its sides for the heavier marks.

When taking colour from the palette board, turn the pencil round, charging it with grey, white and yellow grey on different sides. This gives a soft blended effect as the brush is turned round on the surface.

The painting of the veins is done more loosely than it would be for Black and Gold marble.

A small fitch should be used to fill in the openings inside the stone shapes in varying tones of grey, keeping well clear of the edges near to the white and thus leaving a black margin.

Some of the insides of the stone shapes should be left with the earlier sponging exposed, while a few may be filled in with a light grey.

The edges of the colour are removed by softening gently with the hog-hair softener.

The three painted examples show the three stages in the reproduction of this marble. None of the examples is complete in itself.

Number one shows the sponge texture, two the pencilled veining, and three the filling of the open stone shapes.

In practice these operations follow one after another while the colours are still wet.

Glazing

Glazing is only required if a careful representation of the marble is desired.

It should be carried out in the same colours.

The ground is oiled in with a clean rag, a small amount of black being introduced.

A small amount of zinc white or titanium should then be used; these materials not only bring out the white lights to perfection, but they also maintain their pristine whiteness for a long time.

Two coats of the white and the lighter greys are required to give body and solidity, and they should again be applied with pencils and fitch.

The surface can be broken up a little by charging a clean fitch with turps and striking it against the palette knife held about six inches away from the work.

Black, White and Grey Colours

It is worthwhile to examine a little more closely the colours used for this type of marble.

Black to be perfect must be void of colour and destitute of reflective power.

It is the last and lowest in the series, the opposite extreme to white.

At the same time, if it is added to white in small quantity, it makes the white more neutral, more solid and local, with less of the character of light.

Impure black is brown; but black in its purity is a cold colour.

White is the most advancing of all colours; that is it comes forward and catches the eye before all other colours.

If mixed with other colours, it renders their tints lighter and more vivid; hence it appears to make other colours recede when they are placed near it.

White is the nearest ally to yellow, and is in itself a cheerful and pleasing colour. White takes every hue, tint, and shade and harmonizes with every other colour.

Grey being a mixture of black and white, partakes of the qualities of each according to the amounts used. Grey agrees well with other colours, adding to their brilliance when used near them.

Scotch Pine

Mr. Dobson includes in the illustrations for this article a mural employing pinewood as a background, and also suggests the colours of paint and wallpaper, etc., which can be used to advantage in schemes with pine woodwork.

MANY millions of pine trees have been planted in the British Isles in the last fifteen years. The true home of this fine timber is the Highlands of Scotland, chiefly on the slopes of the Grampian mountains, but there are many sizeable plantations in other parts of the country.

Of the ninety different types of pine-wood, Scotch Pine is by far the most popular and I have therefore chosen it as the subject for this article. Other types will be dealt with in later articles; the varieties include, in addition to Scotch Pine, Austrian, Black, Damar, Bull, Pitch, Cypress, Golden, Rosemary, Sugar, Yellow and White.

As a decorative wood, pine is at its best either in its fresh new-cut state or in a bleached form after it has matured.

A few days ago, my attention was called to some pine graining that was being carried out on an attractive private building estate at Bolton-le-Sands, Lancashire.

The grainer was busy on the flat doors of a staircase. The few minutes spent on the graining of the pine markings on each door made a wonderful improvement. The additional decorative effect given to the whole staircase was just right, and the purchaser of the house was very pleased with the painter's efforts.

Scotch Pine

Scotch Pine is not a very light coloured wood; it varies from a dull yellow to an orange brown. The heartwood markings are clear and well defined; they are only a tone darker than the ground and not quite as striking as those of Pitch Pine.

The lines of the side grain are clear, slightly waved and not quite as deep or varied in colour as the heartwood markings. Glazing is only found near the centre of the knots and rings and is of so little importance as to be hardly noticeable.

Knots, though few in number, are large and prominent; no knots occur in the long straight trunk where there are no branches.

A peculiarity of pine is that the soft edges of the heartwood markings and the annular rings are on the inside, whereas those of, say oak, are on the outside.

Materials and Method

Pine should be grained from a buff ground, medium to light according to the example being worked. The scumble used for gilp may be a proprietary one specially made for pine graining or

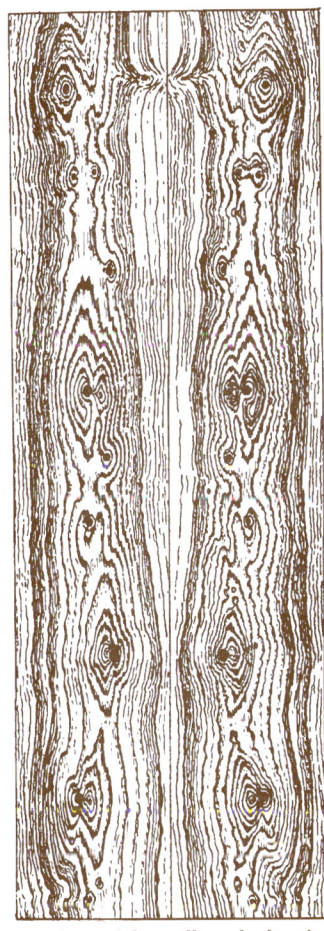

Drawings of the well marked grain of Scotch Pine

one mixed by the decorator from raw sienna cooled with a touch of raw umber.

Burnt sienna should be added to the two colours for the grain markings, which are best worked from a small palette in a semi-prepared state.

The tools required are few in number; they include steel graining combs, brush grainer, a few sizes of fitches, and a hog hair softener.

The light thin ground glaze is prepared in a small kettle from raw sienna with a touch of raw umber and thinned with one of oil, one of glaze medium and two parts of turpentine.

The panel to be grained is rubbed in with a medium coat of scumble, and subsequently some of the colour is rubbed off with the brush side where the heartwood markings are to go.

This last operation helps to balance the tone, also allows cleaner working and ensures that the lines show without being too dark.

The work is evened up with a piece of rag, care being taken not to remove all the oil from the surface.

The heartwood markings are drawn in with a partly worn fitch, using a light red brown colour a little darker than the scumble and working from the base of the panel upwards.

A few knots are a feature of pine graining; they should be placed in position before the work is far advanced and the lines of grain worked round them.

The side scumble should be examined and made good before combing: it should shade off gently from the strong markings to the edges.

The combing may be carried out with the steel combs or with the brush grainer as desired, and should follow the outside line of the drawing made with the fitch.

It is essential to make a good joining between the fitchwork and the combing.

The grainer should not be easily satisfied but should rub up the work and comb it a second time if the joint is untidy.

All the rails and styles should be cut in cleanly, the rails being combed before the styles are rubbed in.

When the work is partly set, a clean fitch is used to soften the inside edges of the heartwood markings, and the hog hair to soften the work gently, working outwards from knots and heartwood centres.

Glazing

A little shading, carried out with rag near the knots, will give a lighter tone, which is often all that is required. No mottling is found in Scotch Pine, but the area near the knots or the centres is a little darker than the remainder, and a thin glaze of vandyke brown in water, softened away with the badger softener, will produce this effect if desired.

Harmonising Colours

In wallpaper and painted surfaces, white and orange cream go well with pine woodwork, whilst blue, medium blue, gold, orange and brown are suitable for smaller areas such as pattern, ornament and lining.

Botanical

Balmoral Castle is built of red granite and stands amongst the pine forests of Aberdeenshire.

It was almost totally enclosed with high trees giving it great privacy up to three years ago, when a severe storm destroyed many of them in a few hours.

They were thrown into such an entangled mass that great difficulty was, and is still being, experienced in removing them.

Such was the number of trees felled by the storm in Scotland that it greatly influenced the freeing of timber from controls at that time.

Scotch Pine also grows in the Scandinavian Peninsula, Lapland, Germany, and the

U.S.S.R. In Sweden and the U.S.S.R., turpentine is extracted from the gum, whilst tar is obtained from the roots.

The odour of the turpentine is so pungent that it is unsuitable for domestic work.

Probably as much pine wood has been used in the construction of buildings in the past century as all other woods combined.

The botanical name is Pinus Sylvestris, and I have before me a few tufts of foliage that I collected the other morning high on the slopes of the Pennine Range.

The needle-shaped foliage grows in pairs in one sheath: they are just over two inches in length and face inwards.

Several male flowers are growing near the base of the leaves, of a pinky red with a bright yellow tip. At the tip, one small purple female flower is visible and this will later arow into a cone.

Scotch Pine is one of the most picturesque of our forest trees.

It has the interesting christmas tree shape when young, but in maturity it changes to a mushroom shape at the top with a long straight trunk. It grows rapidly.

The foliage is of a dark blue green, growing densely on the twisted and gnarled branches and the bark is of a red brown.

A mural by Mr Dobson, showing an industrial scene against a background of pinewood

The male flowers produce a bright mustard-yellow pollen in the springtime the cones take a two-year cycle to mature, often remainine on the tree for three years before scattering.

Illustrations

The large grained panels in the illustrations have been carried out in line drawing. This method should show up the graining clearly.

The mural drawing shows the use of pinewood as a background. The theme is a simple one – a tree, a few clouds, a large sheet of ply or laminated wood, with a number of modern factory buildings in the foreground.

The floating stratus clouds indicate fine weather on a summer evening, ard help to give distance.

Interest is given to the picture by the alteration of the scale; the clouds and factory buildings being small make the tree appear large, whilst the pine board appears to be very large.

Lacewood

The delicate markings of the figure are the chief characteristic and, from the decorative point of view, the main attraction of Lacewood, and Mr. Dobson describes how these are worked in the grained representation of the wood.

Railway Coaches

LACEWOOD, one of the lighter woods, is still popular for interior decoration.

My attention was drawn to a clever piece of cabinet work in Lacewood while I was waiting for a train in York Central Station recently.

A number of new coaches were drawn up on an adjacent platform; they were clean with the smell of paint and the smell of new upholstery.

All the interiors were lined with well-marked woods, straight out of the building shops.

The coaches were of the open type, and had white painted ceilings, which showed up the light warm-coloured wood to advantage.

All visible constructional woodwork, seat ends, doors, and so on, were of the same type, whilst the wall fillings had been veneered with selected pieces of Lacewood.

In many of the panels the wood had been reversed, but throughout, the flow of the grain had been maintained at the correct angle.

Without this care in placing, Lacewood could look very disturbing with its rather flamboyant, shaded bands of warm light brown.

Description of the Wood

Botanists differ as to the origin of Lacewood; some attribute it to the Oriental Chenar tree, others to the hybrid Plane of America.

It has, however, been growing in London for the past three hundred years, and although it is a slow growing wood a beautiful specimen was well established in the palace grounds at Lambeth in 1837 and had then reached the lofty elevation of one hundred and fifty feet.

Despite the smoke-laden atmosphere Lacewood grows at its best in the counties centred on London.

Its botanical name, Platanus Acerifolia Willd., is of importance because there are other varieties of the tree, with leaves and fruit similar and the wood only slightly different.

The name Lacewood comes from the delicate markings of the figure and the delicate texture found on the bark of the tree.

The general colour is a light warm brown, similar to that of satinwood, viewed from a short distance away and minus the mottle. Lacewood is one of the few trees that produce figures; these are very graceful and about half the size of the figure of Oak; they lie close together and are rather darker in colour than the ground glaze.

A painted example of Lacewood

The shapes and contortions of the figure are similar to those of the larger figure in Oak, but perhaps not quite as violent in the changes of direction.

The largest figure is no longer than two inches, compared with six inches in Oak, and the figures generally lie more horizontal and are square in the drawing.

Lacewood figure runs in vertical bands some four to seven inches in width and small figure runs down the sides of the tapering bands.

Large figure is always displayed down the centre, although a number of bands are made up of small figure only.

Bands of slightly heavier, light brown glaze colour are found on the plain parts, never over the figure; they run away to nothing top and bottom whilst the edges are softened away into the ground.

Very little ground texture is noticeable – no more than can be produced with the side of a badger softener – and only the outline of the small figure appears sharp.

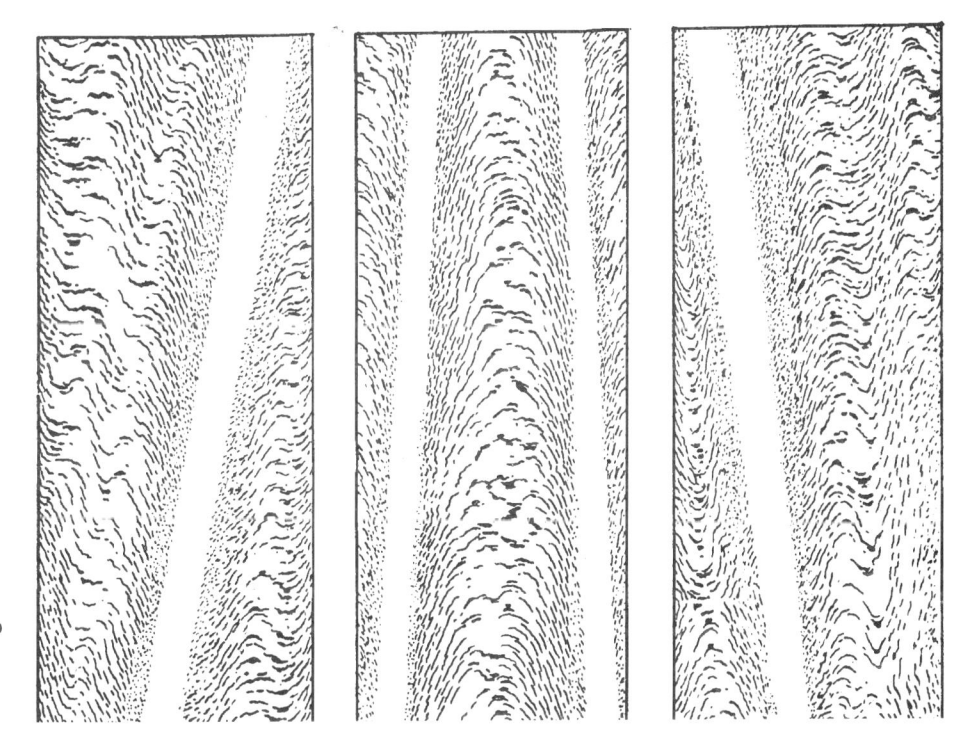

Drawings showing the fine figure of Lacewood

Method of Graining

A two-process method is employed for the graining of Lacewood. The small figures, being darker than the ground are best produced by the wipe-out method. A light opaque coating is used for the gilp on a darker buff ground which is intended for the figure only, a transparent wood coloured glaze being used on the top when dry.

A ground colour of medium buff is prepared and this should be close to the deepest colour to be found in the figure. When this is hard and ready for graining, a white or pale yellow buff oil paint is rubbed in, this colour being so formulated that it will allow ample time for graining and not overrun the edges of the smaller figure. Most white undercoatings of quality will be suitable if a few drops of linseed oil, a spot of glaze and a few drops of turpentine are added; experiment will show the exact quantity required of each ingredient. Care should be taken not to over-thin this opaque gilp, for good coverage is required and it must be rubbed out well to keep it in its place.

In rubbing in, it is best not to over-brush the gilp, and there should be no crossing of the work.

A few brush marks running the same way as the grain of the wood do not matter and may even improve the appearance of the finished work.

Applying the Figure

The figures are now worked on this wet light paint, the larger ones being produced in the traditional manner by means of a narrow graining horn with rag folded over it, and the finer small figures (which would of course take too long to grain in this manner) with a clean graining comb.

The small figures can be worked in very quickly by means of two combs, a one and a three-inch coarse steel, with every other tooth bent back so that it does not operate.

The operation is from the top downwards, and the combs are used in short strokes, almost with a stippling motion, working carefully the way of the grain.

The broader comb is used whenever possible, and the empty spaces are then filled in with the narrow one.

To prevent the colour from running on the edges of the figure, the end of the comb should be wiped clean after every few strokes.

For a smart job, all the finer points such as length of figure, space and general direction, must be carefully watched.

The small figures should occupy from two thirds to three quarters of each band. As some bands have no large figures, it is best to put the small figures in first.

Spaces should be left clear of figures between the bands, which can be arranged according to the amount of time to be devoted to the graining. (One grainer whom I know grains with figure only in two narrow bands on a one-panel door).

After the small figures have been inserted down one band, the larger ones are added with the narrow graining horn covered with rag.

A fair amount of weight is required for a clean-cut figure, and the graining should be so well done that the joining from small to larger figure does not show. In places the comb may have to be used a second time.

When the figures are completely drawn in, no other mark must be made until the work is dry.

The work will look a little raw until the glazing is carried out, for the deeper buff will be grinning through and a few brush edges will be showing; but after glazing these defects will probably help with the wood effect.

Glazing

Glazing should be carried out in oil medium, using either a manufacturer's prepared scumble or one of your own mixing.

The colour required, a light warn brown, can be obtained with two parts of raw umber to one part of burnt sienna, although if the latter is of good quality with high staining strength a little less will suffice.

Thin the colour to an easy working consistency with two parts turpentine, one of raw linseed oil, one of clear glaze medium and a few drops of terebine.

A little of the stiff colour (the colour as the scumble, but unthinned) should also be mixed on a small palette.

The door or panel is rubbed in with the scumble, and where the plainer spaces are situated a little of the stiffer colour from the palette is applied to form a darker band as previously described.

The grainer should work with the run of the grain and endeavour to obtain the desired effect with a minimum of brushing. There should be no crossing of the scumble.

A small fine hair stippler is then used to stipple in the work gently but avoiding the dark bands, with should be gently flogged with the side of the badger softener or with a fairly new and soft hog hair.

This should complete the work, but if the dark bands are too striking they can be flogged a second time to take off a little more of the colour.

Crown Elm

Elm is a tree that grows profusely throughout this country and its wood is used for both interior and exterior work. Mr. Dobson introduces his article as usual with details of examples which he has seen in decorated interiors.

I WAS fortunate enough earlier this year to find a new restaurant lined with Crown Elm panelling from the floor to the cornice, the doors, windows and all the fixed wooden fittings being finished in a natural, soft green brown colour.

Where possible the heartwood markings in the graining were arranged vertically and many were well marked but not vigorous.

The staining and polishing had been carried out extremely well, particularly the process known as colouring out, where the highlights are kept in check by the use of a thin coat of green or black.

A good wallpaper representation of Crown Elm was produced a short while ago by a leading manufacturer, and I have noticed that this has been used in a waiting room and bar at Leeds Central Station.

The hanging, and in fact the workmanship generally, was of a high order, and the heavy duty called for at a busy station speaks well for the serviceableness of wood-grain paper.

The Tree and its Markings

The Elm tree grows well in the northern part of the Western Hemisphere, and there are some eighteen species. The common European Elm is considered to be a native of England, where it grows well and sometimes attains a height of 150 feet; in maturity this tree develops a wide crown, hence its name. The branches are numerous (covered with the same rough bark as the trunk), spreading well out and often pendulous at the extremes.

The colour of the wood is at first a greenish white which later becomes a brownish shade; it is close grained and much of it is free from knots. The wood is rugged and heavy and has considerable strength; it does not easily crack and will withstand water.

The Scots or Wych Elm, which grows in Great Britain, has drooping branches, smoother and thinner bark, with larger and more tapering leaves.

The markings of Elm are fairly vigorous and chiefly heartwood, but many smaller shapes are contained inside the larger ones.

It is only quietly marked pieces however that interest us in graining, and the first illustration is of the continuous simple heartwood showing only a few small knots.

The wood has a fine texture which can be reproduced with the flogger, while the many

A painted example of Crown Elm

curly lines found between the wider markings may be produced with the steel graining comb.

The dark lines forming the inside of the heartwood grain are a quarter of an inch wide and coupled with a light line a little wider. These double lines are anything from one inch to three inches apart, with the fine combed lines worked between.

Shading near the centre of the heartwood and about the smaller knots is another feature of the wood, but it is not good graining to over-stress this feature.

The colour may range from a light cool cream to a green brown, worked on a cool buff ground.

Parts of the work are inclined towards pink, and this colour is also found on the side grain and near to the knots.

Method of Graining

A cool buff ground is prepared from white, Italian ochre, and a touch of Brunswick green. A prepared scumble can be used or one made with raw umber and a touch of burnt sienna, suitably thinned.

The glaze is rubbed in thinly, working with the grain, which will act as a preliminary drawing.

A fitch and a piece of canvas are used to work in the centres and the small knots with a touch of burnt umber, and the shaded effect is worked in with a few twists of the canvas. The darker parts are painted in with the fitch. A heavier line of colour is run down the side, with the fitch almost dry, and softened well into the ground glaze. A little pink may be introduced in places by using burnt sienna rubbed out very thin.

The wipe-out of the grain should be commenced at the bottom of the panel (or from the centre of the lowest shape in the third illustration).

The grain should be wiped out with a narrow graining horn covered with rag, which should he changed frequently to avoid a dark line on both sides of the light line.

It is best to draw or wipe out the centre portion with the horn where there is a variation in the widths of the spaces; the side grain can be grained much quicker with an open steel comb with the teeth some half an inch apart and covered with rag, which gives a softer graduated effect.

The comb is used lightly as the lines should not be very prominent.

A small short fitch should be used to work in the narrow dark lines of grain on the inside of the light lines and towards the top only, working away to nothing down into the side grain.

The last operation of the graining is the combing between the large grain markings, which is carried out with a one-inch fine steel comb, working in a wavy manner.

This little bit of combing gives a most

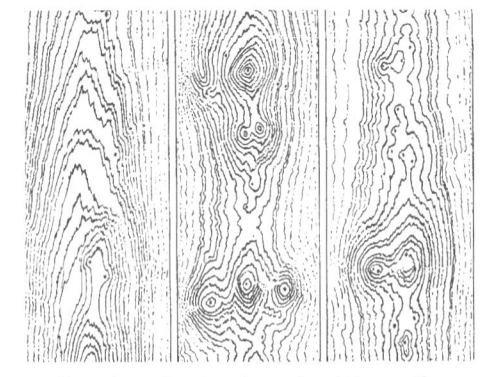

Drawings showing the grain of Crown Elm

realistic effect, and with the comb being narrow it can be controlled easily and care taken that the lines do not pass over the previous graining.

Glazing

Glazing gives a touch of quality to all forms of graining, and in the case of Elm, as a soft effect is desired, it is best carried out in oil colour. The colour used should be the same as for the graining. The mottler will give all the shading that is required near the knots. No sharp cutting is required.

A more vigorous type of Elm is used for the covering planks of half-timbered houses, and this timber shows up well after a few years of weathering.

Elm also produces a very fine show of burr which is found on the trees with the blisters, but this will be dealt with in a future article.

Verde Antique

Mr. Dobson returns to the subject of marbling, which he believes is slowly returning to favour. He deals with Verde Antique, a complicated green marble, the representation of which calls for much skill and patience.

ALTHOUGH there is comparatively little demand for marbling today, either in its painted or natural form, some small pointers lead me to believe that it is slowly returning to favour.

I have had more enquiries for information about marbles recently than for many years past, and Verde Antique has headed the list.

A number of interior designers are adopting marble as a material for wall fillings in many forms, and I noticed that good use had been made of marble-painted papers in the exhibition of craft work held at the Manchester College of Art just before Christmas.

This dull marble effect had been quickly painted and answered admirably as a background – the fine lettering, the beautiful pencil work and the modern paintings all standing out well against it.

I saw another good example of the use of marble effect when I called for lunch recently at a new road-house on the outskirts of Newcastle.

I found that the entrance hall, staircase and galleries were lined with a yellow brown marble of the Napolean type, while the ceilings and a deep frieze were treated with a thin application of plastic paint of low relief. Bright colour was introduced by narrow borders of decorated lincrusta, brilliant lighting fittings and coloured glass ornaments of contemporary design. The whole scheme was very pleasing.

Description and Origin

Verde Antique is a complicated green marble of the breccia group; it is coloured in tones of green from medium to almost black and some examples contain white. We also find the feathery lines usually associated with serpentine marbles, and a fine matrix filled in with broken parts of dark green, white and blue.

The drawing and painting of it is difficult and calls for patience and much skill. Although its use is often restricted to small areas it requires accurate and sharp representation.

Greece is the real home of this marble, but it is also found in the Swiss Alps, Turkey and the U.S.A. Strange as it may seem, although the largest quarries are found at Thessaly in Greece, the Greeks have used it sparingly, preferring stone and the lighter marbles.

The Romans, on the other hand, were very fond of it. Probably the first time that horizontal banding was used in a scheme of interior decoration was with marble in the famous church of St. Sophia at Constantinople. The plan was based on the cross shape, and there is also a large cross in marble on the floor of the chancel.

Painted example of Verde Antique

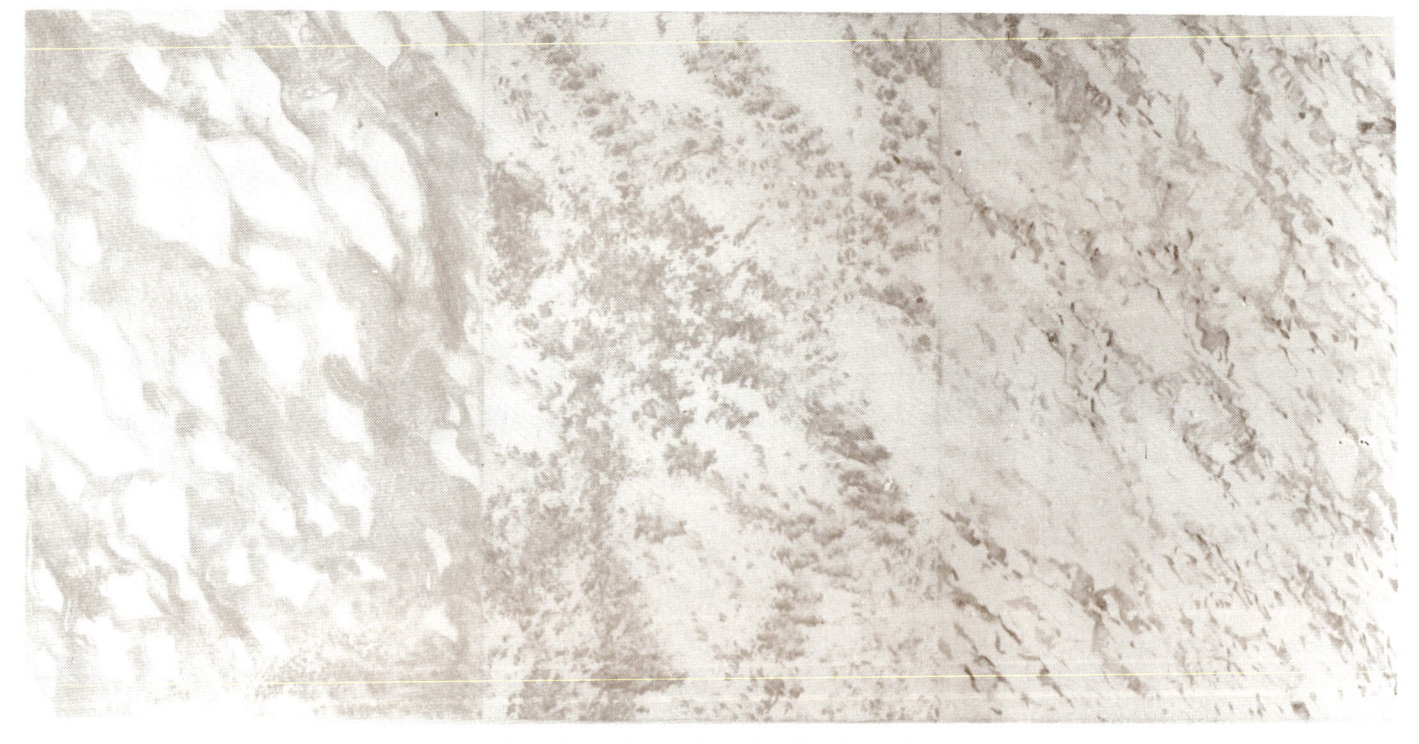

Painted panels showing method of working Verde Antique

Operations and Colours

Verde Antique effect is produced by three operations; a sponge is used for the matrix, a feather for the lines, and a fitch and wipe-out for the stone shapes.

In marbling the control of colour strength must be mastered before good results can be obtained. The basic colours required in this instance are White, Lemon chrome, Oxford ochre, deep Brunswick green, Prussian blue, Black and Venetian red, preferably in decorators' tube quality.

I work from a palette for any surface up to a few yards in area, but for very large work where it is desired to have a number of areas all similar (as in the case of columns in a large hall) I would prepare colour in kettles and store in sealed tins.

The colours are affected by the size and shape of the areas to which they are applied, and also by the proximity of other colours.

In Verde Antique, the large amount of black, white, grey green and sage green is surprising in what appears to be a bright green marble.

A glaze of grey green is first worked in on the off-white ground, light, medium or very dark, according to the depth desired. At this early stage it is helpful lightly to draw in with the tool the outlines of the larger stones, working in the general direction of the marble. The small fine texture of the matrix is worked in with a sponge charged with a light grey green using a stippling action.

The colour should not be mixed with the sponge or the sponge applied on the work with a heavy hand. As most of the sponging will show on the finished work a good job should be made of it. Many of the large stones can be stippled in with very dark colour, for, as they are worked on a light ground and the panel is on the wet side, sparkles of light will show every time the sponge is applied. Turpentine may be sponged on quite freely in places, but it should not be allowed to run.

A feather with the end cut off is then used to work in the criss-cross lines of the serpentine veins; these light green lines are few in number but their placing is important – they must all run round the spaces allotted to stone shapes. The feather should be used very lightly and charged with colour often, a dabbing action being used to empty or use up the colour. To obtain a steady effect, the lines made with the feather must run in one general direction only.

Working in the Stones

The broken shapes of the larger stones are painted with a colour darker than the ground using a fitch. The large stones, which are few in number, should next be worked in with a colour very little removed from that of the ground, but some may be lighter than others; these shapes and colours are important for they contribute much to the stability of the marbling. Spaces must of course be left for the smaller stones that surround the larger ones.

The finer green lines around the stones are produced with a sable pencil, and in places a touch of red or black should be added to the green to give interest. A rag moistened with turpentine is used to remove the colour from the inside of the lighter of the stone shapes, the thumb, a graining horn or a flat piece of wood being used to form the basis of a pad for this purpose.

Often the small amount of colour left on the ground forms a pleasing tint if softened out with the finger or a clean fitch. The wiping out is continued and a few tones of light stones are produced by extra cleaning or otherwise. More small stones are painted in and the veins pencilled in until the result is satisfactory.

The little brighter colour may be worked in at this stage or it can be included in the glazing operation; if the example is on the light side the former course is best. The calcite shapes should be sharpened up with a little titanium white and a few more bright green lines inserted with the double writing pencils. A springy fitch should then be splashed over the work to open it out a little, and give texture to the plainer stone shapes and more sparkle to the sponged matrix.

It is easy, incidentally, in this type of work to overdo the amount of detail, thus destroying the bright green sponging of the matrix.

Glazing

For a first-class example and when a dark representation is required glazing is essential. The surface is softened with a rag moistened with oil and turps, and subsequently sponged over with a light grey green, and in a few places pure green, keeping it more to the small stones, the feathering and the matrix. The glaze, which must be thin and transparent but not running, is softened gently. Glazing can be made to intensify or reduce the boldness of the ground work as desired.

The fitch is used to work in a few more sharp dark stones in places, while others may be lightened by clean wiping with rag or with the addition of a little thin white. Restraint must be exercised with both the light and the dark or the stones will appear to jump from the surface. All work must be near in tone to the general level of the ground and not too contrasting or colourful.

Finally, small glazes of colour are applied to many of the stone shapes in greens and greys. These careful finishing touches will produce work of quality.

Satinwood

Before dealing with the painted repesentation of Satinwood, Mr. Dobson describes in detail some very attractive examples of the actual wood which he found in a collection of furniture at a country house.

THE fine cut of its mottle and its golden colour makes Satinwood on of the brightest and most attractive woods. Some examples have a small amount of heartwood marking but they are not typical of the wood as found in decoration and furniture in Britain. The painted repesentation of this wood has been favoured by craftsmen of national repute for many generations.

Works of Art

I have natural example of Satinwood in my possession and although the area in which I live is rich in both fine furniture and good craftsmen, all of whom are helpful in allowing me access to their work, I had little success in my first efforts to find examples for the purpose of this article.

As I was preparing my material, however, I had a visit from a master painter who required advice in connection with a job he was doing at a certain house.

I made the journey with him to inspect the rooms and contents and had a most enjoyable time amongst a valuable collection of works of art which included many pieces of Satinwood.

Four tables that I saw were probably the choicest specimens of fine grain ever made at the Lancaster cabinet works of Waring and Gillow Ltd.

The top one of them contained two pieces of Satinwood reversed from the same cut of about five feet by two. The edge of this top was treated with cross-banding of the same wood, a narrow line of ebony being let in to divide the panel from the cross-banding.

The top of another, gate-legged, table was a most delicately marked piece of Satinwood, which had been cut from a tree some forty inches wide.

All the mottle conformed to a pattern and was displayed in bands of seven clearly marked divisions; these of course worked into each other but were not exactly alike on each flank.

Further examination showed that all the mottle radiated from the soft heartwood markings running down the centre of the panel. On one of the outer sides a second series of lesser markings indicated where a large branch once grew.

The background to the markings was well shaded, with one or two cuts of mottle grouped about nine inches apart to coincide with the light grain. Working outwards on both flanks was a four-inch band of mottle with cuts about ¾" apart. Another band could be clearly seen

Satinwood panel worked in oil scumble

Painted panels showing in enlarged detail some of the variations in the mottle and colour of Satinwood

rather wider than the first (perhaps seven inches) and full of closey packed mottle no more than ½" apart. A further band was some five inches in width with fine mottle, while interest was provided by plain bands about eight inches in width.

This was the most interesting piece of Satinwood that I have seen, for it gave a complete picture from bark to bark.

Other Examples
I found another piece of Satinwood on the end of a wardrobe. It was a large evenly marked board of some ten square feet, marked from edge to edge with fine mottle: the cuts were all at an angle, and most were 1¾" to 2" in width and about 1" apart.

I also found a few examples of this wood without any mottle which is quite contrary to the decorator's idea of what the wood should be.

They were of the orthodox colour and displayed some fine texture, but their chief point of interest was in the heartwood markings.

These were after the style of Hungarian Ash, containing a number of oval shapes.

The grain markings were ⅛" or less in width and many were no more than half an inch apart. Changes in direction and a slight amount of wave in the lines gave added interest. No knots were visible but a few oval shapes were incorporated in the work, as is found in Hungarian Ash.

The markings were flat and broad, with three or four lines together and then a space. Shadiness occurred in places as it does in the glazing of most decorative woods.

John of Gaunt, the fourth son of Edward the III, built the older portions of this mansion that I visited for use as a hunting lodge when he was created Duke of Lancaster in 1362.

The Satinwood however only dates from the nineteenth century.

At that time a member of the family living here was a General who became attracted to the wood while serving in India.

He had furniture made of it on his return home, and today this house probably contains the finest collection of Satinwood in Great Britain, and I consider myself fortunate in having had the opportunity to examine it.

Panels of Satinwood incidentally were used as grounds for painted medallions in the latter part of the 18th century.

Botanical
Satinwood (its Botanical name is chloraxylon Swietenia, after the famous Swedish botanist) is a near relation of mahogany.

The finest marked timbers of this type come from India, while smaller quanties are grown in Ceylon and the U.S.A.

The tree is broad and stumpy and never grows to any height – ten feet is a good length for a plank.

The leaves grow on both sides of a centre stem, as in the ash tree, twenty to forty in number and about one inch in length; unlike other leaf groups of this type, however, there is no odd leaf at the end.

The cream-white flowers grow in clusters, springing from a point between the leaf and the stem.

The wood is heavy and varies a little in colour from golden yellow to a red cream; in a full cut taken across the centre of the log it will be seen that the heart is slightly darker than the outside edge.

The texture of the wood is close and even, whilst the narrow lines of grain are twisted and complicated.

To obtain the most beautiful markings the timber must be cut on the quarter, that is radially from the centre.

Method of Graining
This wood may be grained in either oil or water colour, or in a combination of both.

It can be grained in water colour at one operation with skilful use of the mottler.

A resonably satisfactory panel can be produced in only a few minutes by this method.

The ground colour varies from white to a pale chrome yellow. Raw Sienna ground in water is suitable for most examples, but it can be warmed up with orange and cooled with raw umber.

The water colour is rubbed in rather wet, working in bands from top to bottom of the door or panel, and the mottler or cutter is used with a rocking motion.

All the mottle in any one band should be roughly the same size as in the example illustrated.

The work is completed by softening very lightly with the bedger in a horizontal direction.

When a better repesentation is required the dual method should be used.

For this a thin glaze of oil colour is applied on a white ground, the fine lines of grain are wiped out, as in the accompanying drawing, and the work is allowed to dry.

A glaze of raw sienna or a prepared scumble of Satinwood is laid in and the mottle produced with a cardboard cutter as previously mentioned and as shown in the illustration.

After the work had been allowed to set for a few minutes it is softened in the ordinary manner.

Softening immediately with the hog hair without allowing the work to set damages the fine cuts.

Californian Red Wood

Although similar in some respects to straight-grained mahogany, Red Wood has most attractive markings which make it eminently suitable for painted representation.

THIS useful and interesting wood bears a close resemblance to plain straight-grained mahogany without mottle, and when recently I saw stacks of this timber ten feet high and fifteen feet wide, stretching for many hundreds of yards, I thought at first that it was mahogany.

Many such stacks are to be seen along the docks at some of our northern ports. I had gone with a party of students from the college on an educational visit to one of these ports and we were well rewarded.

We had an opportunity of examining, at first hand, large examples of this light pinkish brown wood.

Markings

Red Wood is fairly even and constant in colour with the brilliance of light red mahogany. The heartwood markings, unlike those in mahogany, are several tones darker than the ground; they are inclined towards a raw umber brown and not a burnt sienna red as one would expect.

The markings show quite a number of long oval shapes, some of which are open whilst many of the smaller ones are solid. Sharp saw-like points are found in the thin narrow markings, interspersed with oval, chainlike shapes in a most original manner which is peculiar to Red Wood.

The great height of the tree must affect the drawing of the markings for they fill in the centre space of the trunk.

The Red Wood Tree

My earliest recollections of a Red Wood tree was from a geography book at school, where a roadway was shown cut through the trunk, and a covered waggon drawn by several horses was passing through. Red Wood is not the largest tree grown, but very nearly so.

I quote from the Gardeners' Chronicle, describing a grove in the Yosemite Valley : "The grove contains between ninety and a hundred big specimens of the Sequioa Gigantica. The 'Father of the Forest,' a great prostrate trunk, measures 435 feet in length and 110 feet in circumference. He must have been much longer when living. Along the inside of the trunk is a tunnel 35 feet long and eight feet high. The 'Mother of the Forest ' is a gentle smaller tree of 325 feet and 90 feet in circumference."

As most of the tree is bare of branches up to 100 feet or more, quite a lot of the timber is

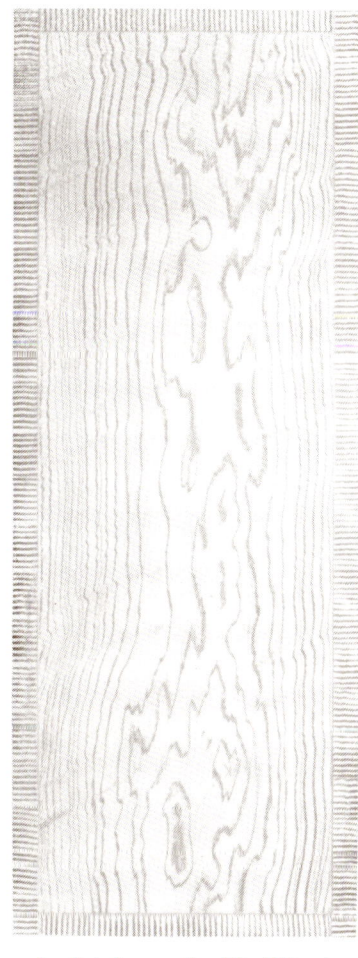

A painted example of Red Wood

straight-grained. This timber is free from knots and has a steady, beautifully marked grain.

It is little wonder, therefore, that the Red Wood is regularly cut, and that up to forty million cubic feet of timber may be harvested in one year.

Redwood, which is classed as a hardwood, is used for most cabinet work and the graining is both interesting and unusual.

As the name implies this tree is a native of California, where large trees are found in great abundance.

Like potatoes, turkeys, tobacco and many other good things, they were brought to Europe by our pioneers and explorers.

Seeds were planted in this country in the Victorian period; it is not known how large they will grow but some have reached 100 feet and are still growing.

Colours and Tools

The ground colour should be of a medium brown colour, prepared from approximately equal quantities of raw umber and white to imitate the finished colour of the brown veins.

As the work is done in reverse the ground will be much darker than is required for the finished effect.

The palette consists of white, burnt sienna, burnt umber and crimson lake, ground in oil. The tools required for the graining are-graining horn, steel or rubber-combs, hog hair softener and a few clean rags ; and for the glazing-leather, sponge, mottlers and badger hair softener.

Three parts of turpentine to two of linseed oil and a few drops of terebine will be required in the dipper.

Method of Graining

A gilp is first prepared from the palette of a dull pink colour, a few tones lighter than that required for the general finishing colour.

This gilp is made up of white and burnt sienna with a touch of umber and lake; the gilp need not be too warm in colour, for the warm transparent effect can be obtained by glazing.

This is thinned with vehicle from the dipper, trials being made to ensure that consistency and colour are both correct; the colour should be about three tones lighter than the ground, and thin enough to give a little transparency.

The colour is rubbed in with the grain and laid off carefully without any crossing of the work.

All brush marks must be hidden most carefully, going well into the corners, under the mouldings and so on, for any such marks will show in the finished work.

The drawing of the heartwood markings is then commenced with the horn; the rag should be firm and tight and both hands used all the time.

This operation needs to be done firmly and cleanly, and a change to a clean place on the rag made every few inches.

There are few knots in this wood, but any important part in the drawing near the top is suitable for a starting place, working from this down the centre.

The markings must be kept narrow, which rules out the use of the thumb.

The side grain, which is quite open, should be carried out with the rubber or steel combs.

One or two of the straight veins near the curly drawing may be wiped out, as the veins are quite often wide apart and should be gradually reduced towards the outer edges.

The comb should be cleaned with the rag at the bottom of each stroke.

If the combing does not come up to standard the first time, it is best to rub it up and start again without disturbing the carefully wiped-out portion.

The whole of the combing, like the graining, is very open; the ground left plain is three times the width of the combing.

The work is softened gently with the hog hair softener in the direction of the grain, which will take out all untidy joints and wiping. Softening, however, has the effect of narrowing down the lines, therefore do not over-soften.

Breche Violet Marble

The painted representation of Breche Violet Marble is being used as a most effective background for window and other displays as well as in other decorative schemes. In this article, Mr. Dobson describes the method of marbling and illustrates this with examples.

BRECHE VIOLET is a light, gay coloured marble used for lining the walls of many public buildings, a notable example being the Royal Hall at Harrogate.

I have recently found a number of painted representations of this marble; one of these, which is mentioned again below, was being used in a window display at Kettering in Northamptonshire.

Display Backgrounds
My advice was recently sought in connection with the redecoration of a gown shop in a grim industrial town.

The manageress wanted something against which to display her dresses to advantage. The job was to be a quick one, and the finished result clean and smart and different from her last few schemes.

The shop had a substantial turnover and money was no deterrent. We decided on a scheme that I thought was very daring and the work was subsequently carried out to the proprietor's satisfaction.

A little later, however, whilst on business in the shoe manufacturing town of Kettering, I came across a more daring scheme than my own. It was a painted representation of Breche Violet in a draper's display window; the scheme was most striking, attractive and well carried out.

More recently, I picked up the largest and most expensive fashion magazine published in Britain. Here again, Breche Violet was being used as a background, this time for a ladies' fashion display.

The black-cloth was a quick painted example in full colour; as regards the marbling, however, the artist had much to learn from the man in Kettering.

Origin and Colour
Breche Violet is found in Tuscany, an Italian province near the centre and south of the Appenines which only became part of Italy in 1861. Its compostion is a double limestone breccia cemented together with the oxides of copper, iron, feldspar, etc.

All the colours contained in a panel of Breche Violet mixed together would probably make a pale violet colour, but the name is rather misleading because white and pale grey form the larger part of the ground of this marble. A small amount of orange cream, dull pink and pale yellow are also found in the background.

The brilliant, contrasting colours of the veining are not the easiest to handle; they need to be

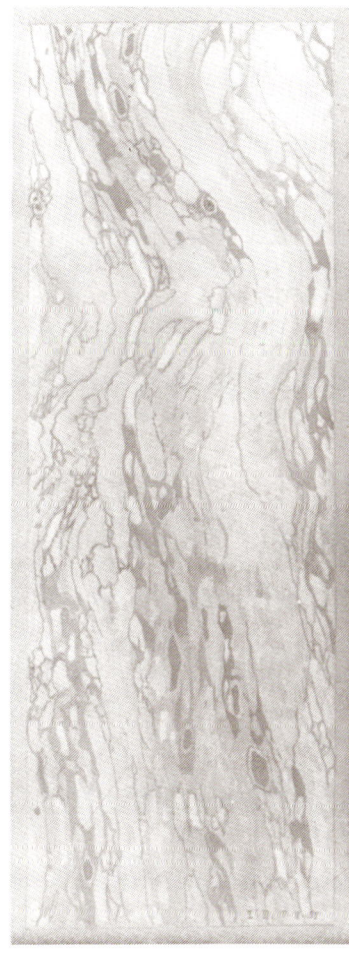

A painted example of Breche Violet

kept separate and used in a clean manner. The veining consists of voilet, crimson and grey, interspersed with purple brown, a little red and some orange.

Heavy breccia markings predominate, but narrow carrara type veining is also found both lighter and darker than the ground.

Most of the stone shapes are filled in with colour close to the tone of the veining; the largest ones, being narrow in proportion, have a most graceful appearance. The stone shapes and the various colours used run in bands from top to bottom of the panel.

Method of Working
The painted example is worked on a white to pale grey ground. A thin coat of white is first rubbed in, with yellow cream, grey and pink in places.

With the sponge, areas of these colours are stippled or rubbed in a little stronger and made more broken, including tints of blue grey and orange.

Any two of these colours are large enough for a panel of some 8sq. ft. – only in very large work would all the colours occur on the same piece of marble.

If the work is too colourful a part can be cleaned off with rag or by rag-rolling; it is best to keep the work very light at this stage.

For the larger veins I prefer a fitch, and for the finer ones I use sable pencils. The action of the fitch in either pencil or square form is to move the ground glaze and fix itself firmly to the ground. The sable on the other hand being soft slips over the glaze, making a firm clean line.

The fitch is charged first with a tone of light grey touched with a dash of crimson lake, and work commenced on the larger more important stones. This is followed with pale blue and crimson, and then orange and crimson.

Similar colours may now be applied on the finer work using two sable pencils in a chain movement down the sides of the larger stones.

The stones forming the main structure of the marble are up to 3 ft. in length, with a width of 6 or 7 in. The inside of this large area is a broken texture made with the sponge and divided with fine lines of pencil work. Turpentine sponging should also be used amongst the fine pencil work, but not over the heavy masses of veining, which have to be dealt with along with the glazing.

A rag over the thumb or a graining horn should next be used for wiping clean the inside of a few stones, others may be only lightly cleaned. If there is a tendency for the colour to run, rag-rolling should be adopted. A few stones should be filled in with colour resembling the breccia markings running to the side but slightly darker in tone.

A dry fitch is used to paint on some pure colour in small areas on the darker markings – ochre, vermilion, violet, pale blue and orange. The work is then allowed to dry.

Glazing
For a fine representation of this marble, glazing is necessary and should be carried out with the same colours. The ground is softened with a thin glaze of oil and turps from the dipper, and a small amount of black is worked in with it.

A little sponge stippling should be carried out with turps and with thin white in different places. More violet should then be worked with an almost dry brush down the principal veins. The stone shapes may be filled in with bright or cool colour as desired.

The quality of the finish depends on the amount of time spent on the glazing. One guilding factor is the size of the surface being decorated.

If it is small, the glazing calls for more attention than is required with a large surface when colour and scenic effect are all that are called for. When I intend to glaze to any extent I spend less time on the first process of the marbling and keep the work light to allow for the use of more colour.

The Illustrations
The painted examples reproduced with this article were all carried out in one day; glazing was not done as a separate operation.

In the small panels of enlarged detail, the first one shows the wood-like effect found in Breche Violet. This was worked with a sponge and fitch only, without softening. The second displays a sponge stipple background, with breccia markings painted with a fitch and fine lines with a sable pencil. A few stones have been filled in with darker colour.

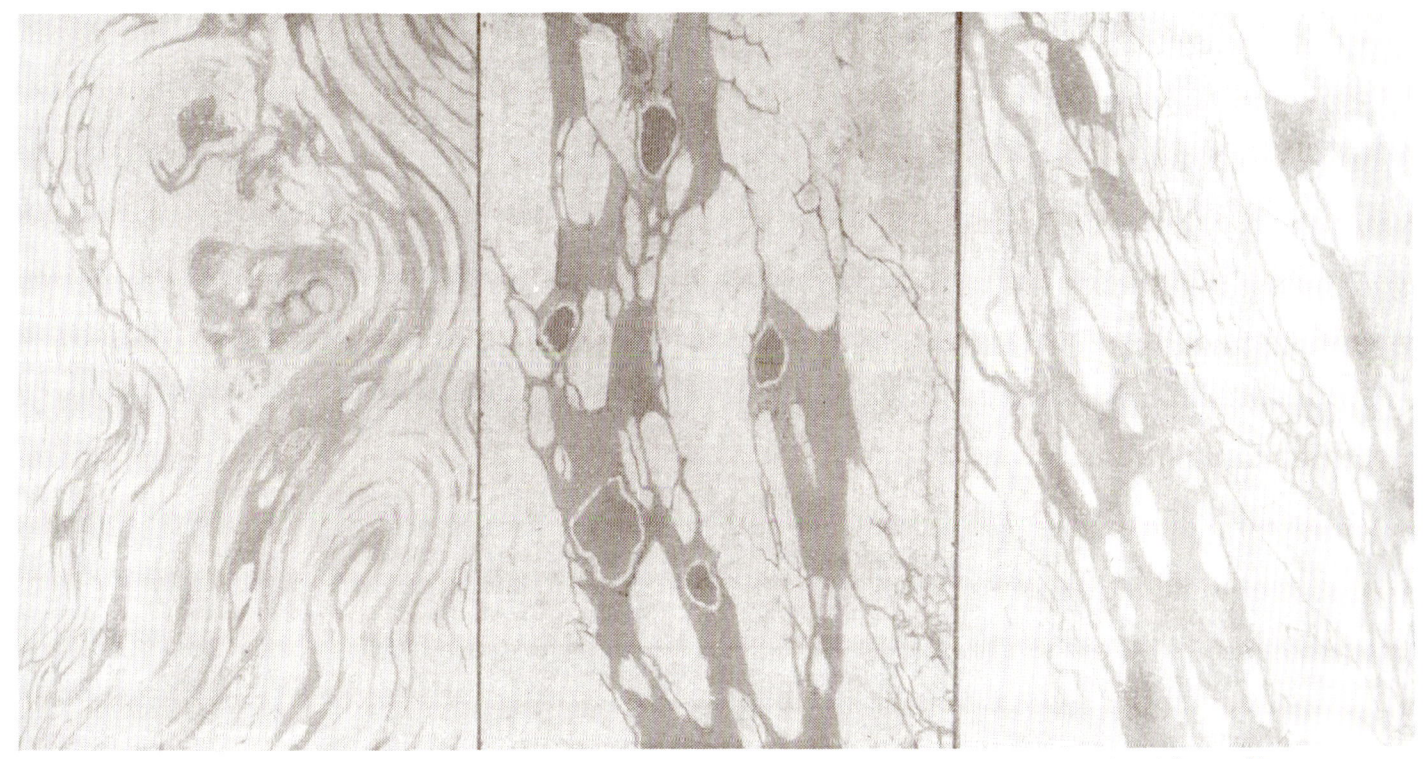

The last example shows most of the narrow cararra type markings dult softened, and stone shapes filled in with both dark and light colour.

Painted panels showing enlarged details of Breche Violet marble.
The panel on the left shows the wood-like effect found in the marble and was worked with a sponge and fitch only, without softening.
The centre panel displays a spinge stipple background, with breccia markings painted with a fitch and fine lines with a sable pencil, a few stones having been filled in with a darker colour.
The third panel, on the right, shows most of the narrow carrara type markings duly softened, and stone shapes in both light and dark colour.

Brown Oak

The example of graining that prompted the choice of Brown Oak for this article was on an entrance doorway originally part of the home of the Washington family at Bolton-le-Sands (now Morecambe).

BOLTON-LE-SANDS, which forms the nucleus of present day Morecambe, was a small fishing village some 800 years ago. The Washingtons once lived there, and the home of this family, which gave America her first President, was still standing some twenty-five years ago. It was pulled down to make way for a market, but the entrance door and doorway were spared.

These are to be seen to-day less than 300 yds. from the promenade at Morecambe, on the left-hand side of the Town Hall, near the entrance to the borough architect's department. I saw them when I visited the department recently in connection with the plans for my new house.

A Historic Doorway

The town hall is a fine new building standing in several acres of gardens and parkland, and I found this old door neat and freshly grained in Brown Oak, with decaying stone archway and massive supporting masonry, almost hidden amongst the trees. There is a neatly written plaque giving the history of the doorway which reads:

"This doorway preserved from the Old Bolton Hall, which until 1932 stood on the site of the market, is the original entrance to the Manor House of Bolton-le-Sands, owned in part during the 15th and 16th centuries by President Washington's direct paternal ancestors whose main residence was at Wharton."

The heavy double doors are solid and massive, probably made of good English oak under their many paint coatings. The graining is a sound job covering all trace of the wood's identity; I could not see any signs of the pith markings associated with oak.

The door is now some 400 years old, proving how paint protects, whilst the heavy blocks of Yorkshire stone, which have been left unprotected, are now crumbling with the action of the wind and the rain.

Each door has six panels, held together with large hand-made studs. The knocker is hand-forged in the shape of a large ring, and must have been used many times by the grandfather of President Washington.

Description of the Wood

Only a few trees live long enough to change the colour of their timber to brown. Because many branches near the ground have been continually cut or damaged by the elements, the figure inside the tree is affected.

Brown Oak is the central portion of a tree near the base; Root Oak is found below it and Pollard on the outside. This portion of the trunk unfortunately is the first to decay so that many fine examples are lost whilst the remainder is sound.

Brown Oak is of a grey brown in colour; it has a well textured ground with a few knots and swirling figure.

As the knots and figure are near in tones of brown, the general appearance is much quieter than the name would suggest.

Lines of brown such as are found in Pollard Oak are prominent in the texture under the figure.

Other colours – green, burnt sienna and a touch of blue – are intermingled with the brown in places, but these are not sufficient to interfere with the brown itself.

The swinging of the texture is a characteristic feature of this wood; the figure runs with it to form small sections or pockets.

The knots are few in number and appear to have strayed from the Pollard portion of the oak.

Some larger knots which run almost across the panel are different in shape and type; these are the anchors of very early branches and they are usually light in colour on the inside and shaded dark on the outside.

Some four fifths of the surface of this wood is covered with figure, which is fine and close. Small figures are found on all the sides, the few larger ones being in the centre.

Reversing of the same figure below and above a space is common practice and makes the graining so much easier to do.

Most of the figures are lighter than the ground scumble, but a few are darker and some almost black.

Method of Graining

The ground colour for the graining should be a cool medium buff, and this must be extra hard before graining is attempted.

Most prepared scumbles of a cool dark brown colour are suitable for this wood, including dark oak, walnut, and antique oak; or the grainer may prepare his own from black, raw umber, burnt sienna and a touch of green.

These colours will make any type of brown required by using varying quantities of all or some of them.

I find it best to rub in a thin glaze of scumble from the kettle and then work in a little brown or green, etc., from the palette board.

A well worn brush should be used for rubbing in, and some lines of direction can be worked in with the brush side.

These lines are followed down in a wavy manner with the steel comb and some darker lines put in with the fantail, followed by touching over again with the comb.

Some of the smaller knots are then put in with a fitch touched with umber; a small piece of sponge may also be used for this purpose.

The work is well softened down the outer edges so that the combing is almost knocked out.

The figure is next wiped out with the horn and clean thin rag, and darker figure is painted on; a pad of rag is then used to soften well between the figure.

Glazing may be carried out in water colour to quieten the figure or put shadows near the knots. Vandyke brown only will suffice.

Drawings showing the figure of Brown Oak, The drawings were made from the panels of the Washington doorway which is also illustrated

Colour Combing

Although colour combing is a technique easily mastered by the competent craftsman, its possibilities in decorative schemes do not seem to be fully appreciated. In this article, Mr. Dobson describes the methods and tools employed and gives six examples of the effects that can be achieved.

COMBS have been used for the ground texture in oak graining for a great many years, and no other treatment was even thought of when I commenced as a boy to learn the trade.

Since then many grainers have gone over to the brush method, but combs still have their value; they produce an effect that no other treatment can equal and many fine craftsmen still use them for their best work.

I use the brush method for 80% of my work, and the small amount of combed work I do is reserved for the medium to the lightest oak graining.

Although very few craftsmen can be sure of making a first class job of graining, most of us can with a little study master colour combing.

Many schools have taught it as a specific subject, but, as is the case with many other school subjects, its practical application in decorative schemes is not made sufficiently clear. I saw an excellent example of its practical application, however, on the woodwork of a large hall and staircase in a boarding house which I visited recently at a fashionable seaside resort.

I am not anticipating a run on colour combing as a result of my article, but it is gratifying to find enterprising men who have remembered their early training and are now adapting it to everyday needs.

Treatment for Hall and Staircase

The treatment I saw in the boarding house was clean and attractive. It had been produced by the manipulation of two combs in bright colour on a wet painted surface.

The doors were contemporary in design and included much glass so that there were only a few wide spaces to be combed.

The wallpaper used for the wall-filling was a newer type of small design, and the dado had been stippled with a fine hair stippler, using the same blue grey scumble as that on the woodwork.

The grounds of the wallpaper and dado were both white, whilst the ground for the woodwork was a yellow cream, giving a slightly stronger effect to the architectural features.

The blue grey scumble on the woodwork was only slightly darker than the ground, making it just possible for the combing to be seen. At a distance of a few feet the manipulation and the colour made it possible to discern small heartwood shapes and areas of figure, which were repeated at almost regular intervals. No broad areas were combed, as all panels were of glass, so that the combing was simplified.

Colour Combing Technique

The principle on which combing is based is the displacement of colour down both sides of furrows made by the steel teeth in a wet coat of colour. Some colour is taken up by the comb and should be cleaned off with rag after each stroke, but most of it is left thick down the edges of the furrows.

This accumulation of colour is liable to run back over the clean lines left by the comb unless suitable precautions are taken.

One way of preventing this is to use a substance such as metallic stearate in the medium. Nearly all the prepared scumbles to-day contain metallic stearates. Another method is to allow the glaze scumble to set just sufficiently to hold before combing. The time to be allowed for setting, can be ascertained by the timing of a few small tests.

Yet another method, perhaps the hardest, but a certain one is good brushing out. This operation is inclined to leave the glaze colour shady, but it will not matter very much because the combing tends to even things out.

Interesting effects can be produced with combs of different widths and degrees of fineness but no more than two combs should be used over each other. With more than two, you may obtain a soft effect, but the tendency is to cancel out the first strokes and your efforts are wasted.

In wood-grain combing I often use a few widths of combs, running over the ground several times, but in colour combing two runs over are sufficient for a good decorative effect. If more than one colour is used each must be used separately and allowed to dry hard before the next one is applied and combed.

Part of the unusual effect obtained with colour combing results from the intersection of the lines, coupled with the colour piled up on the edges.

When the combs are brought down a slight turn of the wrist will give a longer cross-over at one side than the other, more colour is spread down one side and a darker patch is formed. It is possible to produce hundreds of large and small heartwood shapes in a matter of minutes when the proper technique is mastered.

For this work all the combs must be clean and sharp, with a square end to each tooth. Combs have a tendency to wear to a chisel point, which does not clean out the colour to the best advantage. For sharpening I use the small emery wheel on my garage bench, and by holding a few combs together for support the job is quickly completed.

A flat piece of sandstone sprinkled with water or a piece of wet-or-dry paper laid on a flat surface can be used to produce a square end with very little rubbing.

Illustrations of Combing

The examples illustrated with this article are all straightforward in technique and execution. Others requiring a slightly different technique and calling for more skill in manipulation will be dealt with in a future article.

Example One: Example number one was combed with a coarse open comb, tooth width 3/1, in., space width about 1/2 in. It has been done at an angle but could be carried out with a straight square. The combing was worked with a free hand and may have a tendency to wave ; I prefer this technique. The material was from a tin of graining colour merely thinned with turpentine.

Example Two: The second panel was carried out in the same manner as the first, with the same material and comb. The pattern effect was obtained by overlapping the last tooth in the first and second lines of the previous combed stroke. Thus four lines appear close together, forming a lighter band down the edge, and when the same treatment is repeated in the opposite direction it forms a lozenge-shaped pattern.

Example Three: An alteration was made to the comb for number three; two teeth were near together and the next one was bent backwards. Further effects could be obtained on these lines by arranging the teeth of the comb in many other positions. (The first three patterns could be carried out with vertical and horizontal lines, and this is important on panelling for we cannot work at an angle against moulding and sunken surfaces.)

Example Four: The combing in example number four was carried out with a fine 2 in. comb with a 1 in. space between the strokes. Three clear tones of colour were obtained with this simple combing. On this type of decorated surface, a small amount of plain colour is restful.

Example Five: Example five is a simple plaid effect, using three-comb variation. The horizontal lines were first put in with a 1 in. fine comb, 1 in. space, and a 2 in. coarse comb, 1 in. space. The vertical lines are both 1 in. wide; the first was done with a fine tooth comb, then a 1 in. space and the other with an open 1 in. coarse comb. If I were combing a number of large areas I would fasten a few combs together to save time.

Example Six: In the sixth panel a new note is introduced by use of a wavy line. First the vertical bands were combed in with a 2 in. fine comb, and a 1 in. coarse comb was run down the centre over these. The wavy cross lines were combed with a 3 in. open coarse comb.

Example One.   *Example Two.*   *Example Three.*

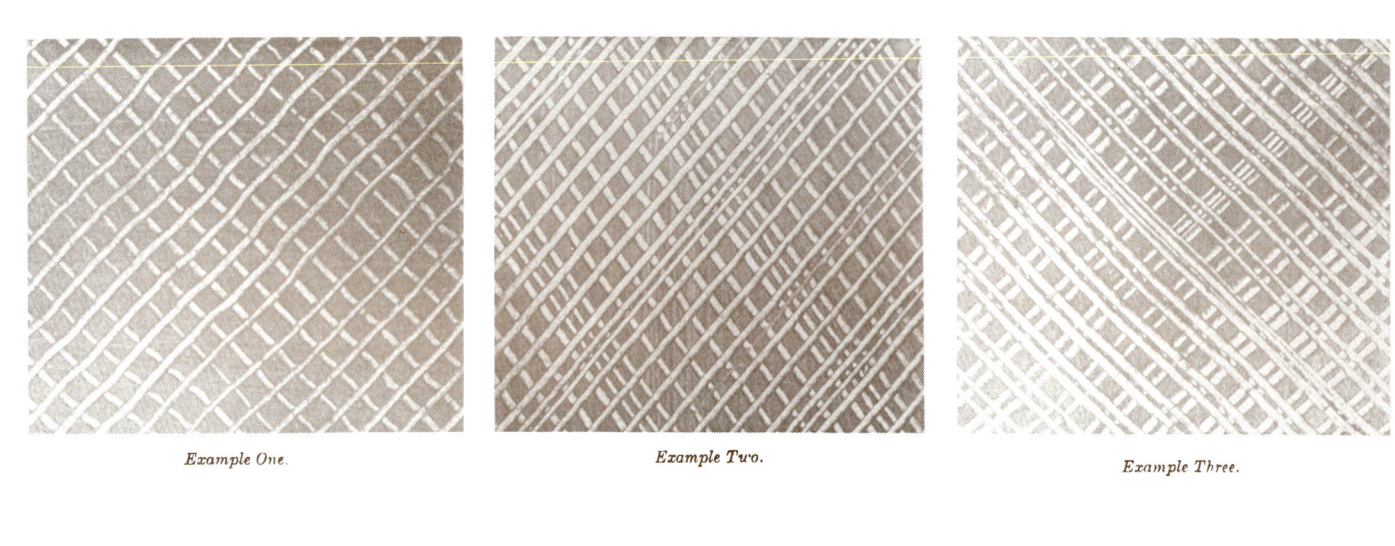

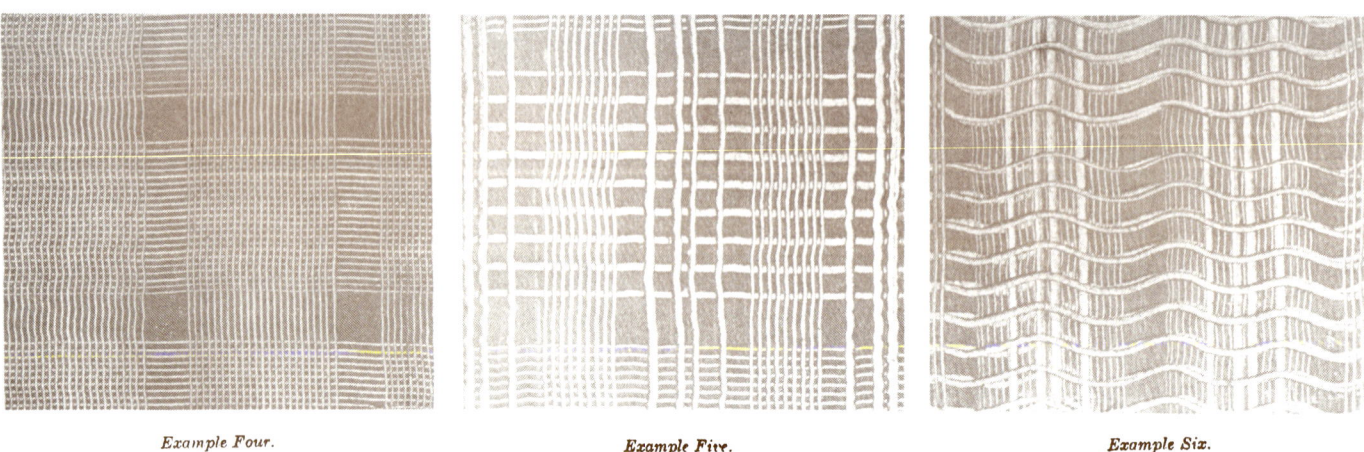

Example Four.   *Example Five.*   *Example Six.*

Drawing of Flat Door Grained Australian Oak

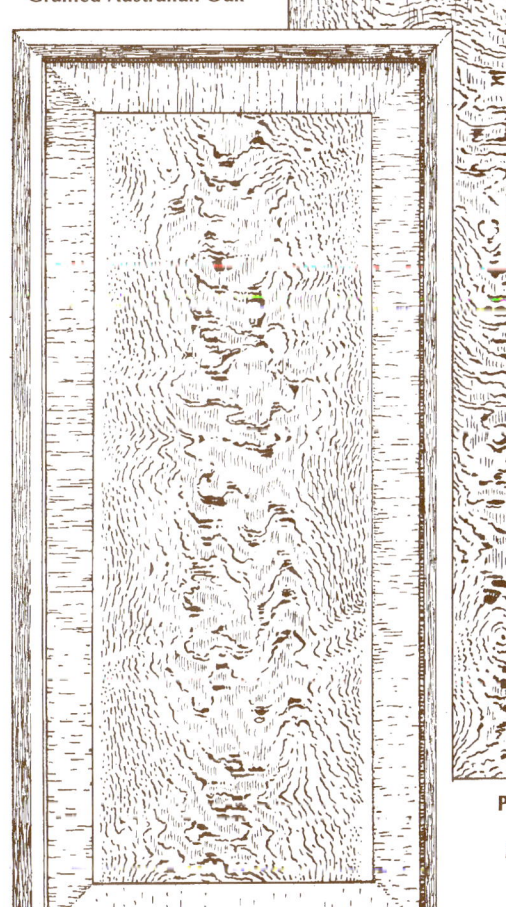

Panel of Oak by Mr Dobson

Graining a Flat Door

As a figured oak panel enough for a complete door can only be otained from a very large tree, such panels are rare and their painted representation is a little more difficult than the normal run of graining. In this article Mr. Dobson explains how design principles are applied to this type of graining.

THE graining of a flat door is the same as the graining of any other normal surface except that there is more of it and it is not broken up into smaller panels.

If it is to be properly grained, the plain spaces and areas of figure, the direction of the grain and the size of the figure must be studied carefully.

Good and Bad Examples

In a few doors that I have examined recently, the figure that should have been used on a small panel had been enlarged from four to six times its natural size and left at that.

It would have been much better to have kept it to its orginal size and used it down the edge of the door, giving the remainder a plain flogged texture or brush graining it.

I must add in all fairness that other doors I have seen were models of what can be accomplished by a skilled grainer.

The large flat door presents the skilled craftsman with a fine opportunity of demonstrating his skill, particularly when the figure of

239

oak is to be grained. Few large examples of figured oak are to be found, so that most of us are at a disadvantage when areas of say two square yards are to be grained in this way.

In the course of my travels both home and abroad I have seen only one or two examples and the Town Halls of Leeds and Brussels stand out as having the finest large panels in figured oak.

I believe the panels in Leeds Town Hall are Australian Oak and must have been cut from very large trees; they are well covered with figure and many of them are larger than domestic doors.

From time to time I visit timber yards to examine examples of actual wood, often moving tons of wood to find just a few finely marked pieces.

To-day in order to produce the finest marked specimens, most of the oak is cut into one-inch planks straight through the tree and sold to the trade in this manner.

Large examples of the figure of oak with a broad display of continuous figure are rare because of the division that takes place down the centre of the tree.

All rays radiate from the centre, none cross over it; thus we have two separate sets of figure markings occurring.

Down the centre we find mostly straight grain some four or five inches wide, containing a few heartwood markings. (These markings are not important to this article, but there is roughly one to every three inches.)

The finely marked figure occurs only on the few planks cut from the centre of the tree, which is built up as follows.

On the outer edge there is a fairly straight grain for one and a half inches, followed by small figure varying from one to three inches; next comes the heavier more open grain which may be from five to twelve inches wide, returning in the centre to small and straight grain similar in width to that on the outer edge.

The figure sizes are repeated on the other side or half of the tree but not the display, which is completely different.

The quantity and size of the figure are balanced on either side of the tree, but the figure is never exactly the same in drawing.

Root growth and disposition of the branches both have some influence on the direction of the figure, and these are never the same on both halves of the tree.

All my working life I have been searching for a true reversed example of the figure of oak, and am continuing to do so; some day I may be rewarded.

Principles of Design

Most men that are doing a worth-while job in the trade to-day have had training in art or technical colleges, where drawing and design have been included in the curriculum.

To my mind this training in design is most helpful for large scale graining.

Three useful terms are laid down as guides in design – space-filling, balance and symmetry, and these same guides can be used in the graining of a flat door.

The space-filling technique can be applied in may ways to the door whether it is treated as one plank of wood, as two or three vertical boards, or divided into geometric shapes.

All these treatments may be used with a broad surrounding style.

The general idea of space filling in design is to draw in the flowers, leaves or motif first and the construction lines last.

The masses of heavy figure are equivalent to the ornament, and the plainer winding variety represent the construction lines.

Thus a good method is to grain the large open figures first, then the long figures packed close together, which are used to fill in the central space, and last the small figures the majority of which can be worked in with an open coarse comb.

If it is decided to have a full panel, use say a four-inch style running round the edge to reduce the total area.

The first band of bold figure can be taken almost straight down the centre, working out towards the edges with medium then small and lastly plain grained texture.

Another method is to keep to the central band as before, start the figure small at the top and work steadily larger all the way down until the bottom two feet are reached, when a good display of open heavy figure can be worked.

Yet another idea is to use the same central band and work two groups of heavy figure one at the top and the other at the bottom, filling the intervening central space with fairly large plain figure, worked close together.

Anything large, unusual, awkward or different from what you have done previously calls for a sketch.

A large flat door takes a fair amount of filling with oak figure and I strongly advise the use of a small drawing to scale.

Such a drawing helps with the display of the figure and gives confidence to the grainer, and I have noticed that where a drawing is prepared the quality of the work is often much improved.

A sketch may show that the plain areas can be enlarged, so that much is eliminated.

The Actual Graining

Most of us use prepared scumbles to-day. They are so good and convenient that only when we have special colours to match do we prepare them ourselves.

In the thinning of the scumble we must take into account the time that the graining will take.

Most manufacturers specify turpentine only as a thinner, but often a spoonful of linseed oil and a few drops of varnish added to the turpentine will allow more time for graining of the figure.

Many scumbles refuse to dry if a slight overdose is given, and it is best to give it a trial on the previous day if you are not sure of the material.

Work from a kettle with the prepared colour and rub in the door as one piece.

A small amount of help can be given to the graining by directing the brush strokes the way the grain is to travel.

Steel combs can be used for the grain, though more often to-day a brush-grained background is provided.

With a wide expanse I find that a cheap six- or seven-inch distemper brush is a time-saver.

For bright clean lines a brush with fibre works wonders, cutting the colour like a knife.

To prevent shadiness it is best not to have too great a contrast in tone between the ground colour and the colour used for graining.

Many methods are used for the reproduction of the figure, all of which have their merit, but the wipe-out method with clean rag is still the mainstay of figure graining and this is what I propose to deal with here.

I use a graining horn for this operation because it is both faster and cleaner, and because I find that the thumb takes the pressure better on the under-side rather than on the top.

To work a long day without a graining horn is very tiring for the thumb.

A hard piece of rubber is another useful tool for a clean wipe-out; with a square end it performs its duty well.

No softening is required after graining.

If a subdued effect is required for the figure it is better to over-glaze with oil or water colour and lightly brush grain.

MISCELLANEOUS
See also:

Tools and Brushes for Graining	30
A Grainer of 1851	102
Drawings of Brushes	166
Knots in Graining	172
Knots in Graining (cont.)	176
Colour Combing	236
Wood Grain by Pencil Rubbing	255
A Glossary of Terms	313
A Look at Watercolour	325

A Quick Method of Graining Walnut

FOR a number of years I have visited East Anglia in the warmer months. One of the attractions for me is that an old friend runs a boarding house, or rather his wife and daughter run it, for he himself is a builder and decorator.

In this area it is popular for decorating and building to run together, which helps to fill in the 52 weeks of the year.

A Valuable Grainer: Whilst there last autumn I noticed that the outside painting of my friend's shop premises was being held up for want of a grainer.

I offered to help with the two doors to be treated so that the job could be completed, but my offer was gently turned down as it was not certain how this regular grainer would take it. There was no other member of the staff who could do the work, and so the job waited.

In the meantime I went along with my friend to see his old and valuable grainer at work.

Walnut was a wood favoured by this craftsman and I was interested to see how he carried it out.

He worked with confidence and his outfit was the simplest possible. The three tools he used comprised two rubbing-in brushes, a

> **Mr. Dobson describes in this article how the painted representation of English Walnut may be produced with no more than three tools. Although only the medium coloured variety can be satisfactorily grained in this way, the decoration is suitable for any surface where hard wear is expected.**

one-inch and a two-inch, and a one-and-a-half inch for most of the graining.

Walnut is prolific in the number of its varieties, over thirty being recorded in the timbers of the colonies. The graining of Walnut therefore covers a wide field, and obviously one cannot produce an intricate burr or a complicated piece of Italian grain with such a simple outfit.

The grain of English Walnut, on the other hand, can be worked in this manner, for it is straight in growth and even in colour, whilst the lines of the grain are not violent in direction.

Although with simple tools the lines of grain will only show softly, they will be hard enough for a representation of English Walnut.

A slight shadiness is desirable in the graining, and a few bands of stronger colour should be used on the side grain.

The heartwood oval shapes have the appearance of being darker on one side, because of the reflection of light; this can easily be produced with the brush. A slight kink or wave in the side grain is another method of providing interest.

The tool that is used for most of the graining should not be worn or even broken in, for a worn brush fails entirely to leave the lines of grain required. The small amount of mottling that is found may be produced with the two-inch rubbing-in brush.

Method of Graining: I now propose to describe this quick method of graining English Walnut.

The ground is first prepared in a medium buff colour. I prefer a warm ground and a cool gilp rather than the other way round.

As this wood is of a medium to light colour, I use one part of of walnut to two parts of medium oak. The standard prepared walnut scumble is on the dark side for this purpose; it is quite transparent but contains a fair amount of black.

The consistency of the gilp is important. Turpentine is the usual thinner; gum, driers, and oil are used in quantity to allow for thinning with the turpentine only. Should too much thinning occur, the gilp will run and the delicate lines of the brush will be lost.

The panel is rubbed in, working in the direction of the wood and leaving it shady. The area to be rubbed in for a start will depend on the time taken with the graining.

You should manage a flat door at one rub-in, but if you have an assistant, do not let him get too far ahead. Continue to draw in the grain markings with the medium-sized tool.

Hold the brush near to the work in a horizontal position; in this position with very little effort you can draw in the grain, apply colour or remove it.

Apply little or no weight, just allowing the brush to touch the wet scumble. A fine set of lines should result if the consistency of the scumble is correct. The overlapping of strokes at the top of the ellipse will probably make a darker line which is desirable.

The whole panel when completed will probably be flat and of one tone. This can soon be remedied.

Take off some of the colour in places by scrubbing with the brush side, after the manner of washing off with a distemper brush.

Colour may also be added by drawing the brush down and giving it a little more weight, but do not be tempted to dip the brush into the kettle, as this will soften all the work near it and leave an unconnected blob of colour.

Some mottle can be produced with the two-inch brush by using pressure quickly in the narrow space where the work is to be darker, and repeating the motion of heavy and light pressure.

Mottling can only be used on the side grain, which should be on one side only, preferably towards the bottom of the panel.

Where waves occur in the side grain, some dark may be added to the underside.

I prefer to work the side grain with my left hand on the right hand side and my right on the left side; this gives clear vision and at the same time balances the shading of the colour.

For added interest an occasional knot may be introduced, using the corner of the tool and a little stiff colour, the knot should be ringed round with a light line by running round the wooden brush handle.

A grained door should be finished off well top and bottom, and cleaned well up against any mouldings.

Decorative Effect: With this type of graining an even decorative effect is to be aimed at rather than a display of graining skill.

Cleanliness of working is important. Joinings of rails and styles can be helped by rubbing out the gilp a little on the rails, leaving them a tone lighter than the styles.

One of the best methods I have found for keeping the joints clean is to lay a piece of glass paper over the finished rail (rough side to the wet paint) and then to use a stippling motion with the colour on the style; the joint comes out perfectly clean, almost as if it has been cut with a knife.

A small amount of grain may be worked on the rails, but the longer styles are best left straight-grained.

Windows, skirtings and architraves cannot be grained to look smart by this method; they are better treated in coloured gloss paint, stippled or brush grained.

This method of graining Walnut is suitable for the medium-coloured variety only. For a light finish it would not show up well enough to justify the labour involved, whilst on a very dark ground it would come out heavy and muddy.

The medium coloured Walnut, with two coats of strong hard-drying varnish, is suitable for any surface where hard wear is expected.

Illustrations: The painted examples prepared to illustrate this article were carried out with a one-and-a half-inch tool.

Near the centre of the heartwood markings I used a small new stencil tool, which gave the work a fine sharp finish. This tool was a number 6 black bristle Hollins stencil brush, the edge of which was straight and clean cut.

This is the first time that I have used a a stencil tool for this purpose but it stood up to the work so well with the bristle being thick that I shall adopt it as a standard tool.

Three painted examples of English Walnut by Mr Dobson carried out with a 1½in. brush and given a fine sharp finished by the use of a small stencil brush near the centre of the heartwood markings

Vert-de-Mer Marble

An example of marbling used in a room scheme on television recently prompted Mr. Dobson to devote this article to Vert-de-Mer marble and its painted representation. He suggests that this somewhat out of the ordinary decoration could be used more frequently by the decorator to-day.

I HAVE seen a number of examples recently of Vert-de-Mer marble used in interior schemes. With a little guidance any craftsman of ability should be able to produce an attractive representation of this marble, although not all the examples I have seen were first class.

Striking Examples: One example worth mentioning was in the entrance of a certain club in the Midlands which had been painted and marbled. The display was most striking, although I would have kept the green a little cooler. The same decoration had been used on a number of plinths or bases at an engineering exhibition which I visited, but the work left much to be desired. Another good show was on more pliths in the window display of a large tailoring establishment; Italian walnut formed the background to the window, and the whole effect was very attractive. It was the marble that I saw first in the window, but I naturally examined the other goods in the window before I came away so that the decoration served its purpose.

I was most interested to see this marble used in a scheme for a bedroom shown in a television scene the other evening. There was a band some twelve inches wide running round the dado, the top edge of which would be about 3ft. from the carpet. The wall-filling and the remainder of the dado below the marble were painted in plain colour, which helped to set off the Vert-de-Mer. All these examples suggest to me that this somewhat out of the ordinary decoration could be used much more frequently in interior schemes.

Origin and Description: Vert-de-Mer is quarried in the French Pyrenees, the Italian Alps and the mountainous island of Corsica, and although these places sound a long way apart they are all within 300 miles of each other.

This marble is formed from a compressed bed of carbon that has been shattered many times by volcanic action, and the cracks in which have been filled by coloured limestone carried by water. Hardening has taken place over millions of years through the great weight of further erupted matter.

Green has been the dominant colour in the many examples that I have seen, about one third of the surface being black or dark grey with a few lines of the veining in white to light grey. Both shades and tints of green are to be found in the fine spidery lines that break up the shapes most effectively and provide the main interest in this marble. The tones of green vary from very dark inside the smaller shapes to light in the larger ones, while the lightest colour is reserved for the main lines of veining. This colouring helps to subdue the effect, for the largest shapes are near in tone to the main lines in the veining. No matrix is found in Vert-de-Mer.

The detail of the feathering is shown in the stone in the bottom right-hand corner

245

Method of Marbling: For the painted representation of this marble, a ground of black or dark grey is prepared, and colour applied in the form of a sponge stipple. I used decorators' tube colours and prefer a palette board for mixing; white, Oxford ochre, black and Prussian blue being my basic colours.

A few variations of tones of green should be prepared on the board, and thinners made ready in a dipper or small kettle. The thinners consist of two parts of turpentine to one part of linseed oil with a few drops of terebine dryers; a pale synthetic varnish may be used in place of the linseed oil – this varnish works quite well and is a little quicker than linseed.

The ground is oiled-in with the thinners, which should be applied sparingly but give a good coverage. If a soft effect is desired the thinners must be applied more liberally but kept inside the running stage. A shade of green prepared from Prussian blue, ochre and a touch of black is then sponge-stippled in the ground. Both the colour and the amount applied may be varied slightly in different areas according to taste.

To ensure that only the points of the sponge touch the work the stippling should at all times be carried out very lightly. At this stage very little of the stippling is likely to show but it will look effective later. If the sponge becomes clogged-up with colour or becomes lifeless with the hammering it receives, it should be put on one side and another piece used; the original piece will revive later with washing in hot water.

A little white or pale green can now be used to draw in the principal lines with a short hog hair fitch, but these are intended as a guide only and may be dispensed with if the outlines can be carried in your mind. For the lines proper the feather is charged with thin white paint and worked over the dark green stipple. Short strokes should be used, almost horizontal, rounded off at the ends and brought back almost over the same ground, after the manner of the Carrick bend or the Overhead knot – two favourite knots from the pole and scaffold days. (The large stone at the bottom right-hand of the example illustrated shows the detail of the feathering).

Provided the ground is still moist and the colour being used is not too stiff, the work of feathering is comparatively easy. The feather may be used for most of the veining down the edge of the large stone shapes, as it gives a more natural line than a brush. I prefer to work with thin white paint only, for much of the green stipple works into the white and the white is then best subdued by glazing over the work when dry. Where such glazing is not worthwhile green should be added to the white for the feathering process. The white lines of the main veins can be sharpened up with the fitch; some prefer to use a sable for this work but it gives too clean a line for my taste.

To return to the stone shapes; at this stage some of them may look too hard and I have found that the feather can be used in a stippling manner to add a little more colour and to produce a different texture. All the corners of the shapes should be well filled with the white or light green worked with the tip of a small feather. The work is then softened gently with the run of the marble. This will have the effect of bringing the green stipple through the white lines, but it should be stopped before the white lines start to spread.

Glazing: For the glazing, oil-in the panel with medium from the dipper using clean rags. This should be rubbed out bare just sufficient to soften the work so that it will take colour easily. Shades of dark green are then prepared on the palette from Prussian blue and vandyke brown, or Prussian blue and burnt turkey umber; both these combinations will give a cool green that is transparent.

This colour is stippled on different areas with a piece of sponge, giving a duller green effect and toning down the general appearance. In order to see exactly the amount of colour being applied it is best to soften the work in stages. One advantage of glazing is that the colour can be taken off in places without doing any damage, and rag-rolling is a splendid method of doing this.

Zinc white or titanum oxide should be used with a fitch, applied in a dry state and well rubbed out, to sharpen up points of light.

Maple

Mr. Dobson describes how the painted representation of Maple was used in the redecoration of a small hotel in the Lake District, and goes on to explain and illustrate how this wood, and in particular the Bird's Eye variety, is grained.

ON a cold day in January I called for lunch as a small hotel in the Lake District. Business is quiet in these parts in winter, but it was extra quiet on this day because the decorators were in.

The decoration was almost completed – in fact the men were just working the last few brushfuls on the entrance hall. All the public rooms had been painted, and the decorators had produced a creditable, smart and up-to-date interior without stripping the plastic paint previously applied.

A Tasteful Interior

The doors, which were substantial with well sunk panels and broad, well moulded architraves, had been grained in a light cool Maple (a few years ago they would probably have been a deep mahogany or rosewood). There were broad cornices, and rich plaster centres adorned each light fitting.

No alteration of the fabric had taken place since it was built some sixty years ago, but the decoration had been brought up to date.

Pleasing colour had been introduced with a small amount of palette work on the plastic in the lounge, showing taste and artistic skill far above the ordinary. The wall filling, previously carried out in plastic and glazed in a raw seinna brown, was now painted white and finished white semi-gloss.

The acanthus-leaved centres and the ornate cornice were treated with the same white paint, whilst the flat of the ceiling was papered with a crimson paper with small white stars.

Grange-over-Sands is a quiet clean town without any industries. It caters for a good type of visitor – the type who would appreciate this sort of scheme.

Visiting the hotel just as the job was being completed, I could see the effect even before the carpets had been replaced. The large area covered with the plaster decoration on the ceiling easily balanced the maroon of the ceiling paper, and the paper gave a clean apperance to the whole scheme.

The Maple Tree

Maple, a close relation of the sycamore family, is found in most countries of the world; it prefers a moderate climate, but the finest types are grown in Japan and North America. The tree is often grown merely for the decorative value of its foliage.

In Gt. Britain, one variety produces a bright red leaf for its spring and summer adornment, and altogether there are some one hundred and ten species growing for utility and ornament.

Most of the wood grain markings in this tree are of the fine heartwood type, with pale straw coloured defining lines. Another important feature of Maple is the mottle, and boards are found with an even distribution of mottle on a straight grain some eighteen inches wide and six feet long.

The most popular with our profession of course is the Bird's Eye Maple, which is covered with small knots that look like eyes in the timber.

We find a great deal of difference in the number of eyes distributed on various boards; some have every inch covered, while in others heartwood markings are inter-mixed with the eyes. The display of the eyes is remarkably like the arrangement found in the figure of oak, with its lines, runs and open spaces.

Trees growing the Bird's Eye are rare, no more than one in fifty, and this is only by accident.

The eyes are attributed to a small insect that sets up an irritation inside the growing tree. The new wood grows round the insect totally enclosing it, and so produces the beautifully marked and shaded cabinet wood.

247

Method of Working

Maple is readily worked from white ground, and I find that most of the delicate colours in light Maple can be obtained by careful mixing of the graining scumble. The strong golden yellow colour sometimes found in the deeper varieties can be obtained by the addition of a little satinwood scumble to the maple, and the ground for this may be darkened by a touch of ochre and umber. The method used in the example that I am about to describe was in straight oil colour scumble, which is quick and clean to work. (Working in water colour will be the subject of a future article).

A number of paint manufacturers turn out good reliable graining scumbles that can be safely used. They should be thinned with turpentine only to an easy working consistency.

A good sized area, say the whole of a flush door, is rubbed in with a two-inch tool. The scumble should be applied liberally within the running stage; the more there is applied the longer it will hold up without setting.

The colour may be a little darker than is desired for the finished work, for some of the colour is lost with the grain manipulation.

The graining of the eyes is done with the sponge only, commencing at the bottom left hand corner and working upwards. You should hold the clean sponge firmly in the right hand, spread the four fingers on the top of one of the longer sides and the thumb on the under-side, keeping the hand level all the time.

Work very lightly on the wet scumble, using short downward sliding strokes about two or three inches in length. A small amount of colour is collected each time the sponge touches the work, and this is deposited when the hand is withdrawn at the bottom of the stroke. Repeat the process across the bottom of the door, altering the place where you take the sponge away each time so that you do not have a straight line across the door. Continue sponging in this way until all the door is grained.

Most of the spaces between the eyes are narrow, but some are up to six inches in width, and this wide space can be used when the area is very large or according to taste and the detail required.

The strokes of the sponge should all be in the same direction on the same door or panel. I prefer to work vertically all the time. You may of course change the direction of the grain slightly by sliding the sponge to the right or to the left when a number of panels or doors are near together and you wish to introduce a little variety. A wild snow storm effect is obtained if the direction is not properly controlled. As the sponging proceeds, you should cover up all the places where the sponge first touches the panel by overlapping the top of the stroke below it. This covers all the marks from the rubbing-in brush and gives a more even set of eyes. Each time the sponge touches the work it makes a number of light points whilst it leaves a set of darker ones when you take it off; it is the darker ones that are required.

All good graining displays a certain amount of design, and a little thought should be given to where the broader spaces are to occur and where the figure is to be closer together. For a flat door I prefer open figure down the centre with closer down the two sides, and for a narrow panel open figure down one edge and narrow down the other.

On no account should the sponge be dipped into colour to make the eyes stronger, but you may rub the sponge into a piece of clean rag to get rid of the excess colour and thus prevent it becoming too soggy. Very little pressure should be applied otherwise the sponge loses its spring and fails to produce the fine points; should this occur it is best to discard the sponge and get another clean piece. It will be found useful to dip the sponge into cold water before using; this softens it quickly, prevents the points from breaking and enables it to do its work more effciently. On completion of the work, the sponges should be washed out in soap and hot water so that they will be ready for the next job.

If the glip is of the correct consistency no softening should be required; if a little softening is required, it must be done very lightly indeed in a horizontal direction. Some fine lines of grain may be drawn in at this juncture using the pry handle end of the fitch. They will not be as prominent as when the crayon is used, but will suffice if a delicate effect is being aimed at.

This method is the quickest possible for the graining of Bird's Eye Maple, and should offer no difficulty to a good craftsman.

The colour may be too sharp if thinned with turpentine only, and I have found that the addition of a small amount of pale synthetic varnish will slow it down and help the stay-put qualities. Finally, do not be tempted to put in any large eyes with the end of the finger tips. These are much too clumsy to suit the delicate markings that are found in Bird's Eye Maple.

The Illustrations
The first of the painted examples was carried out with the sponge only, the strokes being drawn down slightly from left to right. No softening was used, just the run of the material. The second was carried out with the material a little rounder; no running is to be found, every mark is hard and scratchy and the eyes are not as prominent. This condition could have been improved with softening. The heartwood markings have been put in with a wax crayon. In the third example, fairly round colour was again used, a little darker but thinner than in the second. Grain markings were worked in with the end of a fitch, giving a more delicate effect than the crayon used for the second example.

249

Alabaster-Marble Limestone

Mr. Dobson describes the marbling work in one of the famous civic buildings in York and goes on to discuss the painted representation of Alabaster for use in many decorative schemes.

Marbling in York

"The contract included £4,000 for the painters' and decorators' work, and the largest item was for the marbling of the broad high pillars."

These words still ring in my ears as clearly as the day they were spoken by the master painter who has just completed the redecoration of the hall interior. I believe it was in the capacity of Sheriff of York that he was taking us round the famour Assembly Hall of that city.

This tour of the fine historic buildings ot York rounded off the summer short course arranged by the Ministry of Education for Craft Teachers in 1953. I had just completed a series of lectures and demonstrations to the young men on the course.

Lord Burlington, the famous architect and designer, built the Assebly Hall some three hundred years ago, but today it is looked upon as a modern building.

The hall is well lit and the floor is probably the largest and finest to be found in Yorkshire. One of the reception rooms is covered with murals painted in outline and and depicting the hectic life and adventures of Lord Burlington.

A painted example of Alabaster-Marble Limestone by Mr Dobson

No particular type of marble was strictly adhered to in the decoration, but a general marble limestone effect well coloured was attempted and successfully achieved.

The excellence of this marble effect can be judged from the fact that the fashion designers for Vogue magazine have since used it as a black-ground for the photographing of their show of spring models of ladies' wear.

Whilst proudly showing us this work the master painter implored us as teachers not to drop marbling from our curriculum.

The decorator might come across only one such job in a lifetime, but without training in the schools in the elementary principles of marbling this job could never have been carried out.

Work on the pillars was commenced first and carried on long after the plain painting was completed.

One particularly fine craftsman was given the work on the front of the pillars, setting a high standard, whilst others assisted on the side and backs.

In a short time the assistants were competent enough to undertake pillars of their own. I had great difficulty in finding any divisions of work, and I think the job is a credit to all concerned.

Limestone
– Origin and Colours

It is not my intention to describe this decoration in detail, for I did not examine it with this in my mind, but I shall deal with the painted representation of Alabaster which is the nearest marble to what was attempted here.

Marble limestone is considered too soft for classification as a marble proper, although it would qualify by its colour and appearance.

Limestone is found in certain areas of Great Britain in large quantities, and it is interesting to note that heavy clay subsoil and limestone beds are sharply divided.

The limestone areas are a little warmer than other areas and in consequence living conditions are usually more pleasant.

Where the limestone beds are situated on high ground as in the Craven district of Yorkshire, some deposits were carried down to lower ground by the ice in the Ice Age. A little of the limestone brought down by the glacier formation was found in the streams round Burnley.

The colours of the limestone that I noticed last week on the banks of the River Kent, brought down from Westmorland, were grey to almost white with some cream to light buff. Deposits abound on the Lancashire coast brought down from the Lakeland mountains.

The rubbing and buffeting that these stones receive in transit gives the impression of an opaque material, but limestone when polished is very, which contain traces of iron in their colouring. The stone before

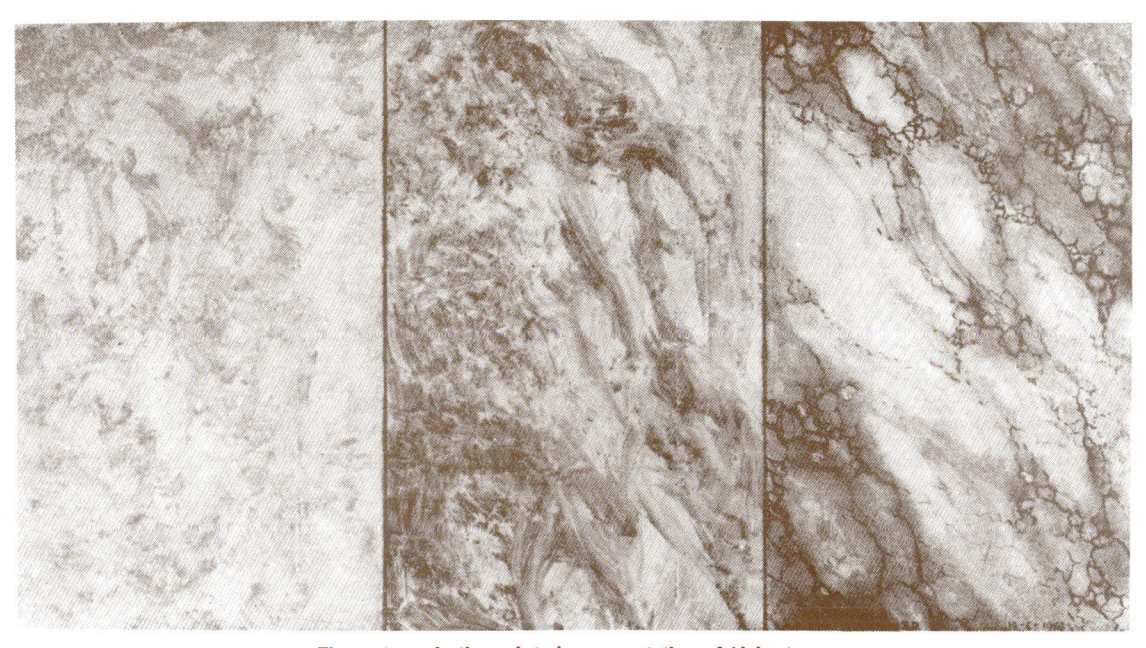

Three stages in the painted representation of Alabaster

burnishing is very fine in texture and easilt recognisable.

The veining consists mostly of tints of grey, with tints of ochre following a close second, a smaller amount of orange to burnt sienna, with a little olive green and some parts almost black. Large pieces are found of one colour only, some have two, but I have never found all the colours on any one piece. One of the largest chemical manufacturers in the country uses no less than four train loads of limestone per day from the Derbyshire beds alone. It is used in the manufacture of gypsum, which is the base of most of our hard plasters, and for many other purposes.

Painted Representation

The materials required for this marbling are – clean washed rags, sponge, fitches, worn sable pencil, tools and hog hair softener.

The ground colour is off-white for all varieties, which will give the necessary transparence to the marble and vein colours.

The colours used are white, black, ultramarine, ochre and burnt sienna, of decorators' tube staining quality.

In order to have a fairly even standard of colour on a large scale operation it is advisable to prepare three tints suficient for the whole job and store them in air-tight containers, taking from them a little at a time and sealing the lids immediately to keep them fresh as long as possible.

A pale glaze of light grey prepared from black, blue and a touch of white is first rubbed in.

The use of white gives longer life to the grey by allowing more stainers to be included before the colour becomes too dark.

For thinners I have used five parts of turps to one of alkyd varnish, but glaze medium or linseed oil are also satisfactory.

The binding portion should be adjusted according to the size of the work and the speed of the craftsman.

Almost two thirds of the total area should be covered with the pale grey, a second tint of grey is applied unevenly over other smaller areas, and then a tint of burnt sienna is used to work in a few patches in other places.

You will find that you can overlap the red on to the grey, but not the other way round.

All the surface is covered with the three tints, which should be much darker than the finished background colours to allow for wiping out and stippling.

Large scale work should never be done in a haphazard way; it is best to make a drawing in the quiet of the studio, indicating where the heavy distributions of colour will be, before the actual job is commenced.

A handful of clean rag is employed to wipe off some of the colour, dabbing, twisting, rolling and completely wiping out in some places to obtain the desired effect.

A good method is to wipe out the cleanest where it is lightest, dabbing only lightly where it is dark and in other places leaving the surface alone. This will result in broader contrasts of tone.

With the sponge previously softened in cold water, some slight opening out with turpentine may be carried out in places; for this the turps must be lightly splashed or poured on to the palette and picked up with the sponge – the sponge should never be dipped in the turps.

Veining

The previous work on the basic glazes will almost indicate where the darker lines of veining should be placed. In a well marked example they are similar to those found in Sienna marble, but the colouring is of course much cooler.

A worn sable held loosely at the extreme end of the handle is employed to paint in the grey colour first, ochre sceond, thin burnt sienna next and a little black or olive green last. The pencil is rolled between the fingers as the work proceeds and extra weight is applied to give heavier marks as the brush is brought down.

The line that we use in leter work should be avoided as this makes the veins much too heavy in appearance, and the areas using different coloured lines must be kept quite separate. Do not fill in every available space, and leave all the finest lines until last.

The panel may now be finished by cleaning up a little more. The insides of a few of the stone shapes may be wiped out until they are white, some places can be rag-rolled and others touched with the almost dry sponge to break up the veining a little more. Finally, the work is softened with the hog hair and a few lines are put in with a fine sable.

By altering the palette this method of marbling can be used for almost any colour to fit in with most schemes of decoration.

Bleached Heartwood Markings of English Oak

The attractive exteriors of houses in a Suffolk seaside town prompted the author to devote this article to the painted representation of bleached oak. He suggests that this treatment is most suitable and durable for garage and house doors, particularly when the garage is built into the house.

LAST summer I spent a short holiday at Frinton-on-Sea, a small seaside resort in Suffolk, full of charm and with many small new beautiful houses. It is a quiet residential district where one sees plenty of gardeners and painters at work. The houses are well designed and everything is clean and well-painted. There are many masterly and some unusual colour schemes to be seen there, and I found several examples of clever exterior graining.

Two of the latter, one in pine and the other in bleached oak, were of outstanding merit, of good colour and equal to any that I have seen in England. The grainer obviously had good taste as well as great skill. From the road no detail of the bleached grain could be seen, and only by coming close to the work could the detail be distinguished.

Treatment for Garage Doors

To-day, with the high cost of land and building, many new detached houses have the garage premises well forward, built-in but protruding from the front of the house. This considerably shortens the drive, making it much easier to reverse the car out, but it also brings the garage doors into a very prominent position.

The old batten doors have given way to newer styles of well-framed, smartly designed doors for which the green or brown gloss treatment is no longer suitable. Staining, polishing and even varnishing are not good enough treatments for finely marked timbers exposed to the British climate – in fact such treatments are a complete failure.

It is difficult to tell how long a house has been up when there is no smoke to blacken the stone and no green moss to change its appearance, but the house I examined had been built since the war and the graining was about two years old. Built with honey coloured stone, with roof of green Westmorland slate, windows ivory gloss, ironwork yellow grey and the doors grained in bleached oak, it looked most attractive. In order to satisfy myself that the garage and other doors were grained I asked permission to examine them, and only by close examination could I convince myself that

A panel of English Oak by Mr Dobson

they were painted and not English oak that had been bleached.

Heartwood graining is carried out by two methods, "the wipe-out" and the "paint-on", and there are several variations of both of them. The paint-on method is the neatest and shows to the best advantage in the lighter woods; it is also much quicker to execute unless one is really expert. Wipe-out is inclined to look spidery or clumsy.

The garage and house doors of this residence had been grained by heartwood markings only, the grainer using a fitch and adopting the paint-on method. It is possible for me to give a fair representation of the markings of heartwood, but I am unable to show the colour in the illustration. I can best describe it as a green cream. Many prepared scumbles to-day are of good colour, and probably one was used here for a few bleached and lighter effects have been added to the manufacturers' range in the last few years.

The colour was not from a standard stainer such as raw umber, but it could have been prepared from umber and a touch of blue or black with plenty of glaze medium to make it transparent. I took it to be a standard preparation because it was even in colour and the lines of grain were a tone darker than the ground scumble but appeared to have come from the same can.

Graining Method
The work is carried out as follows. The colour to be used as glip is thinned to a

254

working consistency in a small kettle – a prepared scumble requires only thinning with turps, as the manufacturers' instructions indicate, and the one that you prepare yourself will be similar in colour but slightly different in the medium.

A touch of white undercoating or even white lead is desirable in the graining oils to obtain the semi-opaque transparency found in bleached effects. A little white also allows the use of more staining colour without making the work too dark. This is particularly useful as most pale colours bleach out quickly when exposed to the elements.

The door is rubbed in and slightly brush-grained straight down the entire surface. If a strong contrast is desired with the heartwood markings, some of the colour where the markings are to be drawn in should be scrubbed out with the brush side or with a handful of clean rag and the brush grainer run over these parts again to give some texture.

The markings are then drawn in with a small fitch ¼" to ½" wide and nicely worn. A fitch scrubs in the colour more accidentally than a sable pencil, it is quicker on the job and the result is more natural.

The colour may be used fairly round, almost straight out of the tin, with an occasional dip into the kettle to ease it, but if a very delicate heartwood marking is desired the thinned colour out of the kettle will suffice. The next step is to run down the sides of the markings again with the brush

grainer, making sure that the grain and the background texture blend well together. It is of course possible to work away to a soft edge with the fitch, by using less colour down the sides of the graining, so that the brush grainer is not required a second time.

A long horse hair flogger is useful for quietening the markings down to a smaller extent, working outwards from the centre, but care must be taken not to over-flog or the markings will be obliterated.

With the rubbing-in tool some of the colour can be pulled together to form shadows in a few places, and the fitch can be used in the centres to give a semblance of knots.

No glazing is called for in a light wood of this description, and on the garage doors I saw no more than one third of the area had been worked, the remainder being left plain brush-grained.

Illustration
The illustration is in the form of a black and white drawing, showing four styles and rails with half round mouldings running down either side of the heartwood markings. Knots, shaded parts, rapid changes of direction and many other interesting features are included.

Prominent lines of pith run behind the figure in the small delicate centre panel; two branches are indicated by the grain towards the top left hand side, with interesting heavier figure near the centre running down to the base.

Wood Grain by Pencil Rubbing

Mr. Dobson describes an inexpensive method of obtaining an exact reproduction of wood grain markings as an aid to good graining. He gives three examples of markings produced in this way.

CERTAIN types of wood lend themselves to reproduction by pencil rubbings, and by this method an accurate replica of the drawing shape, and texture can easily be made.

It is not easy to improve your graining once you have reached a certain stage because you find yourself making the same markings as you did many years before.

A good reproduction of the actual wood by the method I am going to describe can, however, be a great help, particularly if the results are mounted on a card to help preserve them for future reference.

Some, of course, will turn out disappointing and can be dispensed with, but the few good ones will amply repay all your effort.

Aids to Graining

I have used a number of aids from time to time for the reproduction of wood. One of these is drawing or sketching, but the use of it is dependent to a large extent on training.

Photography is another, but the cost of a suitable camera is often prohibitive and the dark nature of our subject does not lend itself to amateur photography. Two friends of mine who have obtained good results from modest equipment, however, are Mr. Alletson of Salford and Mr. Pollard of Manchester.

Books on graining are few and mostly out of date, and writers on the subject in the past fifty years can be counted on the fingers, so that one must to a large extent develop one's own resources, and they must not be too costly.

For a long time rubbings have been taken of old carved lettering and decorative brasses in cathedrals; they give sharp and clear results on account of the clean edges of the stone or brass catching the colour.

I have not, however, heard of this process being used previously for the reproduction of wood grain, although it may have been.

Rubbings are cheap to produce, easy to store and to carry about and there are unlimited examples from which to take them. Rubbings can be taken from any wood, although the figure of oak is not a good subject because of the extreme thinness of the medullary rays.

Equipment

Paper, pencils and a few drawing pins are the only equipment required. For paper I prefer the thin typing kind that we use for taking copies, which gives better results than say cartridge drawing paper. I find that it is easier to work on a number of smaller sheets of 8 in. by 10 in. than to try to hold larger sheets in position.

It is most essential to keep the sheets flat and free from creases, before use, and a piece of cardboard placed in the envelope in which they are stored is all that is required.

Any pencil of medium hardness will do. I use either B, or HB, and my favourite is a joiner's pencil – the one that I have at present is a giant size over a foot in length. Wax crayons are also suitable provided the timber is well weathered, giving a sharp edge between the soft and harder portions of the surface markings.

A little experimenting with the different pencils is required in order to decide whether a harder or softer pencil will give the best results in any particular instance.

It is often impossible to fix the paper with drawing pins because of the valuable nature of the wood from which the rubbing is being taken, and the paper must be held with the hand. On a country fence or a field gate, post pins are just the thing.

I find that with vigorous rubbing of the pencil the paper is liable to stretch, but this can be allowed for by securing only the top of the paper. Adhesive tape one inch in width can also be used in most instances for securing the paper.

The Rubbing Technique
The rubbing itself is really a form of drawing. The pencil is held lightly near the end, between the thumb and the first finger.

The markings are all produced by the pencil striking on the edges of the grain or pith, so that it is best to work with a quick flick of a stroke and not use much pressure.

Working in a slow deliberate manner will produce a clean dark line, without showing any grain or texture, but a little practice will soon show the technique required. The pencil should be kept low near to the paper, swinging some four or so inches, and brought a sixteenth lower with each stroke. The aim should be to make the general tone fairly even.

There is no need to cover all the paper up to the edges but only to take the most interesting parts down the centre of the panel. On a coarse, well defined heartwood of say pine, a black wax crayon may be used and will give good results, but where the grain is closer a B pencil is required.

Selecting Woods
In selecting grain markings everyone will have his own ideas as to what will be most waluable, but it is no use collecting just ordinary markings; it is best to look for out of the ordinary, ornamental and intricate parts which can be put to good use later.

Although they are fast being replaced by thin interlaced strips of pine, there are still many outdoor fences of oak and ash and other hardwoods. The main sources of good marked timber are of course colleges, abbeys, minsters, churches and public buildings, which have large areas of clean unpolished woodwork that will supply all our needs.

New smooth-planed woodwork will not produce good markings, and surfaces bearing rough saw marks cannot be used, but there are plenty of examples on which to work.

Figure of oak is not too good but you may find some old panels of untreated wood that will show results. As this figure is slightly above the level of the surface, it will of course come up black on the drawing; this is misleading as most figure is lighter in colour than the wood itself. For myself I find it much clearer to draw the figure of oak.

Much good timber of the cedar type is being used to-day for summer houses, garages and similar types of building. Most of it has been treated with wood preservatives and takes the rubbing treatment well.

The Illustrations
The examples illustrated are of Teak, Ash and Pine. All are interesting examples of the heartwood centres of their own types; each is completely different from the others and shows up the characteristics of each timber very well.

As most grainers keep the centres plain, with the result that the work lacks interest, I introduce the knotty centres first and refer to the other features of the grain markings later. I have left the edges of all the three drawings uncompleted, showing only part of the side grain; this is as far as I go, and it gives a better idea of the pencil strokes.

The first example is of Burma Teak. It has a graceful centre commencing with two good-sized oval shapes which have a separate existence for four years shown by four annular rings. Next are another four that surround them and form an island.

Interest is added by a slight difference in size and by their not being set opposite to each other. In Teak all the grain markings are narrow – no more than $1/8$in. to $1/4$in.

The side grain is almost straight down one side, with just a swelling where it passes the knots; on the opposite side a more wild appearance is produced by the grain running round a number of imaginary knots.

Many changes in the width of the spaces on one side only is another feature of interest; down the other side the spaces are an equal distance apart narrowing only a little opposite to the knots. A fine net texture covers the whole of the surface. Round the top centre, the lines of grain are displayed in pairs, and advance from $1/4$in. to $3/4$in. in some four inches. The width of the grain markings is shown with a light line, which of course on the wood itself is a darker line than the actual ground.

The second example, Ash, attracted my attention by its fine sweeping curve and the centre knots. I regret that I cannot show it in full. It was situated on the edge of a piece of weather-board forming part of the covering to the outside of a seaside café.

The centre starts with three small knots of varying shapes, separated with four and five annular rings respectively. As these rings vary considerably in width a splendid shape has evolved before they are enclosed by the main veins running down the centre. Travelling in one direction with the bold curve, the lines of the grain are even and composed of the fine lines of grain that we associate with Ash.

In the opposite direction, the grain is broken into small curves, such as we find in Hungarian Ash, although it was taken from a good example of English.

As it was only the centre that I wanted, the larger and more distinguishable Ash markings are missing.

The Pine, in the third example, consists of a two-knot centre of unusual shape. One appears to be growing out of the centre of the other, yet both have had ten years to their credit before they are encircled with an enclosing ring. The rings in one knot are complete, whilst the second and the largest are springing from the first, similar to what we find in Rosewood. It will be noticed that the lines are typical of pinewood and easily recognisable.

Examples of the heartwood centres (l. to r.) Burma Teak, Ash and Pine reproduced by pencil rubbing

Illustrations of Quartered Italian Walnut with the styles worked in Burr Walnut

Bleached Italian Walnut in a Bedroom

Bleached Italian walnut is a finish very much in favour at the present time for furniture, and in this article Mr. Dobson describes the graining of this wood as part of a decorative scheme for a bedroom.

ITALIAN walnut in its bleached form is the softest, the most pleasant and the most decorative type of walnut that I know. Its colour is a very pleasant semi-opaque green cream, interspersed with tints of raw umber.

The delicate heart-wood markings are somewhat different from those in the normal type of walnut, in that they have a slight festoon arrangement near the tips.

Sometimes these festoons form a complete oval shape which is filled in with a light form of grain that cannot be described as a knot.

The grain is soft and has the appearance of having run a little during the graining process, whilst the markings occasionally cross over each other, making the ends into a net shape texture.

The contrast in tone is weak, the texture and the grain being only slightly darker than the ground colour, although frequently towards the centre of the heartwood shape a smaller area is noticeably darker.

As with the more expensive woods, this Italian walnut is used chiefly in the form of a veneer, good use being made of reversing or quartering.

Origin

Supplies of walnut from Italy in the past 30 or 40 years have been small, but with improving international trade they are now flowing more quickly.

The home of this special walnut is centred round Ancona but the timber that is selected and marketed by merchants in this area is often grown further afield, the southern slopes of the Alps providing a fair amount.

The more northerly slopes of the Alps produce a grey coloured wood with a less pronounced figure.

The tree grows to a height of 40 to 60 feet, with a massive trunk and, at first, a grey smooth bark which furrows and becomes rugged with age.

The head of the tree is wide and spreading with glossy green leaves formed of lance-shaped leaflets.

A green fleshy case encloses the nut or seed in a hard wrinkled shell. The fine oil pressed from the nut is used in the manufacture of good varnish and for grinding in the finest of artists' and decorators' colours.

Fashion in Graining

After well over half a century in the painting and decorating trade, I am still puzzled by the way fashions come and go and colour, decoration and graning go on changing.

It is impossible to say how these changes originate, but so far as graining is concerned, the

Panels showing the first two processes in graining Bleached Italian Walnut: (left) the rubbing-in of the glaze scumble and (right) the overgraining

various types of wood in vogue change with the changing fashion in furniture.

Bleached Italian walnut is a popular furniture wood at the moment, and I am therefore dealing with the painted representation of this wood in a bedroom scheme.

As the graining must be complementary to the furnishings and the remainder of the decorations, I will describe these briefly.

The ceiling was finished in flat white paint on a lining paper, the walls were papered to the ceiling and a one-and-a-half inch border was used round the top of the wall filling.

The wall behind the bed was hung with a striking paper – large blue roses with natural green foliage on a white ground.

On the three remaining walls was a pink grey paper of medium tone, with a not very striking small white spot pattern, which formed a suitable background for both the furniture and the graining.

Wine colour was selected for the close-fitting carpet adorned with a large pattern in light tints of raw umber.

Tools and Colours

A hard white to off-white ground colour is used for the graining.

The tools required are sable or camel hair pencil overgrainers, two-inch and one-inch tools, mottlers, fitches, a piece of clean coarse canvas and softener.

The final processes in graining Bleached Italian Walnut. Panels showing (left) fitchwork and (right) mottling carried out with a pad of canvas

A new two-inch tool may be used in place of a mottler if desired.

Sometimes I use two large camel hair water colour brushes, dividing the bristles of each in half with thread and fixing the brushes side by side to give me the equivalent of four pencils.

I also find that the softer hair gives me a better performance than the firmer sable.

A small palette is desirable for carrying and mixing the colours, they should be let down with say four parts of white.

White, raw and burnt umber are the main colours required, but others that can be used for a delicate effect are emerald green, cobalt or ultramarine blue and black, all ground in oil.

Colours ground in turpentine are inclined to fix themselves too firmly to the ground, making it difficult to soften out the grain.

Most manufacturers make a suitable scumble which should be thinned with turps in accordance with the instructions, but if this goes off too fast a small amount of oil and glaze medium can be used as well as the turpentine to slow it down a little.

Method of Graining

The door or panel to be grained is first rubbed in with the scumble.

A very thin glaze is used to give a shady effect so that the work looks partly grained before any of the markings are put in.

The centre should be the darkest and all the brushmarks should be left in, following the lines of the grain.

Some of the colour down each side should then be removed, either with the brush side or with a rag; the surface, however, must be kept moist as it is most difficult to grain or flog if the ground is too dry or partly set.

At this stage, other delicate colours or tints may be introduced from the palette, tints of grey, green or the umbers, but not all of them should be used on one panel.

I have seen examples of bleached walnut with a blue cut relieved only with a small amount of umber.

The next step is the painting in of the lines of grain with the overgrainer. The brush is first touched in the turps, some of the light colour is picked up and the drawing of the heartwood markings is commenced.

This drawing should start from the centre of a knot near the middle of the panel, or, if the work is to be fairly plain without knots, from the bottom centre of the panel.

You should use up all the colour in the overgrainer before recharging, moving it about and working a few places at a time so that the markings become lighter in colour as the overgrainer is applied.

By leaving a few plain spaces, other colours can be put in later to add to the beauty of the finished panel.

The work should be left for about fifteen minutes while the colour partially sets.

The overgrainer is then shaken in the turpentine before being worked over the graining in turps only.

This will open out the lines still further and may help with the softening by running slightly to give the work a more natural appearance.

If the colour runs too freely and appears to be getting out of hand, the work can be rag rolled lightly and all the surplus colour picked up without damage.

A fitch is next used to scrub in a little darker colour in order to outline the more important shapes. This can be done in green, grey, brown or dull grey.

A few small knots can be worked in at the same time; these are run round with the end of a fitch and must not be prominent.

The work is softened lightly with the grain – this should be done with the greatest care and if the work is too wet the operation should be delayed for a few more minutes.

Any mottle required is done last with a good firm hog hair or a pad of canvas.

Mottling if overdone is not good, and I find it best to work on one side all the time.

The work should be finished off with egg-shell or flat varnish where possible, as it gives a more suitable surface for this type of decorative graining.

The wood chosen for this article is a type seen only rarely. Its painted representation lends itself to schemes in which an attractive but subdued effect is desired.

Feather of Oak

EXAMPLES of the Feather of Oak are rare. I have known only a very few, but I found a new one this week that had recently been cut from a fine log of oak.

Touring in Yorkshire

After attending the Harrogate Conference I spent the following week in the Yorkshire Dales, North Yorkshire and on the North East Coast.

Here, almost forty years ago I spent my late twenties and early thirties teaching at the Northern Command Training Centre. No classes were held for apprentices in this area at that time and I gave lessons to many boys privately.

One old friend and teaching colleague that I visited I found had taken to woodcarving in his retirement, and he was busy equipping his workshop with the many electrical aids now available.

Amongst his recent purchases of carving timber was an example of oak feather grown at Cowthorp, Yorks, south of Knaresborough.

A number of fine trees of exceptional size are to be found growing there; others have been left too long and are hollow in the trunk.

The whole complement of the local silver band recently gave selections from their repertoire inside the trunk of one of these large trees!

The fine example of oak feather was supplied by the firm of Robert Thompson of Kilburn, the world famous ecclesiastic wood carvers, who use a mouse for their trade mark.

I understand that much of their carving is carried out by deaf and dumb people whom they have trained for this specialised work.

Description of the Wood

The plank displaying the feather is a solid affair, one and a half inches thick and eighteen wide. Unlike the figure or medullary rays which are very thin, the feather grows deep into the timber and it shows on both sides of the board in identical shape.

The feather is striking in its beauty on account of its rarity, but it is quiet in tone, being only two shades darker than the remainder of the wood.

In my illustrations it tapers slightly towards the top but it grows the other way up or hanging downwards from a branch. Compared with mahogany this wood has a very quiet appearance, there is nothing dashing or flamboyant about it and the shapes are rounder and softer. It would be very suitable for work on a dining room door that calls for subdued treatment.

All the edges of the feather part are soft, the shading is very gradual and plenty of softening is called for in the graining.

As in other woods the feather is formed over a series of lines of heartwood shape. The whole is small compared with say satinwood, fifteen inches to two feet being the largest that I have seen, which is only half of the common size of mahogany.

The heartwood markings which form the base of feather of oak are spaced approximately half an inch apart, free from knots and well rounded at the ends, narrowing to about quarter of an inch down the side grain.

All the side grain is steady and even in colour with a narrow dark line on the outside, or the side away from the crutch of the tree branch. The dark line, composed of short dark lines of grain, is about one sixteenth of an inch wide and most prominent in the heartwood above the feather.

All the shadow cuts made by the mottler are wide and well softened; none are less than three inches and a few are more. Most of the mottling is displayed down one side, where about two thirds of the area is covered. On the second side just a few are found and these more or less divide the feather edge from the side grain.

A small amount of figure is found working its way amongst the mottle and in the same direction, again on one side only. This is not prominent or striking. In the original wood it would probably be found growing on the inside of the tree, where the timber would be much older. I never like to use figure with any other treatment in oak, although it is of course found that way in nature. Small cracks of figures or radiating lines are to be found running down the centre similar to those we see in mahogany.

In colour the example illustrated is cool and dull, probably from a tree some four to six hundred years old. Raw umber cooled off with black on a grey or cool buff coloured ground would be required to reproduce it, using an Antique Oak scumble.

Method of Graining
All types of feather are the same in general design and shape, with minor alterations in detail. Therefore the method and tools are the same. Many grainers use the mottler and the rubbing-in brush as the sole means of producing a feather often with great success. One outstanding decorator who adopts this technique is Mr. Arthur Lane of Shipley, who during his long career has carried out many excellent commissions. Mr. Lane gave a demonstration a short while ago on the ue of the mottler to the Association of Painting Craft Teachers at the School of Art, Shipley. Mr. Lane was also responsible for the greater part of the graining carried out by Messrs Bagnalls of Shipley, the well known painting contractors.

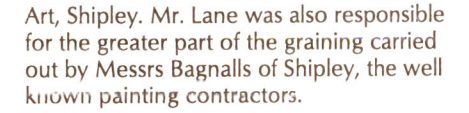

To make any reasonable kind of representation two processes are required. Both may be in oil colour, or the graining may be in water colour and the overgraining in oil. Antique Oak prepared scumble of vandyke brown in water may be used for the graining in the first process. This is worked with the mottler to give the shape and the shading of the feather and the few shadows of mottle near the feather. The overgraining of the heartwood markings tends to keep

263

the feather subdued, which is what we are aiming at.

The Stages Illustrated
In the first illustration (left), a glaze of colour suitably bound has been rubbed in. This is in medium oak scumble thinned with turps and a spoonful of hard-drying synthetic varnish.

All the brushwork can be followed from this; it can be seen where a little darker antique was added to form the centre of the feather. All the colour was used on the thin side to allow for mottling.

In the second illustration (second left), mottling has been followed along quickly before the colour had had time even to set. Very little softening was required as the colour flowed out well.

The few cuts of mottle must run at right angles to the grain of the heartwood, so that for the most part the top edge of the mottler should be in line with the rubbing-in marks. All subsequent lines of combing will follow in exactly the same places at right angles to the mottling.

In the graining of a large panel or flat door it is only necessary to work in the feather area, as mottling is not general in oak graining. The colour may run out to nothing a few inches beyond the edge of the feather.

When the work is thoroughly dry the next process is to oil in for the overgraining of the heartwood. This must be done gently so as not to disturb the graining of the feather.

A comb is then used as in the third example (second right). The comb that I used was made by cutting into the edges of a stout piece of card with a razor blade; this picked up the oil scumble well without disturbing the graining. The small cracks down the centre were removed with a small sharp knife.

Another small point of interest is the use of a lighter scumble over a darker one to give a most realistic effect over the feather mottling.

For clarity in the third example I left the cross combing, but this is carried out in the fourth (right).

Poupre Violette Marble

MANY large industrial concerns are again adopting marble for interior decoration, and some of the finest rooms, halls and staircases in new office blocks, mansions and even town halls are receiving the same treatment.

This trend will probably be reflected in an increased demand for painted marble, which should make the decorator's job much more interesting.

I recently visited two interiors in which marble had been used, one was part of an industrial block and the other a fine new addition to a town hall.

Both had been lined with Poupre Violette panels surrounded by pink marble styling.

The combination of these two marbles immediately attracted my attention because I recalled that the same combination had lined the head office of the Bank of Belgium where as a student I used to cash my cheques many years ago.

Description and Origin
Poupre Violette is one of the most suitable of marbles for large scale wall decoration.

Its open markings and its tints of yellow cooled off with grey make it striking in its beauty but not aggressive.

This marble is of the breccia type and the veins and smaller stones are of a purple

> **The author says marble is returning to favour for the decoration to entrance halls and staircases in new office blocks and large public rooms. The marble he deals with is one of the most suitable types for large scale wall decoration.**

shade, being a true complementary to the large yellow shapes.

The markings of the deep purple stones against the ground form its most striking feature and account for its name.

When the veins are deep in the transparent yellow marble it rather greys the purple but has little effect on the reds and ochre yellows.

Large stones are even in tone and merge into the dark matrix round the edges; the blended contrast is not too sharp.

A number of the smaller stones are much lighter in colour, a few of them being almost white.

Pavenazzo and Paonazzetto are other names by which our subject is known in the few countries where it is quarried – Algeria, France, Italy and the United States.

Owing to the soft nature of the darker parts of this marble, it is difficult to cut, handle and move.

The type to which these notes refer, containing the most crimson in the purple, is quarried in the Pyrenees.

This range of mountains dividing Spain from France and part of the Cambrian chain is some 270 miles in length and in places 90 miles wide.

Evergreen oak, box, fir and pine forests abound on the lower slopes.

The geological formation of the Pyrenees shows distinct signs of volcanic upheaval, thermal springs exist up to the 8,000 ft. mark and important mineral deposits have been worked for many centuries, all of which have an important bearing on the pleasant colouring of the valuable marbles found there, some of the finest in the world.

Method of Marbling
For the painting of this marble a palette of white, chrome yellow, ochre, crimson lake, black and Prussian blue is required.

A white ground is used and this should have stood for a few days; it is best semi-gloss just hardened with a few spoonfuls of hard varnish.

Some thin white paint should be prepared in a kettle with at least one quarter of

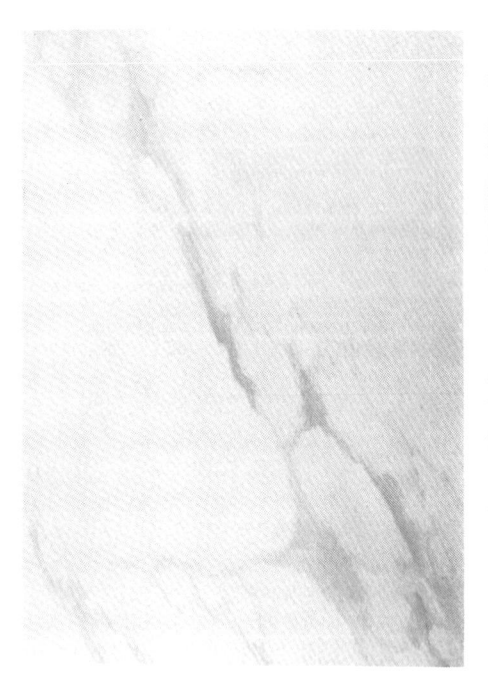

To imitate Poupre Violette Marble, first pain the colour on the wet, white ground...

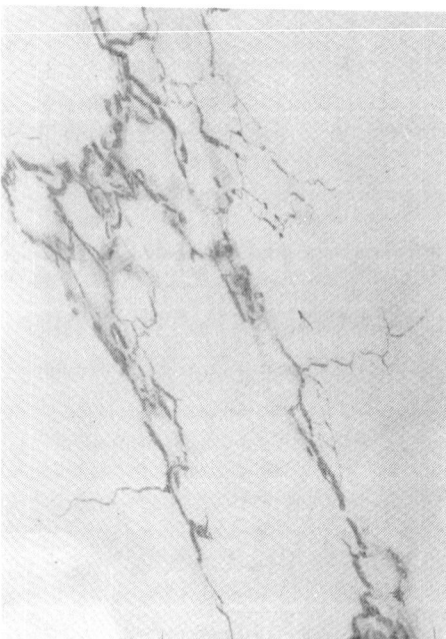

...then draw in the lines with soft and hard black crayons...

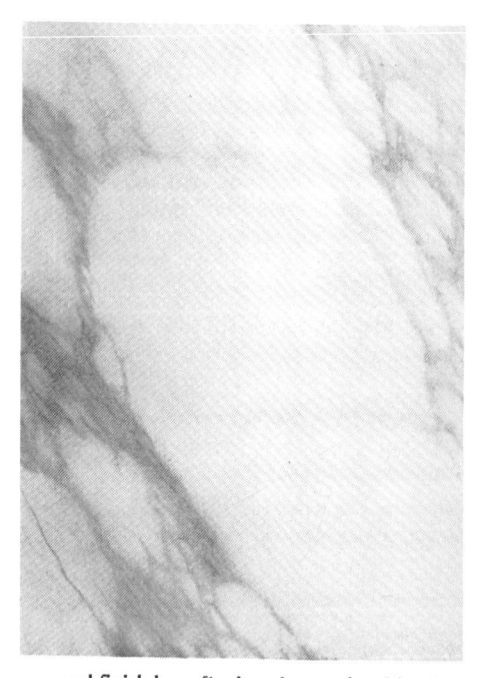

...and finish by softening vigorously with a hog hair softener

linseed oil in its mixing to make sure that it remains wet long enough to soften well.

A few drops of terebine should be added as all forms of black are bad driers.

One or two tools and large fitches will be required to rub in and place the colour – a hog hair softener, a hog hair pencil and sponge, together with two grades of black

crayon (for the soft one a black chalk will answer.)

The method of marbling is then as follows.

With white from the kettle, paint in the ground, brush as little as possible and leave in the brush-marks. Proceed with a clean tool to work in the yellows and creams of the stone shapes, using chrome, ochre and

white. This colouring can be on the strong side as much of it will be lost in the softening process.

Next work in the purple shades using a clean fitch on the principal veins that run between the larger stone shapes.

Most veins are of purple colour, a few of the larger straight veins are backed with crimson, whilst the smaller shapes are backed with ochre.

A few lines consist of grey without the addition of any colour.

The next step is to draw in the lines with the soft crayon.

The lines can be made a little heavier and a little more rugged in places by working the crayon backwards and forwards in a few short strokes.

A few short cracks loose at one end should be added; they will be found to come up well after softening.

Use a harder type of crayon for the finer lines in order to ensure that they do not rub away later.

Do not be afraid of applying plenty of black, for it forms the basis for softening.

The colour comes up much lighter after softening and when the glazing is completed.

Follow immediately with the softening, using the hog hair softener quite vigorously in a vertical direction, but only lightly across the panel.

Where the lines are near togther amongst the smaller stones only a very little softening should be undertaken, otherwise the lines will come up smudgy.

The quality of the finished effect depends more than anything on the success of the softening, which can be carried on almost to the point of the work setting.

The process of course itself accelerates drying by causing the turpentine to evaporate and forcing oxygen into the binders.

If the centres of the large stones come up rather dark after the softening, rub in some white with a stiff brush and soften well towards the edges.

Glazing
It is worth-while spending a few minutes on glazing.

First, moisten the surface with clean rag and a spot of oil and turps and rub out to a thin film.

Sponge stipple more than half of the area, over all the finer work and most of the veining, and knock back still further most of the delicate lines.

Then, with a fitch charged with purple, strengthen a few of the darker lines; apply the same treatment to the others using black. This completes the glazing.

MARBLES
See also:
Grand Antique Marble	42
Breche-Verte Marble	44
Sienna Marble	46
Carrara Marble	52
Levanto Marble	54
Poupre Violette	60
Irish Green Marble	64
Rouge Royal Marble	68
Granite Marbles	72
Marbling Vert Campan	84
Verde Antique	90
Alabaster: Marble Limestone	98
Skyros Marble	114
Cipollina Marble	122
Napoleon Marble Limestone	128
The Marbling of Breche Violette	132
Blue Fleuri Marble	136
Breche Blanche	140
Black and Gold Marble	146
Serancolin Marble	152
Convent Sienna Marble	158
Black and Gold Marble	162
St. Anne Marble	168
Dark Dove Marble	174
Waulsort Marble	180
Swedish Green Marble	188
St. Anne Marble	212
Verde Antique	223
Breche Violet Marble	231
Vert-de-Mer Marble	245
Alabaster-Marble Limestone	250
Connemara Marble	275
Rose Campan Marble	282
Henrietta Marble Limestone	290
Rouge Royal Marble	299
Skyros Alpha Marble	305

Mr. Dobson describes the painted representation of English Ash on a shop front. The treatment looked far more attractive than plain painting and at the same time was more hard wearing.

English Ash

THE use of Ash in graining to-day is popular because of its light colour and the fineness and delicacy of its grain. Its drawing for the most part is simple, pleasing and effective and it holds a high place in the curriculum of most good grainers.

Ash grained woodwork provides a more decorative and hard wearing surface than just plain painting; it has more interest than plain brush graining and avoids the heavy lines that tend to distort the architectural features.

An Attractive Shop Front
My attention was drawn recently to the outside of a wireless and electrical shop that had been painted in the autumn. It had been carried out in light Ash graining and looked fresh, clean, and charming, despite the fact that the shop was on a busy narrow road of a shopping centre so that the outside painting was subjected to much rough usage.

The light Ash graining also harmonized with the contemporary papers used for the interior and the valuable contents of the shop display.

A pale yellow ground had been used for the graining on the narrow window frames, pilasters, cornices and architraves, and it could be seen that the greatest attention had been paid to the graining of the door, which is in line with the ideas put forward in the article by Robert S. Back in the January issue of this Journal.

The English Ash
Ash is a native of the British Isles (growing widely over most of the temperate zones of Southern Europe and the United States) and we have four varieties.

In this article I am dealing with the original English Ash, Fraxinus-excelsior; the others, which are more complicated in the grain, will be dealt with later in the series.

It grows to a height of 60 ft., and will occasionally attain a height of 100 ft. on suitable, moist, well-drained soil. Fully grown trees have a diameter of 3 ft. but few trees are left standing long enough to become so large as there is a quick demand for the smaller sized boles.

An interesting feature of the Ash tree is that in growth the branches often bend downwards and then upwards towards their extremities. The twigs are thick and knotted, due to the large lateral and terminal buds, which are protected by black scales.

The bark of the tree is grey and with its compact texture produced by deep groves has a bold appearance. Minute flowers appear before the leaf buds in late April or early May. The leaves are compound with long leaflets, and a grooved mid-rib which will absorb water. Seven to eleven leaflets are found on each leaf, one terminal and the remainder in pairs opposite each other. The average length of a leaf is about 1ft.

Ash is a pleasant light coloured wood varying from an almost white to a pale brown and occasionally has a pinkish tint.

The colour of the most common variety is no darker than pale maple, while the darker type is a medium cool oak colour. The strong yellow colour that we sometimes see in older examples comes from the use of deep stained spirit or oil varnishes.

The heartwood markings of Ash are broad and open, composed of fine lines of a light brown colour. The texture is closer than that of oak, but it has lines of light running through the veins as though a steel comb has been drawn through after graining.

The points of the heart grain are rounded, never sharp, and this is one of the characteristics by which it can be distinguished from light oak or chestnut heartwood.

Method of Graining
Tools required for the graining include pencil, brown or black crayon, leather or well washed rag, steel combs, fitch and hog hair softener. The ground colour for the door in the shop front mentioned above was a pinky buff, similar to that for light

mahogany. The windows were worked on a white ground. The method of working used by the grainer was unorthodox, but I could see instantly that he must have been a man of great experience.

The wiping out, combing, crayon marking and use of the mottler were clearly not "do it yourself" tactics, but good graining methods by a sound craftsman. A heavy coat of white oil paint was applied to the pink red ground of the door. The heartwood markings were then wiped out to a width of a quarter of an inch, the wiping being only carried over the end curves, one in three running a few inches down the side.

To complete the first process of the graining steel combs were used, but very sparingly, just sufficient to indicate the direction of the grain, as shown in the small grained illustrated example. Some combing was also worked on the edges of the wiped out markings with a fine comb no more than 1in. in width.

The markings here went deep into the white paint, so that the comb had to be cleaned at every stroke, or the colour left on the comb would have run over and filled up the lines. About one quarter of the space was left empty of markings with the fine narrow comb, and more than three quarters of the side grain was left clean. At this stage the work, which would look very hard and stark, was allowed to dry.

The next step was to rub in a thin scumble of Light Ash oil scumble, or a scumble prepared from white, raw sienna, raw umber, and a touch of black.

This is thinned with turps, a touch of glaze, terebine, or a spot of flat varnish, the speed of drying and the slip being regulated as necessary. The glaze of colour should be left smooth without brush marks before the markings are worked in with the crayon.

Some four or five lines are worked in as shown in the illustration, and the hog hair is then drawn through them to break them up into short lines. One or two small knots made with the crayon could be included with the side grain.

A few short lines of crayon can be drawn in any place that looks too empty; the centres of grain can be sharpened up much more easily with the crayon. The softener is dragged through, but softening with a brushing motion should be avoided.

Glazing
On the shop door some glazing was done with vandyke and the use of the mottler, which softened down the hardness of the previous graining. All the mottling was confined to the knots in the side grain, but the whole received a thin coating of vandyke and was lightly shaded.

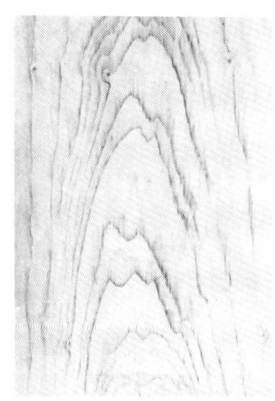

Graining illustrations: These show the three processes for reproducing English Ash described in the article – (top left) the graining, (top right) the overgraining and (bottom left) the glazing – and (bottom right) the finished panel with all the processes combined.

> Apart from its attractive name this wood has a fine curly grain and delicate mottling which give distinction to any interior scheme in which it is used.

Makore Curl

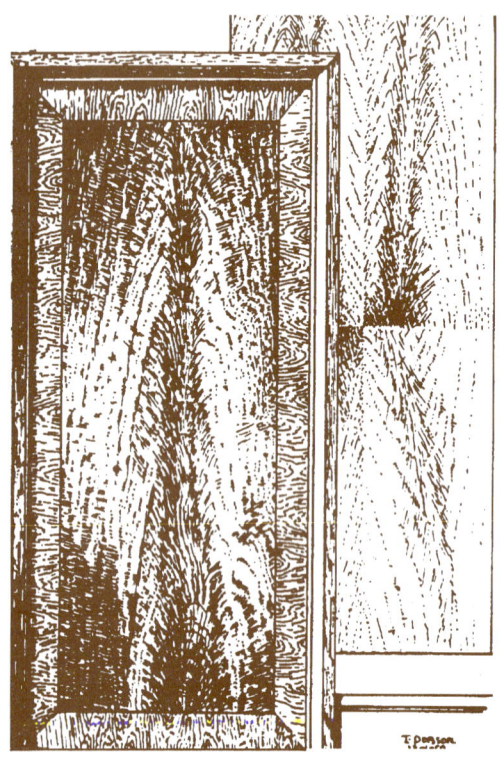

Illustrations of panelled doors grained in Makore Curl

THE name Makore Curl fascinated me the first time that I heard it.

It is of course French, for this finely marked wood comes from the forests of the French Ivory Coast and finds its largest market in Germany.

In salesmanship I understand that a good name or a particular number helps an article to sell; it is a great advantage if it is easy to remember and sounds attractive.

It was not the name, however, that first attracted my attention, but the fine curly grain or feather of a piece of the wood some 5 ft. high that a friend of mine had in his possession when I was up in Durham recently.

Large veneers have a tendency to appear coarse, but this did not and for fine delicate mottling in such quantity I have never seen its equal.

It must have been cut from a massive tree, yet it had kept its delicacy.

I do not claim that it is something new, but it is rare.

The Latin and family names are Mimusops Lecelii (Pierre) H. Lec., and Sapolaceal; these are not important to us but they convey a wealth of meaning to some people and they are useful internationally for tracing a particular variety.

Makore is found growing in all the forest region of West Africa.

The tree grows remarkably straight without large buttresses and the base is often up to 40ft. in circumference.

The bark is of a grey colour with fissures for most part running up and down the tree; when this is cut with an axe the sap exudes in the form of a sticky milky juice.

The leaves, which are crowded together at the tops of the branches, are thick and leathery in texture like those of the laurel.

A new-felled tree does not cut easily as the saw soon gums up. New logs are heavier than water and will not float until they are partially dry, so must be seasoned first or transport is difficult.

Makore was selected for the furniture and wall panelling in the state rooms of R.M.S. Queen Mary.

Description of the Wood
The best description that I can give of the colour is a rather milky brown pink, obtained from crimson lake, burnt sienna, ultramarine and a touch of blue black.

A cool buff or a light leather colour is

used for the ground; the final colour is by no means dark so that it is best to keep the ground from medium to light, otherwise with graining, glazing and overgraining it is not easy to keep the final work light.

The graining part of the curl is obtained with good fine mottling which follows the curl round the top and down both sides.

It follows the fountain or fan shape that we associate with mahogany or satinwood, but not as dark, so contrasting, or as deep cut.

The top of the curl is nice and round, perhaps on the narrow side compared with the others, and on the whole it is remarkably even though inclined to be narrow towards the top.

Down the side grain a few dark lines are found anything up to 15 in. in length, some up to ¼in. wide, mostly cut with mottle on both sides a few on one side only.

A wave of the grain with a few kinks makes the side grain more interesting and the mottle follows these variations, keeping carefully at right-angles.

Fine texture is to be seen in the lighter parts, such as can be produced with the badger side or with fine flogging.

Painted examples of Makore Curl. The first (top left) shows the drawing, worked with one side of the tool, and the second (top right) the lines brought out with a thin mottler. In the third (bottom left) the softener has been used with vigour and some texture has been worked in with the side of the softener. A few darker lines have been painted in the fouth (bottom right) and much cuttings has been carried out with the cardboard cutter, a stout piece of board with a slightly convex edge. All the examples are worked in thin oil scumble, diluted well with turps.

Mottling completely covers the whole of the centre part of the curl making it darker than the sides, where only one third is adorned with mottle.

Hard, sharp cut and vigorous is a near description of the mottling; all of it, however, is on the fine narrow side, nothing above 1½in., most of it 1in. in width.

Dark cloudy parts are to be found down both sides of the flanks slightly subduing the mottling.

Most of the light flashes are found in the usual place down the edge of the centre band, the latter being some 1½ to 4 in. in width, and in places these flashes of light follow the lines of grain down the flanks 18 in. to 2 ft. long, becoming very narrow as they near the bottom edge of the panel.

Method of Graining
The method of graining is as follows.

Rub in a thin glaze of burnt sienna in water, add a touch of crimson down the centre and a little blue on the flanks.

Draw in the heartwood with the sponge or the mottler.

Most colours to-day are ready bound but you should test them and bind if necessary in your own manner.

Recently I have been using both poster colour and fine tube water colour for these small special jobs; they are finely ground and well bound and when your job is only small the slight additional cost does not matter.

Take the sponge and draw in the large heartwood shape, using only a few points on one side; in order to obtain the height without too much width, work two short curves at the top additional to each one that runs down the flanks.

The whole operation should not take more than a few seconds.

Any slight variation in the grain must be made now in the first drawing with lines following rigidly afterwards, and wipe the sides down fairly clean.

If there is time available after it has set, fix the work with a thin coat of varnish.

For the main graining process, which includes all the mottling, use an oil-based prepared scumble.

You may mix one or two scumbles together to obtain the desired tone, choosing from mahogany, rosewood and grey.

Thin with turps to a nice working consistency.

Rub this in, following the grain in an uneven manner.

Some of the colour may rub up but this will not matter – work gently over without much brushing.

For mottling use a short cutter or a curved piece of card, which works quite well and cleanly. Wipe the edge of the mottler frequently as you work, or the colour picked up and drawn together will tend to spread out or run.

Work towards and downwards from the centre with the mottling until it is completed; this will take some time, but fortunately the oil colour will allow for this.

Soften gently across the mottle, to carry the colour away from the lighter parts of the cuts, and lightly flog with the side of the hog hair between the lines of the mottling running down the sides.

Glazing
The glazing process is optional, but it improves the general appearance and should be carried out with vandyke brown in water.

Rub in a thin coat of colour, wipe off with the leather all the parts that should be left light and mottle others in a broad manner only.

Parts may be left plain and slightly darker to be softened into the other work with the use of the badger softener.

Limed Oak

The graining of Limed Oak is dealt with in this article in response to a request from a Newcastle-upon-Tyne member. Although the graining and rolling of this wood is regarded as a straight-forward job there are a number of pitfalls to be avoided.

LIMED Oak is produced by the application of lime to oak timber after drying or during growth. This alters its appearance and makes it more valuable for interior decoration.

The beautiful effects that are obtained by the use of lime are not by any means the same on all classes of timber. We find that new fresh-cut oak will darken slightly on being subjected to the action of lime whilst its figure will remain light. Mature wood on the other hand will bleach out, and its figure will often go darker.

Treatment of the Wood

It is quite easy to produce the limed effect in graining with a slightly alteration in the colours and the addition of the white pith marks with the graining roller.

The graining itself calls for skill; the colour must be kept in harmony with other parts of the scheme and it must at all times be of the correct consistency, or the results will be disappointing. Lime cannot be used in our painting process, as it is too transparent when varnished, and we have therefore to use a solid metallic-based pigment.

To day, lime is used less and less in the cabinet making industry, for the colour changing process is too slow and as it must be applied direct to the bare wood it raises the grain and entails more work in scraping and smoothing prior to finishing.

Some time ago I treated a number of pieces of wood as examples for the cabinet makers in my employment and I still have many of these. I found the following method the most satisfactory, working direct on to the natural wood.

The pores are scrubbed out with a wire brush and then the wood is coated with a thin solution of clear shellac varnish. For a darker example I used a coat of hard drying stain.

A coat of thin white enamel is next applied, allowed partly to set and then the face is cleaned off, by rubbing across the grain, to leave the surface milky and the pores full of the white. When thoroughly dry the whole is polished with a bleached lac polish.

I carried out a similar type of treatment in cellulose with even greater success. The grain was cleaned out, then a fairly heavy pigmented coat was given with the gun.

This had the effect of filling up much of the grain, leaving only the deeper texture which it showed up to the best advantage.

White grain filler was next applied, fine steel wool was used for cleaning off purposes and afterwards the work was sprayed with matt or glossy cellulose.

Painted Representation

Limed Oak varies in colour from a light green cream to a cool medium brown. In grained work it is best to work as dark as possible consistent with the particular job, otherwise the white lines of filler will not show up to advantage.

It is best to keep the figure well open in character to allow more clear space for the short white lines, which should be cleaned off the figure. The milky appearance can be easily produced by a glaze of thin white scumble.

The changing of the brown lines pith to white is the crowning distinction of Limed Oak. The grain is just the same as we find in English Oak, and, as it has both figure and heartwood markings, combing or brush grained texture may be used as the background.

The tools and sundries required include hog hair softener, combs and brush grainer, graining horn, rags, check roller and supply brush. This supply brush is most important, but most painters seem to lose it after the first few days of service or use it for some other purpose.

An ordinary tool will suffice when using the roller in black or brown because these are

273

colours that are both good covering and light in specific gravity. For white however this brush is essential, as it feeds evenly allowing the roller to run at a fast speed and giving off a moderate supply of colour while doing so.

The colours and thinnres required are raw umber, raw sienna, black, white and a small amount of white enamel, linseed oil, turpentine, glaze medium and a touch of terebine.

You carry out graining as follows. From the colours prepare a small amount of gilp in a kettle. (For a medium toned example I would use seven parts of umber to one part white, for a lighter colour three of raw sienna, one of the umber and one of white). Rub in, soften the combing or brush graining well before figuring, then work the figure in an open manner to allow for a good subsequent display of white grain.

Glazing

With a thin coat of milky white scumble, go over the whole surface, wipe out the centre of all the panels and stipple the remainder lightly with a fine hair stippler. Prepare a small amount of white for the roller, comprising one part white enamel and three parts flat white eased with turps but still left in a fairly round state.

Experiments must be made to obtain just the right consistency; if it is too round it will only make faint markings, if too thin the colour will be too poor to give as bold a mark as desired. When the consistency is correct proceed with the roller markings and clean off with rag all the colour on the front of the figure.

Should the figure appear too hard, it should be softened in the same direction as the grain.

Finally varnish with a pale varnish in either flat or gloss, remembering to keep the film thickness down to a minimum to prevent the yellowing of the surface later.

Painted examples of Limed Oak showing (top left) the brush grained background, (top right) the well softened ground with wiped out figure on half the panel, (bottom left) the white pith grain worked with the check roller, and (bottom right) the completed panel with the roller marks cleaned away from the front of the figure.

Connemara Marble

The painted representation of Connemara marble is dealt with here at the request of a Sunderland member now engaged on a job calling for this type of decoration.

CONNEMARA is a green marble and like many other marbles takes its name from the district where it is quarried. This is an area to the west of County Galway, Ireland, consisting largely of mountains and loughs, typical holiday country and celebrated for its wild and romantic scenery.

Limestone abounds there. Marble was formerly a valuable export from this part of Ireland, chiefly to France and Spain, along with wool and salmon (the river Shannon drains a large part of the area).

Architectual Features
Banks, churches and many important public buildings make use of Connemara marble in their architecture. It is most suitable for use along with others in building up luxurious interior schemes. The effect when used alone on large areas of wall-filling is not good because of the prominent wavy bands.

Two rather poor examples of its use spring to mind as I write these lines, one in a large banking hall and the other on a two-tier pulpit in an important minster.

The wall-filling of the banking hall was lined from the dado rail to the picture rail; three of the sides were quite good as they were broken up with doors and windows, but the fourth completely spoiled the effect. In the pulpit the effect would have been improved by the use of other marbles of lighter or darker tones and with less formal wavy bands.

Another hall that I have visited has six heavy pillars and a three foot dado in Connemara. On the dado the slabs are twenty-one inches wide and used in threes; the first one has the marble running vertical whilst the next pair are reversed with the lines arranged at a gentle slope. The pillars are built up of circular slabs some two feet in diameter by eighteen inches thick, all the lines running horizontally.

Painted examples of marble should be positioned so far as possible in exactly the same way that natural marble would have been.

Origin and Description
Connemara is a crystalline rock, composed of coloured grains of the mineral calcite, calcium carbonate.

It results from the crystallization of pure limestone under the influence of solutions and increased temperature or increased pressure and is thus mainly metamorphic rock. Quartz in the limestone gives rise to wollastonite, calcium silicate; with some magnesium carbonate present.

The original dolomitic limestone contained quartz with magnesium silicate fosterite which hydrates to the green sepentine and provides sepentine marble or othicalcite, as exemplified by the Connemara marble.

Light green predominates in this marble, covering more than one half of the total area, and this is broken up with other tints of green, browns and blacks and bands of white. A few of the wavy bands of green are up to six inches in width, but most of them are narrow. The edges of many of the broad bands are shaded darker, whilst all the single dark bands are narrow.

The texture is mostly fine, little of it being clear or definite, and a large amount of the colour is smooth without any texture. Often the drawing of the outline of the bands gives the impression of root oak in a bright green colour.

Connemara marble is most conveniently worked in oil colour with raw sienna, Brunswick green, Prussian blue, black and vandyke brown. Off-white is suitable for the ground colour.

Method of Working
The painted representation of this marble is carried out as follows. Work with a mixture of turps, or turps and a little flat varnish, which will give sufficient transparency to all the colours. Prepare a few tints of greens and greys on the palette board.

Rub the panel over with thinners from the dipper to prevent the colour from getting too firm a grip on the white ground. With a small tool lay in a number of the lighter clours first; these tints of warm green will form the drawing, which must not be crossed over.

Half or more of the area should be covered, all running in the same general direction. Continue to add other narrow bands of colour and greys to the edge of the first bands or down the edge of each other, some on the paler green.

Charge the sponge with turpentine and proceed to stipple or dab to break the surface up into a fine texture. Follow the lines of colour in the direction of the marble without turning your sponge until you have got to the bottom of the line.

For the darker lines a fitch should be used with tones of brown and darker grey for the colour concentrated in one or two areas. To soften these dark places I find it is best to roll lightly with a pad of rag. Continue to work with the fitch, sponge, and rag until a satisfactory arrangement is obtained.

Glazing
Glazing may be used in two ways, either to tone down the effect that has been produced or to brighten it up by giving it additional contrast. Oil in the surface and add glazes of tones of green, shaded to follow the lines of the marble.

To clean up, take the rag and wipe out in places, soften vigorously but do not add any white. With a clean fitch splash on some turpentine by striking against a second fitch which should open out the small amounts of colour on the surface.

Do not be over liberal with the turps or it will run; allow a few seconds for it to work, when small rings of dark will appear near a light spot.

The illustrations show (top left) the effect obtained with the brush after rubbing in the ground colour, (top right) the results of running a sponge down the wavy lines, (bottom left) the addition of more colour with a fitch and pencil to sharpen up the edges of the bands, and (bottom right) the additional texture obtained by the use of turps and sponge stippling.

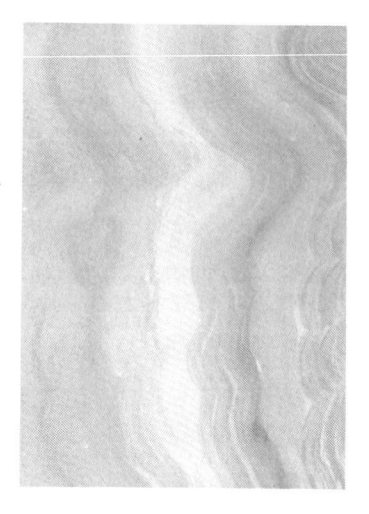

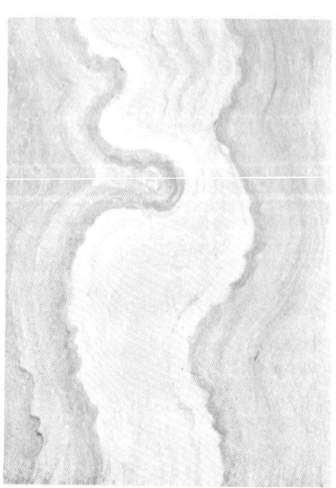

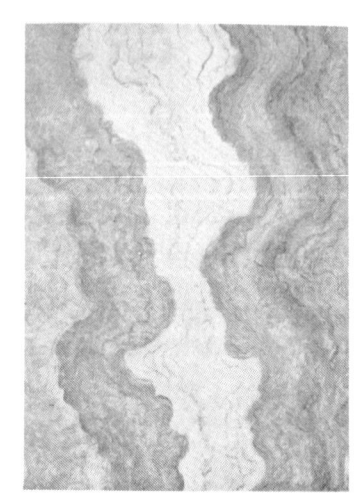

Walnut Burr

This is one of the most valuable of woods and in veneer form is in great demand to-day for radio and television cabinets.

THE walnut tree is well known throughout the world for both its beautiful wood and its tasty nuts.

About seventeen species are identified, half of which we recognise for graining purposes as being different in colour and grain.

The tree is classed as one of the noblest of the hardwoods; it may live for centuries growing to some 150ft. in height with a proportionate spread of crown and a trunk up to six feet in diameter.

It is from the lower part of the trunk of these large and valuable trees that burrs are found growing.

The burrs are sometimes only a few inches deep but others go very deep even through the bole.

If the burrs commence to grow early in the life of the tree, the knots will be deep and the burr much thicker, and the number of small twigs growing out appear continually to increase in numbers.

Large pieces however are rare, and the wood is always cut to the best advantage.

Many examples contain parts of heartwood markings, but the finest are those containing nothing but the burr.

Much of our finest furniture is enhanced by the skill of the cabinet maker in quartering or reversing the veneers.

We can add to the value and interest of our graining by adopting many of the cabinet maker's methods.

Masking tape and patience work wonders with this form of graining, and one of my friends successfully uses tracing paper for quick and accurate quartering.

Walnut Burr is a sure test of a grainer's ability, calling for great skill in the manipulation of the tools of our craft.

Many of the fine, large T.V. cabinets are of walnut and the more expensive are of burr.

One that I examined recently had doors 15in. by 36in.; these are being turned out in the thousands each week but the workmanship was flawless. No joints or repairs to the veneer could be distinguished.

The decorative value of this elaborately marked wood is so high that it is worthwhile making good weaknesses in the burr veneer and repairing cracks and loose places.

Origin and Description

Walnut grows in greater or less quantities in most countries with a moderate temperature.

Italy probably provides us with the choicest marked examples, whilst Africa supplies us with the quantity and the largest boles, some up to twenty tons in weight.

Only a few of the walnut trees grown in any country produce burrs, for they must be large and advanced in years before doing so and most are cut before reaching this stage.

Fruit is the sole reason for growing walnut in several countries, where a fine flavour is produced and no timber exported.

Most of the wood is a medium blue or purple brown colour, the Italian contains much olive green colour, but all types are flat in tone with very little contrast.

Two thirds of the area is covered with knots of many shapes and sizes, singly or in poorly defined groups of up to ten in number.

All the knots are darker than the other markings, some being almost black, and usually well softened into the ground leaving nice shaded edges.

Comparing it with pollard oak, I find that the main points of difference are – all the markings of walnut burr are much rounder, the colour is much cooler, the softening more pronounced and the overgraining much more subdued.

I well remember two trees that I visited

often as a boy; one was birch and the other wilow and both were well adorned with burrs.

    The first ten feet of the trunks were covered with burrs, and as they were growing almost up to the branches they were much easier to climb.

    The largest burrs were growing on the willow tree – they were up to two feet in diameter.

    On both trees the burrs were bristling with small twigs, whilst the adjacent parts of the trunk were perfectly clear.

    In the graining of burr walnut quite a large area is left devoid of markings, with only a little mottled shading covering it.

    If any lines of heartwood are to be introduced, they will be less than one quarter of an inch wide, about a third of an inch apart, nicely curved, and well softened.

Method of Graining
The graining may be carried out in several ways, but I have adopted water colour for the actual graining and a prepared oil scumble for the glazing.

    This method has two major advantages – it allows the work to be completed more quickly and

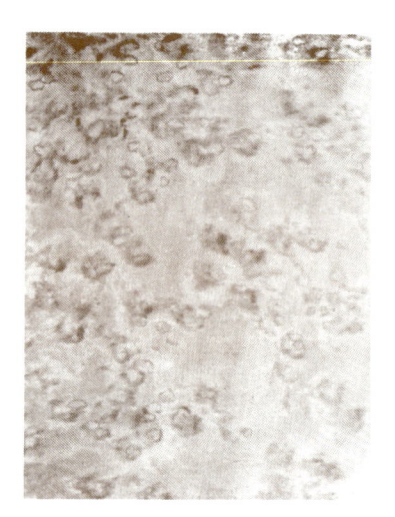

Burr Walnut
The first illustration, top left, shows the preliminary rubbing-in, left in its rough state. The second, top right, shows the knots worked in with a sponge. In the third illustration, bottom left, additional work has been carried out with a fitch between the knots. The fourth, bottom right, shows the glazing, mottling and softening.

the finished effect is much softer.

For the first graining stage I used vandyke in water with no special binder added (I had just opened a new tin and the new material always appears to be better bound).

Raw, burnt sienna, and black may also be included in the palette for special colour requirements, but all are inclined to be loose and require binding.

A ground of medium buff will answer for most requirements, as we want to avoid a great contrast between the ground and the finished work, and two or more glazes of brown can soon make work darker than we require.

About two square feet are rubbed in with a tool, leaving the colour rough and shady without any attempt to lay it off.

A little more colour should be applied than is required as a little is lost in the graining process.

Often the lines of the rubbing in can be used as a guide for the graining.

The knotted portion should be worked with a small portion of sponge, artificial or otherwise.

A little colour should be rubbed into the sponge at the start so that we do not clean up the area too much where the first few knots are made.

The knots are no more than three quarters of an inch and as they must all be worked separately we must work quickly to cover the area.

Filling in can be carried out with a stippling action with the sponge but this must not be overdone as the softening will knock most of it out.

The softening is done quickly in almost every direction with the badger softener.

If it is desired to work in any lines of grain, these can best be carried out with a round hog-hair pencil, which will not pick up the colour or leave the lines very prominent.

Should you desire to make the lines more prominent, a worn sable may be used, but guard against making the lines of grain too startling and do not leave the second softening too long.

If you are working a large area, say a one-panel door of almost two square yards, break this into two or three parts.

Try to keep the joints alive and cover any small jointing marks with the oil glazing colour.

Glazing

Glazing should be carried out with prepared walnut oil scumble, thinned with turpentine and rubbed straight on to the hard dry vandyke.

If you wish to put any further detail into the graining, it is best to bind the vandyke before glazing with a coat of thinned varnish or goldsize, but normally this is not called for

and a little care in light rubbing in and as little brushwork as possible will be found effective.

The mottling is best worked with a thick solid three-inch mottler, and softened with the hog hair softener.

Glazing should be focussed near the knots, and the whole treated as an overall pattern.

A few of the knots may be strengthened with a fitch and a little stiff colour.

The fitch, mottler and softener can be applied until you are satisfied with the results.

WALNUT
See also:
The Graining of Walnut (1) 94
The Graining of Walnut (2) 100
The Graining of Walnut (3) 112
Italian Walnut 118
Italian Walnut (cont.) 120
Italian Walnut (cont.) 124
Walnut 144
Satin Walnut 160
Bleached Walnut 170
Australian Walnut 186
English Walnut 197
A Quick Method
of Graining Walnut 242
Bleached Italian Walnut
in a Bedroom 258
Feather of Walnut 284

Oak Heartwood

Oak heartwood is one of the most popular subjects for graining and it is usually produced by the wipe-out method described here.

GRAINING to many of us to-day still means oak graining, either heartwood or figure, produced by the wipe-out method. I have always been grateful to my father, who insisted that all his sons should master the art of oak graining at an early age. Painting and decorating generally has provided me with a very interesting life, and I have moved about England a lot in the pursuit of my calling.

Glasson Church

Before the industrial life of Lancashire had settled down to its present pattern, Glasson Docks, not very far from where I live, were in use for the early import of cotton. They are still being used to-day by British Railways; large warehouses have been built on the wharf and the large tanks for the storage of imported linseed oil have been repainted. Glasson is situated near the estuary on the south bank of the river Lune, where a small community resides, many working on the docks and others on the rich agricultural land that surrounds them.

I recently visited the fine old church there that had just been decorated. It was a clean smart job carried out with taste and dignity. There was no painted ornament, no decoration and no lining, but the woodwork was grained in medium oak graining, with wipe-out heartwood and figure markings – the only fully skilled job about the whole work of repainting. The final effect was excellent; the sun was shining brightly through the richly coloured stained glass and I saw everything to its best advantage. Incidentally, I noticed that one of the memorial windows belongs to a family that has descended from John O'Gaunt, who at one time resided in the castle at Lancaster.

Much of the painting and graining would be done on the top of oak, but it had now been treated to make it all appear alike. Additions and alterations over centuries give an odd look to a building; often one or two kinds of timber are used, and the colours vary according to age, so that the whole can be evened up only by painting.

I am glad that the church authorities chose the graining of English oak to level up this work, for it looks well, it will wear well and it is in keeping with the tradition of church decoration. I cannot give the decorating firm or the grainer a pat on the back, as I do not know who they were; they probably came in by their own transport from a distant town, for the area to-day is thinly populated with no painter's shop in the village.

Description of Markings

To the untrained eye, the drawing of oak closely resembles that of ash, and at times they are difficult to distinguish, though normally the markings of oak are not as coarse. One important feature of the drawing of oak is the spoon-shaped end followed by a number of ringed markings with dull or rounded points of varying widths.

Perhaps a small knot or other interesting shape occurs to one side, followed by another series of plainer markings.

Most of the markings are fine because it is such a slow growing timber. The annular rings are close together, and this keeps the spaces between the heartwood markings narrow. A new set of annular rings are made with each branch, which work into the pattern of the central design.

Heartwood markings in any timber are, as the name implies, in the timber cut from the heart or centre of the tree. In oak, the finest marked heartwood is always obtained from a position two or three inches away from the dead centre.

This heartwood is often referred to as "sap", probably because the word is shorter, but the sap is of course to be found on the outer side of the trunk, just under the bark.

Timbers differ as to which side of the heartwood markings the heavy short lines of grain are displayed. In the case of oak this is on the inside.

Method of Graining

To describe the method of graining oak, we will take the woodwork in the bright, clean Parish Church, at Glasson, Lancs., as our example.

A medium buff ground should be prepared, made up from raw sienna with a touch of raw Turkey umber, or a prepared scumble of medium oak will suffice. This is thinned to a working consistency, rubbed in and well brushed out.

I prefer to darken the centre, by rubbing in a little extra colour from the can bottom or a touch of umber from the stiff oil stainers.

For the actual wiping out, washed cotton material is the best, for linen, nylon and other hard fibre will not pick up the colour at all well. A small piece of cloth about eight inches square folded double will be found ideal.

Both hands must be used to hold the material steady and taut; the bulk is gripped in the palm of the hand and a little passed over the thumb, the end being secured with the second hand.

As the work proceeds the rag is passed through the hand over the thumb so that the part being used is always clean and soft. You should not be afraid of going back to wipe out more colour or broaden a line; the final width of a line is not easy to determine as the work proceeds.

Most of our work is grained on the rails, and for this you should commence in the centre of a knot and work outwards. On a vertial panel I prefer to start at the bottom and work upwards.

On the best work where really good drawing is called for, a good method is to use the end of a fitch to make the preliminary sketch and then to follow these lines with the thumb wipe-out.

A small worn fitch is very useful for softening the outside edge of the wipe-out, whilst the inside is left in its hard state.

The side grain is now combed in, using leather, rubber or a coarse steel comb according to the work being done.

If a **soft effect** is required, a piece of rag may be wrapped over the comb.

In order to break up the lines a little more, a two or one-inch comb is often used over the work, radiating towards the centre of the heart or knot; this gives a quick, starling effect and should be used with caution.

Finally the work is softened lightly with the hog hair softener, again towards the centre.

Oak Heartwood: The first illustration (top left) shows the shaded rubbing in done with a sash tool and the second (top right) the lines drawn in with the fitch and part grained. In the third (bottom left) the whole of the panel has been wiped out, whilst in the fourth (bottom right) a little more attention has been given to the wiping, the edges have been softened with the fitch and some combing has been carried out.

Rose Campan Marble

The attractiveness of the Campan marbles lies in their bright colours, and Rose Campan is one of the brightest and most attractive.

TWO things attracted the attention of a friend and I when we entered the Royal Station Hotel, Newcastle-on-Tyne, recently; the first was the bright colour on the dado, the second the homely smell of paint. The friend who accompanied me was a brillant young decorator who had made a name for himself in the North Eastern Region of the Federation. Our eyes went straight to the dado and we gave the red marble a passing glance before going about our business.

Without examining it carefully, we passed off the marbling as a recently painted example that was not too well carried out. Dust sheets were covering the fine furniture and fittings, whilst scaffolding was stacked in most recesses; the painters were obviously working somewhere.

Just before leaving the hotel I touched the dado and found it cold – obviously it was the real marble, Rose Campan. We were both slightly disappointed. My friend was trained and educated in Holland, attended the same college as myself in Brussels and is one of the experts in our craft, but he was misled just as I was.

Decsription
Rose Campan, as the name implies, is the red variety of the brightly coloured Campan family. The outstanding feature are the bands of colour in tones of red and for the most part six inches in width. About one tenth of the area is in the complementary green, and added interest is obtained from glazes of colour slightly darker than the ground. The shaded ground is covered with many small almond-shaped shells, which give the appearance of a coarse texture. The shell shapes vary in size from ½in. to 1 in. in length and they change direction along the bands of colour in much the same way as markings in oak grain.

Veining, white to light grey in colour, is prominent in some examples and appears to hold the work together. Smaller amounts of gold and orange are also found in the light veining.

Origin
Rose Campan is quarried in the French Pyrenees. The river Adour runs through the Campan valley there; one side is adorned with green hills, and on the other are precipitous crags among which the marble is quarried. The quarries yield a profusion of brightly coloured marbles, largely built up of nodules and small shells embedded in a coloured matrix.

In the Percy collection, housed in the Sedgwick Museum, Cambridge, seven varieties of Campan marble are exhibited, all from the Pyrenees. These varieties are Isabelle, Melange, Rose, Rouge, Verte, Verte-Verte (a very pale green) and Griotte.

Method of Marbling
All the Campan marbles are best worked on a shaded ground, painted in as shown in the first illustration. The ground for the Rose variety should be painted in pinks, red and blue. White, Indian red and vermilion should be used for the pinks, and a little Prussian for the blue band, which is repeated about every fifth band. Care must be taken with the preparation of those bands as they show up prominently through the glaze of the marble. On a dado they are best arranged in a vertical direction, whilst on panel work they should follow the long side of the panel.

The painting in is done with a small tool or large fitch, and the edges are softened well with a dry brush. No attempt should be made to produce a textured surface – in fact I like to include a little gloss paint in the preparation of my ground because it flows out well, blends better and forms a smooth hard ground.

Stippling
The next task is to rub in glazes of reds prepared from crimson lake, Indian red and, for the most interesting colour, a dull green. I prefer to work from a palette board. For the thinners you can use any composition that you have to hand but it should include a

small amount of oil or varnish, so that it will open out well when stippled or splashed with turpentine.

If a rubber stippler is to be used for the shell impressions, it can be loaded with stearate glaze medium, which will stay put and is quite effective on the shaded ground.

For the sponge method, up to ten minutes is allowed for the work to set before the stippling is proceeded with. The sponge is softened first in water then in turps and squeezed out well after each soaking. Both the fine and the coarser sides of the sponge may be used on different areas.

Petrol is also quick and clean for producing a coarse texture. It the sponge stipple opens out quickly and commences to run it can be arrested by rolling with clean rag.

For the longer shell shapes a sliding motion may be adopted, and the sponge should be rinsed out frequently in the turps to obtain the sharpest results.

If you follow along too quickly with the sponging after rubbing in, the colour will have a tendency to run; on the other hand, if you are too long and the ground glaze is set too much, it will not open out and it will be necessary to rub it up with the thinners and re-stipple.

The sponge stipple will sometimes be a little weak in places, but this can be improved by running a few fine lines round with a little colour on a fine sable. Misses can be replaced with wiping-out using a graining horn and rag; the ground glaze will be set too hard for additional sponge stippling.

Vein Markings
The chain or vein markings, as shown in the last illustration, may be worked immediately if the work is small or if it is wanted quickly, otherwise it is as well to allow it to dry. To ease the pencil it is best to soften the surface with thinners from the dipper and rub over with rag.

The sable pencil is charged with white, touched with ochre on one side and light grey on the other. It is rolled between the thumb and first finger whilst being worked to blend the colours together in a pleasant manner.

This pencil work should not be too striking, the colour should be subdued, particulary on the larger veins, and softened lightly. The amount of pencil work varies from one tenth to one quarter of the area.

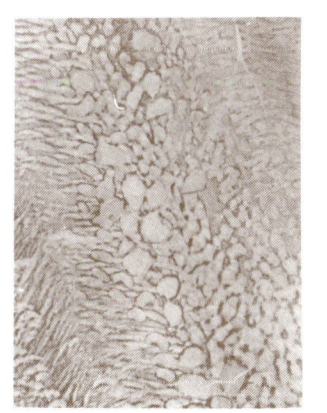

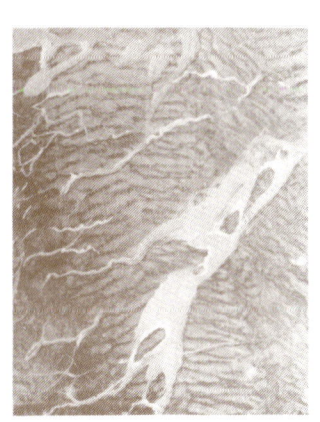

Rose Campan Marble: These illustrations show (top left) the painted shading of the ground, (top right) the effect obtained by stippling with the rubber stippler, (bottom left) the small shell shapes produced with the sponge and turpentine, and (bottom right) the heavy veins for which the colour was applied with a sable pencil.

Feather of Walnut

Although the feather is not the most popular feature of walnut its use is recommended for doors and large vertical panels to be treated as one flat area.

THERE are a number of decorative cabinet woods that have an interesting feather, but with the exception of mahogany feather little use is made of them by the average painter.

The feather we select is the one that has been passed down by tradition as typical of the particular wood – we speak of the knots in pine, or the bird's eye in maple, of the burr in walnut, and of the figure in oak, but all these fine cabinet woods have other attractive features.

In my small collection of veneers I have a well marked specimen of walnut feather, which was given to me by a cabinet maker friend in Yorkshire.

Fountains

Last week I met an old customer of some thirty years ago, now retired from his wool merchant's business, walking leisurely on the promenade with his wife.

After we had exchanged greetings he turned to the subject of painting and decorating in which he always took a great interest.

He told me that all his walls, which included a number of murals, had been painted and flat varnished and most of his doors had been adorned with sprays of flowers, but the tit-bit was that his doors in the hall and the staircase were all like fountains.

He was of course describing the walnut feather to which this article is devoted.

It was indeed very fine work and it appealed to his imagination.

The decorator responsible I knew well. He is one who carries out his own graining and takes a pride in it, and he was the first decorator I saw using a spray gun to grain a door in oak figure.

I wonder how many of you will remember this outstanding personality.

Description and Graining

The feather of any wood takes on a colour similar to that of the wood from which it is cut, and as the tree must be a well developed one there is a tendency for the feather to be on the darker side. The specimen I have is of a medium toned green-brown.

A drab colour is the best description I can give for the ground. A buff would be too warm.

Raw umber, white and a little burnt sienna will cover all our requirements for slightly lighter or darker ground colours.

For the graining a standard walnut scumble, which is both dark and cool in colour, will fill our needs.

Coming from a very hefty bole, the shape for drawing is broad and thick-set.

Down the side nearest to the centre of the tree the lines fall away sharply, whilst at the other side they reach out almost at a right angle, radiating in a slow curve towards the branch.

When you come to the graining of the feather, this feather is useful but as the side where the lines come down sharply takes up so little space it must be placed out of centre.

At the base it should be from one quarter to one sixth of the panel width nearer to one side, working back in a curve towards the centre as it proceeds higher up the panel.

The lines working out at right angles at the base should fall towards the top to balance with the opposite side.

As in other forms of feathering, the darkest part, formed by the lines of grain and the mottle, is to be found down the centre.

Dark, fairly broad lines of grain passing

over the top of the arch of the feather are typical of walnut.

Some are broad, others narrow, with small points or with scalloped meanderings, and a few cross over each other.

The scalloped edges coincide with the mottling, which in places is found only on one side whilst in others it runs clean down the centre.

Mottling is not over elaborate.

Only a few of the longer cuts are used, varying in length from four to six inches and about half an inch wide.

Smaller ones are found on the outside edge of the dark centre shape, and both large and small are well softened, the former heavily.

Down one side there is a finely drawn heartwood shape, similar to those we associate with mahogany.

It is of course smaller and less important than the feather.

The lines of grain are only about one third the width of those of the feather; they are much wider apart and most of them are light in colour.

Two rather bold knots will be found to improve the effect, and

Feather of Walnut
The first example (top left) shows the effect obtained with the rubbing-in tool and the second (top right) the addition of colour and the first sponge markings. The fitch and cutter have been used for the third example (bottom left) and the final example (bottom right) has been glazed with vandyke brown in water.

they also enable more mottle to be displayed.

Short pith markings are prominent, particularly down the sides, and unlike those in mahogany, they flow with the grain.

These pith marks are comparatively easy to produce with the flogging process; as they are fine and short, a badger should be used – a long bristled flogger would be too coarse.

Light delicate mottling is found down the flanks, and this again is best produced in the traditional manner.

A thin glaze of vandyke brown in water should be rubbed in and the undulating surface mottled with a good hefty broad brush.

In colour and texture and the smallness of the knots the flanks are similar to those we find in good Italian walnut.

Uses
Quartering, crossbanding and the dividing of a door surface into geometric shapes are no longer very popular, whilst only a few woods are suitable for graining a door in one large flat area.

A feather overcomes this difficulty, and I find that cupboard fronts, large vertical panels and most other architectural features in wood are suited to the display of a large feather.

Illustrations
In the graining of the examples illustrated I used a manufacturer's prepared scumble thinned with turpentine, to which was added a few drops of linseed oil and a touch of glaze medium.

The latter slowed things down and also helped with the manipulation of the colour.

Black and ultramarine decorator's tube colours were also used – black to make the centre of the feather more intense and a touch of blue to grey the gilp in places down the sides.

In the first example only the rubbing-in tool was used. Some black and the sponge were used on the second.

I do not favour the use of the sponge in oil colour because it soon becomes messy and soggy, but to open out the colour in a coarse manner I find the sponge as good as any material; it is best to have a number of changes and wash them out together on completion.

My cardboard cutter, which works well in a prepared scumble, was brought into play on the third example.

A fitch was also used on the edges of the top portions of the side grain with a little additional colour.

The whole was then well softened and the short grain worked in last.

Glazing only was carried out on the last example.

This was worked in water and vandyke after the first three processes were hard and dry, but could have been done equally well in the oil scumble.

WALNUT
See also:
The Graining of Walnut (1) 94
The Graining of Walnut (2) 100
The Graining of Walnut (3) 112
Italian Walnut 118
Italian Walnut (cont.) 120
Italian Walnut (cont.) 124
Walnut 144
Satin Walnut 160
Bleached Walnut 170
Australian Walnut 186
English Walnut 197
A Quick Method
of Graining Walnut 242
Bleached Italian Walnut
in a Bedroom 258
Walnut Burr 277

Pencilled Figure of Oak

The pencil graining to be seen in Acklam Hall, Middlesbrough, inspired the author to devote an article to this subject.

THE pencilled figure of oak recalls very sharply to my mind a number of very fine craftsmen and two in particular who were amongst my closest friends.

One operated in North of England and the other in the West Riding. Both were gifted public speakers who made a good name for the craft and for themselves – one alas! passed on quite recently – but it is their pencil graining that I want to describe here.

A Stately Home

Acklam Hall, Middlesbrough, one of the stately homes of England, has dominated this part of the country for centuries.

Here the cream of craftsmen have had an opportunity to give of their best.

Not long ago all the painted woodwork was carried out in the pencilled figure of oak, representing probably the largest graining job within a hundred square miles.

The woodwork of the main staircase and in many of the rooms is of carved oak, whilst the large doors in the hall and dining room are the finest mahogany doors that I have ever seen.

Many of the lofty, well designed rooms are decorated with Italian plaster ornament equal to anything to be found in Europe.

The green bedroom, painted all over in a medium dull green colour, always interests me.

This room was used by Charles the First in the early seventeeth century whilst he was visiting the North or passing through to Scotland during his troublesome reign.

The decoration of the room has not been changed since its Royal occupation.

It is not surprising that painters in the area still talk about the long runs and the good work that was carried out there.

What a credit it was for the local grainer who was given a job there, and how well he was ready to acquit himself when given the chance.

Sometimes outside specialists were called in, even from as far afield as London, but the work that I now refer to was carried out by a local craftsman.

The Hall is no longer a residence but a school, but most of the fine decoration is still preserved.

I hope that the grained work will continue to give good service for a long time to come, for almost two thirds of the woodwork throughout this large building is grained in the pencilled figure of oak.

The trees in the park-land and down the long avenue to the Hall are mostly beech but they are very large; the oak must have been cut and used for the decoration of the interior.

Building has taken place on much of the border land of the park, but the trees were allowed to remain and they make a fine setting for some well designed post-war houses.

I am indebted to the late Alderman Ellis Whatley and Mr. Fred Simpson of Middlesbrough, and to Mr. Croft of Stockton-on-Tees for the details of their experience at Acklam.

Method of Graining

The grained work throughout the building was all of the same colour, the ground being on the light side for a medium oak and brush-grained with a gilp prepared from raw umber.

This brush-graining was very clean; every piece was run with the grain into all the corners with the brush held firm and given a slight wave.

Each piece had been rubbed in separately

and then grained, with the result that all the joints were well up to standard.

The work was allowed to dry and the pencilled figure then applied on the hard ground after a rub with an oily, turpy rag to prevent the pencil work from "cissing".

Figure was mostly displayed on the panels but a little was used on the rails; all the styles were clean brush-grained and no heartwood markings were introduced.

The colour suggests that the gilp may have been used with the addition of some tube stainers to help with the covering.

No softening had been carried out for the work was clean and sharp, just as the sable pencil had left it.

The quantity of pencil figure throughout the building is enormous and must have taken months of a grainer's time.

The figure was on the small side and there was no evidence of haste; the drawing was good, if perhaps a little formal, and in keeping with the remainder of the decoration throughout and Hall.

Near Perfection
My other close friend and grainer of the pencilled figure served on

No.1 The oak figure worked on a wet ground to give the softest possible effect.

No.2. The figure pencilled in after the ground is partly set.

No.3. Strong pencilled figure worked on a dry ground.

N.4. Figure softened out with turps and then run over with a brush-grainer.

the school advisory committee whilst I was teaching in South Yorkshire.

He brought this art to near perfection. All his oak graining was carried out by the pencil method; in some instances it was laid on with a gilp, and at other times he would remove the figure with the turpentine method.

All the figure was applied on the wet brush-grained, stippled or combed ground, and a dry brush was drawn gently down the work afterwards.

The secret of success in this, of course, is to allow the ground gilp time to set before applying the figure.

It is not easy to fix this time which may vary between 15 and 45 minutes, but my method is to rub in two doors at a time and then follow along with the graining of both.

A good idea is to take careful note of the time allowed for setting when the best results are obtained and keep to it as near as possible.

Grounds suitable for pencil graining may vary between a white and a medium ochre buff; darker work is not suitable for this method.

Short stumpy figure is not good for pencil reproduction, but the longer type of figure can be reproduced at a rapid rate with a good meaty sable.

For the softest effect, use the same gilp or scumble for the figure as for the rubbing-in and apply it with the sable without any attempt to wipe out.

Pencilled figure should be drawn in carefully, for one figure out of alignment will show up badly on the finished panel and cannot be put back into place without rubbing up the whole door or panel.

A pencil charged with colour is much easier to handle than one charged with turps, as the latter is invisible.

Turpentine in a sable has a nasty habit of starting with a round blob, particularly if the pencil is well worn or too heavily charged with turpentine.

Illustrations

The painted examples show how soft and hard effects can be obtained by the pencil methods.

In number one, showing the softest possible effect, the figure was applied as soon as the graining scumble had been brush-grained.

The scumble was taken straight out of the kettle used for the rubbing-in process, and some softening was carried out between the figure.

Tube colour was added to the scumble for number two, and the ground was allowed partly to set.

Although the ground was softened well between the figure, the effect produced is much harder.

The hardest effect is obtained in number three where the brush-grained ground was allowed to dry before any figure was applied.

Colour was again added to the scumble; no softening was carried out.

Turpentine mixed with fat oil from the top of the glaze medium was used for the pencilled figure in number four.

I find that the small amount of oil prevents the turps from evaporating and helps to give a cleaner wipe-out with the hard stiff brush-grainer.

Rag-softening between the figure was carried out as a final treatment.

The turpentine wipe-out method will be dealt with more fully in another article.

OAK – See also:

Figured Oak	74
English Figured Oak	76
Oak Trees	82
Turkey Oak	88
Oak Graining: The Heavy Figure	110
Oak Graining: Heartwood Markings	116
Graining of Brown Oak	134
Heartwood Markings of English Oak	142
Graining of Pollard Oak	148
Oak Graining: Larger Figures	154
Graining of "Natural" Oak	178
Knots in Oak Heartwood	184
Light Oak and Linen Fold	206
Brown Oak	234
Bleached Heartwood Markings of English Oak	253
Feather of Oak	262
Limed Oak	273
Oak Heartwood	280
Australian Silky Oak	296
Bog Oak	311

Henrietta Marble Limestone

Mr Dobson deals in this article with an attractive marble which he saw being put to good use in some of the new buildings in the city of Liverpool.

MOST of my life has been spent near great inland industrial centres, so that when I visit Liverpool it is always a pleasure to me to watch the ferry plying between Liverpool and Birkenhead and the bigger ships passing up and down the Mersey.

I had a weakness too for the overhead railway; it was a splendid place from which to watch the activities at the many docks, and I was sorry when it closed.

Buildings in Liverpool

Attending the Institute meeting in Liverpool in the springtime, I found myself with time to spare and so I walked down from Lime Street station to the river.

This area is alive with interesting things. I passed the Agricultural Hall and could not resist spending half an hour in the Model Railway Exhibition – a very good show.

The next attraction I came across was the decoration of the entrance to a ten-storey block of offices.

Much of the property in this area consists of head offices of large public companies who spend levishly on decoration.

More permanent materials are often used instead of the usual painted plaster surface, and my attention was attracted to the glossy surface of a light brown Henrietta Marble in one entrance hall.

The whole of this fairly large hall was lined with rectangular blocks from floor to ceiling, the woodwork being of solid English walnut, of a medium yellow brown colour polished to a high gloss.

The walnut had been selected for its plain straight grain, and mottling was its only relief.

This was all to the good as it gave all the interest to the marble on the wall-filling.

Almost plain textured grain appeals to me, being harder to work than the more vigorous kinds that are always in demand.

Green and white granite or marble chippings had been used for the floor, giving a light green effect to the smooth mosaic surface; it was well washed and looked bright and clean.

Also on my way down to the river I found another interesting use for marble. Panels had been placed between the windows of many of the new shop fronts.

Inside massive oak frames, thin broken or roughly-hewn pieces of light coloured marbles had been set in a bed of cement leaving a bold margin of cement rendering in light grey between the large irregular shapes.

Description and Origin

The first impression of Henrietta Marble is of a well textured marble of a light cool brown colour.

In places, green, grey or pink are mingled with the ground colours, though not in any quantity to alter the brown effect of the whole, and at ten feet the variation of colour is not visible.

Veining is narrow (a three eighths inch line would be a broad one), and of a meandering type, like a river on a map.

White is used on a few smaller veins but three parts of them are brown, a tint of umber slightly darker than the ground markings.

Changes in size, shape and colour occur in the intersection of the veins.

This marble possesses the most interesting texture that I know, far more interesting than the Campan marble which we considered in an earlier article.

Henrietta marble originates in the Pas-de-Calais area of France, and in a group of quarries near Boulogne the export and home use of decorative marble is again being developed.

The honoured name given to the marble is from the French Princess Henrietta, the youngest daughter of Henry IV of France, who became Queen of England when she married Charles I in 1625.

It will be remembered that Parliament was closed for a period of ten years during this troubled reign, and Charles started, amongst other things, the billy-goat trim for beards, which from some reason still remains popular with artists.

Calcite, silliminite, corundum and diorite occur in this marble limestone, but the spheriodicle structure is not common in Europe, although it is found in marble limestone elsewhere.

It arises apparently from the repeated and intermittent crystallisation of the rock-forming minerals in successive stages.

The magma might be impoverished of a particular substance, and another of a different kind would follow producing a zone of a different colour.

Painted Representation
I prefer to work from a white

The shaded ground on a panel of about one square foot

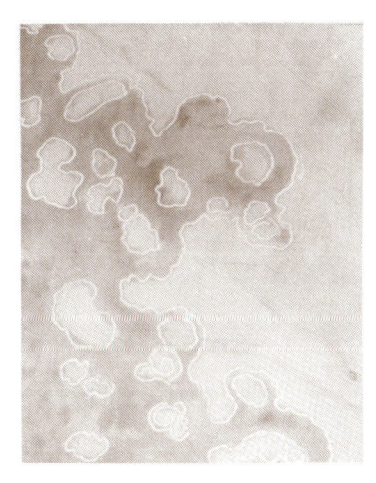

The fitch work with the outline drawn with the point of the wooden handle

This example shows mainly the fine cross veins worked on the plainer spaces

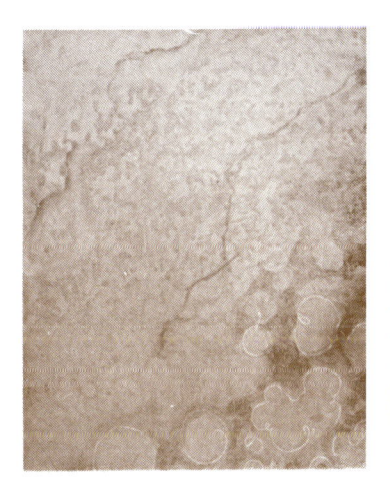

Mainly sponge work on the completed panel, including the glazing process

ground, but pale grey, broken white, cream or light stone may be used to fit in with any particular scheme.

A few stiff colours are required on the palette – burnt umber, black and Oxford ochre, with a small amount of stiff white in a kettle and four parts of turpentine to one of linseed oil and a few drops of terebine in the dipper.

A two-inch tool is used to paint in the ground scumble in a shaded manner, using all the colours from the palette in turn and a little white.

A general tint of umber brown, somewhat lighter than the finished work is what we require.

Part of the colour may be used transparent without the use of white; no laying off should be attempted, the colour being applied with short strokes in any direction, then softened vigorously in any direction.

Next, the more violent parts are worked in with the use of a quarter or half-inch fitch in or around the stone shapes and the divisions where the veinings are to be placed.

The fitch work, in a slightly deeper tone of umber, forms the drawing of the main shapes, none of which will be prominent when the panel is completed.

Stippling
Next we come to the sponge stipple. The stippling shown on the painted examples was carried out with a natural sponge.

A synthetic sponge is quite good, but care must be taken with any square block sponges if the square shape is not to show up on the finished work.

I had a special brush for this purpose which I brought from the Continent, but it has worn out long ago and I shall have to buy another on my next trip.

It was similar to a large stencil tool made from good length fox hair; it came to a number of fine points when charged with colour, and one of its advantages was its cleanliness in working.

The many tints of greys and browns are prepared with the palette knife, and the sponge is softened in water.

With the sponge in this damp condition the colour is picked up and stippling commenced.

The aim should be to get as much variety as possible out of the sponge, slightly twisting or sliding, stippling very lightly in places and using the colour thinner in others.

At no time should the sponge be dipped into the thinners, otherwise a large blob will be the result.

The sponge should be worked lightly at all times, or the fine points will be hammered flat.

A certain amount of filling-in should be done with the fitch, again using tones of brown.

The pebble shapes are irregular; a number of round and oval ones are found down the edge of the darker mass, not unlike a chain in black and gold.

Veining
Lastly the veins are worked in with a sable pencil, in narrow, wavy lines – a few in white, the remainder in tones of brown.

These are softened with the hog-hair, and many lose their identity in the wet ground, but sufficient colour remains to fulfil our purpose.

Glazing may be carried out (in the same colours) to improve the general appearance.

First the ground is oiled in; then a thin sponge stipple of white is applied over most of the surface and lightly softened.

Pencil and fitch work should have more attention in thin brown and grey, care being taken not to cover too heavily the narrow light lines drawn with the end of the fitch handle.

Pine Laths

The incorporation of wood laths in decorative schemes for both interiors and exteriors is becoming increasingly popular. The painted representation of pine laths, as the writer makes clear, should present few difficulties to the competent decorator.

ALL varieties of pine, except perhaps curly pine, may be used in the form of laths, but I shall discuss here pine lath graining generally without going into detail as regards any particular form of pine.

Garage Front

I have recently had some alterations carried out to my garage doors.

As I now have a smaller car, I have had the doors made narrower and they now fold with hinges so that they are much easier to manipulate in gusty weather.

My old doors were each 4ft. x 6ft. and at times were almost unmanageable.

The three feet space left between the new door post and the corner has been filled in with horizontal laths of wood some three inches wide, slotted in the form of weatherboard.

I was helping the joiner to do the job, and I could not help but think as he stood back to admire his work that a panel of this type, composed of narrow boards, would have been out of place only a few years ago.

Materials in use are basically the same as they have always been, but the methods of using and the places where we use them are continually changing.

These particular oak boards had seen service previously on the fence before being dressed and fluted for their present duty.

Several of the pieces are well-marked and they will now be painted over and finished in pine along with the concrete gate posts.

This lath type of decoration is becoming popular, both for interior and exterior adornment, on facias, wall panels, doors, dados and wall-fillings.

Televison "Sets"

More and more use is being made of grained woodwork on television "sets"; this is all to the good as it is of course being carried out by an expert grainer and not by a scenic artist.

The scenic artist in Great Britain seems to be much better at producing marble effect than representing wood grain.

Films imported from abroad are also interesting from this point of view; the quality of even the grained pine from Hollywood is so good that one can almost tell what type of pine it is intended to represent.

Ted Ray in his half hour on the television last Friday evening performed in front of some superb graining of pine.

It was a live show from one of the London studios, probably Riverside, and the "set" appeared to be a new one, as I have not noticed such striking pine graining previously.

It was boldly carried out and good use was made of the knots, which are of course a prominent feature of most forms of pine wood.

The flat doors were divided into five or six vertical divisions, grained with heartwood markings towards one edge and with straight grain towards the other.

Although the graining was not over-elaborated, a fair amount of time had been spent on it and in my opinion more straight grain would have improved it.

Shop Fronts

The design of premises is continually changing, the owner or occupier finding it well worthwhile to invest in a new front, new display material, decoration and fittings.

The use of vertical laths as a background for lettering is a recent innovation; the letters are of the cut-out type, often painted white, and fixed on the face of the lath, and they show up remarkably well.

Pine Lath Graining
Combing only was used for the three lighter laths. It was carried out with two steel combs, one coarse and the other fine. One in every three teeth in the coarse one was bent backwards, and the comb was then covered over with rag to give a cleaner wipe. The darker boards were worked on the wet gilp, a fitch being used first, and then the grain markings were strengthened on the edges with a sable pencil and some tube umber. All the work, including the lining, was carried out at one time while the ground glaze was soft.

Stained woodwork may look pretty on the outside of a building when it is new, but it cannot stand up to the elements and very soon becomes shabby, spoiling the appeaance of the finest architectural facade.

Painting with several coats of paint and graining in oil colour is the best for permanence.

It is quite a simple job to a grainer, as the use of elaborate figure or grain is not called for.

Description and Method of Graining
The two main points of interest about pine lath graining are the tones of colour used and the simplicity of the graining itself, which can be undertaken by almost any bright craftsman with a few years' experience.

The monochromatic use of graining colours is not new to grainers; it was obtained formerly by the use of vandyke in water over an oil scumble.

The graining should be carried out in such a manner that no markings are visible at a distance of a few feet.

The heartwood markings, which form the larger part of the adornment, are simple and include a few knots, centres and half-shapes, drawn as falling away from the edges; roughly three fifths of the area should be plain comb or brush grain.

For the side grain, a brush effect is rather soft for our purpose and I prefer a coarse steel comb covered with a piece of rag.

Cut-out cork may be used on the lighter work, which will help to give contrast and be fully in keeping with the pine graining.

No overgraining, mottling or glazing to form shading is called for.

We find three types of staining in connection with pine lath graining.

First we have the medium tone with the boards all of the same colour; these are often convex with the mould ploughed down one edge.

Some small amount of relief is found in the lighter colour where the grain markings occur.

In the second type, two different tones of laths are used and placed at random; whilst in the third type many different tones are used, ranging from light cream to a very dark brown coloured grain.

Type one should be grained on a pink buff ground, pitch pine or medium oak scumble being used for the rubbing-in process.

Part of the colour is removed with a piece of rag, and the lines of grain worked in with a ⅜in. fitch, using fairly open markings along with a number of knots as in the illustration.

This is softened lightly, working outwards from the centre of the heartwood shape as the thin edge of the grain is on the inside.

The side grain may be worked with a coarse steel comb covered with rag, or with a fantail overgrainer charged with a small amount of colour.

The second more contrasting type, can be worked on a similar coloured ground.

Two different coloured scumbles are used; the darkest one is applied first and allowed to dry, which means cutting in the edges and wiping them clean.

Graining is carried out as for the first type.

The second graining colour is used a few hours later.

The third type requires three different grounds – white, a pink buff and a deep cool buff.

Two graining colours are sufficient but should be worked separately as with type two.

Graining is the same as for the other two.

The arrangement of the laths should be as haphazard as possible, often with two or more of the same colour together.

Australian Silky Oak

Travellers by rail will have noted the tasteful use of some of the newer woods in coach interiors. Australian Silky Oak is one of the more adaptable of these and its painted representation is capable of many uses in interior schemes.

I WELL remember the occasion when I had almost an hour to wait in a train at Skipton, Yorks.

It was in mid-winter and we had missed the connection to a cross country service owing to fog.

Normally I should have been very annoyed, but my annoyance soon disappeared when I looked around me and the time passed all too quickly.

The railway coach was a new one, and one of many that I have travelled in recently that have been lined with the newer types of woods.

The special thing about this particular coach was that the wood used was Australian Silky Oak.

For hundreds of years it has been the height of the interior designer's ambition to line important rooms with finely marked cabinet woods.

Here in this long, open saloon coach someone's ambition had been realised; all the wall filling, panelling, seat supports, doors and fitments were adorned with silky oak and the effect was warm and cosy.

The graining of this wood was a favourite with my father. He always liked the small figure of silky oak and would always use it when he wanted to grain a special door.

He was a fine grainer, having had much practice both before and after commencing in business on his own, and in my time grained the best door of silky oak that I have ever seen.

Origin

Silky oak is for the most part grown in Queensland, the northern right-hand state of Australia.

The leaves that grow on this massive tree are pointed and flat like those of the chestnut, affording good shade in the warm sunshine.

The tree has been introduced into India and other tea-growing parts of the Commonwealth, where it is used to provide shade in the many young plantations.

It is much quicker maturing than our British oak and often attains a height of 120 ft. with a girth of 12 ft.

The wood has a soft, silky touch, is rich in appearance and has plenty of figure, but is not classed botanically as an oak tree.

The timber that it produces is considerably lighter in weight than our native oaks.

It was one of the first of the Empire timbers to find favour with the cabinet makers of this country and rightly so, for it is very adaptable and can be carved, bent, veneered, stained and polished with equal readiness.

Description of Grain

The many examples that I have examined have all been of a medium nut brown colour.

Small, dumpy figure covers the whole of the surface, but it is orderly with a sense of design running through it.

Some of the figures are broad, others narrow, with different spaces between them.

Softening occurs between the larger figures and also down one side of a few of the more prominent ones; a line of darker colour runs on the underside.

This dark line is not difficult to work as the colour collects during the wipe-out process, due to pressure from the horn or the thumb nail.

Additional work on the figure with some softening

The line effect obtained with the rubbing-in tool

The completed panel glazed in oil colour

Combing and figure work

Australian Silky Oak

297

The lines of grain, texture and overgrain are all quite vigorous for a wood with such small figure.

At regular intervals we find clear streaks or bands free of the comb grain markings.

These are difficult to leave clear, as the combing, if only run over the surface twice, is apt to cover up the whole of the ground scumble.

Combing at all times distracts from the beauty and skill displayed in the figure, and there is a tendency to-day to dispense with it, which is to be regretted.

There is finally a set of lines, running over the figure and the grain, which we produce with the glaze of colour.

This glazing subdues the figure into its proper setting, giving the wood grain a steady finish with greater depth.

Method of Graining
Silky oak should be worked on a medium cool, buff coloured ground.

The prepared scumbles of medium oak, antique oak and walnut are all suitable for the graining process, the medium type being suitable for the warmer and the walnut for the cooler varieties.

To prevent the combing and the figure being lost, it is best to rub in on the dry side and keep the scumble round.

If you prefer to prepare your own scumble, burnt turkey umber forms a suitable base colour. Considerable help can be given to the line effect of the ground glaze by the rubbing in; this should always be worked the long way of the panel with no crossing of the brushwork.

In the first illustration, part of the colour was removed with the brush side, a handful of rag was then used and it was finished off with a tool and some stiffer colour.

Combing is clean and prominent – more so that for our British oak – and only one width of comb should be used, i.e. ten teeth to the inch.

In order to leave a darker line, one tooth in every four should be bent back.

The comb is run down the panel twice, first straight and second in a wavy manner.

Use say a four-inch-wide comb and run down the same width each time, trying not to fill up the space left where the teeth have been bent back.

For the wiping out of the figure, I used a narrow bone graining horn, and clean-washed cotton rags.

The horns in my collection are of many shapes; the one that I used here has a square end with rounded corners, in all no more than ¾in. in width.

A suitable comb or leather may be used to put in the smaller side figure at a quicker rate.

Before leaving the figuring, give a little more attention to the shape of the more important, larger figures.

Softening
Perfection in graining is a matter of care with a number of smaller points.

One that is sometimes omitted is the softening, which should be carried out in two stages.

First fold the rag into a pad and proceed to dab lightly between the main figure on the combed grain of the scumble; in places a sliding motion may be used to remove a fair amount of colour.

Care is needed not to desrtroy too much of the combing and not to leave light blobs that compete with the figure for prominence.

The whole of the figure work should then be softened lightly with the hog hair softener and a few of the more important figures can be heavily softened on one side.

Glazing may be carried out, in either oil or water colour, by rubbing in a thin glaze and then running down with the badger or the brush grainer.

Rouge Royal Marble

The painted representation of this marble, while presenting something of a challenge to the craftsman, provides great scope for individual skill.

ROUGE ROYAL – what a charming name to give a hard cold marble!

Rouge can be associated with many things, all of them pleasant, from jewellery to make-up.

Many examples of Rouge Royal contain crimson red, but colcothar, the finely ground ferric oxide also known as jewellers' rouge, is on the yellow side compared with the royal red of this marble.

At the end of the first world war in November 1918, I spent several days with my Division up the Meuse and Sambre valleys, where Rouge Royal marble is quarried.

The quarries and working buildings were quiet, no one was there and I saw the plant just as it had been left (no doubt in a hurry) with all the tools scattered about.

The workshops themselves were intact and a large column of marble was in a lathe, part of it still in the rough whilst three of four feet had been turned to a smooth circular finish.

Only here in Belgium in the Province of Namur can this marble be obtained, for there are few places on the earth's crust where the hard red marbles belonging to the "Devonian" age have been thrown up near enough to the surface to be quarried.

Cathedral Church of St. Asaph

Last year I visited for the first time the famous Cathedral Church of St. Asaph, North Wales and found what is probably the finest display of this marble in Great Britain.

Generally, Rouge Royal looks very complicated and difficult to imitate, but if the work is tackled in the proper sequence it is not beyond the good craftsman.

The marble at St. Asaph, however, is not over elaborate in its markings; it relies on its rich colour for effect, and the bold white lines of the final working show up in a splendid manner on the warm red matrix.

The interior decoration of the cathedral consists of dressed building stone, enlivened with clean, fresh and brightly coloured marbles. A number of varieties are displayed in the chancel, which is panalled up to the frieze line, and many architectural features in the nave are adorned with marble.

The Rouge Royal is contained in two long lines of four-column pillars that carry the large, high roof of the nave. The pillars are bright and glossy, each containing many cubic yards of solid marble.

The craftsmanship is superb; the work must have been carried out by hand for the four columns in each pillar are cut out of one block and built up with horizontal joints.

(Here at St. Asaph, incidentally, is to be found a rare decorative stone known as Penmon marble. Several small columns on the west wall and the vestibule are carved from this scarce Anglesey marble which is of a brown colour. I learned that Edward II showed a partiality for Penmon in the few castles that he built in the 13th century.)

On closer examination of the pillars, we find that the colour is inclined towards pink, and broken with grey.

Relief is given by a number of heavy white veins running over the red, in places slightly tinted with grey. A small amount of yellow, no brighter than a tint of ochre, is found mostly amongst the grey.

Description

My remarks now are based on a fairly plain example of the red variety, although there are panels where grey predominates and only a few patches of red are found.

In all cases the red is milky, say a tint of Indian red, dulled with burnt sienna or brightened with crimson lake, and a little white.

I can best describe its texture by saying that it consists of fitchwork, sponging and pencil work, in that order. The fitchwork is of large motifs of fossil shapes, arranged in spot pattern formation, all of which are neutral in

Rouge Royal Marble

1. Showing the ground glaze, and the first drawing of the knot

2. With the addition of the sponge stipple, centre of knot filled with yellow and softened

3. Red colour added with white cross lines painted in

4. Completed panel, with a little more detail added, and lightly glazed

colour – white, greys and a little yellow. They are drawn with many fine lines, mostly of grey, running parallel to the outside edge with yellow in the centre.

These shapes, many of which resemble the centres found in walnut burr and are up to one foot in length, form the basic pattern of the marble. I prefer to limit their use to say one-tenth of the area, but in complicated examples five-sixths of the surface is covered.

Stipple or sponge work covers the remainder of the ground. This may be either fine or coarse as we find in granite, partly in grey but chiefly in red colour.

There is great scope for individual skill in this sponge work, and I have known three masters of it who could execute a good panel in a very short time – Ernest Sanderson, the late Zeth Carr and William Riley of Burnley.

White veins up to one inch in width cover the whole area thinly; they are heavy and in parts quite solid in colour. Along with the fossil shapes they call for careful drawing.

Large cream to yellow shapes with much shading are also found in some examples of Rouge Royal.

Method of Working
An oiled ground may be used if a quick transparent effect is desired.

I prefer to work on a thin wet coat of grey colour and finish with a transparent glaze of largely red, but this takes slightly more time. The method of working is as follows.

First prepare three tints of light grey from white, black and a touch of yellow ochre.

Commencing with the lightest colour first, rub in the ground, using the different tones in separate areas and twisting the brush about to leave an uneven surface.

Using a large fitch, draw in the basic shape as in the first illustration with a tint of grey slightly darker than any of the previous colours.

By keeping the brush on the dry side and working on the wet ground it is easy to obtain an effect of a number of fine lines.

Work slowly. Continue placing these shapes, of different sizes, over the area to be marbled in the form of a pattern, all however running in the same direction.

Next, proceed to stipple with the sponge the space between shapes in a medium grey tone; use the sponge lightly with a fair amount of turps in the colour. Soften lightly with the hog hair softener and then work in some pinky red sponge stipple in the same manner.

Base your pinky red on a tint of Indian red, warmed with crimson lake and in places cooled with burnt sienna. Use the red with discretion. A handful of rag can be used at this stage to remove part of the colour, by rolling or gently wiping, and it will be found that it comes up well on the white ground.

More work can be put in with a fitch, using a little stronger grey and red, and continued until the general colour and drawing arrangement are satisfactory.

A small amount of yellow should now be painted in the centre of the knots, whilst others can be cleaned out with rag and left in white.

As the whole of this work will have taken some time, the first applications will be partly set so that we can now proceed to paint in the large white veins with a sable pencil. Hold the pencil lightly between the thumb and first finger and roll it a little as you work.

A few of the finer lines may be put in with a smaller brush, or cleaned to the ground with the end of a fitch. The large veins may also be cleaned out with a piece of rag soaked in turpentine. A splatter of turpentine on the stippled part, applied with a short fitch, will improve the general appearance and should complete the job.

Glazing
If the first effort is too light or too dark and you wish to improve it, or if you wish to make a really first-class panel, you can do this with glazing. All the same colours are required.

First, oil in the ground, then sponge stipple in white on the darker parts and in red on the lighter ones and soften lightly. Small glazes of fine colour should also be worked in, near and about the knotted parts.

The painted representation of Silver Spruce is comparatively easy to carry out and adds distinction to a brush-grained ground without the high cost normally associated with the more complicated woods.

Silver Spruce

SILVER spruce is a popular member of the pine family, and because the graining is simple and easy to carry out it is of high value to the decorator.

It adds distinction to a brush-grained ground without the high cost which makes the use of the more complicated types prohibitive.

In this article I shall describe the graining in detail, but the emphasis will be on the drawing of unusual pieces of pine that I have seen in various places.

A Tree in Glen Nevis

Last year on my way to the Highlands I spent a few days at Fort William to explore the surrounding country, and it was there near to the entrance to Glen Nevis, about two miles north of the town, that I found a silver spruce that was one of the finest trees I have ever seen growing in the British Isles.

It is growing on the roadside on the northern boundary of the forestries plantation where many thousands of seeding pine trees are being cultivated.

As I write these notes the Billy Butlin £5,000 walking contest from John O'Groats is in full swing.

The first man has just reached Fort William, while the remainder are strung out down the side of the Caledonian Canal and will all soon pass near large nursery gardens at Nevis, where this tree is growing.

Nevis is a charming picturesque valley only a few miles in length, nicely covered with trees, with many waterfalls and torrents rushing down the mountains.

Glen Nevis is well protected from the north winds by the highest mountain peak in Great Britain (Ben Nevis, 4,406ft.), the summit of which was covered in snow even in June when I was there.

I am indebted to the glen forester for the following information about the tree.

It is over two hundred years old, which is in itself remarkable for most trees of this variety mature in about one third of this time.

The tree is in sound condition and is still growing, its present height being in the region of 200ft. It produces many hundredweights of seed-cones annually.

At eight feet from the base, the trunk is twenty feet in circumference, and ninety feet up it is still no less than fifteen feet around it.

The trunk is clear of branches for the first thirty-five feet, which accounts for the timber being free of knots. It is separated from the river Nevis by less then forty feet, and drinks an estimated 3,000 gallons of water per year.

It started its life about the time that the Young Pretender, Charles Edward Philip Stuart, was marching on England to claim the English throne on his father's behalf.

Description of the Wood

My first impression of silver spruce is of a quietly marked wood, light in colour, the grain of which is scarcely discernible from a few feet away, having neither shading nor mottle.

Compared with the general run of pine woods, silver spruce is very light indeed; it is worked on a white ground, and a bleached or blonde oak scumble will suffice for the brush-grained of flogged ground.

Grain markings are narrow, up to a quarter of an inch in width, and slightly darker on the inside; this shading is so delicate that it is observed only on close inspection.

All the grain is clean with no glazing or over-graining noticeable.

The lines of the side grain are delicate but clearly defined and, compared with most other woods, wide apart.

Another feature of the side grain is that

Silver Spruce

Sable pencil work on a wet ground

The brush-graining

Grain markings worked on dry brush-graining

Graining done with a fitch on a wet ground

some of the lines do not taper or run parallel; they appear to wander from side to side in the space allotted to them.

This feature occurs also in pitch-pine, but only rarely.

Knots are a common feature of the pine woods, but silver spruce is renowned for its freedom from knots and for the long clean pieces of timber that it provides.

In the days of the light wooden fighter planes, such as our own Spitfires, silver spruce was used in aircraft construction because of its low specific gravity.

Method of Working.
The method of graining (assuming that a door is being executed) is as follows.

First prepare the ground in white or yellow cream, according to colour required for the final finish.

If you wish to work with a prepared scumble, bleached oak will be suitable; if you require to match a particular example raw sienna and raw umber will produce any tint that you are likely to meet with.

Proceed to rub in the whole door, leaving the centre parts of the panels slightly lighter, and brush grain to leave the joints clean in a finished manner.

Allow the work partially to set, the longer it can be left the better, but not less than twenty minutes should be allowed.

If you have the time and plenty of work on hand, I suggest that you leave it to dry hard and grain the following day.

If, however, you must get on with it, strengthen the scumble with a little of the two colours and proceed to work in the lines of grain.

Either a well worn sable or hog hair fitch may be used, but I prefer a sable.

With the ground partially set, very little colour will be required as a sable is soft and works on the top without distrubing the wet ground of the scumble, and the line that it paints is both clean and accurate.

A hog hair fitch more or less scrubs its way immediately to the ground colour, and for this reason the colour must be stiffer and darker to counter the action of the brush.

For the side grain a hog hair over-grainer should be used, charged with colour and drawn through a coarse hair comb.

A number of the lines should be painted in with a fitch, and if desired two fitches can be used held in one hand slightly apart.

In the case of moulded panels, very little side grain will be required, but with the flat door you should work in some grain down the side but allow it to run away into the ground scumble in order to avoid having to fill in the whole door surface.

After the graining, some flogging with the long horse hair flogger is desirable to add texture to the grain and break up the smooth edges left by the sable. This must be carried out with caution depending on how wet the ground is and how strong your colour.

With a few gentle trial strokes you can soon tell how much it will take.

Where the ground scumble has been allowed to dry, soften the surface with a rub of oil and turps on a piece of rag.

Then proceed to paint in with a fitch, afterwards flogging when the work has partly set.

OTHER WOODS
See also:
Graining Rosewood 39
Graining of Obeche 126
The Graining of Sycamore 130
Graining of
Bleached Rosewood 182
Graining of Beechwood 190
Juniper 194
Willow 203
Lacewood 218
Crown Elm 221
Satinwood 226
Californian Red Wood 229
Makore Curl 270

Skyros Alpha Marble

The bright colours of this marble make it an attractive decoration for large interiors.

SKYROS ALPHA is a coloured marble containing a large amount of orange to dark red veining on a tinted and white ground.

In the Sedgwick Museum, Cambridge, seven varieties of this marble are exhibited, of which Alpha number 314 is the most handsome, being a little lighter and brighter in its colour combinations than the others.

Kinmel Park
During an autumn tour of North Wales, I found a well decorated foyer lined with Skyros Alpha in the hall of Kinmel mansion in Kinmel Park.

This mountainous stretch of country attracts many visitors in the season; it is noted for its splendid scenery, and many business and professional people have made their homes in the area.

Kinmel Park of course is known to many as an important military training place of former years.

Along with friends I was invited to pay a visit to the hall and inspect the decorations, and it was a most rewarding task.

The hall is approached by a long drive through the parkland, which was looking its best in the late autumn sunshine, the grounds and the gardens of the hall being well maintained by a large staff.

The principal object of my visit was the examination of the marble foyer, which I found in fine condition.

It is of course of recent date, probably installed during some big renovation in the early part of this century.

One of the splendid features of coloured natural materials is that with a little attention they retain their brightness for a long time.

Here at Kinmel the marble has not only retained its colour, but many of the iron-based colours such as yellow, orange and red have slightly developed.

For this reason, the display of Skyros Alpha seen on a bright day gives one a great deal of enjoyment with an almost breath-taking display of colour.

The Foyer
The foyer is rectangular in shape and lofty, with windows running the full length of the outside wall.

A balcony runs the length of the opposite wall with access from a broad, short, central staircase.

The lively, bright, clean marble we are considering is used for the lining of the wall-filling, from the plinth to the frieze rail.

Woodwork is wax polished light oak, which harmonizes well with the many colours of the marble filling.

The frieze, cornice, and ceiling are all well designed in delicate plaster ornament, finished in flat white.

The large high, clear, leaded windows illuminate the foyer direct from the large fore-court, giving a spendid glow of light to the many hundreds of square feet of Skyros.

At present the hall houses the Clarendon School for girls, who were in session as the headmistress took our privileged party round.

Later, we were given an outline of the work being carried on there in boarding and educating some two hundred or more girls with a deep religious outlook.

Description of the Marble
The white ground of this marble is broken with pink, pale grey, and yellow, separated from each other by the veining, sharing with the white, second, third and fourth places respectively in area of distribution.

A small amount of carrara type mesh is

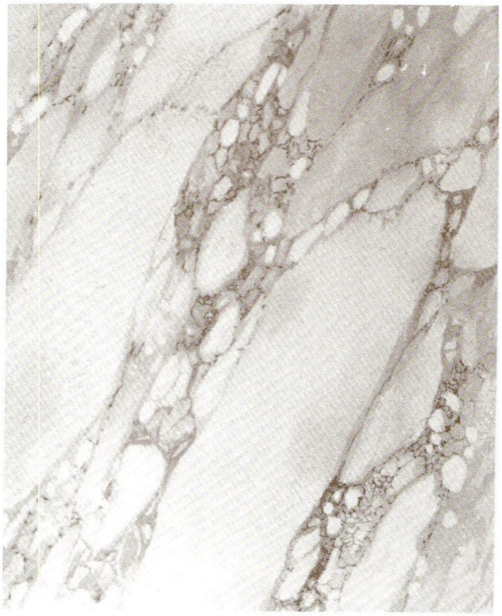

The heavy, darker breccia markings

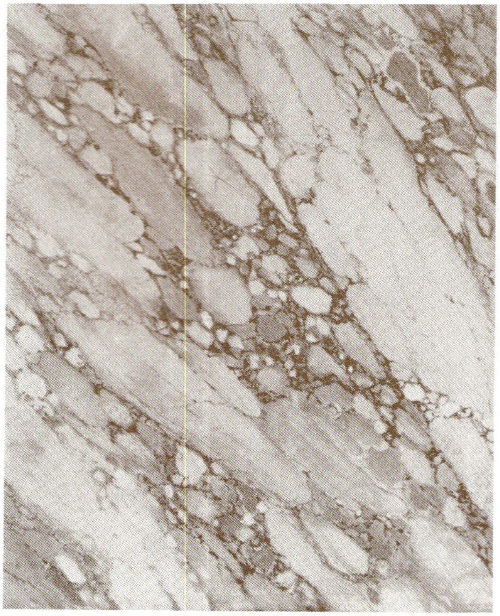

The light, well softened ground for Skyros Alpha Marble

The glazing of the completed panel

The arrangement of the larger stone shapes, worked with a fitch

Skyros Alpha Marble

306

worked into the larger stones in colours a few tones stronger.

In construction, the main veining is of the breccia type, with quite strong colouring, although this does not appear too heavy as the markings are wavy and delicate.

Tints of orange, yellow lake, Indian red, Venetian red with a little crimson lake, vermilion, black and ultramarine are worked as mixtures in smaller quantities.

Much of the veining is transparent, white flashing through in several places.

A few of the smaller stones are filled in with strong colour – yellow, salmon red, medium red, dull red and almost black.

Several of the large constructional shapes are up to four feet by eighteen inches in width, the smaller ones being some three to five inches high.

Because of the existence of the large stones, almost five-sixths of the ground is showing and most of the insides of the stones are worked over with some form of treatment – glazing, shading, delicate colour or veins.

Method of Working
The marbling is carried out as follows.

Rub in a thin glaze of white, prepared from a good class white enamel thinned with three parts of turpentine and one part linseed oil or glaze medium.

With the rubbing-in brush, work in patches of delicate tints of orange, yellow and pink, keeping the colours clear of one another, and soften well with the hog hair.

Next, draw in with a number six hog hair fitch charged with a tint of orange the spaces that the larger figures are to occupy.

If you make too many they can be filled in later, but it is best to know where the larger shapes are to go early in the proceedings.

All the areas where the finer parts of the breccia markings are to be displayed should now be stippled in with colour from the sponge, in strong, fairly cool tints of yellows, reds and greys.

The whole should then be softened lightly, forming a bright, broken-coloured background for the pencil work.

Two hog hair or sable pencils should be employed to work in the stronger deeper veins.

A mixture of orange, white, black and vermilion will form a suitable general colour, and other colours from the palette may be used in turn with the same brushes to give a little variety.

It is best to start with fairly light colours and darken them progressively, using smaller amounts of the purer colours on smaller areas.

Soften the work at intervals as you proceed and before the colour sets.

The panel should now be almost covered, and you can put in a few carrara-type lines in yellow and orange, both as part of the finer work on the breccia and for the decoration of the larger stones.

Next, with a fitch proceed to fill in a few of the smaller shapes with fairly dark colours – red, dull purple and orange cooled with grey.

Some deep grey to black should be added in parts to the breccia markings to give additional depth.

The use of bright colours in juxtaposition is not easy; it demands much study and practice to achieve good results.

Glazing
Glazing is carried out in the same colours, after a rub of oil soften the surface.

First, sponge stipple in snow flake form, then add purer colour in places and lighter in others until a satisfactory result is obtained.

Hungarian Ash

Hungarian ash is a high decorative wood which, although laborious to produce by orthodox graining methods, is brought within the scope of any good craftsman by the use of the mechanical aids described here.

HUNGARIAN ash is a variety of Fraxinus excelsior, one of the well known ash trees found growing in our countryside, and it is not confined to its homeland Hungary.

The figure of this wood is round and curly which makes it highly decorative and explains the name of "ram's horn" figure, by which it is known in the industry.

Finely-marked pieces are valuable, often being converted into veneers.

This beautiful ram's horn figure may grow on any tree, and is difficult to account for, only about one tree in thirty being so marked.

A short while ago the Manchester College of Art re-equipped their painting and decorating department with hard-wood furniture and many of the tables were made of this finely marked wood.

I would not have been writing of the graining of this wood a few years ago, as I considered it too laborious for the results obtained.

We had several sample panels in the classes at Bradford, and I well remember the struggles of the industrious young men endeavouring to imitate them.

To-day, however, there are a number of aids to assist us with the graining of Hungarian ash and with these it is now within the reach of every craftsman to make a good workmanlike job of its graining.

Description of the Wood
Long lines of small, broad, heartwood markings running down the centre of the panel, with a lot of bright dazzling mottle, are the first impressions one grains of this light-coloured wood.

Wavy lines fill in the side-grain, coupled with plenty of mottle all the way to the edge of the panel.

The general colour is a pale yellow to a light brown, prepared with say a glaze of sienna on a white ground, while some examples lean towards pink.

The markings of the grain are of the same hue, strengthened with a small amount of raw umber, whilst the lighter part is broad and firm occupying about one third of the distance to the next line.

Fine pith marks make up the lines of grain, which are darker on the inside towards the centre of the knot and work away to nothing.

A good flogging of the ground will produce all the markings of the fine grain much better than will a graining comb.

The graining is the most striking feature of our subject consisting as it does of a large number of broad, fairly square, heartwood shapes.

The arrangement is perhaps nearest to that of curly pine, but more regular in layout.

Heartwood shapes are staggered above each other up the centre of the panel, with wavy side-grain filling the remainder.

Most panels have a single row; I have come across some with a double and a few with three rows of oval shapes, but these are rare.

All examples are true to type with the markings of even size and running down the centre; two or three rings form shapes with the centre filled in or wiped out.

I have seen examples eight feet long, decorated with the delicate central ornament; as might be expected a tapering or gradual diminishing occurs from bottom to top.

The first mechanical aid for this work is a roller with the markings cut out on the rubber face; this will roll off the small heartwood shapes with great ease on the soft, fresh, rubbed in scumble.

Glazing as a separate process, mottled in oil colour

The rubbing-in and the commencement of the wiping-out

The completed panel, glazed in oil colour after the graining had dried

The wiping-out conyinued, and some mottling carried out on the wet graining

Hungarian Ash

Next we have an absorbent paper that can be laid on the wet surface to make a natural impression on the light ground.

This paper is a print reproduced from an actual photograph of a piece of wood.

Another method is to make use of lincrusta to cover the larger flats and the one-panel doors, and the Hungarian ash on the lath-type licrusta is very suitable for door covering.

Hand Method of Graining

Although I am in favour of any aids that will help to achieve results, this article deals now only with the hand methods employed in the process.

There are two methods that can be used – first the paint-on, and second the wipe-out, and it is with the latter I shall deal here.

The method is as follows.

On an off-white or cream-coloured ground, rub in a prepared ash scumble, or, if that is not available, a mixture of light and bleached oak.

For cleaner wiping-out add a spoonful of linseed oil or clear glaze medium, and apply the scumble rather darker down the centre.

Next, proceed to wipe out the shapes with the rag and graining horn as shown in the illustration.

There are a lot of them to wipe out but they are all similar so that it should not take very long.

Change the position of the rag often and work as quickly and cleanly as possible.

Be sure to wipe out the centres of the shapes with rag on the ball of the thumb; this has a quietening effect on the general appearance.

Run the side grain down with the horsehair brush-grainer; working carefully in and out with the oval shapes.

If the surface has been marked with the wiping out, run it over again with the rubbing-in brush until it is quite even.

Try to produce a certain amount of shading with the brush-grainer to help with the general effect.

Glazing

Take the short hog-hair cutter or thick well worn mottler and remove some of the lights to represent the glazing.

In this operation, run with the grain and try not to obliterate it; this should not be difficult.

Quite a lot can be picked up from a well-ground scumble while it is soft, but the cutter must be lifted clear of the ground after each cut.

The cuts of light should be made near the top of the curve opposite to each small oval shape, and as you proceed outwards towards the edge of the panel the cuts should be smaller and nearer together.

There is a similarity here with the mottling of maple, particularly towards the edges of the panel.

If the glazing or shading comes out hard or strong, it can be softened either by flogging or with the use of the hog-hair softener.

The glazing and mottling can be carried out more safely after the graining has been allowed to dry, but this adds to the time.

ASH
See also:
Ash 48
Ash (cont.) 50
English Ash 268

Bog Oak

The author deals in this article with one of the more expensive woods generally used for quality furniture.

BOG Oak is a well-known Irish product that gives the decorator full scope for his graining skill; the figure and heartwood markings are similar to those with which we are accustomed, the difference being in the use of colour.

Lyme Hall

Of the work carried out by the Institute of British Decorators, the educational visits to the great mansions with well decorated interiors must always stand high in importance.

It was on one of these visits, to Lyme Hall, Cheshire, that I first became acquainted with the best examples I know of Bog Oak.

Many of the oil paintings and most of the furniture in this remarkable home are the original pieces that were in use when the hall was a family home, and much of the carving is attributed to Inigo Jones and other equally famous men.

The hall and extensive grounds are open to the public (being classed as an ancient monument they come under the Ministry of Works) and are well worth a visit.

I have now been on several occasions to examine the interior, but the visit I remember best was under the guidance of Mr. Alferd Garner of Stockport, who was taking members of the Northern District of the Institute on a tour of inspection. High tea was served to us in a clean and bright dining room, which had just been decorated in period style by Mr. Garner's company.

The examples of Bog Oak are to be found in the suite of furniture in one of the bedrooms in the northern block on the first floor of Lyme Hall.

The wood is of a rich brown colour, very old, and the pith markings are the finest that I have ever seen, clear and well defined of a medium grey green – a fine natural example. The suite is well polished, in a good state of preservation, and has the best of attention in a well heated building.

I had better add that part of the decoration of this mansion has been carried out by painting staff of the office of works. Appropriately, they have confined their attention to the kitchens, back staircases, and other secondary apartments.

Much of the woodwork has been grained, but this is not well done – in fact, it leaves much to be desired. I would not like anyone to associate this with the splendid work carried out in the state rooms by Garner and Sons Ltd. of Stockport.

Description and Origin

Most of the supplies of Bog Oak come from Ireland, and a considerable industry is carried on in Dublin in furniture and ornaments made from it. As the name implies, it is the decorative wood of trees that are found beneath peat bogs, changed in colour and in a good state of preservation. A limited number of other hardwoods also change their colour when submerged under the same natural treatment.

Not all specimens of this oak are very dark; I have a few examples that are more of a medium grey colour than brown. This suggests that the colour varies according to the length of time the wood has been submerged, and no doubt the variety of oak will also have a bearing on it.

Those specimens which are more of a charcoal grey than brown have probably sprung from the large tree Quercus Valentina, which of course is a black oak to start with and the only changes in the wood are the green markings in the pith grain.

The figure and heartwood markings always come out in a blackened state; I have never found any that were lighter than the ground colour. The greatest change takes place in the pith markings when they take on greenish grey colour which is considerably lighter than the ground.

The wood hardens with age, and because of this and also on account of its mellow colour it is much in demand and the price is high.

In consequence it is only found in valuable furniture and smaller fittings used for decoration. Much thought and skill is often devoted to the polishing of light fresh-cut oak to give it the appearance of Bog Oak, but the process is often carried to extremes and the wrong colour results.

The markings of the pith should never be of emerald green colour, nor should the figure be of a lighter tone than the ground. With care over these few points, however, a very fine job can be produced with the use of stain and filler.

Method of Graining
The method of graining is as follows. A scumble of cool grey brown, either a manufacturer's preparation or a "home-made" gilp, is rubbed in on grey or cool buff ground. The colour where the heartwood markings are to be placed is wiped out with the brush side, and then the whole is lightly brush grained.

The most practical way of producing the small amount of figure that is required is by the paint-on method using a worn writing sable. Having regard to the tone of colour, it is best to allow the work to set almost before laying on any colour.

A fitch should be used for the heartwood markings; the short serrated lines can then be worked with much more freedom. No glazing is required with graining of this weight, for the depth of the work can be balanced by the use of a suitable graining colour.

When the graining is set, the pith marks should be added with the check roller. I have found that a willow-green gloss paint, slightly let down with turps, works well for this purpose, although the colour may require some slight adjustment.

The use of the rollers was dealt with in a previous article of limed Oak; the method is the same and it is now only a matter of changing the colours.

Cutting tools may be used in place of the check roller if a better quality job is required. Briefly, they are used in this way: the marks are cut when the graining is dry, filled in with colour and wiped off.

Most readers will be conversant with this interesting process, but I propose to devote more time to it in a later article.

Illustration
For the illustration I have made use of a line-drawing, which is clear and easy to follow.

The heartwood markings shown on the styles and the mouldings are most popular when the cutting process is used. The figure, on the other hand, is more easily executed with the sable pencil.

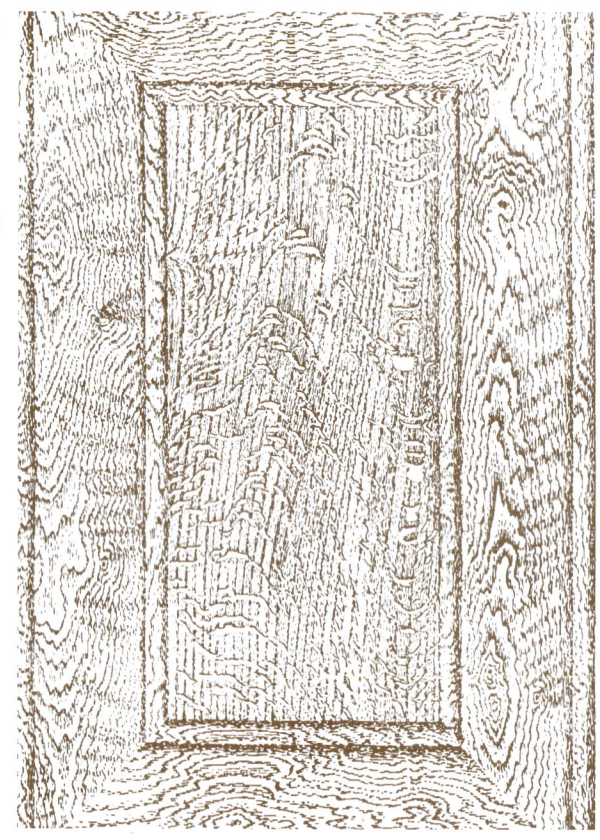

Drawings of the figure and grain of Oak by Mr E. Dobson

The drawings in the illustration could of course be used for almost any form of oak graining.

A Glossary of Terms

The terms used in this glossary may have a wider meaning in the context of painting and decorating, the definitions used here however are restricted to the craft of graining and marbling.

BADGER SOFTENER
The badger is used in both graining and marbling for softening hard effects, clouding, blending and getting "lift" in graining. It is only suitable for use in water-colour.

BINDER
Binder is the material which binds the ingredients of paint, scumbles and stains together, as far as graining and marbling is concerned raw linseed oil acts as a binder for oil stains, and the traditional binder for water stain was stale beer or vinegar, nowadays acrylics are the preference for water-based graining and marbling products.

BLENDING
Is the act of achieving a gradation of colour, or blending two or more colours in a piece of work. It applies mainly to marbling and is best achieved by a careful application of colour, then a first blending with the paint brush, and a final softening with a hog or badger softener.

BRUSH GRAINING
Is the most basic element of oak graining, it is produced by applying graining colour on a suitable ground then using a dragger pull it down through the work to simulate a woody effect. Dragging has now been adopted by interior designers as a decorative treatment in its own right.

CUTTER
The cutter has a similar shape as the mottler but is much smaller and with a short length-out bristle. Usually made of camel hair. It is used primarily in water-colour to shape the feather of Spanish mahogany.

CHECK ROLLER
When graining we can imitate the dark pores of oak by the use of the check roller. It has serrated metal teeth mounted on a barrel and is fed with a ordinary paint brush or mottler. The brush and roller are held as one piece and run through the work leaving a deposit of small pore like markings.

CISSING
Unless an oil painted surface is treated a water based scumble is likely to adhere to the surface, i.e. a continuous distribution of colour on the surface is impossible because the water based scumble will collect in globules. To remedy this the oily surface may be "flatted" with fullers earth or whiting, this will effectively de-grease the surface.

CLOUDING
A semi-transparent glaze coat often used in marbling, it acts to alter an existing colour but does not obscure it.

COMBING
Is primarily used in graining to imitate the fibrous nature of timber (sometimes called tic-marks). They are also used for decorative treatments.

FULLERS EARTH
Is an alternative binder for traditional water colour media, but its main purpose is to prevent cissing when water colour is used on a oily surface. Fullers earth comes in powder form and is mixed with water to a creamy consistency, it is then used to wash the oily surface and cissing is prevented.

GLAZE
Glaze is a semi-transparent liquid that has many uses in painting and decorating. When graining with oil colour a small amount is added

to the mix to ensure that the initial rubbing in holds up whilst the material is manipulated by combing and figuring. In marbling oil glaze is useful because it allows very thin colour can be used in the glazing process. Glaze also has a wider role to play in getting many broken colour effects.

GLYCERINE
Glycerine can be added to water colour medium to extend its open time, it does this by slowing down the evaporation rate of the water content in the water medium. Too much however will stop the drying process completely, so as little as possible is added.

GRAINING
A reproduction of the decorative qualities of natural wood grain achieved by manipulating semi-transparent glazes over a painted ground of solid colour.

GRAINING COLOUR
The term used by the painter to mean a thin stain, scumble or semi-transparent glaze which is brushed on to a grounding of solid colour and which is dragged, combed or otherwise manipulated to produce brush graining or figure graining.

GRAINING COMB
Steel combs with teeth of varying widths, and pieces of rubber, cork or linoleum with the edges serrated to form openings of various widths, which are used to reproduce the plainer kinds of wood markings and which are used in combination with various other effects in figure graining.

GRAINING HORN
A short piece of celluliod or perspex over which a piece of folded rag is doubled and which is used by the grainer to "wipe out" or lift wet graining colour in order to reproduce grain markings. It is a less painful and more hygienic substitute for the old-time grainer's method of using his own thumb nail, allowed to grow unnaturally long for the purpose.

GRANITE
One of the hardest of the rock family, it is used extensively in construction. It comes in a variety of colours and can be readily imitated by sponge-stippling various colours on a suitable ground colour.

GROUND COAT
A coating of solid colour applied to a prepared surface to which glazes and scumbles may be added to simulate graining, marbling and other broken colour treatments.

HEARTWOOD
If we sliced a tree trunk vertically down the middle it would reveal the markings we call heartwood. Towards the outer edge we find the silvergrain or dapples. These are the main characteristics of oak heartwood that the grainer tries to imitate. Heartwood is found in all timbers, some are less prominent than others.

HOG HAIR
Hog hair is best known in graining and marbling as the filling that is used in softeners that we use with oil glazes and scumbles. They are a sister brush to the badge hair brush which is used with water-based glazes and scumbles.

KNOTS
Hard cross-grained disfigurements in timber which are formed where the parent stem puts out the shoots which develop into branches.

Since the resin ducts run parellel with the growth, the resin which is in the knots flows to the surface of the timber. If the exposed surface of the knots is not sealed before paint is applied the resin, being the same substance from which turpentine is obtained, bleeds into the paint film to cause staining and in severe cases exudes in the form of sticky unsightly tears.

The most effective treatment in the case of large knots is to cut them right out and plug the holes with sound wood. Where this is impracticable an alternative method is to cut the knot back below the surface and fill the cavity with a water filler which when hard is sandpapered down to the level of the surrounding wood.

The normal method employed where the knots are small and not too troublesome is to seal them with shellac knotting, although occasionally metal foil is used as the sealer.

KNOTTING
A solution of shellac in methylated spirit which is used to prevent resin from exuding from the knots in woodwork and softening and affecting the paint film.

The knotting should be applied sparingly and allowed to extend well beyond the edge of the knots, being feathered off so as not to leave a prominent ridge.

It is better to apply two thin coats rather than one thick one, as there is a tendency for the spirit evaporating from a thick film of knotting to develop pinholes through which the resin can pass, and in any case it is difficult to avoid the formation of a ridge.

Cheap grades of knotting should never be used as they are frequently adulterated with colophony (rosin), a material which is readily soluble in paint oils and thinners, and they are therefore incapable of holding back the resinous matter from the knots.

Knotting should be kept in air-tight containers to prevent the thickening and darkening which takes place on exposure to air.

A variety of knotting known as stop-tar knotting, consisting of shellac and methylated spirit with the addition of a plasticiser, is used to prevent materials such as creosote from bleeding into paint.

KNOTTING BOTTLE
A metal container with a glass lining, with a wide neck in which a close fitting stopper in inserted.

The stopper is pierced so as to grip the handle of a small soft-haired brush, the brush and stopper being firmly joined together to form a complete unit; thus when the stopper is replaced in the neck of the bottle the brush is suspended in the knotting.

It is most desirable that knotting should be used from a properly made container of this kind; the common practice of using discarded varnish tins and other makeshift receptacles is very unsatisfactory.

Even the heaviest tin plating used for protecting the iron of cans is disintegrated in the presence of knotting, and if there are any imperfections in the lining the corrosion which takes place is very rapid indeed.

This causes the knotting to become contaminated with soluble iron salts, and also sets up an electrolytic action which affects the resin by producing acidic substances.

It used to be the practice for knotting to be supplied by the manufacturers in large earthenware jars; nowadays it is often sold in metal cans but the metal has been specially protected with a lining of mineral waxs.

It is not generally realized that when the knotting is transferred to smaller containers for use on the site its properties are often adversely affected.

LIME OAK
Oak which has been pickled by the application of a coating of lime, which is subsequently brushed off the surface but allowed to remain in the grain. The surface is usually left unpolished.

The painter and decorator is sometimes called upon to match the woodwork of a room to an existing suite of limed oak furniture or to carry out a scheme in limed oak, and there are various methods by which the effect can be reproduced.

When the woodwork consists of real oak, whether in the form of solid wood or of sheets of thin veneer used as panelling, the treatment usually resolves itself into staining the work to the required depth of colour and applying one or two sealer coats, usually of clear shellac varnish; a paste of white material is then prepared stiff enough to cling in the grain and this is either brushed or knifed across the surface in such a way as to fill the pores, the surplus material being removed from the face either with a soft cloth or a squeegee.

The white paste can be made up with a proprietary brand of water-mixed filler or with an oil-bound water paint.

When Lincrusta has to be matched to limed oak it presents a smooth face and after it has been stained to the required colour it may be found that a paste of flat oil paint mixed with glaze medium clings in the surface better.

Softwood doors and architraves can be matched to limed oak very successfully by painting them with a suitable ground, incising the grain pattern by a "needle oak" process with proprietary cutting tools, staining to the required colour, and filling the grain with stiff water paint of flat oil paint and glaze medium.

Alternatively, a straightforward graining technique may be used on a smooth painted ground with a graining colour composed of glaze medium tinted with flat oil white, which by judicious combing, cross-combed with a fine toothed steel comb and supplemented where necessary by light figuring, can be made to achieve a passable representation.

LINSEED OIL

Raw linseed oil is derived from the seed of the flax plant and has traditionally been known as a drying oil. For graining and marbling it has been and remains an invaluable ingredient of oil glazes and scumbles.

For example a mixture of two parts of turpentine to one part of raw linseed oil plus a small amount of driers makes up a glaze that can be used in the oil process of graining and marbling, and also broken colour work.

Its only drawnback is, that it has a tendency to yellow with age.

MAHOGANY

A light harwood; one of the best known and most widely used of the hardwoods. The orginal Spanish mahogany which in the 18th century became so popular for the production of furniture was introduced into Britain in the first place as a ballast cargo from Cuba and Central America; it is now rare, its place having been taken by another species from Central America and by African mahogany from Nigeria and Ghana.

Spanish mahogany is very close grained with a fine silky texture and is often beautifully figured particularly where forking of the stem occurs to produce the "crotch".

Central American and African mahoganies are lighter in colour and coarser in texture. A number of other tropical woods which bear some resemblance to it in colour, grain and texture are sometimes described as mahogany but strictly speaking only woods of the true mahogany or Meliaceae family are entitled to the name.

Mahogany is important to the painter and decorator in two connections.

In the first place the wood is widely used for constructional purposes, advantages in its favour being the fact that it shrinks very little when drying and also the fact that when dry it is very durable and largely free from twisting and warping; it is employed in the construction of doors and panelling, in high class joinery work of all kinds and in the production of veneers.

A white lead primer of the tradtional type is suitable for mahogany but some difficulty may be experienced due to the closeness of the grain resisting penetration by the paint; adhesion is improved if the primer is thinned with up to 10% of white spirit.

In the second place the popularity of mahogany in the making of furniture means that it is a wood that the decorator is often called upon to imitate by graining.

It can be reproduced in either oil or water medium, but it is generally agreed that the effect of its characteristic silky appearance is achieved more faithfully in water medium.

A common fault in mahogany graining is the use of a rather unsuitable pink ground, upon which the necessary richness of colour can only be obtained by means of a two-warmly coloured reddish glaze; far better results are achieved if the warmth is introduced into the ground colour and the glaze colour is kept on the cool side. A suitable ground can be made up with Venetain red, burnt sienna and ochre, or Venetain red and orange chrome, and the glaze may consist of Vandyke brown, Vandyke brown and mahogany lake, or mahogany lake and blue-black.

There are innumerable methods of producing the figure; it is usual to build it up in stages, using the flogger to produce the pore marks, a feather, a sponge or a mottler, coupled with overgrainers, to produce the main figure, and a mottler to produce the final faint mottling, all work being softened with the badger.

Mahogany is a wood that takes a high degree of polish and the decorator is often called upon to finish such items as mahogany doors and shop fascias in French polish.

MAHOGANY FEATHER
The highly decorative figuring which occurs at the forking of the stem.

MAPLE
A tree of the same family as the sycamore, the wood of which is used as a decorative veneer and is also employed in furniture making and to some extent for flooring and stair treads.

Maple wood is very light and clean in colour and is characterized by a beautiful silky silvery mottle, but when exposed to air and light it darkens to an unattractive yellow colour.

The grain markings are indistinct; sometimes the outer parts of the wood are dotted with "birds' eyes" where tiny branches have sprung.

The graining of maple is usually carried out in water medium on a ground of white or ivory, a very thin glaze of raw umber and raw sienna being used.

After the glaze has been mottled and softened with the badger, grain markings may be inserted with a crayon.

"Birds' eyes" are put in with burnt sienna by means of a maple dotter; they can also be put in with the finger-tips or with a piece of rough cork, but these devices produce an unnatural effect.

MAPLE DOTTER
A simple tool with which the small horseshoe shaped "birds' eyes" can be inserted in maple graining. A useful dotter can be made by singeing the centre out of a water colour brush with a red hot needle; dotters can also be cut from pieces of rubber, chamois leather, felt, etc.

MARBLE
Marble is a metamorphic rock made up primarily of calcium carbonate, with various veinings of oxides and vegetable matter. It varies from pure white (cararra) to the more flamboyant breches which display beautiful colouring.

MARBLING
A surface treatment by which the texture, pattern and broken colour effect of polished marbles are imitated in paint. The work is prepared and grounded out in a suitable colour, and the marbling is generally executed with opaque oil colour, blended and softened as required, although glazes are sometimes used to give added depth and the appearance of translucency, and crayons are sometimes used for the veining.

MEDIUM
A confusing term has many applications in painting and decoration. In graining for example the medium binds together the ingredients of the graining colour i.e. strainers and thinners, in marbling it has a similar use. It also can lubricate a surface before glazes and colour are added for the reason that it can increase the open time for tool manipulation.

MEGILP
Is one of the oldest terms used in graining. Before modern advances in paint technology, lime-water, soft soap and other exotic substances were added to graining the colour to prevent it flowing together after combing and figuring. Nowadays ready mixed scumbles contain a clear oil glaze to do the same task.

METHYLATED SPIRIT
Is widely used in the manufacture of French polish, and shellac knotting. Its usefulness to the marbler is, that if it is applied to a water-based glaze coat it can slightly open up the work in the same way that turpentines does in oil colour, though not to the same extent.

MOTTLER
A brush consisting of a ferrule and hog hair bristle. They come in various sizes and are used in graining to form the lights and darks, and mottle which chararcterise many timbers, in particular walnut and mahogany. They can also be used to construct the central figure in many woods. They are used in both oil and water.

MOULDINGS
Ornamental and continuous lines of projections or grooving used to embellish the face of a structure and showing, in profile, a complex series of curves; they may, for instance, form part of a cornice, may surround the panels in a piece of woodwork, may surround a door or may be part of a capital or arch, etc.

Any individual part of a moulding is called a member, and any member which is ornamentally carved is said to be enriched.

NYLON BRUSHES
Brushes with a filling composed of nylon filament.

Because of the scarcity of hog hair, the possibility of using nylon as an alternative is a matter of great interest especially as none of the other alternative types of filler apart from nylon can be used successfully on their own for ordinary paint brushes.

Nylon filament offers several definite and distinct advantages over other types of filler.

In the first place they are most remarkably hard wearing and resilient; comparative tests have proved that when bristle brushes and nylon brushes are subjected to a similar degree of hard usage for an equal length of time the length of the nylon has only decreased by a small fraction of an inch when the bristle has been completely worn down.

In the second place, nylon is considerably cheaper than bristle and the gap in price is constantly widening as bristle becomes more and more scarce.

In the third place, nylon is not adversely affected by any known paint solvent, nor is it affected by alkaline materials.

On the other hand in its present state of development nylon has not yet become a satisfactory filling for a paint brush.

When dipped into paint kettle the brush does not become charged with paint as effectively as bristle, and when charged it does not spread the material efficiently, which means that the painter cannot produce an even level coating; in addition, the rate of application is slowed down. Nor can paint be laid off satisfactorily, and this results in a coarse, ropey finish.

Attempts have been made to improve the spreading qualities of the of the filament by grinding it down to produce an artificial taper, and a further refinement has been to form and artificial flag at the tip of each length of filament; naturally, however, when the flag is worn away it cannot be replaced wheras the flag of a hog hair bristle is constantly renewed throughout the life of the bristle.

A further disadvantage is that the springiness of nylon filament leads to far more paint being splashed about than when a bristle brush is used.

There seems little doubt that the attractive qualities of nylon will give rise to further endeavours to improve its performance and it may in due course become an acceptable brush filling.

It should be noted, however, that nylon brushes are quite unsuitable for the application of creosote or any material of an acidic nature.

OAK
A hardwood of the greatest interest and importance to the painter and decorator. The oak is a tree of the genus Quercus, which is

widely distributed throughout the world; there are some 250 different species, of which the best known and most important commercially are the European oaks, which include English oak, Austrian oak, American oak and Japanese oak. 'Australian oak', however, is quite unrelated.

At one time the oak covered large areas of Great Britain, and was an important factor in its economy. Quite apart from its vital role in the development of the nation's sea power, it was the material that the Anglo-Saxon people turned to for domestic building, it was the timber used in the fine roofs, the benches and the stall work that were such important features of medieval churches, it was widely used in Tudor domestic building not only in the main structures but also for panelling, and at least from Norman times up to the Restoration in the 17th century it was the principal wood used for furniture.

Although the last period in which extensive planting took place was in the Napoleonic wars, it would appear that the long tradition of the use of oak coupled with the beauty and the distinctive grain of its timber have made an indelible impression on the tastes of the British people so that to this day there is a constant demand for oak effects in decorative work, a steady market for wallpapers, relief goods and veneers for the simulation of oak panelling, and a call for the painted and grained imitation of oak which exceeds that of any other type of wood imitation.

The colour of natural oak varies from a rich honey colour to a yellowish brown. The heartwood grain markings, although similar to ash, are far more rugged and varied in shape, and a peculiar feature is that the outer edges of the elliptical curves are sharply spiked and tend to open out into spoon-like shapes at the extremities.

Due to the breadth of the medullary rays, oak wood presents a most beautiful silver-grain or flash when cut on the quarter. The wood takes stain well but shows to better advantage if left unstained so that its unrivalled natural colour and grain are not obscured.

Oak graining is generally carried out in oil graining colour, which should afterwards be overgrained in Vandyke to develop the subtle variation of high light. Much of the commercial graining that is seen is hopelessly crude in colour, due to the fact that the ground colour is too muddy and the stain made too warm in an effort to redeem it.

For natural oak a ground colour of white and raw umber alone may be used, for medium oak and Pollard oak and white may be tinted with raw umber and golden ochre, for dark oak burnt umber and golden ochre stainers are used and for antique oak the pigments are burnt umber, ochre and black. The stainers used to make the graining colour for each of these types are respectively raw umber, raw umber and raw sienna, burnt umber and raw sienna, and burnt umber and black.

The grain markings may be produced by the wipe-out process or by pencilling in with a one-stroke writer. The characteristic pore markings are sometimes added by means of a check roller. An excellent imitation of oak can be produced with patent graining wheels of various kinds which are used to cut or incise the grain markings and pores into the ground colour or into the wood itself prior to staining.

Oak timber is used for various constructional purposes, including door frames, window frames, sills, staircase treads and risers. The painting of these and similar oak surfaces is complicated by three factors:

(i) the wood contains a high proportion of tannin which may retard the drying of the primer coat, (ii) the close grain prevents penetration of the primer, thus affecting adhesion, unless the primer is thinned down with 10% of white spirit of turpentine to assist penetration, (iii) the pronounced and open pores cannot be bridged satisfactorily with undercoatings or finishes, the paint tending to recede from the edges of the gaps; this necessitates filling the pores after priming, and a filler composed of paste white lead and gold size or powdered slate and gold size is recommended for the purpose. Gypsum filler does not accommodate itself sufficiently to the movement of the timber.

When oak is used for exterior doors and gates the wood is very often given a preservative treatment of boiled oil so as not to obscure the natural beauty of the grain, the oil being applied copiously and the surplus wiped off after a lapse of some two hours, the work being then rubbed briskly with a soft cloth to produce a slight sheen. It is important that the wood should be thoroughly clean before the treatment is undertaken, and that the finish should be maintained in good condition by periodic re-oiling. For interior work the recently developed catalyst wood finishes give excellent results.

It should be noted that wherever iron, in the form of wedges or nails, is in contact with newly cut oak a blue-black stain of the same composition as writing ink rapidly forms, due to the action of the woods' natural tanning upon the metal.

OBECHE
A tree found in tropical West Africa producing a sodt light timber which is also known as Nigerian whitewood of West African satinwood and which is used in coach building, plywood manufacture and for shelving.

OVERGRAINER
A brush used in graining for the purpose of producing a series of parellel lines in thin glaze colour, either in oil or water media. It is a thin long-haired brush with a filling of hog hair set in a metal ferrule; very often the ferrule is packed with wood or with cork composition. The width may vary; the usual widths are 1½ inches and 2½ inches.

The overgrainer is charged with colour and is then passed through an orinary hair comb in order to break it up into separate strands. in addition to the normal type of overgrainer there are variations known as pencil overgrainers and fantail overgrainers which are especially useful for certain types of wood grain.

OVERGRAINING
A process carried out with thin glaze over the top of figure graining in order to simulate the subtle light and shade effects seen in natural wood. It is usually carried out in a water medium such as Vandyke brown but oil medium may also be employed. Though often omitted on the grounds of economy, it is very necessary if an accurate representation of true wood grain is desired, for it is impossible to convey a really natural effect in one single figuring operation.

PALETTE
A term with dual meaning, firstly is any thin board containing a thumb piece, and secondly it is a selection of colours chosen for a specific task.

PENCIL OVERGRAINER
An overgrainer consisting of a series of small pointed brushes similar to writing pencils set in a row along a metal bound wooden stock.

Several sizes are available in varying widths. The best kind of pencils of sable hair, but this makes an expensive brush. The pencils should be spaced irregularly so as to give variation of width between the lines. Pencil overgrainers are excellent for the imitation of many woods, being particulary useful for American walnut.

PINE
The name given to a large and important group of coniferous trees providing softwoods for building and constructional purpose. It covers such woods as Scots pine (a tree native to Britain), Cembrian pine, Columbian pine, Weymouth pine (white or yellow pine), pitch pine (a very resinous tree and consequently providing a very durable wood), Corsican pine, etc.

POLLARD OAK
Wood displaying a large number of small knots and an irregular curly figure, due to the pollarding of the tree, i.e., the lopping off of the top part of the tree or of the main branches in order to encourage it to form a large number of side shoots.

Willows and poplars are normally the only types of tree to be pollarded nowadays, but there is a constant demand for an imitation of pollard oak effects in graining; the effect is generally reserved for the panels of doors, etc., so as to contrast with the plainer rails and stiles. It is carried out in oil medium on a light buff ground, the graining colour being made up from burnt umber, raw sienna and burnt sienna, and should always be overgrained.

PUMICE STONE
A substance of volcanic origin; a light form of acid or silica-rich lava which became spongy and porous due to the escape of steam or gas while the lava was cooling. Pumice stone is used as an abrasive, with water as the lubricant and is especially useful for the initial cleaning down and preparation of previously painted and enamelled surfaces prior to redecoration.

Pumice stone is supplied in lumps of varying size and is prepared for use by cutting a lump across with an old hack saw blade so as to provide two pieces each presenting a flat face; the faces are then rubbed on a wet stone to make then smooth. The operative then takes a piece to rub the surface with a circular motion. The stone soon becomes clogged up; to prevent this, and to maintain the stone is useful condition, the two pieces are periodically rubbed together.

A good quality of pumice stone will float in water. A poor quality sinks, which indicates that it is not porous enough to abrade a painted surface properly.

RAW SIENNA
A yellow-brown earth colour consisting chiefly of iron oxide and containing smaller amounts of silica, alumina, oxide of manganese and calcium carbonate, found principally in Sicily and Italy and taking its name from the Italian town of Sienna. It is a somwhat transparent pigment, and for this reason is very useful in the tinting of glazes, when it makes a rich golden colour, and in the mixing of graining colour. Due to its manganese content it is a better drier than ochre although otherwise similar in composition.

RAW UMBER
An earth pigment similar in composition to ochre and sienna but containing a higher proportion of oxide of manganese, and consequently a good drier. It is a good stainer, and like all the earth pigments, is fast to light, durable and inexpensive to produce. Mixed with white it produces a fine range of cool subtle colourings.

ROOT OF OAK
The wood obtained by cutting across the base of the tree where the growth of the root system is developed; the grain is very much twisted and curled and the wood is dark in tone. The graining is undertaken in much the same way as pollard oak.

ROPINESS
Is the defect of heavy lines left in the paint preparation because either the paint coating was too thick, or poor craftsmanship in its application when graining and marbling it is essential that surface is smooth and free from defects.

ROSEWOOD
A type of tree found in Brazil, Argentina, the West and East Indies and India. The wood which is brown, red-brown or a dark brown which is almost black, has a striped grain suggestive of marble markings, and is used for veneering, furniture and cabinet making and shop fitting. The grained imitation of rosewood may be carried out in oil or water colour with a graining colour of Vandyke brown, mahogany lake and black on a ground of bright terra-cotta. Overgraining is carried out with mahogany lake and black.

RUBBER COMBS
Tools made of rubber, used in graining for the purpose of imitating the straight grain of wood. They lift the graining colour from the ground more cleanly than steel combs. Rubber combs with teeth of varying widths can be purchased, a familiar pattern being the triangular shaped combs which present three separate sides each with a different tooth arrangement. Many grainers, however, prefer to make up their own combs by cutting notches in the edges of a piece of rubber-flooring; with the home made article it is possible to devise teeth of varying widths and of a size and patern suited to the individual piece of work in hand.

RUBBING IN
Is often regarded as a necessary chore, but in fact it is essential that it is carried out correctly if any degree of success is to be obtained. Basically it is applying a very thin material on a prepared ground and you must ensure that it is well brushed out on flat and moulded surfaces.

SCUMBLE
A semi-transparent stain or glaze which is applied over a hard dry ground of a different colour; while the scumble is wet it is manipulated in such a way as to expose portions of the ground colour. It differs from a glaze in that it is used to produce a broken colour effect by means of a sharp distinction between the scumble colour and the ground colour, wheras a glaze is used solely to modify the ground colour and is similar in colour to the ground.

The essential features of a scumble are that it should remain open long enough to be manipulated but should retain the markings made in it without flowing out.

A scumble may be made of oil colour or water colour; oil scumbles include proprietary scumble stains and mixtures, made up on the site, of transparent glaze medium tinted with various stainers, and water scumbles are made with powdered pigments bound with fuller's earth of stale beer with a little glycerine added where necessary to retard the drying.

SCUMBLE STAIN
A semi-transparent oil stain, often of a rather pronounced colour, used fro graining (especially brush graining) and other broken colour effects. Some excellent proprietary brands of scumble stains are available which work far more smoothly then home mixed varieties and which have the capacity to remain open longer for manipulation without the drawback of flowing out and losing their clarity; proprietary scumbles are usually ready for immediate use, merely requiring thinning with white spirit and sometimes easing out with oil. Scumble stain may also be used as a stain applied directly to bare wood.

SCUMBLING
The production of broken colour effects by means of scumbles applied over appropriately tinted grounds and suitably manipulated. The methods by which the effects are achieved include graining, brush graining, combing with steel or rubber combs, rag rolling, rubber stippling, rolling with crinkled paper, and in the case of plastic painted or other textured surfaces, wiping with soft cloth to reveal the highlights.

Dark brown scumbles are often applied over metallic paints and then wiped to produce antique leather or oxidized effects. When water scumble is used for this purpose it may be applied directly on to the metallic paint, but if oil scumble is being used the metallic paint should be given a buffer coat of clear lacquer before scumbling is commenced.

SIENNA
A type of marble distingguished by its warmth and richness of colour, with groups of stone-like shapes of various sizes linked by fine veining. It is imitated on a white ground with a palette of raw sienna, burnt sienna, chrome yellow, Indian red, ultramarine blue and white; the effect should be of soft masses of pale cream, rosy red, grey and deep yellow, with veins of purple, reddish grey and brown.

SPONGE
An essential part of a painter's kit. Natural sponges are a primitive form of animal life, those sold commercially being found in the Eastern Mediterranean. Synthetic (cellulose) sponges are now becoming popular both for house painting and industrial work; it is claimed that they hold a greater quantity of water and the flat face covers a greater area at one sweep.

SPONGE STIPPLING
A decorative effect readily produced in flat oil paint or water paint. The technique consists of painting the wall surface with a suitable colour in the normal manner and allowing it to dry; the colours to be

stippled on are then mixed and a little of the darkest of these colours is placed on a flat palette board.

A dry natural sponge, cut across the centre to present a flat face, is used to pick up the colour from the board and transfer it to the wall; the stippling is carried out with a light dabbing motion, the wrist being continually turned to and fro so ad to avoid and reguralrity in the pattern. This is followed by stippling in each of the other colours in turn, the lightest colour being applied last of all.

STAIN

(i) A discolouration or blemish.

(ii) A fluid which is used to colour a surface by penetrating without obscuring it; in most cases the surface to which stain is applied is woodwork. Woods of good quality are stained in order to enhance the beauty of the grain markings and generally improve their appearance; inferior timbers may be stained in order to hide defects and to give the semblance of better quality; sometimes wood is stained in order to bring it to a colour matching or harmonizing with other parts of a decorative scheme; in many cases staining is used for reasons of economy because it is one of the cheapest methods of colouring the woodwork.

The term "stain" includes a number of different types of materials. Water stain usually consists of vegetable dyes such as logwood, saffron, etc;, in solution, but it can also be made up of semi-transparent pigments such as Vandyke brown or sienna bound with gum arabic. This type of stain tends to emphasize the grain markings, especially those of a softwood, because it penetrates freely into the springwood but is rejected by the hard resinous summerwood. It has the drawback of raising the grain of the wood.

Spirit stain consists of spirit soluble dyes such as nigrosine, turmeric, etc., in solution with shellac. It evaporates quickly and needs careful handling to produce an even effect. It tends slightly to subdue the grain markings, and if used too strongly gives a "bronze" semi-opaque effect.

Oil stain consists of semi-transparent pigments such as sienna, crimson lake, etc., ground in linseed oil and thinned with turps or white spirit. It is less penetrative than water or spirit stain and can therefore be more evenly applied, especially on softwood. Because the colouring matter is pigmentary it has the effect of subduing the grain markings.

Varnish stain is a pigmented hard varnish which leaves a top coating on the surface. It is generally used by amateurs rather than professional painters. Chemical stains are sometimes used by the French polisher; they may consist of an aqueous solution applied direct (e.g., permanganate of potash) or of a fume process (e.g., ammonia).

It should be noted that a true stain is a solution containing soluble dye. Pigmentary materials do not give the same measure of purity and transparency.

TACK RAG

A device for removing dust and grit from a surface prior to painting. It consists of a length of cotton fabric impregnated with a non-drying tacky or adhesive substance and folded so as to form a pad of convenient size for handling. When passed across a piece of work it picks up any dust which is present, the dust clinging to the pad, in contrast to a duster brush, which flicks the dust away but sends it swirling into the surrounding air from whence it gradually settles back again on to the work.

A tack rag is designed in such a way that when one face has become clogged up and too dirty for further use it can be folded over to present a fresh clean face, a process which can be repeated several times over so that one pad proides thirty-two clean faces.

Tack rags are widely used in industrial and coach painting, but are not yet used to a great extent in painting and decorating and certainly not used as much as they should be.

In the initial stages of a job, at the burning off, rubbing down and priming stages, it is probable that the conventional duster brush is more effective than a tack rag in clearing away the debris, but in later stages of the work when undercoats are being applied, and particulary in the finishing stages when gloss materials are being used, the tack rag is undoubtedly the most efficient form of dust removal and ensures a much cleaner piece of work than can be achieved with a duster.

TEREBINE
A very strong liquid drier made by dissolving drying agents such as lead or manganese salts in linseed oil at a high temperature, usually with the addition of rosin, and thinning down the mixture with white spirit. It is rather dark in colour, which restricts its use in paints of pale colour, and it paoduces a somewhat brittle film. Unless used very sparingly it can readily lead to cracking. It is very often wrongly spelt as "terebene", which is a totally different substance.

UMBER
A natural brown earth pigment derived from coloured clays composed of hydrated silicate, the colouring being due to the presence of iron oxides and a high proportion of manganese oxide. The best quality comes from Cyprus and is known as Turkey umber, but umber is also found in Italy, France, the U.S.A. and Great Britain.

Like all the earth pigments, it is permanent, stable and cheap to produce; it is a much better drier than ochre or sienna because of its manganese content, manganese being a powerful drying agent. It possesses good staining strength; the natural product, raw umber, has a peculiar greenish cast and when mixed with white it produces a fine range of cool subtle colours.

Raw umber can be calcined to produce burnt umber, which is a rich dark brown colour and when mixed with white gives a muh warmer range of colours. Burnt umber has only moderate staining strengths, but is very useful in the production of stains and graining colour because of its partial transparencey.

VANDYKE BROWN
A deep brown richer in colour than burnt umber, which used to be derived from a natural peaty earth found in Germany but is now prepared by the partial decomposition of beechwood bark or cork. It is a semi-transparent pigment and besides being sold as an artist's colour it is used by the decorator in making up graining colour and glazes for graining. Although it is esteemed for its rich colour it is a very unsatisfactory material to use. It is a very poor drier and has a retarding effect upon oil, and it is very prone to fading; it is used chiefly in water medium, but even in this form it has a bad effect upon the drying of a superimposed varnish film. It is also strongly inclined to cracking.

The material which is sold to the decorator nowadays is not usually true Vandyke brown but an imitation made up from ochre, oxide of iron and lampblack; this is a more durable material but lacks the richness of colour of genuine Vendyke.

WAINSCOT OAK
Another term for quartered oak.

WALNUT
A highly decorative wood obtained from a tree of the Juglandaceae family which is native to Asia Minor but which is now widely distributed in many parts of the world. It is used to a considerable extent in furniture manufacture and cabinet making, being a wood that works easily and takes a good polish.

The grain is rather obscure, but the colouring gives a strong impression of grain markings. Walnut shows very great variations of colour ranging through grey-brown, grey-green, greyish yellow and grey-red, the curly bands of the contrasting tones flowing over the surface regardless of the boundaries of the annual rings. Burred wood, obtained from the Mediterranean countires, is in very great demand by cabinet makers. Walnut is a favourite wood with grainers and the methods of imitating the wood are legion. it may be grained in either oil or water medium.

WIPING OUT
The production of decorative effects by means of lifting part of a coating while it is still wet in order to reveal the ground, e.g., in glazed and scumbled effects, in figure graining, etc.

A look at Watercolour

INCREASINGLY water-colour mediums and coatings are being used in graining and marbling, two main areas are worthy of discussion:

* Surface Preparation

* Scumble and Glazes

Preparation for graining and marbling relies very much on traditional methods; for example, surfaces that are sound require a thorough washing down, wet abrading, spot priming, making good and then adequate coatings to obtain a smooth non-absorbent ground coat.

Damaged surfaces must have their coatings removed either by heat or paint remover remembering of course that coatings that pre-date 1960 may contain lead and removal must conform to health and safety regulations.

Then after knotting and priming the paint system listed above may be employed.

Similarly new work must be knotted and primed with a suitable primer, all defects made good and again built up to a ground colour that is very smooth and non absorbent.

Interior and exterior coatings are worth mentioning.

On exterior work an oil based paint system is preferred and on interior work we have a choice between oil based and water based paint systems.

Using oil or water based scumbles and glazes is very much a matter of personal choice, oil based scumbles and glazes live quite happily with both paint systems mentioned above, water based scumbles work best on acrylic paint systems.

They have a difficulty with oil coatings in that unless they are cessed down with fullers earth or whiting the old problem of water on oil will occur.

If we are asked which are preferable oil or water mediums, it is a matter of choice, but choice must be based by extensive use of both mediums, only then can a valid judgement be made.

Also we must mention the use of a mixed media approach to graining and marbling.

Traditionally water colour had a wide use by the early grainers but with the advent of oil scumbles and glazes their use was very much reduced.

Now the wheel has almost gone full circle with water colour increasing at a rapid pace, and it is now usual for both oil and water mediums to be used on one piece of work, remembering of course to fasten down before water goes over oil.

The trend toward water base products is a reflection on modern legislation, they are in the main enviromentally friendly, much favoured by architects and planners in the public domain.

They dry quickly, are non flammable and non yellowing.

The manufacturers have some way to go before thay can be judged superior to oil based products, for example they lack flow and thus are subject to the defect of ropiness their open times are limited.

But having said this continous use and planning our work does let us build the skills needed to produce good examples of work.

Index by subject

ASH

Ash	48
Ash (cont.)	50
English Ash	268
Hungarian Ash	308

MAHOGANY

Graining Mahogany	32
Graining Mahogany (cont.)	34
Graining Mahogany (cont.)	36
The Graining of Mahogany	164
Mahogany (Sapele Variety)	209

MAPLE

Maple	56
Maple (cont.)	58
Grey Maple	62
Maple	247

MARBLES

Grand Antique Marble	42
Breche-Verte Marble	44
Sienna Marble	46
Carrara Marble	52
Levanto Marble	54
Poupre Violette	60
Irish Green Marble	64
Rouge Royal Marble	68
Granite Marbles	72
Marbling Vert Campan	84
Verde Antique	90
Alabaster: Marble Limestone	98
Skyros Marble	114
Cipollina Marble	122
Napoleon Marble Limestone	128
The Marbling of Breche Violette	132
Blue Fleuri Marble	136
Breche Blanche	140
Black and Gold Marble	146
Serancolin Marble	152
Convent Sienna Marble	158
Black and Gold Marble	162
St. Anne Marble	168
Dark Dove Marble	174

Waulsort Marble	180
Swedish Green Marble	188
St. Anne Marble	212
Verde Antique	223
Breche Violet Marble	231
Vert-de-Mer Marble	245
Alabaster-Marble Limestone	250
Poupre Violette Marble	265
Connemara Marble	275
Rose Campan Marble	282
Henrietta Marble Limestone	290
Rouge Royal Marble	299
Skyros Alpha Marble	305

MISCELLANEOUS

Introduction	28
Tools and Brushes for Graining	30
A Grainer of 1851	102
Drawings of Brushes	166
Knots in Graining	172
Knots in Graining (cont.)	176
Colour Combing	236
Graining a Flat Door	239
Wood Grain by Pencil Rubbing	255
A Glossary of Terms	313

A Look at Watercolour	325

OAK

Figured Oak	74
English Figured Oak	76
English Figured Oak (cont.)	78
English Figured Oak (cont.)	80
Oak Trees	82
Turkey Oak	88
Oak Graining: The Heavy Figure	110
Oak Graining: Heartwood Markings	116
Graining of Brown Oak	134
Heartwood Markings of English Oak	142
Graining of Pollard Oak	148
Graining of Pollard Oak (cont.)	150
Oak Graining: Larger Figures	154
Graining of "Natural" Oak	178
Knots in Oak Heartwood	184
Light Oak and Linen Fold	206
Brown Oak	234
Bleached Heartwood Markings of English Oak	253
Feather of Oak	262
Limed Oak	273
Oak Heartwood	280
Pencilled Figure of Oak	287

Australian Silky Oak 296
Bog Oak 311

OTHER WOODS

Graining Rosewood 39
Graining of Obeche 126
The Graining of Sycamore 130
Graining of Bleached Rosewood 182
Graining of Beechwood 190
Juniper 194
Willow 203
Lacewood 218
Crown Elm 221
Satinwood 226
Californian Red Wood 229
Makore Curl 270
Silver Spruce 302

PINE

Pitch Pine 66
Curly Pine 70
Scotch Pine 215
Pine Laths 293

STONE

Sandstone 86
Reproduction of Stone of the British Isles 92
Sandstones of Britain 200

TEAK

The Graining of Teak 138
The Mottled Graining of Teak 156

WALNUT

The Graining of Walnut (1) 94
The Graining of Walnut (2) 100
The Graining of Walnut (3) 112
Italian Walnut 118
Italian Walnut (cont.) 120
Italian Walnut (cont.) 124
Walnut 144
Satin Walnut 160
Bleached Walnut 170
Australian Walnut 186
English Walnut 197
A Quick Method of Graining Walnut 242
Bleached Italian Walnut In a Bedroom 258
Walnut Burr 277
Feather of Walnut 284